Praise for *Y2K Risk Management* . . .

"It is naive to think we will all be prepared for Y2K by December 31, 1999. This is an important and timely book in which the authors provide clear and cogent advice for managing the entire spectrum of Year 2000 business and legal risks. Whether you have Y2K well in hand or are just getting started, this book is essential reading for every executive, manager, and technical professional who might soon face the consequences of Year 2000 failures."

—Dr. Edward Yardeni
Chief Economist
Deutsche Bank Securities

"As we enter the eleventh hour of the Y2K project, we face a litany of litigation. This erudite recital of risks and ways to manage and mitigate them is your protection against the inevitable lawsuits. Read it and ready yourself for the final phase of Y2K."

—Peter de Jager
de Jager & Company Limited
Speaker on Change & Year 2000

"This is a great reference book for the Y2K uninitiated as well as the battle-scarred Y2K professional. It contains a multitude of information all in one place that can help answer questions posed by end users, suppliers, customers, internal legal counsel, and even the board of directors. A must-have for the Y2K reference library."

—Ann K. Coffou
VP, Managing Director
Giga Information Group
Year 2000—IT Practices

"Even if your business does everything possible to address the Year 2000 problem internally and with external business dependencies, problems will still occur. Business relationships can survive Y2K if both parties work together toward a solution. *Y2K Risk Management* gives you a clear picture of the challenges every business will face, and the steps you should take to ensure business continuity and avoid litigation."

—Harris N. Miller
President
Information Technology Association of America (ITAA)

"This is one of only three books on Y2K that I believe makes a real contribution to the problem resolution. I believe that every public and private enterprise, whether they have a well established Year 2000 risk management program or not, would benefit from this book. It may well become the Year 2000 manual for every risk management professional and team leader."

 —Richard Bergeon
  Cofounder of Systemic Solutions
  and author of Managing 00 and
  Countdown Y2K with Peter de Jager

"Three wise men illuminating the management and legal darkness of the year 2000 problem."

 —Leon A. Kappelman, Ph.D.
  Co-chair, Society for Information Management Year 2000 Working Group
  Associate Professor, College of Business, University of North Texas
  Associate Director, Center for Quality and Productivity

"*Y2K Risk Management* contains many of the answers that health-care providers need to protect their organizations and their patients from the potentially devastating effects of Year 2000. The book is full of rock-solid information, thorough checklists, and sound advice for staying out of harm's way. Every Y2K project will benefit from this outstanding book."

 —Joel M. Ackerman
  Executive Director
  Rx2000 Solutions Institute

"For every organization in our economy, the risks associated with possible Year 2000 problems impose challenges of management attention, budget, human resources, and quite simply, for many, basic credibility considerations of an unprecedented quality. Goldberg, Davis, and Pegalis address these issues with a clarity, thoroughness, and eye to functional utility not yet seen in other works. This volume, with its business-based organization, extensive reference to understandable lists and templates, and carefully researched references to additional external resources, has a place in the Y2K arsenal of every organization."

 —Michael A. Aisenberg
  Attorney-at-Law
  Member, President's Y2K Council Working Groups
  Washington, D.C.

Y2K Risk Management
Contingency Planning, Business Continuity, and Avoiding Litigation

Steven H. Goldberg
Steven C. Davis
Andrew M. Pegalis

Wiley Computer Publishing

John Wiley & Sons, Inc.
NEW YORK • CHICHESTER • WEINHEIM • BRISBANE • SINGAPORE • TORONTO

Publisher: Robert Ipsen

Editor: Marjorie Spencer

Assistant Editor: Margaret Hendrey

Managing Editor: Marnie Wielage

Text Design & Composition: North Market Street Graphics

Designations used by companies to distinguish their products are often claimed as trademarks. In all instances where John Wiley & Sons, Inc., is aware of a claim, the product names appear in initial capital or ALL CAPITAL LETTERS. Readers, however, should contact the appropriate companies for more complete information regarding trademarks and registration.

This book is printed on acid-free paper. ∞

Copyright © 1999 by Steven H. Goldberg, Steven C. Davis, Andrew M. Pegalis. All rights reserved.

Published by John Wiley & Sons, Inc.

Published simultaneously in Canada.

No part of this publication may be reproduced, stored in a retrieval system or transmitted in any form or by any means, electronic, mechanical, photocopying, recording, scanning or otherwise, except as permitted under Sections 107 or 108 of the 1976 United States Copyright Act, without either the prior written permission of the Publisher, or authorization through payment of the appropriate per-copy fee to the Copyright Clearance Center, 222 Rosewood Drive, Danvers, MA 01923, (978) 750-8400, fax (978) 750-4744. Requests to the Publisher for permission should be addressed to the Permissions Department, John Wiley & Sons, Inc., 605 Third Avenue, New York, NY 10158-0012, (212) 850-6011, fax (212) 850-6008, E-Mail: PERMREQ@WILEY.COM.

This publication is designed to provide accurate and authoritative information in regard to the subject matter covered. It is sold with the understanding that the publisher is not engaged in professional services. If professional advice or other expert assistance is required, the services of a competent professional person should be sought.

Library of Congress Cataloging-in-Publication Data:
Goldberg, Steven H., 1954–
    Y2K risk management : contingency planning, business continuity,
  and avoiding litigation / Steven H. Goldberg, Steven C. Davis,
  Andrew M. Pegalis.
        p.   cm.
    "Wiley computer publishing."
    Includes bibliographical references and index.
    ISBN 0-471-33352-2 (pbk. : alk. paper)
    1. Year 2000 date conversion (Computer systems)   2. Risk
  management.   I. Davis, Steven C.   II. Pegalis, Andrew M., 1968–
    III. Title.
QA76.76.S64G65   1999
005.1'6—dc21   98-53409
                                                                    CIP

Printed in the United States of America.

10 9 8 7 6 5 4 3 2

To my sweet wife, Janet Louise Klein, my great kids, Hilary and Addy, and my loving parents, Lenny and Sandy Goldberg.

—STEVE GOLDBERG

To my lovely wife, Wendy, and my darling children, Ben and Abby, who have supported me and tolerated my many long hours "dealing with the Year 2000 problem."

—STEVE DAVIS

To my family, friends, and business partner for their unwavering support.

—ANDREW M. PEGALIS, ESQUIRE

CONTENTS

Acknowledgments		xv
Introduction		xvii
Chapter 1	**Year 2000 Business and Legal Risks**	1
	Y2K Casualties: Your Business, Customers, and Career	1
	Sources of Risk	1
	Potential Consequences of Y2K Failures	8
	Failure Horizons	11
	The Expected Legal Fallout	13
	Types of Lawsuits Anticipated	13
	Year One of Year 2000 Litigation	14
	Factors Complicating Y2K Suits	16
	Denial or Loss of Insurance Coverage	16
	Shifting Market Forces	17
	Preparing for 2000 and Beyond	19
	Who's Driving the Bus?	19
	What's Next?	20
Chapter 2	**Building an Effective Year 2000 Risk Management Program**	21
	Risk Management Program Scope and Goals	21
	System Remediation	22
	Project Resources	23
	Risk Management Planning	26
	Risk Management Planning Phases	29
	Planning Steps	29
	Project Plan Process	33
	1. Define Criteria for Mission-Critical Processes	34
	2. Business Process Risk Rating	34
	3. Determine Cost Impact on Your Operations	34
	4. Define Recovery Processes, Costs, and Time Frames	36
	5. Identify Processing Alternatives	36
	6. Formulate Strategies Based on Optimum Cost-Benefit	36
	7. Revise and Develop Contingency Plans as Needed	37
	Key Elements to Risk Management Planning	37

	Where to Start	39
	Management Responsibilities	40
	Business Risk Assessments	40
	Triage and Risk Ratings	41
	Legal Audit	42
	Due Diligence	42
	Conclusion	42
Chapter 3	**Fast-Tracking a Year 2000 Project**	**45**
	It's Never Too Late	45
	Risk Analysis and Prioritization	46
	A Contingency-Planning Approach	47
	Y2K Fast-Track Planning	48
	The Project Management Plan	49
	Select a Good Project Manager	49
	Identify Technical and Management Representatives	50
	Project Organization	50
	Project Scoping and Triage	51
	Cost Estimates and Budgeting	53
	Develop Accelerated Administrative Processes	55
	Decision-Making and Reporting Structures	56
	Establishing a Y2K Plan	57
	Awareness	57
	Assessment	58
	Renovation	59
	Validation	59
	Implementation	60
	Post-Implementation	61
	Project Checklist	61
	Establish Compliance Standards	61
	Conclusion	62
	Project Checklist	62
	Project Initiation Checklist	63
	Project Life Cycle Checklist	64
Chapter 4	**Reducing Y2K Liability Exposure**	**69**
	Not Just for Lawyers	69
	Executives, Managers, and IT Professionals	69
	Lawyers of Every Kind	70
	Exercising Due Diligence	70
	What Due Diligence Means	71
	Year 2000 Due Diligence	71

Legal Issues Checklist	72
Overview of Y2K Liability Risk Management Areas	72
Causes of Action and Defenses	78
The Elements of Legal Cases	78
Dissecting Y2K Lawsuits	79
Directors and Officers Liability Exposure	89
Fiduciary Duties	90
Directors and Officers Legal Protections	90
Checklist for Directors and Officers Legal Risk Management	93
Protecting Technical Professionals	95
Errors and Omissions Insurance	95
Y2K Risks for IT Workers	95
Cooperating with Employers	96
Indemnification	97
Conducting Y2K Legal Audits	98
Audit Objectives	99
Conducting the Audit	101
New Contracts—Stopping the Bleeding	105
Define Y2K Compliance	105
Year 2000 Warranties	106
Other Y2K Contract Clauses	110
Year 2000 Remediation Contracts	112
Manage Remediation Contracts Closely	113
Other Contract Provisions	114
Independent Verification and Validation Contracts	114
Protecting Y2K Vendors and Consultants	115
Contractual Risks	115
A New Approach	117
Avoiding Liability from Selling Noncompliant Products and Services	118
Take Stock of Your Compliance Status	118
Assess Your Legal Obligations to Customers	119
Communicating with Customers Under the Year 2000 Information and Readiness Disclosure Act	119
Regulatory Compliance	122
The Evolving Year 2000 Regulatory Landscape	122
Developing a Y2K Regulatory Compliance Program	126
Conclusion	127
Chapter 5 **External Compliance Strategies**	**129**
Understanding Business Dependencies	129
Presumptions about Resource Dependencies	130
Multilevel Dependencies	132

	Output Dependency Risks	134
	Sole-Source and Affiliated Suppliers	135
	Electronic Trading Partners	135
	Responsibilities Within the Organization	136
	Assessing and Managing External Business Dependencies	137
	Communications Program (Disclosure)	139
	Standardized Responses	145
	Quid Pro Quo Inquiries and Statements	146
	Consideration of Alternative Resource Dependencies	148
	Embracing Sole-Source Dependencies	149
	Anticipating Marketplace Changes	149
	Conclusion	150
Chapter 6	**Contingency Planning**	**151**
	Overview	151
	How Bad Will It Be?	152
	Why You Need Contingency Plans	153
	Contingency Planning Project Phases	154
	Assessment Phase	154
	Planning Phase	157
	Plan Execution	167
	Recovery	167
	Emergency Management	168
	Conclusion	172
Chapter 7	**Major Corporate Decision Making**	**173**
	Disclosures and Communications	173
	Mergers and Acquisitions	175
	Year 2000 Mergers and Acquisitions Due Diligence	175
	Oversight of Discoverable Potential Liabilities	176
	M&A Disclosure Requirements	177
	Technical and Business Risks	177
	Business Process Improvement	178
	Role of the Decision Maker	179
	The Y2K Factor (Internal Systems, Embedded Systems, EBDs)	180
	Business Improvement Programs	181
	Conclusion	182
Chapter 8	**Substantiating Due Diligence**	**183**
	Reasons to Substantiate Due Diligence	183
	Documentation	185

	Disclosures to the Securities and Exchange Commission	187
	Effective Date	188
	Required Disclosures by Public Companies	188
	Statutory Safe Harbors	192
	Disclosures by Private Companies	193
	Internal and External Audits	194
	Y2K Role of Internal Auditors	194
	Y2K Risks Facing External Auditors	198
	Working with External Auditors	203
	Conclusion	204
Chapter 9	**Insurance Issues**	**205**
	Year 2000 Residual Risks	205
	Unknown Exposures	205
	Risk Finance Techniques	207
	Risk Transfer: Insurance	209
	Insurer Alternatives	209
	State of the Industry	212
	Applicability of Existing Coverage	213
	Property Insurance	213
	Directors and Officers Liability Insurance	217
	Errors and Omissions Insurance	220
	Fiduciary Liability Insurance	221
	Y2K Questions on New or Renewal Applications	221
	Grounds for Voiding Coverage	222
	Risks for Insurers	224
	Bad Faith Claims	225
	Collusion	225
	Reinsurance	225
	Subrogation	226
	Loss Adjustment	227
	Disclosure of Y2K Insurance Coverage	227
	FFIEC Disclosures	227
	Mergers and Acquisitions	228
	Y2K Specialty Policies	228
	Aon's ARM2000	228
	J&H Marsh & McLennan's 2000 SECURE	229
	American International Group	229
	Other Policies	230
	Commentary on Available Insurance Coverages	230
	Conclusion	231

Chapter 10 Alternative Dispute Resolution — 233

- Example of Year 2000 Disputes — 233
  - The Moral of Both Stories — 236
- Differing Perspectives on Y2K Failures — 236
  - Buyers — 236
  - Sellers — 237
- The Burdens of Y2K Litigation — 237
  - Judicial Relief — 238
  - Preparing the Case — 238
  - The Court's View — 240
  - How Will Juries Regard Y2K? — 241
- Special Risks for IT Companies — 241
- Objectives of Year 2000 ADR — 242
  - Sharing Compliance Information Safely — 242
  - Preventing Supply-Chain Breakdowns — 243
  - Settling Disputes and Avoiding Lawsuits — 243
- Types of ADR — 243
  - Negotiation — 244
  - Case Evaluation — 244
  - Mediation — 244
  - Arbitration — 245
  - Court-Ordered ADR — 245
- Building Corporate Y2K ADR Programs — 245
  - Gaining Management Support — 246
  - Program Development — 247
- Conclusion — 254

Chapter 11 Litigation Planning and Management — 255

- Selecting and Managing Litigation Counsel — 255
  - Qualifications — 256
  - Litigation Guidelines — 259
  - Fee Arrangements — 260
  - Litigation Budgets — 261
  - Allocating Work between In-House and Outside Counsel — 264
- Communications Planning — 265
- Cost Recovery Suits — 266
  - Phase 1: A Loss Is Suffered — 267
  - Phase 2: Suit Is Filed — 272
  - Phase 3: Discovery — 274
  - Phase 4: Moving toward Resolution? — 275
  - Phase 5: Preparing and Trying the Case — 275
  - Phase 6: Post-Trial — 276
- Managing Multiple Lawsuits — 276

	The Need for Coordination Counsel	277
	Selecting Coordination Counsel	278
	Joint Defense Agreements	278
	Conclusion	280
Chapter 12	**Post-2000 Risk Management**	**281**
	Predictions for 2000	282
	Crisis Management	283
	Failure Scenarios	284
	Recovery Strategies	285
	Financial Concerns	286
	Liquidity Shortages	286
	Possible Credit Crunch	287
	Post-2000 Investment Opportunities	287
	Legal	288
	Post-2000 Litigation	289
	Insurance Claims and Coverage	289
	Conclusion	289
Appendix	**Y2K Resources**	**291**
References		**297**
Index		**305**

Table of Planning Templates, Resources, and Matrices

Figure 2.1	Risk-Rating Methodology	35
Figure 3.1	Typical Y2K Program Management Organization Chart	51
Figure 3.2	Typical Y2K Budget Breakdown	54
Figure 3.3	Administrative Process Ideas	56
Table 4.1	Classification of Probable Year 2000 Lawsuits	81
Figure 5.1	Overview of External Business Dependencies	133
Figure 5.2	Business Dependency Template	138
Sidebar:	Sample Vendor Survey Letter	140
Sidebar:	Sample Year 2000 Questionnaire	141
Sidebar:	Sample Definition of Year 2000 Compliance	142
Figure 5.3	External Business Dependency Tracking Spreadsheet	144
Figure 5.4	Disclosure Tracking System	147
Figure 5.5	Importance of Tracking	149

Table 5.1	Guidelines for Securing Alternative External Business Dependencies	149
Figure 6.1	Contingency Planning Phases	155
Table 6.1	Contingency Planning Matrix	158
Table 6.2	Contingency Planning Matrix Examples	159
Sidebar:	Year 2000 Contingency Planning Resources	171
Table 8.1	Examples of Y2K Documentation	186
Table 8.2	SEC Examples of Forward-Looking and Historical Fact Statements	193
Sidebar:	Example of a Subrogated Y2K Claim	226
Sidebar:	Year 2000 ADR Resources	248
Figure 11.1	A Sample Y2K Litigation Budget	263

ACKNOWLEDGMENTS

There are many people we would like to thank for leading the way, sharing their insights, allowing us to reprint their work, or just plain putting up with us. With apologies to anyone we have inadvertently omitted, we extend our sincere thanks to Joel Ackerman, Kevin Ashworth, Marty Cosgrove, John Donohue, Lew Eisenberg, Donald Evans, Tim Feathers, Michael Hale, Bill Harvey, Edwin Jackson, Leon Kappelman, Tom Kiley, Sandy Lish, Bob Lonis, Tony Montagnolo, Scott Nathan, Marc Pearl, Rhonda Prokos, Chris Ricci, Bob Rosenthal, David Schaefer, Matt Schemmel, Jonathan Small, John D. Stewart, Jr., Doug Turner, Carl Valvo, Steve Wakeland, and Rick Will.

We are particularly grateful to our editor, Margaret Hendrey at Wiley Computer Publishing, for her steadfast support of this project and her light touch in guiding us along. It is a wonderful thing to be able to say, in effect, "this stinks," without giving offense. Thanks to Marjorie Spencer for finding merit in the book proposal. We also appreciate the efforts of Marnie Wielage and her copyediting and production crew. Are we paying you guys enough?

Steven H. Goldberg

Steven C. Davis

Andrew M. Pegalis

INTRODUCTION

"Many things which cannot be overcome when they are together, yield themselves up when taken little by little."

—PLUTARCH

It is 1999. On October 19, 1998, President Clinton signed the Year 2000 Information and Readiness Disclosure Act, in which Congress made the following sobering findings:

> (A) At least thousands but possibly millions of information technology computer systems, software programs, and semiconductors are not capable of recognizing certain dates in 1999 and after December 31, 1999, and will read dates in the year 2000 and thereafter as if those dates represent the year 1900 or thereafter or will fail to process those dates.
>
> (B) The problem described in subparagraph (A) and resulting failures could incapacitate systems that are essential to the functioning of markets, commerce, consumer products, utilities, government, and safety and defense systems, in the United States and throughout the world.

In less than one year, the century odometer in your date-sensitive hardware and software will roll over from "99" to "00." Maybe you've been working on making everything Year 2000—Y2K—"compliant" for a year or two or more. Maybe you've barely started. Either way, there's not enough time to finish everything. You and everyone else on the planet aren't going to successfully fix and test *every* line of computer code that contains a date field, repair *every* data interface, rewrite *every* date field in *every* corporate database file, and replace *every* electronic component containing an embedded microchip that reads dates. Heck, you might not even find them all.

Truth be told, you know you're not going to make it. Your compliance program didn't start in earnest until much later than everyone would have liked. Your Y2K team made countless expedient decisions, took many unavoidable shortcuts, and dropped important applications, assets, and suppliers from the "mission-critical" list just because it became too long. You have far more test scripts to run than time will allow. Your company has lost Y2K staff, and the schedule has slipped and never fully recovered. And even though the project grew bigger the deeper you waded in, your resources didn't keep up.

For most companies, Y2K compliance has been a tough sell, the most expensive nonproductive investment most businesses have ever made. How do you pitch a multimillion dollar project to management when the CFO says its return on investment is zero? The problem went from virtual obscurity a couple of years ago to a subject of ridicule, superficial media reports, and scare tactics by consultants and lawyers in 1997 and 1998. But 1999 brings with it increasingly strident journalistic and political rhetoric. How could management have been so short-sighted in the first place? Even worse, once awareness became commonplace, why have so many companies responded so lethargically? Everyone is starting to worry about protecting their backsides. Most information technology (IT) professionals have never seen so many lawyers, much less worked so closely with them.

You have Y2K risk, big time. If it makes you feel any better, so does everyone else.

The Year 2000 problem is much too big and much too messy just to fix and test the code and then see what happens. Maybe if Y2K conversions had been handled as a routine maintenance project over the past decade, you could have gotten away with that. But rushing the project through in the last couple of years means corners have been cut and hard choices have been made that make it almost inevitable that something has been overlooked or that you remain vulnerable to the ripple effects of failures outside of your corporate boundaries. Everyone knows that 1999 is the time for contingency planning, but as you'll soon see, there's quite a bit more than that to mitigating the business and legal risks of Y2K.

Overview of the Book

In the 1935 Marx Brothers movie, *A Night at the Opera,* Chico makes a speech in his false Italian accent about "how we fly to America":

> The first time we started, we get-a halfway across when we run out-a gasoline and we gotta go back. Then I take-a twice as much gasoline. This time we-a just about to land—maybe three feet—when whaddya think? We run out-a gasoline again and a-back we go again to get-a more gas.

Y2K risk management is a lot like that: a last chance to go back and pick up what you missed the first time through.

Of the many disciplines required to manage an effective Year 2000 program, risk management has not been recognized as a separate set of integrated and identifiable tasks designed to mitigate the hazards of imperfection. That is our goal here, to provide as comprehensive a treatment as possible of the many elements involved in controlling the organizational, financial, managerial, technical, and legal risks of Y2K projects. Many readers will be familiar with some of the issues we discuss, but we believe that this book is the first time all of these disparate elements have been brought together under one roof.

Even though it is quite impossible to run a perfect Y2K project, it is our firm belief that much greater success can be achieved—irrespective of when you started or how far along you are—by focusing on reducing risk as a distinct management objective for the final year of the twentieth century. (Yes, we know the century *technically* begins on January 1, 2001, but we're going to adopt the popular convention that the new millennium starts in 2000.) Because complete success is unattainable, residual risks remain, and they are serious enough to merit your focused attention. By taking a broad, best-practices view of risk management, we hope to help you cross the date boundary in much better shape than you otherwise would. Along with testing and deployment, risk management is one of the great unfinished tasks of Y2K programs. 1999 is a good time to "go again to get-a more gas."

How This Book Is Organized

We've divided our discussion into the major risk areas and risk management processes that most organizations must address to effectively mitigate the anticipated fallout from Year 2000 problems.

In Chapter 1, "Year 2000 Business and Legal Risks," we lay out the universe of risks that are the subject of this book. As you will see, much more than fixing your own computer systems is involved. Computerized equipment, electronic data interchange, and external business dependencies, including your customers and supply chain, are vulnerable to Y2K failures and must be brought under control. We'll discuss the consequences of the various categories of risk and when they might occur, and we'll focus closely on legal liability, insurance coverage, and market impacts, all as a foundation for understanding what's ahead.

Chapter 2 is a guide to "Building an Effective Year 2000 Risk Management Program." Here we introduce the scope and goals of a comprehensive Y2K risk management program, with particular attention to the steps and process of planning the project. The discussion is designed to enable you to build a risk mitigation program from the ground up or, if you've already started, check to see what you may have overlooked. Topics include where to start, management responsibilities, business risk assessments, and triage and risk ratings.

The most important risk management strategy is having a well-organized and effective Y2K compliance program. In Chapter 3, "Fast-Tracking a Year 2000 Project," we provide a soup-to-nuts course in starting a project from scratch and structuring it so you can complete the essential tasks in time. From planning the project quickly, to developing an accelerated remediation plan and establishing compliance standards, we walk you through the work that comprises the critical path to success. The chapter closes with a quick-and-dirty *Project Initiation Checklist* to get you up and running quickly, plus a detailed *Project Life Cycle Checklist* to make sure that nothing essential falls through the cracks.

Chapter 4, "Reducing Y2K Liability Exposure," will help you make the best use of 1999 to avoid Year 2000 litigation, or at least take steps to improve your position if you do get sued. The concept of *Year 2000 due diligence* is introduced, and a detailed *Legal Issues Checklist* is discussed at length. We describe the different types of lawsuits that are anticipated, the probable theories of liability, and the most important defenses. Specific strategies for protecting directors and officers and IT professionals are presented next. We then lay out step-by-step approaches for legal risk management, including conducting legal audits, developing new contracting and purchasing policies, protecting Year 2000 vendors and consultants, avoiding liability from selling noncompliant products and services, and taking advantage of the recently enacted *Year 2000 Information and Readiness Disclosure Act*. The chapter closes with suggestions for developing a Y2K regulatory compliance program.

Chapter 5 looks at the important subject of "External Compliance Strategies." The discussion covers the entire range of third-party business relationships, including resource dependencies you need to produce goods and services, output dependencies such as customers and wholesalers, as well as multilevel dependencies, sole-source suppliers, and electronic trading partners. We then explain how to assess and manage those external business dependencies (EBDs), including collecting compliance information from your resource dependencies and providing information about your own compliance efforts to your output dependencies. A sample supply chain questionnaire is provided, together with templates for tracking and analyzing the responses, and guidelines for securing alternative EBDs.

"Contingency Planning," the subject of Chapter 6, is likely to be the primary risk management activity of 1999. We walk you through the five phases of a best-practices contingency planning project—assessment, planning (including alternative strategies for working around Y2K events), testing, execution, and recovery. Detailed outlines of a contingency plan and an emergency management plan are presented, along with a list of contingency planning resources.

Chapter 7 addresses "Major Corporate Decision Making." One of the many difficulties of Year 2000 is that you cannot put the normal demands of business on hold while you finish up your Y2K remediation and testing. Instead of treating your Year 2000 project as something that is separate and apart from your ongoing business initiatives, it makes more sense to incorporate Y2K thinking into your strategic goal setting. We look first at the risks and rewards of integrating disclosures and communications about your Y2K preparedness into your marketing efforts and discussions with customers, shareholders, and resource dependencies. An analysis of exercising due diligence to reduce Year 2000 risks for mergers and acquisitions follows, with a discussion of valuation issues, overlooked contingent liabilities, and technical and business risks that should be considered before deciding whether to combine two enterprises on the eve of the millennium. We close by explaining how inattention to Year 2000 issues could undermine efforts to achieve business process improvements.

Because so many Y2K risks are beyond your immediate control, even organizations with excellent Year 2000 remediation programs may still encounter serious failures. In Chapter 8, "Substantiating Due Diligence," we discuss what you can do now to show regulators and juries that you have exercised due diligence and reasonable business judgment. Topics covered include sound documentation practices, disclosures required by the Securities and Exchange Commission, and disclosures by privately-held companies. We then explain how to use internal audit controls to shore up your compliance efforts and how to work with external auditors on Year 2000 issues, in order to avoid adverse audit opinions that could be harmful to your business.

Chapter 9 covers the vital subject of "Insurance Issues." We first identify the major residual risks for which protection is required and then discuss risk financing techniques to fund uninsured risks. There follows an exhaustive treatment of risk transfer—insurance—issues: the prospects for coverage under all of the major types of existing policies, the workings of the new Year 2000 coverage exclusions that have been approved in most states, handling Y2K questions on new or renewal applications, and a review of the pros and cons of the Year 2000 specialty policies that have come on the market since 1997.

Every business should carefully consider "Alternative Dispute Resolution" (ADR), the subject of Chapter 10, as a legal contingency plan for avoiding costly and destructive Y2K litigation. The discussion begins by looking at the interests and perspectives of the parties who are likely to become embroiled in Year 2000 disputes, and then shows how litigation will often be an unsatisfactory solution to both sides. The objectives and types of ADR are described as a foundation for showing you how and why companies should put corporate Y2K dispute resolution programs in place now, *before* conflicts arise. Strategies for gaining management support, getting the parties to the table, and screening cases are presented, along with sample Y2K ADR contract clauses.

Recognizing that many Y2K lawsuits are probably unavoidable, Chapter 11 provides advice on "Litigation Planning and Management" to help you reduce legal costs and achieve better results. We offer suggestions for selecting and managing Year 2000 trial counsel, budgeting for litigation, and managing cost recovery suits. Because many companies are likely to face multiple lawsuits that will pose difficult financial and logistical burdens, the unique role of coordination counsel is discussed. We focus on when you might need an outside law firm to coordinate simultaneous suits raising similar legal and factual issues, how to choose such a firm, and how to develop joint defense agreements that enable multiple defendants to share information and expenses without compromising privileged communications.

Finally, Chapter 12 looks ahead to "Post-2000 Risk Management." Notwithstanding the difficulty of trying to predict what the world will be like after the date rollover, we present several observers' views about the outlook for Year 2000, wade into the important issue of crisis management, and explore public and private sector recovery strategies. We close with some final thoughts on possible financial, legal, and investment scenarios on the other side of the date line, including concerns about a possible credit crunch in late 1999 and early to mid-2000.

Who Should Read This Book

As you can see, we've cast a pretty wide net because the universe of Y2K business and legal risks is so broad and diverse. The entire book—even the legal sections—is written in plain English that you will have no difficulty understanding. We wrote this book for many different audiences, ranging from employees with highly specialized responsibilities in large corporations to small business owners with just a couple of folks who will have to pretty much do everything themselves. Specific job titles that should benefit from this information include the following:

CFOs, CIOs, and CTOs

Corporate VPs and departmental managers responsible for Year 2000 compliance and business continuity

Y2K project managers and team members

Business continuity, contingency, and disaster recovery planners

Risk managers and directors

Directors, officers, trustees, and other fiduciaries

In-house and outside corporate legal counsel and litigators

Emergency response personnel

Federal, state, and local government emergency planners and managers

After Chapter 1 introduces "Year 2000 Business and Legal Risks," the remaining chapters fall into three overlapping clusters.

PROJECT RISK MANAGEMENT

Chapter 2, "Building an Effective Year 2000 Risk Management Program"

Chapter 3, "Fast-Tracking a Year 2000 Project"

Chapter 6, "Contingency Planning"

BUSINESS RISK MANAGEMENT

Chapter 5, "External Compliance Strategies"

Chapter 7, "Major Corporate Decision Making"

Chapter 9, "Insurance Issues"

Chapter 12, "Post-2000 Risk Management"

LEGAL RISK MANAGEMENT

Chapter 4, "Reducing Y2K Liability Exposure"

Chapter 8, "Substantiating Due Diligence"

Chapter 10, "Alternative Dispute Resolution"

Chapter 11, "Litigation Planning and Management"

Year 2000 is a cross-departmental problem, and many readers will benefit from learning about subjects that usually fall outside their areas of expertise. For example, IT professionals might want to look at Chapter 4, "Reducing Y2K Liability Exposure," and Chapter 8, "Substantiating Due Diligence," to gain an understanding of the legal environment in which they might soon become involved. CFOs and other managers might venture into Chapter 6, "Contingency Planning," to learn why the company needs to devote so much time and expense to planning for the possibility of failure. Readers whose Y2K projects are well along and reasonably on schedule can certainly skip Chapter 3, "Fast-Tracking a Year 2000 Project."

From Here

The Year 2000 was first thought to be a straightforward technical headache. We now realize that Y2K may be perhaps the greatest business problem ever to face most organizations. We hope this book will give you the information and tools you will need to conduct an effective program to minimize your Year 2000 risks. Let us begin with a comprehensive overview of just what those risks comprise.

CHAPTER 1

Year 2000 Business and Legal Risks

"A pessimist is a well-informed optimist."

—REPRESENTATIVE CONSTANCE MORELLA

In this chapter, we will provide an overview of Year 2000 risks, including their potential scope and severity, to help you structure effective risk response strategies. To begin, we will focus on the risks side; in the rest of the book we will describe the affirmative steps your organization can take to avoid Y2K perils and mitigate their harms. As you will see, potential Year 2000 business and legal risks are so vast in their scope and diversity that this entire chapter can serve as only an introduction. In subsequent chapters, we will focus in detail on each of the risk areas outlined here.

Y2K Casualties: Your Business, Customers, and Career

Significant Y2K failures, should they occur, are likely to have extremely serious business and legal consequences. Regardless of how you may view the sufficiency of the efforts being made to prevent Year 2000 problems, if the rate of repair and level of testing are not accelerated, last-minute responses or "fix-on-failure" strategies probably won't be enough to prevent severe business disruptions (Jones, 1998a).

Sources of Risk

Year 2000 risk comes from many quadrants; together, minor but simultaneous Y2K events can form waves of disruptions that may spread throughout the business world and the global economy. Every organization needs to think systematically about multiple categories of risk so as not to lose sight of the forest for the trees. We will start by looking at the basic sources of Year 2000 business risks and work our way up to higher levels of risk exposure. Then, we'll consider the possible business and legal consequences.

Internal IT Systems

Internal IT systems are the most obvious source of potential Y2K failures and the risk most under the company's immediate control. Vulnerable technologies include mainframes, client/server systems, networks, intranets, personal computers (PCs), and other components of hardware and software infrastructure, as well as application programs, utilities, databases, and so on. The nature of Y2K risk often depends on the extent to which components of information systems are under the company's *direct* control. You may have a combination of systems, including applications that were developed entirely in-house, plain vanilla or modified commercial off-the-shelf (COTS) programs, and custom-built systems and applications. Many companies use software developed by third parties to provide expert application and systems development not available in-house. Vendors, however, may not be willing to provide the level of Y2K support you require because they now face risks to their own bottom lines and possible liability exposures from their noncompliant products.

Companies often depend on maintenance and support agreements with multiple vendors responsible for different parts of the system, strung together over time. Dealing with multiple vendors of IT products and services is difficult enough in normal times; it is fair to assume that Y2K will stress these relationships in new and unpredictable ways. The patchwork quilt of interdependent technologies upon which most companies rely creates additional difficulties because Year 2000 requires assessment, remediation, and testing of an entire system for which no single vendor bears sole responsibility. Indeed, it has become common to define Y2K *compliance* (about which we will have more to say in Chapter 4, "Reducing Liability Exposure") by accounting for such interdependencies. For example, the Federal Acquisitions Regulation's definition includes a qualifier that a product is compliant "to the extent that other information technology, used in combination with the information technology being acquired, properly exchanges date/time data with it."

Embedded and Non-IT Systems

Embedded systems are "devices used to control, monitor or assist the operation of equipment, machinery or plant" and are "an integral part of the system" (IEE, 1998). The renowned Year 2000 evangelist, Peter de Jager, says of embedded systems, "Without doubt, this is the area of greatest risk . . . they are the Achilles heel of Y2K" (1998). Embedded chips are nonprogrammable microcircuits hard-wired into other pieces of equipment, many of which include date calculations in their programming logic. The equipment in which the chips are embedded often is not under the control of the IS department but usually is the responsibility of the vendors that supply and maintain it for diverse operational units of the organization.

Giga Information Group of Cambridge, Massachusetts, categorizes embedded systems into four groups: individual microprocessors, small microprocessor assemblies with no timing functions, subassemblies with timing functions, and computer systems used in manufacturing or processing control. According to Giga, only the last two groups are likely to experience Y2K failures, ranging from annoying to aggravating, debilitating, and finally, life-threatening (Coffou, 1998). Embedded chip systems that should be tested for Year 2000 vulnerability include the following:

- Monitoring and control systems, including smart valves and sensors and environmental and safety equipment
- Fire alarm systems, including detection, sending, receiving, and suppression units
- Security systems, including sending and receiving units, video and surveillance systems, and badge readers
- Telecommunications equipment, including telephone switching equipment, call management systems, pagers, and cellular phones
- Medical devices and equipment, including monitoring systems; dialysis, chemotherapy, and radiation equipment; and laboratory, radiology, and other diagnostic systems
- Building infrastructure, including heating, ventilation, and air-conditioning (HVAC) equipment, energy management and lighting controls, emergency generators and lighting, uninterruptible power supplies, and elevators (Coffou, 1997a; Ackerman, 1997; Bailey, 1997).

Embedded systems pose unique Year 2000 risks. Most organizations lack the in-house technical expertise required to inventory, repair, and test these automated devices for Y2K vulnerability. In fact, most Y2K consultants have little or no expertise in this difficult area, and there may not be sufficient technical capacity in 1999 and 2000 to address the problem. It may be, as de Jager suggests, that "the only alternative we've left ourselves is to turn off what we're not sure of" (1998).

The other major problem with embedded chips is that they're everywhere, with literally hundreds of billions of them installed in all kinds of equipment around the globe. Even if, as most knowledgeable experts believe, only a very small percentage of such devices are vulnerable to century-date failures in equipment that could be considered vital, incapacitating and even catastrophic consequences could result. Consider the following examples.

Plant Automation

TAVA Technologies, Inc. of Englewood, Colorado, which, by February 1998, had Y2K manufacturing plant floor experience at more than 400 sites, has reported that "the company has yet to find a single site that did not require some degree of remediation." Computerized factory floor systems store, transfer, output, and calculate dates in a wide variety of management and control systems, including maintenance databases, smart sensors, inventory management, programmable logic controllers, shipping documentation, and energy management. Out of the tens of thousands of manufacturing automation systems and components TAVA has tested for Year 2000 compliance, it has found "more than 20% to be either non-compliant or 'suspect,' that is non-compliant under certain circumstances" (Hagewood, 1998).

Healthcare

ECRI, a nonprofit agency specializing in healthcare technology located in Plymouth Meeting, Pennsylvania, finds that, although most medical devices will not be affected by Y2K problems, "a small number of devices may fail or malfunction." ECRI identifies information systems, medical devices, and general hospital systems as "susceptible equipment," with problems ranging from billing errors, improper supply orders and device lockup, to erroneous patient data and invalid dosage rates. Failures of high-risk equipment used for "life support, resuscitation, or critical monitoring," such as anesthesia units, radiographic equipment, and ventilators, could directly harm the patient. In the case of "medium risk equipment," such as clinical laboratory equipment, ultrasound scanners, and cardiac output units, Y2K failures would not pose "immediate harm to patients," but "[m]ay have a significant impact on patient care" (Montagnolo, 1998).

Electric Power

Much of the concern about the stability of the nation's electric power grid relates directly to the extensive reliance of power-generating and transmission equipment on embedded systems. Rick Cowles states that "Within a typical electric utility, embedded-logic control is prevalent in every facet of operation; from load dispatch and remote switchyard breaker control, to nuclear power plant safety systems and fossil fuel plant boiler control systems. Whole generating units (generally, gas turbines) are controlled from miles away by personnel remotely adjusting system loads in response to peak demands" (1998).

Exchanging Data Electronically

An increasing number of commercial transactions are now handled by direct electronic communication. These include the following:

- Electronic funds transfers (EFT)
- Electronic data interchange (EDI) systems that place, fill, invoice, and pay for orders for parts, supplies, and finished goods
- Medical and other insurance claims processing and payments
- Securities trading clearinghouses and regulatory compliance reporting

Several opportunities for Y2K breakdown exist. First, a basic prerequisite for electronic communication is that both systems must be able to talk to each other, that is, successfully send and receive information. Y2K can disrupt IT systems on either end of the wire, blocking electronic communication, and it can disable the communication linkage itself.

Second, even if both systems have achieved internal Year 2000 compliance, they still may not be able to communicate if they have renovated their systems using incompatible methodologies. For example, if one party converted its code using a *fixed window* and a trading partner used a *sliding window*, the century designation for the date data could become ambiguous after transmission.

Finally, electronic data exchange could *contaminate* compliant systems with erroneous data transmitted by noncompliant but functioning systems of their trading partners. For example, if system A generates data with financial information that is 100 years off and successfully sends that information to system B, the databases of system B could use that data to process transactions and perform calculations that contain unknown errors.

Due to the increasing importance of direct electronic transactions, Year 2000 remediation may require large-scale *end-to-end* testing across many links in a supply chain, such as retailers, EDI clearinghouses, value-added networks, distributors, wholesalers, shippers, suppliers, and assemblers. Substantial technical, logistical, financial, and managerial challenges abound, with corresponding business risk.

External Business Dependencies

Most business organizations, public and nonprofit agencies, and institutions understand that, no matter how well prepared they may be for the century date change themselves, they remain acutely vulnerable to Year 2000 problems if the many third parties with which they do business are not ready to process twenty-first century dates. Although awareness of this external dimension of Y2K increased dramatically in 1998, it remains a difficult problem to address and, hence, an intractable source of risk.

Supply Chain Compliance

The problem of evaluating Y2K risks in the supply chain is a stubborn one for many reasons. The number and diversity of outside dependencies may make efforts daunting. Companies are unable to control or even reliably assess external compliance efforts. Potential failure points that could trigger and result from Y2K chain reactions are unpredictable. All of these obstacles can prove insurmountable when trying to assess supply chain compliance and many initial efforts have proven ineffective. For example, a group of large retailers and manufacturers that rely on thousands of suppliers, including the big three automakers (acting through the Automotive Industry Action Group), were among the first to disseminate detailed vendor compliance questionnaires in an attempt to assess supply-chain Year 2000 preparations. The initial results proved unsatisfactory because of low response rates and unreliable data, and extensive follow-up efforts were required to produce satisfactory results.

Nevertheless, vendor surveys have proliferated widely, albeit with mixed results. Common mistakes include asking for too much detail, requiring *compliance certifications* and signatures that give rise to liability concerns, and adopting an antagonistic tone. In Chapter 5, "External Compliance Strategies," we'll share what we've learned about mitigating vendor risk and suggest an expedited strategy to follow in 1999.

Customer Compliance

There is a real risk that companies unprepared for Year 2000 will be unable to pay their bills or at least will experience significant disruptions. If so, businesses providing goods and services to such companies could take hits to their own cash flows and receivables. The concern is serious enough that the Federal Financial Institutions Examination Council (FFIEC) has required member banks, credit unions, and savings associations to implement customer due diligence plans to evaluate whether Y2K might prevent their material customers from repaying their loans on time (1998). As 2000 nears, all businesses—not just banks—should ask themselves if they are putting too many eggs in the wrong baskets.

Customer compliance problems have the potential to adversely affect an entire market segment. For example, in September 1998, a Massachusetts technology consultant and systems integrator saw its stock price drop 22 percent after the company announced that many of its customers were delaying new projects to focus on Y2K work (Reuters, 1998).

Infrastructure Compliance

Every enterprise, whether public or private, needs electric power; telephone service; water and sewer service; police, fire, and ambulance service; public transportation; cargo ports; airports; and similar services and facilities. Providers of those services and operators of those facilities face the same Y2K risks discussed here.

In many cases, the useful life of aging infrastructure has been extended far beyond its original design by patches, workarounds, and other expedient contrivances, making Y2K assessment and remediation all the more difficult. Because most of us can't build our own electric generating station, sewage treatment plant, or international shipping terminal, serious Year 2000 events in essential infrastructure systems pose risks that would be extremely difficult to overcome. You cannot safely ignore infrastructure risks; to the contrary, every business should formulate contingency plans so it can operate without basic services for a short or extended period.

International Compliance

It would be wrong to assume that all countries are devoting equal effort to tackling Year 2000 problems. In fact, wide disparities in their compliance preparations exist among nations. According to the Gartner Group, which conducts a quarterly Y2K survey of 15,000 companies in 87 countries, the United States is farthest along in its preparations, followed by Holland, Belgium, Sweden, Canada, and Australia. By contrast, Gartner predicts that two-thirds of the companies in Russia, China, India, the Middle East (excluding Israel), Argentina, and Venezuela, as well as half of all companies in Japan, Germany, Mexico, and Malaysia, will have one major mission-critical Y2K failure (Weil, 1998). *USA Today* reported in April 1998 that only 8 percent of German companies had a formal compliance program, as compared to 80 percent of large U.S. companies (Lynch, 1998). Professor Richard L. Nolan believes that "probably more than 70 percent of Japan's CEOs are unaware of the potential of the Y2K problem to disrupt their business and are not providing any meaningful Y2K leadership" (1998). The Federal Reserve Bank has expressed serious concerns about the compliance efforts of many foreign banks, in no small part because many U.S. banks depend on international funds flows and foreign counterparties for funds deposits and processing major financial transactions.

Outside the United States, additional obstacles are complicating Year 2000 conversion efforts. Economies around the globe are currently struggling to recover from failing markets, and others are converting to a single European currency. Because European Monetary Unit (EMU) conversions and economic difficulties have largely preempted international Y2K preparations, U.S. companies are in danger from noncompliant overseas customers and suppliers. Unprepared international subsidiaries and affiliates of U.S. firms also pose financial risks to those companies that maintain consolidated balance sheets.

Potential Consequences of Y2K Failures

Up to this point, we have merely catalogued the various sources of Year 2000 risk. Now let's consider what kinds of damage Y2K could cause.

Operational Disruptions

It should be obvious that serious Y2K problems from any of the sources outlined previously—internal IT systems, embedded systems, data exchanges, and external business dependencies—could prevent a company from conducting business as usual, on either a short-term or prolonged basis. It takes little imagination to come up with a long list of plausible date-related failure scenarios including these:

- Inability to generate invoices, pay bills, or issue paychecks
- Cancellation of customer accounts identified as 100 years past due
- Delays in just-in-time deliveries from key parts suppliers
- Malfunctioning of first-in/first-out inventory management systems
- Termination of lines of credit due to inaccurate credit reports
- Failure of robotics, calibration systems, or process control sensors
- Loss of electrical power, phone service, or Internet access
- Disruption of airline reservations and flight schedules
- Erroneous cancellation of insurance policies resulting from uncredited premium payments or miscalculation of expiration dates

Financial Losses and Business Failures

We need not belabor a self-evident point: Any of the foregoing operational disruptions will surely have financial consequences. It is worth noting, however, that credible analysts anticipate that Y2K will push some companies into bankruptcy, with potential ripple effects for customers and suppliers. For example, the respected software economist, Capers Jones, projects that Y2K problems will lead to a 5–7 percent business failure rate for the approximately 30,000 U.S. corporations that have 1,000 to 10,000 employees. That figure would translate to approximately 1,500 to 2,100 Y2K bankruptcies. Jones has reasoned that "In the year 2000 context, mid-size corporations will probably be late in getting started on their year 2000 repairs, will underestimate and underbudget for their year 2000 work, will not bring in the appropriate tools and specialists, and will probably not have any contingency plans in place on what to do with applications that don't make the changes in time" (Jones, 1998b). His thinking is confirmed by our observations in the marketplace.

Health and Safety

Year 2000 failures are unlikely to actually injure someone, but there is still a risk. Certainly, a great deal of safety-related equipment is computer operated or contains embedded microprocessors. It is likely that the incidence of date-related problems will be lower in health, safety, and security systems than in IT and embedded systems in general. Hardware and software that protect life and health are usually designed with redundancies and fail-safe features that make them more resistant to stresses such as power outages.

Nonetheless, we strongly recommend that every Year 2000 risk assessment consider health and safety impacts of date-related problems. You will need to guard against two primary risks. One is the risk that Y2K problems would actually *cause* physical harm, as in the case of a dangerous piece of equipment that might malfunction or operate unpredictably in 2000. The second is that safety systems—technologies that control building access, fire suppression, or emergency communications, and so on—might fail. Given the vital importance of health and safety systems, ignoring them would be foolish and potentially dangerous.

Of course, the healthcare industry bears a special exposure to Year 2000 problems that could imperil health and safety. Computers control many functions that care for patients and protect them from harm, including monitors, devices that administer medications and control dosage rates, and diagnostic equipment. Most of these systems do not depend on accurately processing date information for their safe and effective operation, but a small percentage do. A senior government healthcare official offered the following testimony before Congress: "For example, an incorrect date or time sequence in the output of a blood gas analyzer could cause confusion when interpreting the sequential results, causing errors in diagnosis and treatment. Likewise, an incorrect date calculation which is stamped on an automated chest X-ray could prompt unnecessary further testing or even cause a misdiagnosis . . . Similarly, if a Year 2000-induced error causes a piece of laboratory equipment to skip a function, or perform a function twice, a patient could get the lab results of the patient who preceded or succeeded him or her, with potentially adverse consequences" (Kizer, 1998).

In focus groups of Y2K healthcare professionals conducted by the Rx2000 Solutions Institute, a nonprofit organization that addresses Y2K issues in the healthcare industry, 67 percent of the respondents strongly agreed and 25 percent agreed that "Year 2000 issues have the potential to negatively impact the quality of health care." Even more disturbing, 58 percent agreed and 25 percent strongly agreed that "Year 2000 issues have the potential to create errors that lead to unnecessary deaths" (Ackerman, 1997).

Career Damage

Serious Y2K failures have the potential to damage many careers. Y2K poses special liability risks for directors and officers, but they can be overcome by the exercise of due diligence. There is little excuse for failing to take the steps necessary to fulfill fiduciary responsibilities, as explained in Chapter 4, "Reducing Liability Exposure." In public companies, directors and officers could be forced to resign if stock prices decline significantly. Unprepared companies can expect that heads will roll at the top of the corporate pyramid, and even in the board room. Executive complacency regarding Year 2000 risks is a serious mistake, one that endangers both your career and your business.

Senior executives in virtually any company will have a lot of explaining to do if their competitors are better prepared for the millennium transition. CIOs—who faced high turnover rates even before Y2K came along—will confront added pressures as 2000 approaches. Y2K project managers could become embroiled in lawsuits, not as defendants but as principal witnesses whose competence and judgment may be called into question.

IT professionals would be well advised to prepare themselves now for difficult adjustments in their daily routines. Careers of computer professionals have been marked in recent years by dizzying highs and lows; in a sense, the instability is nothing new. But the Y2K problem, often seen as a short-sighted failure to prevent major business disruptions due to oversight of a trivial design parameter (two-digit year fields), has engendered much disdain for IT professionals. Public criticism is likely to increase if serious failures start to occur on a broad scale. At the same time, a host of recent developments in the industry, including Year 2000, have put many IT professionals in the cat bird seat, with compensation, perks, and career opportunities the likes of which they have never before seen. Widespread Y2K breakdowns could well bring this short-lived Golden Age to a crashing halt, so it is in the interest of all computer professionals to prepare themselves for a new world order of scapegoating, lawsuits, and governmental regulation. As Paul A. Strassman has observed, "Relying on the year 2000 precedent, government regulators will surely extend their reach into security and safety, standards for electronic commerce and certification of software reliability. In the future, many of the key decisions about IT will be subject to the same scrutiny as originators of pollution, purveyors of tobacco or makers of breast implants. Decisions that should have been made by CIOs and corporate executives now will be shaped by lawyers, government officials, lobbyists and legislators" (1998).

If a Y2K calamity does occur, technical professionals will need to be ready for a steady diet of second-guessing, finger pointing, and worse. Good careers could be ruined, and you could find yourself spending an awful lot of time working with lawyers, preparing for depositions, and wishing you'd documented the decisions you made along the way. We will describe what you can expect from Y2K litigation in Chapter 11, "Litigation Planning and Management." For now, it is worth noting that as unpleasant and seemingly pointless as it may be to spend precious time building a paper trail of Y2K planning and triage decisions, test results, and the like, we hope to convince you that this time is not only well spent in your own fundamental self-interest, but good for your project, too.

Year 2000 is bringing many programmers out of their cubicles and into the wider business environment where different skills are needed to stay out of harm's way. 1999 is not too early to start learning those new skills, and we will do our best to get you started. Year 2000 risk management may be neither glamorous nor fun, but it could prove essential to professional self-preservation.

Legal Liability

We will introduce this important issue in its own section later in this chapter and elsewhere in the book, where we present detailed strategies for reducing liability exposure (Chapter 4), alternative dispute resolution (Chapter 10), and litigation planning (Chapter 11). For now, it is enough to note that legal liabilities are likely to be one of the most significant impacts of Y2K failures and must be an integral part of effective risk management planning.

Failure Horizons

As our information-driven world closes in on 2000, it cannot be doubted that, given the considerable amount of work that remains to be done, time is short. We share the views of many of our colleagues that testing and contingency planning will take at least as long as assessment and remediation, so most organizations will find their Y2K plates full to overflowing during 1999. Unfortunately, there is a widely held and often unstated assumption—supported by most media coverage—that Year 2000 problems will not occur until internal computer clocks roll over to "00" at midnight on December 31, 1999. Such thinking is both uninformed and dangerous.

Y2K failures will occur as soon as twenty-first century dates are entered into noncompliant systems. We know this to be true because a fair number of Year 2000 problems have already occurred:

- The Social Security Administration discovered the problem in 1989, when it was unable to perform long-range actuarial forecasts that extended into the twenty-first century.
- The mortgage banking industry had similar experiences when it tried to calculate payments and returns on 30-year mortgages.
- A 104-year-old woman in Winona, Minnesota, was sent a computer-generated notice to enroll in kindergarten in 1992 (de Jager, 1997).
- A Detroit-area grocery store filed suit in 1997 after its computerized cash register system shut down whenever it tried to process transactions using credit cards with "00" expiration dates.
- On January 1, 1998, a Chase Manhattan Bank software program that normally maintained stop-payment orders on checks for two years treated all that day's orders as "expired" (Sheinheit, 1998).
- A survey of IT directors and managers in 12 business sectors conducted by Rubin Systems for Cap Gemini America in July, 1998, showed that 40 percent of respondents had already experienced Y2K failures, including processing disruptions (87 percent), financial miscalculations or loss (62 percent), logistics or supply-chain problems (44 percent), and customer service problems (38 percent) (Soat, 1998).

It is widely anticipated that Y2K problems will increase dramatically in 1999. Consider the many planning requirements common in business and government that need computers to process information at least one year ahead: preparing budget and financial projections, procurement planning for manufactured goods, determining whether someone is eligible to drive or holds a valid professional license, scheduling annual appointments and follow-up visits, calculating insurance policy expiration dates, and so on.

The *time horizon to failure* can also be foreshortened if fiscal years are used in processing date calculations. For example, most state and local governments operate on July 1 fiscal years, so FY00 starts on July 1, 1999. Many budget systems used to project costs for the coming fiscal year already need to process Year 2000 dates.

On the other side of that wall, Year 2000 problems will probably continue to crop up long after 2000. Many Y2K errors will not prevent systems from operating but will simply generate incorrect data that the system will accept and process. As a result, organizations could encounter major and minor snafus until the errors are discovered and fixed, one at a time. Also, the use of windowing, masking techniques, and other short-cuts to repairing noncompliant systems is likely to degrade the performance of many IT systems and create greater-than-usual maintenance requirements that will adversely affect business productivity. Indeed, as companies rush to complete and test their mission-critical remediation work by the end of 1999, they will find that they must then turn their attention to the many important systems they left behind.

The Expected Legal Fallout

The projections of litigation arising from Y2K are unprecedented. Capers Jones estimates that damage awards and legal fees will total $100 billion in the United States and $300 billion worldwide (Jones, 1998b). Giga Information Group puts the global cost at $1 trillion (Coffou, 1997a). Jeff Jinnett, a leading Year 2000 lawyer, has offered a $1 trillion estimate for U.S. Y2K litigation (Jinnett, 1997a). He also puts the scope of the Y2K liability picture in perspective when he observes that "a $1 trillion cost for Year 2000 litigation would exceed even the estimated total annual direct and indirect costs of all civil litigation in the United States (at $300 billion per year)" (Jinnett, 1997b).

It is important to note that damage awards to businesses and consumers that suffer Y2K-related financial losses will constitute the vast majority of these estimated litigation costs, with attorneys' fees and litigation expenses representing a substantially smaller portion. In any case, the projections are staggering and certainly justify the widespread concern among IT vendors, directors and officers, legislators, and many others (including the authors) about the prospects for crippling Y2K lawsuits.

Types of Lawsuits Anticipated

A consensus is beginning to emerge about the major kinds of Y2K lawsuits we can expect. Capers Jones has developed a useful starting point:

1. Litigation filed by clients whose products, finances, or investments have been damaged
2. Litigation filed by shareholders of companies whose software does not safely make the year 2000 transition
3. Litigation associated with any deaths or injuries derived from the year 2000 problem
4. Class-action litigation filed by various affected customers of computers or software packages
5. Litigation filed by companies that used outsource vendors, contractors, consultants, or commercial year 2000 tools, but Year 2000 problems still slipped through and caused damage
6. Litigation against hardware manufacturers such as computer companies and defense contractors if the year 2000 problem resides in hardware or embedded microcode as well as software (Jones, 1998b)

Note that Jones's list identifies potential plaintiffs and defendants, with only brief mention of the "cause of action," that is, the nature of the allegations. Typically, most commercial and tort (personal injury and property damage) lawsuits allege multiple theories of liability, and Y2K litigation is likely to be no different. We will examine specific claims and defenses in Chapter 4, "Reducing Liability Exposure."

In addition, Jones focuses on *cost-recovery* suits by parties that have suffered some financial or other loss that can be measured in pecuniary terms. Some lawsuits will fall outside the cost-recovery boundary. Four additional categories of Y2K suits may include:

- Suits to determine whether insurance companies are required to provide coverage for various Y2K claims and lawsuits
- Enforcement actions by regulatory agencies and law enforcement authorities for civil and (less likely) criminal violations of federal and state statutes and regulations
- Suits challenging the failure to provide governmental services and suits to determine the validity of immunity legislation that several states have adopted to insulate themselves from Y2K litigation
- Suits by software vendors (probably in the form of countersuits against their customers) alleging that customers violated copyright laws by rewriting noncompliant computer code in breach of the terms of the software license

Year One of Year 2000 Litigation

From August 1997 through August 1998, 20 Y2K-related suits were filed in federal and state courts across the country. They fall into four distinct categories.

Actual Y2K Failures

Only one suit alleges that the plaintiff experienced an actual Year 2000 problem. In *Produce Palace International v. Tec-America Corp.*, a Detroit-area grocery store alleged that its computerized cash register system crashed whenever a customer tried to pay with a credit card with a "00" expiration date. Filed on August 4, 1997, *Produce Palace* holds a place in history as the first Year 2000 lawsuit. If more organizations experience Y2K failures during 1999 as they enter "00" data into noncompliant systems, many more such suits can be expected.

Class Actions

Seventeen of the suits are class actions brought on behalf of business customers and consumers using current or older versions of noncompliant software for which the developer has allegedly refused to provide compliant upgrades without charge. The substance of the allegations is that the developer marketed the software knowing that it was defective and should fix it for free. Software products named in these suits have included accounting, home finance, anti-virus, medical practice management, and voice processing/telephony applications. One of the cases was ordered dismissed in August 1998 on the ground that the plaintiffs had not yet suffered any legally cognizable damages, but the decision has not been reviewed by an appellate court.

Shareholder Suit

One class-action suit was filed by shareholders of Peritus Software Services, Inc. in connection with its acquisition of Millennium Dynamics, Inc., a Year 2000 remediation company. The plaintiffs allege that Peritus made false and misleading statements and failed to adequately inform investors about the acquisition, causing Peritus stock to become artificially inflated.

A Preemptive Strike

On August 28, 1998, a partner in Andersen Consulting LLP filed suit on behalf of the international consulting firm's approximately 600 partners against one of its former customers, J. Baker, Inc. Andersen alleges that between 1989 and 1991 it successfully designed and implemented a computer-based merchandising system in accordance with J. Baker's specifications, but that it was not economically viable at the time to make the system Year 2000 compliant. Andersen has asked the court to "determine and declare that plaintiff Andersen Consulting LLP fulfilled all its obligations to J. Baker and that plaintiff is not responsible for any costs associated with making [the system] year 2000 compliant...." Andersen filed the preemptive suit after J. Baker's attorneys served a demand letter threatening to sue Andersen for more than $3 million in remediation costs.

Nonpublic Legal Disputes

In addition to the 20 publicly filed lawsuits that have been reported, it is likely that other nonpublic disputes and claims are in the works or in the process of settlement. In April 1998, the Gartner Group reported that almost 200 Y2K legal disputes had arisen between IT vendors and customers, largely concerning the cost for Year 2000 upgrades (Caldwell, 1998). In cases of routine Y2K patches or software upgrades for products or systems that are covered by warranties or support agreements, vendors may respond favorably to—or at least be willing to negotiate—customer requests for free or reduced charge fixes to avoid publicly embarrassing litigation.

Factors Complicating Y2K Suits

In the case of Year 2000 litigation, the whole is likely to be considerably greater than the sum of the parts. If current assessments about Y2K preparations prove accurate, several factors are likely to contribute to a chaotic litigation picture.

First, the timing of many lawsuits could be problematic. Companies experiencing operational disruptions, financial losses, and an inability to communicate with their trading partners will find it difficult to shoulder the additional burden of multimillion dollar lawsuits and the tremendous diversion of key employees' time they require.

Second, many organizations, particularly vendors of noncompliant IT products and services, might find themselves the target of multiple, simultaneous suits. This phenomenon has already occurred in 1998, when several class actions were filed against the same software developers for selling noncompliant products: six suits against Intuit, Inc., three against Medical Manager Corporation, and two against Symantec Corporation. If actual failures occur, this trend is likely to take place on a much larger scale for nationally or internationally marketed software and hardware products that are sold in millions of units.

Companies should not underestimate the onerous burdens of multiple and simultaneous litigations. Once thriving corporate giants such as Johns-Mansville and Dow Corning were driven into bankruptcy when they succumbed to the unbearable transaction costs and management distractions resulting from thousands of product liability suits filed across the country and around the globe. Businesses that might find themselves in similar situations because of Y2K need to develop strategies for coordinating and managing such wide-scale litigation well before 2000 to control costs and mount effective defenses.

Finally, the court system will probably not be well equipped to handle a flood of highly technical, document-intensive Y2K lawsuits. When thousands upon thousands of asbestos cases entered the courts during the 1980s, the logistical toll became so great that the federal courts were forced to adopt special procedures to consolidate cases, process motions, conduct hearings, and settle cases. Also, judges and juries often have great difficulty understanding scientific and technical evidence. As a result, considerable delays in handling Y2K cases are likely, so that litigation could continue long after the IT problems have been resolved.

Denial or Loss of Insurance Coverage

It should come as no surprise that the insurance industry is greatly concerned about the potential for unprecedented numbers of claims for Y2K-related losses. A vigorous debate has raged among insurers and their customers about whether existing policies will provide coverage for such claims. Virtually all policies written before 1999 were silent on Year 2000, but insurers argue that Y2K problems will not be *fortuitous* events that were neither *intended nor expected* by insureds, as standard policy language requires. As the saying goes, you can't insure a burning building. On the other side, insureds and their counsel point to the extensive body of case law that requires courts to interpret ambiguous policy language in favor of finding coverage.

Coverage questions defy easy answers. Sweeping statements in news stories that coverage will or won't be available are worth little to companies that need to understand whether they might have to bear potentially enormous Y2K business losses that normally would be covered by insurance. There are multitudes of commercial policies for a variety of claims containing complex definitions, conditions, endorsements, exclusions, limitations, riders, and other provisions that must be analyzed in the light of specific factual circumstances before informed judgments about coverage can be made.

In addition to the many substantive questions concerning which losses might come within the four corners of the policy language, a host of procedural issues affecting coverage will certainly arise. Even if coverage might exist under some circumstances, insureds might lose coverage based on statements they made or information they failed to provide when they first applied for coverage or renewed their policies. Companies could also deprive themselves of the benefits of their policies if they fail to comply with strict requirements for giving notice and presenting claims.

There is likely to be extensive litigation about the availability of insurance coverage for Year 2000, just as there were thousands of such lawsuits filed during the 1980s concerning the availability of coverage for environmental claims. In addition, most state insurance regulators have approved industry-sponsored exclusionary language that could start appearing in new and renewed policies during 1999. We will consider these issues in Chapter 9, "Insurance Issues," and offer strategies for preserving opportunities to insure Y2K losses.

Shifting Market Forces

The many risk scenarios we have described so far present a challenging environment for risk management. Depending on the magnitude and severity of Y2K events, however, still greater hazards must be considered. Many of these macro issues may be beyond the control of any single organization or industry, but that does not mean they can be safely ignored in risk planning.

Impairment of business and industry goodwill. The technology sector has largely fueled this country's phenomenal economic growth during the 1990s. Year 2000 could be the sand in the gas tank. For decades, the IT industry has managed to flourish, despite a track record of failed, late, and bug-ridden products and services. Y2K could galvanize customers into demanding—and getting—better performance and accountability for their money. If the millennium transition becomes rough, the adoring press coverage of whiz-bang technologies and IT millionaires will turn ugly fast.

Y2K credit crunch. Federal financial regulators remember the 1980s real estate crash and resulting S&L crisis as if it were yesterday. As a result, they have required all banks, savings associations, and credit unions to review their loan portfolios by September 30, 1998 to assess the Year 2000 credit risks of their *material* borrowers. Loan customers that have not made adequate Y2K progress will find it more difficult to obtain credit renewals and extensions during 1999. Lending requirements will also become even stiffer for new borrowers.

Capital asset values. Noncompliant information technology and embedded systems will be worth a lot less than their book values suggest as 2000 approaches. And some investments in corporate technology won't be as productive or provide the same return on investment as originally anticipated. Balance sheets, collateral values, and tax planning could all require rethinking.

Loss of market share. Every business should be asking its critical vendors for confirmation that they'll be able to provide uninterrupted service across the date boundary. Although many companies have not been particularly forthcoming in responding to vendor compliance letters from their customers, suppliers that are reluctant to provide reasonable assurances about their Y2K standing will lead many companies to look elsewhere. Look for Y2K compliance to become a strategic marketing theme during 1999.

Investment implications. During 1998, Wall Street wasn't very interested in the Y2K status of publicly-traded corporations, but that is likely to change soon, particularly as the SEC increases pressure on registered companies to provide investors with meaningful disclosures of their Year 2000 costs and exposures. How will your pension funds, 401(k) plans, and corporate investment accounts measure up? Many industries, countries, and currencies are likely to come under scrutiny as differences in compliance efforts become more apparent.

Economic outlook. Ed Yardeni, the highly regarded chief economist at Deutsch Bank Securities, has been predicting a Y2K-induced recession for close to two years. He put the matter succinctly when he wrote "CEOs must prepare now to fly as best they can in a suddenly alien global economy" (1998). Capers Jones of Software Productivity Research has suggested that the projected number of

Year 2000 business failures presents "an open question as to whether the impact of the year 2000 problem is severe enough to trigger a recession" (Jones, 1998b). *Business Week* forecast that the Y2K hit "would be the same size as the expected economic damage from the turmoil in East Asia" (Mandel, 1998).

Preparing for 2000 and Beyond

However strenuously we prepare for Year 2000 in the time that remains, we must accept the fact that "[t]here is not enough awareness, time, and resources to fix every computer system" before "00" arrives at home and abroad (Yardeni, 1998). In 1999, as organizations make their final push to achieve Y2K compliance, they also must plan for failure.

Who's Driving the Bus?

As we gird ourselves for the difficult task of planning for possible Year 2000 failures, we should think for a moment about what economic and institutional forces could help reduce Y2K damages. For example, the one clear exception to the governmental dithering about Year 2000 has been the federal financial regulators, whose sustained and focused efforts have unquestionably contributed to the impressive accomplishments of the banking, financial services, and securities industries. In turn, the relative strength of the financial sector is likely to generate useful pressures throughout the economy. Businesses that can't get a loan unless they improve their Y2K credit risk ratings are more likely to do what is necessary to get the cash they need to stay in business and grow. IT vendors know that they will lose important banking and securities clients if they're not ready in time.

Accountants and auditors will likely play a similar role. Independent auditors, another industry that experienced tremendous fallout after the 1980s boom went bust, will again face exceptionally severe professional risks in 1999. Outside accountants will find themselves in the crosshairs if they fail to provide specific and timely warnings to management about the stability of corporate information systems and business relationships. If accountants don't issue such warnings, they risk being seen as the deep pockets responsible for their client's failures.

As the SEC and the accounting profession force companies to disseminate meaningful information about their compliance status, no one will have to explain to corporate directors that, before long, investors are likely to vote with their wallets. The securities rating agencies and pension funds will have an opportunity to become part of the solution, too.

Insurers and underwriters can apply useful pressure as they take steps to protect their assets from undue risk. This is particularly true with regard to professional liability insurance that is so vital to physicians, accountants, and lawyers, many of whom seem to need additional incentives to get ready for 2000.

Talk of a trillion dollars in lawsuits may have already had a positive effect in increasing awareness of the Y2K problem that no amount of exhortation has generated so far. Now that the attorneys have everyone's attention, most companies will find that taking the steps we recommend in Chapter 4 to reduce Y2K liability exposure will also improve their prospects for avoiding Year 2000 failures in the first place. Paper trails don't work very well if they're just designed to cover your backside; they help only if they document reasonable efforts made. As noted computer expert Ed Yourdon put it, "It's a shame that a complex problem is further complicated by the prospect of expensive lawsuits," but "[i]t's important to get the lawyers involved early, to confirm that you are doing the right thing in your year 2000 projects" (Yourdon, 1998). Lawyers aren't smarter than IT professionals, but they do ask tougher questions.

What's Next?

What will risk management look like after 1/1/00? Surely, a great deal of crisis management will be required, and *SWAT team* is already becoming a Y2K buzzword. As weak links in supply chains begin to break, we will need to reestablish communications among trading partners and build new business relationships. The long-expected flood of litigation will probably begin, just when we need it the least. We will explore these long-range risk management issues in Chapter 12, "Post-2000 Risk Management."

Our focus in this chapter has been on identifying and classifying things that can go wrong to provide a foundation on which to build effective Y2K risk management strategies. Now we can start to deal constructively with the uncertainties and perils that lie ahead.

CHAPTER 2

Building an Effective Year 2000 Risk Management Program

"This [Y2K] is going to have implications in the world and in American society we can't even comprehend."

—DEPUTY DEFENSE SECRETARY JOHN HAMRE
BEFORE A SENATE COMMITTEE; JUNE 5, 1998

Just as awareness of the magnitude of the Year 2000 problem was slow to spread, so too was awareness of the myriad of risk management issues that Year 2000 presents. As you read in the previous chapter, the problem poses many new and increased risks to your organization. This chapter will focus on how to deal with these increased risks by implementing a sound and effective risk management program. Subsequent chapters will cover how to carry out these concepts in more detail.

Risk Management Program Scope and Goals

Traditionally, risk management programs have included efforts to avoid accidental loss or injury and work to reduce the consequences of a loss when it occurs. While your organization may already have a risk management program in place, most traditional risk management programs fail to account for the scope and breath of issues that multiple and simultaneous problems present. By now, the complexity of the Year 2000 problem is clear to everyone. The threat of widespread failures and malfunctions in your electronic and computing systems is compounded by the threats of disruption in infrastructure and supply-chain systems. This widespread and simultaneous failure scenario may have a domino effect, causing even more disruptions to ripple through the business environment—an entirely plausible scenario for which every diligent organization must plan.

Because there is a significant probability of simultaneous system failures and supply-chain disruptions, Year 2000 risk management is a daunting endeavor. Most organizations have begun to address the technical issues of the Year 2000 problem. In stark contrast, few have even acknowledged the possibility that their own Y2K projects will not be completed in time, nor have they addressed the serious risks that external factors present. Your organization must now face the challenge of managing the increased risks that both internal and external problems present. Establishing the scope and goals of your risk management program is an important first step.

This new risk management challenge may be more than your current risk management program is capable of supporting. You should consider putting sufficient resources in place by creating a special risk management team with representation and resources from all of the line-of-business and operational function areas. This team should be delegated responsibility for the special planning and management issues that Year 2000 presents. The risk management team also should be tasked to develop plans for critical operations that include not just computing but building systems, networks, suppliers, personnel, and operations. In the event of a system failure, they should be concerned with how critical business functions will be maintained, what happens if they fail, and how they will be restored in the event of a disaster.

In the section called, *Establish a Risk Management Team or Working Group* later in this chapter, we will describe the players and their roles on your risk management team. Once established, your team will be faced with the daunting task of identifying, assessing, and minimizing the risk of failures in every facet of the business environment from any number of possible failure points. As a result, the scope of a Year 2000 risk management program can become extremely broad. It is important to *triage* your risks and to clearly define your risk management goals from the start. Risk areas that you should address are described next.

System Remediation

Your organization is obviously at risk if your remediation project is not on-track. You should consider conducting an *independent verification and validation* (IV&V) of the project to determine if appropriate methodologies and quality controls are in place. First, you must determine if the project has appropriately inventoried and prioritized all systems. Has the project missed anything? A complete systems audit should have already been completed, but you must verify that everything has been thoroughly reviewed and tested.

Ensure that no one assumed that something is problem-free based on hearsay or a vendor's statement. Thorough testing records should be preserved and kept readily available in case they are needed years later to demonstrate due diligence. Look to see if any mission-critical systems were not identified as top priorities for the project. You should also review the progress of the project. Are project milestones being met? Is the testing program for remediated code sufficient? Chapter 3, "Fast-Tracking a Year 2000 Project," offers guidance that will be helpful in accelerating project efforts.

Project Resources

It is very important that these Year 2000 projects are fully staffed and funded. Check to determine if the project is adequately resourced. Also, system remediation exposes your computers and data to greater risks. Because many changes are being made, and because you are likely using contractors and other outside help, you will need to determine if security measures are adequate. Finally, for business reasons, risk managers should also compare the cost of a chosen system remediation option (repair, replace, reengineer, or retire) with the cost of other compliance options. Remember, however, that you will have to balance cost-benefit with time requirements. Expediency may be more important than cost if the success of the project is at stake. Y2K risks were presented in Chapter 1, "Year 2000 Business and Legal Risks," but as a point of reference, here are some of the key categories.

Personal Safety Risks

While personal safety risks are relatively rare, to the degree that they exist, they may represent the greatest risk to your organization. Personal injury is always a risk that you want to avoid for moral, liability, and good will reasons. Your risk management team should obviously give high priority to this risk area.

Operational Risks

Operational risks are those risks that threaten the actual operation of your business and include the myriad of services and equipment that you depend on to operate. You must examine the many ways that Year 2000 failures will affect your operations and develop backups, contingency plans, and workarounds in the event that they occur. Consider some of the many operational areas that can be affected by Year 2000 problems with computers and embedded systems.

Operational Areas at Risk

The following Y2K risks, affecting a wide array of public and private infrastructure systems, could significantly disrupt business operations:

- Process and manufacturing controls
- Electricity
- Oil and gas
- Water and sewer
- Telecommunications
- Banking and finance
- Police and fire
- Public services
- Health services
- Transportation and delivery

Legal Risks

Legal risks include the risk of lawsuits from customers, business partners, and the public. These suits could stem from personal injury, breach of contract, warranty, and a host of other issues. The best defense is to be able to show *due diligence* in your remediation and risk management projects. How to minimize your legal risk is dealt with in Chapter 4, substantiating due diligence is covered in Chapter 8, and litigation planning is covered in Chapter 11.

Business Risks

Business risks include the issues of competitiveness, insurability, and market share. They include the obvious risk from your inability to do business due to internal problems but also include the risk of losing business as an indirect result of related disruptions, like failures of public services, suppliers, and customers. Your business is at risk of losing both market share and good will if others determine that you are not doing enough to prepare for the Year 2000. Additional business risks are security and confidentiality. Your project will need to assess the business risk to your organization in each of these areas.

Risk to Assets

Risks to assets include the risks to property and capital. Year 2000 malfunctions can damage machinery if safety systems fail, monitoring controls malfunction, or regulators fail. Indirect property losses can result from loss of heat or power. Burst pipes could cause water damage. These risks must be assessed, and steps must be taken to minimize their impact. Your company's capital and investments may also be at risk from the Year 2000 problem, which has the potential to affect the economy; consequently, investment managers should evaluate the safety of their investment mechanisms.

Business Continuity

Business continuity planning is required to address your ability to continue operations in the event of a catastrophic event. Year 2000 failures present additional risks in ensuring the continued availability of essential services, programs, and operations in the event of unexpected interruptions. Although business continuity can include many of the other risk areas described here, we are using the term to describe the process of ensuring that your suppliers and business partners do not disrupt or affect your ability to continue normal business operations. Business continuity planning includes determining if your current business partners are compliant and ensuring that all new business partners are compliant. This includes using contractual language to require the delivery of compliant products and the assurance of a constant provision of services or goods.

One of the first steps in business continuity planning is to survey your various vendors, suppliers, and other business partners in an attempt to determine their compliance. The casual statements "we have a program" or "we plan to be compliant by 1999" are not sufficient. Due diligence requires that you take the steps necessary to determine the risk of business impact due to your supplier's problems. You should aggressively pursue written compliance information from your suppliers and keep copies of all correspondence on file. Send reminders and/or requests for status updates regularly. Some companies have attempted to require vendor compliance certifications, but due to the vendor's possible litigation risks, certification often proves to be an unreasonable request. We will help you solicit the assurance your company needs from vendors in Chapter 5, "External Compliance Strategies."

If yours is a large organization, you may need to decentralize the vendor survey/contact efforts. It is important, however, to make sure that you don't waste resources by allowing duplicate or unnecessary efforts in contacting vendors. Your risk management team should coordinate these efforts to ensure that there is only one point of contact with each important vendor. For example, one of the *best practices* for achieving the required comfort level with your critical business partners is to require joint or third-party testing of processes or equipment. If a partner is less critical you may accept its test results without further testing.

Critical suppliers should be approached through face-to-face meetings. Work with them as partners, and consider joint testing and assistance in helping them achieve your required level of compliance.

Business Recovery

Finally, business recovery planning is required to address your organization's ability to resume operations after any disruptive event. Recovery issues might include restarting manufacturing processes, cleaning up water damage from broken pipes, recalling staff, reissuing incorrect checks, and recalculating account balances, accrued interest, and penalties. Your risk management team must review all available options, provide approaches for recovery, and formulate appropriate alternative operating strategies to enable timely recovery of critical business functions.

Obviously, there are many issues to face in building your risk management program. Your organization's Year 2000 project is likely to be the largest and most challenging management nightmare you will ever face. It is important to realize the scope of the challenge and to understand and manage the various issues that the Year 2000 problem presents. Even though you may not be able to fix and test every system and interdependency, you can do your best to minimize the impact and the risks that the Year 2000 problem presents.

Risk Management Planning

Due to the gravity and scope of the Year 2000 problem, top management should give Year 2000 their personal attention. One of the first objectives of your Year 2000 project should be to immediately establish this senior support and leadership. Without support from the top, Year 2000 efforts will be difficult, if not impossible. Initial briefings and announcements should be well thought out and should clearly emphasize that senior leadership understands the scope of the problem and the consequences of not addressing it immediately.

The best-practice approach is to establish a Year 2000 *policy directive*. Management support should be formalized by issuing this document. It is important that senior management support continue in an active fashion. Oversight groups should be established to monitor progress and identify problem areas.

A *Manhattan Project* approach should be taken to bring the necessary resources and expertise to bear on the project. Given the little time that remains, this project must be the top priority and receive the full attention of the staff assigned to it. Do not think that you can simply appoint staff to a committee and have them maintain their regular duties. It will be necessary to reassign staff to work on this project. Executive-level commitment to and participation in the process are also required and will help ensure the project's success. Top management must give both the Year 2000 project and the risk management effort the priority and resources that they need, including sufficient project staffing.

How your organization should approach risk management planning depends on several factors. You will have to make the crucial decision of how much effort to put into the risk management effort. Determining how much effort is too little or too much is a difficult business decision. Think in terms of cost-benefit and due diligence in planning your efforts. Your stockholders will expect you to avoid wasting money yet expect you to do everything necessary to ensure minimal business disruption. The following are factors to consider in finalizing your risk management approach; these factors will vary from organization to organization.

The size and type of the organization. The larger and more complex the organization, the more difficult the risk management planning will be. Organizations that are large, are geographically dispersed, or have numerous lines of business will face a larger and more complex task in assessing their risks and developing scenarios and plans. International firms will have even more difficulty because variables of even greater complexity will present themselves (the single European currency, for example). On the other hand, if yours is a small firm with a single product line, you may find managing your Year 2000 risks relatively straightforward.

The nature of customers and business partners. Another important factor in designing your program will be the nature of those with whom you do business. Customers, suppliers, and other business partners figure into your planning. How hard are they working to resolve Year 2000 issues? How risk-averse are they? How risky are their operations? Will partnerships with them present an increased risk of loss?

How litigious is your industry? The likelihood of lawsuits may be high regardless of your industry but can be tied to the nature of your industry and its tendency toward litigation. If lawsuits are prevalent, it is likely that you will face an increased threat due to Year 2000. We expect that medical services and other providers with personal safety risks will have the greatest exposure. Other high-risk areas may include financial processing, software development, and electronic equipment manufacturers. Alternatively, if you are a small retailer or service provider, you can expect a much lower risk of lawsuits.

The availability of insurance coverage and vendor bonding options. If you have insurance or bonding options you may be able to transfer some of your risk to others. As you will see in Chapter 9, "Insurance Issues," however, it may be difficult to recover through existing insurance policies or to acquire insurance that provides Year 2000 coverage. Many firms are finding great difficulty in extracting indemnification and warranties from consultants and other Year 2000 service providers. Self-insurance may be an option for some firms; others may have to go it alone.

Dependence on computers and embedded chips. Obviously, the more you rely on electronics, the more likely you are to suffer disruptions. Although supply-chain, infrastructure, and financial services issues put almost everyone at risk, the more you depend on electronics internally, the more exposure you have. You are at especially high risk if you rely on robotics, process controllers, and other automated systems. If you are less automated you have less internal risk, but you still must address those external threats. Working to assess and minimize these critical dependencies is a key factor in your risk management planning.

Propensity for risk. How risk-averse is your organization? How do your directors, officers, and stockholders normally perceive risk? What is their current risk posture? Are they willing to accept risk, or do they prefer a low-risk business environment? Obviously, if you operate in a risk-averse business environment you will want to make every effort to minimize risk; you may design a more complete and expensive risk management program as a result.

Once you have considered these issues the next step is for the organization's leaders to decide on an overall management approach and organize to address Year 2000 issues. Your management approach must be firmly established and publicized throughout the organization. This chapter provides an approach that focuses on a comprehensive, best-practices-based plan for dealing with the Year 2000 problem. To promote success, try to address each phase and every aspect of the Year 2000 risk management process.

If yours is a large or complex organization, you may want to consider using centralized coordination and decentralized execution as an organizational approach. Regardless of your approach, a central project office should be created that will coordinate all activities and serve as a central repository for information and record keeping. Decentralized work groups will be used to conduct assessments and planning. Consider a department or line-of-business level assessment and certification process that is coordinated through a central office for policy guidance and communications with vendors. This approach allows all business units the flexibility to address the problem as they see fit while also benefiting from best practices in a well-coordinated effort. However you choose to proceed, the centralized monitoring of these efforts is highly advisable. Once organizational issues are determined, make sure that the responsibilities are made clear to all units and levels in your organization.

Given the limited time and resources, prioritization of your efforts will be critical. Make the best use of your resources by determining which systems are critical and which will benefit most from repair efforts. Identify systems that can be retired or converted to manual processes. Consider a moratorium on all new projects. Avoid (or, at least, severely limit) administrative changes that will require computer revisions. And finally, constantly and actively assess and manage risks in developing contingency, business continuity, and disaster plans.

Risk Management Planning Phases

The risk management planning effort should follow an overall phasing similar to Year 2000 computer remediation best practices. Specific project planning and processes are covered elsewhere in this chapter, but you can generally think about the project in four basic phases. You should consider using these phases as part of your project management and time-line process. Remember, as with remediation projects, there is no slack in the time line. You will need to ensure that efforts progress at the planned rate.

Awareness phase. The objective of this phase is to raise awareness about the need for risk management, contingency, and continuity planning for all elements of the organization and for all of those business partners and other entities that you depend on to do business. This awareness effort should include business partners, suppliers, customers, and others in the region. This phase also includes initial data collection on what systems and processes are at risk.

Risk assessment phase. During this phase the organization should bring together information gathered in the awareness phase, look at current risk management efforts, and identify additional areas needing risk management attention. Then the organization must prioritize risks in each area of their operation, analyze business impact, and then determine how best to diminish those risks.

Renovation phase. The objective of this phase is to act on the recommendations from the risk assessment phase. For example, you will need to update any internal risk management plans that need adjustment and create new plans where new risk areas are identified. For the external issues, contracts with existing vendors may be terminated and replaced with new ones, or additional contracts may be entered. For some organizations, emergency preparedness efforts should be included.

Validation phase. During this phase an approach to testing must be documented, test schedules developed, and then actual tests of all the contingency plans conducted. Results should be documented and used to determine if a particular area's plans are adequate in the event of a Year 2000 problem or if they need to return to the renovation phase. Emergency preparedness should include desktop exercises and drills on likely Year 2000 scenarios.

Planning Steps

It is important that careful planning measures be taken at the beginning of your project. Given the time constraints, you must quickly establish the organization and blueprint for your efforts. You will need to conduct several specific planning steps to get organized for your risk management effort.

Establish a Risk Management Team or Working Group

Although Y2K was once considered a computer problem, most people now understand that it jeopardizes all business activity, including operations, service delivery, financial management, safety, and customer, vendor, and investor relations. Every executive and IT professional needs to have a working understanding of the risks facing the company and the strategies available to address them. This is no different from many other "non-business" issues with which managers have become familiar in the 1980s and 1990s, such as workplace safety laws, employment discrimination, and environmental compliance. For example, no competent business organization would undertake a commercial real estate project in any urban setting today without exercising environmental due diligence, enlisting advice from competent technical and legal experts, consulting with appropriate regulatory officials, delegating responsibilities to in-house compliance and risk management specialists, briefing directors and officers about potential liability exposures, and, in some cases, providing disclosures to shareholders, auditors, and financial institutions. In 1999 and beyond, Y2K risk management will look a lot like environmental and other types of business risk management.

Risk management professionals, along with subject matter experts, should be used to form the risk management team. You will need to include staff from functional and line-of-business areas both for expertise and staff resource purposes. A good cross-section of your business is necessary to conduct a thorough assessment and to develop scenarios for contingency planning. Consider selecting individuals with planning, finance, insurance, legal, and operational expertise as well as those who are known for having a big picture view of the world.

It is important to rapidly assemble this core team of knowledgeable individuals to develop a detailed approach and then to add staff to develop procedures, and to conduct detailed assessments and analysis as required by the project. In addition, in many cases it would be wise to hire outside consulting expertise and to bring in additional staff for specific issues.

You should consider establishing the risk management team as a separate team from, but coordinated with, your systems remediation team. The staff involved with fixing your computers will be an important resource but should not be burdened with additional responsibilities. Your organization should be structured in such a way as to minimize the impact on your ongoing remediation efforts.

Establish a Steering Committee

Many of the organization's most important assets and mission-critical processes may be affected by Year 2000 problems. Because of the importance of this project, a high-level steering committee is needed to complement the Year 2000 risk management team's efforts. This group could be the same steering committee that may be in place for your remediation project. If your organization is large, both an organizational steering group (for policy direction) and a working group (to directly assist the risk management team) may be needed. The steering committee should consist of senior personnel and should include the Chief Information Officer (CIO) and high-level managers from legal, administrative, and operational departments including those normally involved in resource allocation, procurement, risk management, and major operational and line-of-business activities. The steering committee's role should include resource allocation, policy guidance, and oversight, but this group should be geared toward *facilitating* the project's efforts by helping resolve problems and fast-tracking budget, procurement, and other processes. Having such a group monitor progress and take a high-level view of project issues and how they affect the overall operation is essential. This group also will be critical in making triage and resource allocation decisions during the project. Additionally, if yours is a very large organization you may need to establish steering committees within each major organizational unit to provide continuous coordination with project managers and department staff.

Establish a Risk Assessment Policy

Everyone who is expected to provide input into the risk management planning process must agree to a comprehensive risk assessment policy that addresses the roles and responsibilities of the various groups, the decision-making process (especially for prioritization), and the allocation of resources. Without a formal policy supported by top management, the program faces inattention, low priority, and possible nonconformance. Experienced consultants may be required at this stage to provide needed organization and expertise.

Establish a Review Schedule

It will be necessary to establish a review schedule with identified time intervals between reviews of given systems. As with remediation projects, there is an immovable deadline, and it will take the same level of project management effort to ensure that the project stays on track and meets its milestones.

Perform a Program Assessment

Hire consultants that have the expertise necessary to do a thorough review of your entire Year 2000 program. The consultants should be able to provide benchmarking to industry standards and gap analysis of program comprehensiveness, technical assumptions, conflicting objectives, deadlines, resource allocation, and cost influences. In addition, if not done as part of your compliance effort, the consultants should be tasked to perform independent validation and verification of the technical approach and testing methodologies.

With the assistance of the risk management team and/or your consultants, make corrections or adjustments to current project efforts. This may include identification of alternatives that are faster, less expensive, or technically superior. Develop contingency and business continuity plans for all mission-critical systems based on the study's findings and looking at the potential for impact resulting from system failures and the interrelationships of various systems. Set compliance deadlines (the absolute latest date things can be ready). In general, systems should be repaired or replaced three months before their individual failure horizons.

Perform an Internal Risk Assessment

Review the likelihood, timing, and severity of Year 2000 events in all technical and nontechnical areas:

- Systems interdependence (ripple effects)
- The cost of nonreimbursed losses including litigation, decreased revenues, and remediation costs
- Cost of insurance/self insurance
- Cost of interest on loans, investments, and bonds (from economic fluctuations as a result of Y2K)
- Cost of risk control measures—solution provider fees, contingency planning costs, and so on
- Administrative cost of risk management—consultant fees and expenses of internal oversight personnel
- Societal impact and costs of failures

Perform an External Risk Assessment

Review both computer and noncomputer system issues arising outside of your organization. These issues include operational risks, risks to services, liability risks, risks to revenues, and societal impacts of system failures. Specifically, you should review the risks associated with the following:

- Mission-critical electronic business dependencies
- Mission-critical suppliers
- Infrastructure providers (utilities, telecommunications, banking, etc.)
- Electronic Data Interchanges (EDI) and its format and date standards

Perform a Business Impact Assessment

Business impact assessments are required to quantify and qualify the potential effect that various Y2K risks may have on your business. This assessment will include using your risk analysis to determine the potential impacts that system failures may have on your organization. These effects include potential loss of production capacity, loss of revenue, loss of market share, and loss of good will. Qualified staff will be required to perform the necessary analysis to determine the impact on your business from the various Year 2000 risks.

Perform Risk Control

Take affirmative steps to reduce risks by mitigating problems discovered during the assessments. Obviously, this includes fixing your computerized systems. As time runs out for labor-intensive computer projects, however, it is important that you reduce your exposure by doing the following:

- Perform remediation of external dependencies by working with partners to fix any problems.
- Document remediation and testing efforts to maintain project controls and prove due diligence if sued.
- Develop contingency plans for all affected systems.
- Develop contingency plans for external service disruptions (power, telecommunications, and transportation).
- Conduct business continuity and disaster recovery planning.
- Review project financing, implementation rates, validity of current estimates, and budget allocations.
- Develop an executive summary for senior management and elected officials.

Project Plan Process

By now you realize that you are going to have a lot of work to do. To help you get organized, we have laid out how a typical risk management planning process should flow. Your organization may want to modify this process, but essentially these steps should be followed in completing risk management.

1. Define Criteria for Mission-Critical Processes

One of the most difficult value judgments in a risk management program may be determining what systems are *mission-critical*. The users and process owner of every system will find their system to be critical while the organization as a whole may be forced to differentiate among systems and make judgments about their degree of criticality. You must ask yourself if the system or process is something without which your business can function. This decision will require sound business judgment; you need to take a high-level business survival view of your situation. The best practice in approaching mission-critical classification is to conduct a complete inventory of systems and processes and then to perform a *business impact analysis*. A business impact analysis will confirm the types of business consequences that may arise from failures and serve to identify their likelihood.

To begin your analysis you must first identify the universe of items to be included in the inventory. You should include all business processes, comprising any business function as well as the applications, supplies, equipment, and interdependencies required to carry the functions out. The next step will be to rate the risk from each of these processes.

2. Business Process Risk Rating

Your organization must develop a methodology to determine the relative risk to your business from each of your systems. One method is to use weighted scoring including a number of factors. Figure 2.1 displays one possible risk-rating methodology. You may need to modify it for your organizational environment.

Once the risk ratings have been established, you can use them to sort and manage your inventory. The overall risk rating of each process can be used to prioritize your projects. You should consider using some of the risk categories to determine if a process has an overriding critical risk factor, such as risk to life, and use that information to classify it as a high-risk project, despite an overall low score.

3. Determine Cost Impact on Your Operations

Another important aspect of rating your processes is to determine what the indirect costs of failure represent to the organization. Your operations could

Year 2000 Risk Rating Methodology

Risk Factor	Risk Rating	Numeric Score	Explanation
Degree of Date Dependence	H M L	8 6 3	More than 25% of functions are date dependent More than 10% of functions are date dependent Less than 5% of functions are date dependent
Probability of Successful Replacement	H M L	0 2 3	Probability > 0.5 that process will be replaced Probability < 0.5 that process will be replaced No plans to replace process
Dependence on Automation	H M L	5 3 1	Business functions depend highly on process Business functions depend somewhat Manual operation possible w/o penalty
Criticality of Business Process	H M L	4 2 0	Critical business function—core process Secondary line-of-business Not a critical process
Multi-Organization Dependence	H M L	3 2 0	More than two organizations depend on process More than one organization depends on process Only one organizational element depends on process
Risk to Personal Safety or Life	H M L	20 10 5	High degree of risk to life, personal safety Some risk—potential injuries Little or no direct risk to life
Risk to Property	H M L	4 2 0	High risk of property loss Some risk of property loss No known risk to property
Risk of Legal Liability	H M L	7 4 0	High degree of legal risk—injury or loss Some risk of legal liability Little or no known legal liability
Risk to Revenue	H M L	5 3 0	High degree of risk to revenue—must not fail Some risk to revenue—should not fail No known risk to revenue
Risk to Internal Service Levels	H M L	4 2 0	High degree of risk to service levels—work stoppage Some risk to service levels—work slow down No known risk to service levels
Risk to General Administration	H M L	3 2 0	High degree of risk to administrative functions Some risk to administrative processes No known risk to administration
Inter-operation Priority	H M L	5 3 2	Needed by many critical processes for inter-operation Needed by two to three processes for inter-operation Needed by one other processes
Schedule Priority	H M L	5 3 1	Needed immediately—long lead time, time horizon Needed immediately—low tolerance for outage Short lead time or high tolerance for outage
Cumulative Score		_____	**Risk Rating Score** (Enter the total of Numeric Ratings)

Note: If any risk is not applicable leave blank (score of zero)

Figure 2.1 Risk-rating methodology.

be affected in many ways by system failures, and you will need to look at the cost of fixing systems and processes in relation to the cost of the potential consequences. The analysis should include the cost from potential property losses, legal liability, lost income, opportunity costs, and the loss of good will. Your budget, auditing, and finance staff may need to assist in this effort. Long-term analysis and *net present value* (NPV) calculations will likely be needed to accurately make comparisons between cost of impact and cost of repair or replacement.

4. Define Recovery Processes, Costs, and Time Frames

You also need to determine how you will conduct business recovery actions for each system or process in the event of failure. What steps will be required to recover from a failure and to restart the process? How much will recovery actions cost, and how long will it take to implement the new process? Some processes, like those dealing with molten metals and plastics as well as chemical, pharmaceutical, and food processes, can have significant restart costs if the product cools in pipes or molds.

5. Identify Processing Alternatives

You need to identify all available alternative processing options. These alternatives can include off-site processing, alternative equipment and networks, outsourcing, and manual processes. Advance work to identify alternative service providers or replacement equipment is crucial. A diligent business will have made arrangements well in advance of the problem's occurrence. The most prepared firms will have prepositioned equipment for the most critical processes. Also consider the likelihood of back orders and shortages for equipment and services as your competitors find themselves in the same position.

6. Formulate Strategies Based on Optimum Cost-Benefit

Once you have completed the previous steps, you should be prepared to formulate strategies based on the cost-benefit of the various options. Here you may be required to make some tough decisions. Sound decision making will require good data, sharp minds, and the long view of your business. You will need to weigh the variables of risk, cost, benefit (process improvement, cost avoidance, and so on), and others across many projects. You will have to consider the long-term effect on and possible future benefits to your organization. For example, a system replacement may be expensive, but it may be less risky and may provide long-term productivity and cost-avoidance benefits as well. Consider constructing a matrix that allows you to look at and weigh all of the issues relating to each option so that you can determine the optimum solution.

7. Revise and Develop Contingency Plans as Needed

You may already have contingency plans, but these will need to be revised in light of Year 2000 failure scenarios. Equally important is the need to identify entirely new areas where contingency plans are required. Completion of the business impact analysis will leave you in a position to prioritize your contingency planning efforts.

Once risk management work has been completed you should develop contingency and business continuity plans using the triage process to prioritize systems and services. Contingency planning has always been seen as a business issue rather than an information systems issue. Contingency planning best practices include developing alternate plans, manual workarounds, and fallback procedures for the affected systems. Year 2000 heightens the need for contingency planning and expands it beyond the traditional information systems purview because the probabilities that outages, shortages, and unplanned events will occur are much higher. Although computer specialists normally deal with disaster recovery relating to critical applications, systems, and data, contingency planning for noninformation system disasters similar to those for floods, tornadoes, fires, explosions, and similar disasters will be needed. Planning for these emergencies is normally left to safety officials. Among these safety officials, plans are less common for the types of simultaneous and widespread problems that may result from Year 2000: extended electrical, gas, water, or phone outages, transportation disruptions, and supply-chain disruptions affecting critical resources such as food, raw materials, and consumer goods. For these reasons, many organizations will need to increase efforts to develop contingency plans. Contingency planning is discussed in detail in Chapter 6, but the following are a few key issues to think about:

- Develop test plans and exercises
- Conduct system and process testing
- Perform backup site testing
- Evaluate test results
- Perform process improvements based on test results

Key Elements to Risk Management Planning

Now that we have discussed the what, why, and how of Year 2000 risk management, let's recap some of the key success factors. Clearly, Y2K risk management will require tremendous effort. To be successful, you should keep the following issues in mind.

Leadership. As mentioned earlier, the first step in an effective risk management program is to get high-level buy-in to the necessity and importance of risk management efforts. Ask for leadership and support from the very top of your organization. This is a project with a scope and complexity level like no other that your organization has faced; strong and effective project management skills are essential. It is best that a separate team (not the project team) be established for this effort.

Risk evaluation and control. Begin immediately to identify and prioritize the potential problems and events that could affect your organization both internally and externally. Look for opportunities for quick and effective fixes. Eliminate anything that isn't needed. Fix things that can be easily fixed. Don't let the planning process delay any repair or risk control efforts. Strive to be accurate in estimating the damage that Year 2000 events could cause, the time requirements for service restoration, and the controls needed to reduce both the probability and impact of Y2K problems.

Business impact analysis. Ensure that your team has representatives from all of your functional areas and task them with evaluating the potential impact to business from Year 2000-related failures and losses in both quantitative and qualitative terms. The team should develop and document an impact analysis methodology and a business continuity plan that includes procedures to ensure business continuity as well as business recovery. Ongoing senior management leadership and involvement is needed to establish project boundaries and timelines and to ensure the development of a sound plan.

Physical and logical security. Provide an in-depth analysis of actions to be taken to limit the probability of incidents that may adversely affect business operations and security. Use structured, comprehensive, and effective testing methods to ensure that the environment is secure and that business continuity efforts remain practical and free of errors and omissions.

Develop recovery strategies. Review all available options and formulate appropriate alternative operating strategies to enable timely recovery of critical business functions.

Develop corporate awareness and training. Develop and implement organization-wide awareness and education programs, fostering commitment to the project and ensuring development, maintenance, and execution of the business continuity program.

Emergency response. Prepare plans outlining the actions necessary to respond to emergencies that are likely to occur, have plans for how to stabilize an emergency situation, and determine appropriate actions from the recovery plan.

Develop business backup and restoration procedures. Develop procedures to ensure availability of critical data, information, programs, and instructions under all circumstances. Consider *quick fix* or *rapid rewrite* strategies for the projects that may fail. Similarly, automated testing is a way to finish critical testing on projects that do finish but won't have time for full testing. Automated testing may produce significant savings in time, labor, and CPU usage. Of course, proper testing is needed to minimize risk.

Develop secondary projects to act as backup for the primary projects. Look for alternatives such as time-shifting or simply setting the system date and data back one year; live with being out of sync with the days of the week and plan to go off-line for February 29.

Exercise the plan. Finally, it is not enough just to plan. You must train your staff in the procedures envisioned in each plan and drill your organization on how to use the plans that are developed. Consider using "table top" exercises to take your staff through various scenarios. Use "fire drills" to make sure that your staff is prepared to take necessary actions.

Where to Start

Now that you understand what lies ahead, begin your internal risk assessment by identifying the people and resources required to complete what will be a large and daunting task. Contact your Year 2000 project manager and become familiar with the organization's objectives, plans, system inventories, subcontractors, risk evaluations, and projected solutions. Determine how your organization is addressing the conversion process. Look for assistance and support from staff in the executive, computer systems, finance, legal, and other departments. Once you have a feel for your organizational situation, quickly begin to develop a risk management plan following the guidelines presented in this chapter, but consider the importance of these first quick hits.

Perform a quick internal systems audit, collecting information on all the electronic systems and linkages that affect the organization. Your Year 2000 project office should already have a complete inventory on file, including status of remediation on each system and interface.

Evaluate any previous triage of these systems to validate the conclusions in light of the current state of the remediation project, and perform any additional triage that is needed. Interview your most critical business trading partners and suppliers on their Year 2000 compliance plans. Quantify the risks and exposures, and determine if the risk can be avoided, assumed, transferred, financed, or insured. Review insurance policies and vendor and service contracts for potential exposures. Check carefully on insurance renewals and policy exclusions. Review potential legal exposures as well.

Different industries will have different issues as critical systems and resources vary. For example, the trucking industry relies heavily on supplies such as spare parts, diesel fuel, and tires. Contingency plans should be reviewed and developed in the context of emergency preparedness. Review existing disaster plans, and look for areas not covered such as supply-chain disruptions or communication problems. This issue is dealt with more fully in Chapter 6, "Contingency Planning."

Management Responsibilities

As stated previously, management must exert the effort and take the responsibility to ensure the success of the Year 2000 project. Directors and officers must face issues such as product liability, breach of contract, and securities law issues. Directors and officers are required to meet the legal standard of care in dealing with the Year 2000 problem. There is a serious risk of liability in both the proper operation of the company and in the issues of financial reporting. If the organization fails in whole or in part to fix the problem in their own systems, the resulting disruption of operations will inevitably produce claims by third parties, including business partners, customers, employees, and others.

Business Risk Assessments

The business risk assessment looks at the types of business impacts that may arise as a result of a Year 2000 problem. The risk management team must identify the likely consequences arising from any number of potential failures and identify critical business functions that may be affected. Once critical business functions have been identified, the project plan can be reviewed and amended as appropriate based on the revised scope of the project.

With many other organizations behind schedule in Year 2000 work, you should expect significant disruptions in the supply chain. Due to a heavy reliance on just-in-time inventory, the shelves may be bare and assembly lines may be missing key items before January 2000. Experts say many suppliers are seriously uninformed about fixing their systems for the millennium and are headed for failure. Even if you successfully complete and test your systems, you may still face operations disruptions as a result of Year 2000.

We can all hope that suppliers and other business partners become fully compliant in time, but there's little basis for that hope. According to Lou Marcoccio, research director at the Gartner Group, "The vendor issue is the biggest risk issue and the biggest litigation risk issue and the issue people have least control over, and yet it's where people are focusing the least amount of attention. It makes no sense whatsoever" (Melymuka, 1998).

Clearly, supply-chain issues are a problem for any organization. Government officials must face the added issues that working with nonprofits and others in public–private partnerships present. It appears that many smaller organizations have not even realized that they have a problem.

There are six tasks in the risk assessment phase:

- Determine the critical business functions.
- Identify types of potential business failures.
- Assess how a process failure or unavailability will affect the business.
- Estimate the consequences of business function failure.
- Calculate the likelihood of each failure and estimate its event horizon.
- Develop business continuity, contingency, and disaster recovery plans.

Triage and Risk Ratings

Given the little time that remains, you must realize that everything can't be fixed in time. In addition, it will be difficult to assess and mitigate every risk. This is why triage is so important. Triage (French for sort) is defined by the *American Heritage Dictionary of the English Language, Third Edition,* as:

1. A process for sorting injured people into groups based on their need for or likely benefit from immediate medical treatment. Triage is used on the battlefield, at disaster sites, and in hospital emergency rooms when limited medical resources must be allocated.
2. A system used to allocate a scarce commodity, such as food, only to those capable of deriving the greatest benefit from it.

These are appropriate analogies to the challenge involved in dealing with the Y2K problem. The Year 2000 remediation and risk management projects must both sort through numerous issues to decide which ones are the most critical to the mission of the organization as well as those at greatest risk of date-related impacts. Decisions on allocating or redirecting scarce resources must be made. Because this activity is so sensitive and important, it should be developed at the highest level possible. Senior management must make the difficult decisions, such as which systems to fix, which to abandon, or which ones will not get attention. In addition, senior management should prioritize risk mitigation and contingency planning efforts based on failure scenarios to determine how to plan for manual or alternative operations.

Each organization's Y2K project manager should assist in this effort by providing justification and supporting information including all available assessment information, the customer survey, the inventory, the assessment, the renovation schedule, and perhaps a suggested list of core business processes that are critical to the organization. Beyond that, the steering committee should negotiate the position on the priority list with the customer. It is also imperative that the steering committee supports the project manager on conversion using the priority list and is open and flexible when new information is provided as the conversion moves forward.

Legal Audit

Your general counsel should be brought in to work with the project committee to assess all of the legal exposures presented by Year 2000 issues. Exposures can include risks resulting from any services or products that you provide as well as those provided to your organization. Chapter 4, "Reducing Liability Exposure," covers these topics in detail.

Due Diligence

All levels of management must ensure that reasonable care is taken in carrying out the business of the enterprise. Due diligence in Year 2000-related activities will be ultimately defined by the courts, but it may require that you substantially follow the best management practices described in this chapter. Failure to exert a due-diligence level of effort will leave you susceptible to law suits. This means that developing a risk management program that meets the due-diligence test is vital to your organization. Due diligence is covered in-depth in Chapter 4, "Reducing Liability Exposure," and Chapter 8, "Substantiating Due Diligence."

Conclusion

You now should realize that you have a lot to do and relatively little time to do it. This book will help you in understanding Year 2000 risk management issues and will provide you with some of the best ways to deal with them, but you must use this information effectively to be successful. You will need to convince yourself and your management to give Year 2000 issues top priority at the expense of other projects. You will need to build a sense of urgency in the organization. In this quest, you will be faced with skepticism and denial. You will confront individuals who don't believe that Y2K is a problem, think that someone else should be taking care of it, and still want their other projects to proceed as planned.

You will find that, regrettably, working on this project will likely be an uphill battle all the way. You will have to constantly convince others to give you the resources that you will need. As a result, you will find that the awareness phase will never end. But hang in there, worldwide awareness is increasing every day; in due time, others will realize that you are right in pushing them to deal with this important issue. To succeed, you must plan to conduct effective briefings for management before asking them to make this their top priority. Also, brief the staff that will be asked to support the project, and defer other, less important work. Start thinking about how you are going to build your team and what types of risk management plans you will need to develop.

Since having an effective Year 2000 remediation project is one of the most important aspects of risk management, the next chapter, "Fast-Tracking a Year 2000 Project," will assist you in starting a project in 1999 or accelerating a project that is behind schedule.

CHAPTER 3

Fast-Tracking a Year 2000 Project

"I love deadlines. I like the whooshing sound they make as they fly by."

—DOUGLAS ADAMS

Information technology projects are notorious for missed deadlines. Year 2000 projects that started years ago are missing deadlines as you read this. Even though it may seem impossibly late to start, or to speed up a problem project, you must do everything possible to limit the negative impact of Y2K. If you haven't initiated a Y2K remediation plan, act quickly to establish one. Or, if you are faced with a problem project, you need to get it back on track to meet the deadline. Either way, you should establish strong project management and fast-tracking processes and secure clear top-level leadership support. In this chapter we will walk you through fast-tracking a Y2K project by helping you build a team, plan the project, and manage it effectively.

It's Never Too Late

As we approach the new millennium, experts are exclaiming that it is too late to fix everything and that organizations should focus on contingency planning. Truthfully, it is very late, and as a popular Y2K joke going around says:

Question: "What do I need to do to fix my system's Year 2000 problems?"

Answer: *"Start in 1995!"*

Although managing Year 2000 risks through contingency, continuity, and recovery planning is extremely important, there is no reason why Y2K remediation projects should not proceed *in parallel* with risk management activities. Fast-tracking may mean that you have to do a "quick and dirty" version of a Year 2000 project; but preventing Year 2000 disruptions in the first place is, by far, the most effective way to reduce your Y2K risks. Regardless of when you start, you will have to fix your systems and processes—even if you finish after January 1, 2000.

This chapter caters to your need to "bite the bullet" and get started now to establish a Y2K project. "But isn't it too late?" you ask. Well, it is too late to do a complete best-practices project; the project life cycle will simply be too long. We will try to help you in spite of the fact that you have started too late. Making the best effort possible will improve your chances of success both in business and in court. You are going to have to cut corners, however, and your decisions may later be questioned. In the end, management will have to make and defend difficult decisions about how to best proceed in light of the late date.

Y2K project managers lament their situation on almost any project, but especially on late-starting projects. Even early starters are now wishing that they had more time. What to do? A late-starting project simply needs to have a different attitude and a different approach to Y2K. You obviously can't plan a 24-month project life cycle. You will have to work in parallel on project segments that should be done sequentially. You will not be able to take best-practice approaches in all cases. You will have to focus on only critical systems, and you will have to find the fastest and most effective solutions, often in lieu of the best alternative. Even though there will be a point in mid-1999 when it may be too late to start a project to prevent system failures (yes, you should have started in 1995), 1999 is not too late to start working on the problems that are most likely to occur. Any Year 2000 project effort, even a late-starting one, is better than nothing in most cases. In other words, if you have not yet started a project, it is better to start one now than not at all.

Risk Analysis and Prioritization

Triage is imperative in fast-tracking a Y2K project. We mentioned it in Chapter 2, "Building an Effective Year 2000 Risk Management Program," and we will give you more details in the section *Project Scoping and Triage*. Given the precious little time you have for your project, you must focus your resources on the most important tasks. Your initial systems risk analysis will require an inventory and assessment of all your electronic systems and processes. It is extremely important that you quickly determine which systems have the greatest potential impact on your organization. To the degree that there are easy-to-implement workarounds, you should consider directing resources toward other priorities. Be cautious that you do not spend time on remediation of low-impact systems if there are other, more important, systems to be fixed. The previous chapter discussed the basic concept of building an effective risk management program and includes a risk-rating methodology that may be useful in your prioritization efforts.

A Contingency-Planning Approach

As mentioned above, some experts are now advising companies to take a contingency-planning approach if they have not started remediation projects early enough. Although we do not support giving up on a remediation project, we agree that contingency planning is imperative. As a part of your planning for each system you must include contingency plans—all the more important when there is a risk that you will not complete remediation and testing in time. These contingency plans may include converting to new *commercial off-the-shelf (COTS)* applications or developing replacement programs through *rapid application development (RAD)* using newer-generation *object-oriented programming (OOPs)* technologies. Alternatively, you may plan to create a simple database application or even a spreadsheet as a backup for the existing legacy application. In some cases, you may decide that the contingency plan is a better option than any of the available remediation options. If this is the case, then you may reasonably decide to pursue remediation of selected systems by using the contingent option.

Remediation contingency planning is very different from giving up on your systems remediation and making business-oriented contingency plans. Efforts geared toward carrying out business functions without computer systems should proceed as part of your risk management effort, as described in Chapter 2, "Building an Effective Year 2000 Risk Management Program," and Chapter 6, "Contingency Planning." You should make sure that everyone involved in the project understands the different types of contingency planning that are taking place and does not assume that system remediation stops due to contingency planning. We believe that, even if you choose to focus on risk management activities, you need a remediation project to make a valid (due-diligence) effort to minimize Y2K failures.

A substantial Y2K project will be required to establish due diligence and good business judgment. We have heard of firms that are consciously taking a *do-nothing* or *fix-on-failure* approach. This is extremely risky from both an operational and a legal risk exposure perspective. The failure to establish a best-practice Year 2000 project will raise obvious questions about reasonable business judgment. Your organization has a due-diligence obligation to pursue a vigorous remediation effort as a means of minimizing the impact of system failures. You need to make the effort to inventory, assess, and repair failing systems, to develop contingency plans, and to test systems, processes, and interfaces for Year 2000 compliance. To the degree that you can find easy-to-implement solutions, you should employ them to prevent serious Y2K disruptions.

The key to establishing due diligence is to do as much as you possibly can in the time remaining. In the event of a lawsuit, opposing counsel will try hard to hold you to a very high standard on this point. In a practical sense, the level of effort needs to be commensurate with the risk and the consequences of failure. Given the typical business, if you are starting this late, expect your Year 2000 project to take an extraordinary effort, abundant resources, and endless work hours to accomplish anything meaningful. Do it anyway; if you don't, you will have a very difficult time proving to your stakeholders, business partners, or, in the worst case, a court, that you took a prudent course of action. Due diligence requires that you exert a level of effort that is reasonable given the risks that your Y2K problem presents.

Risk management efforts go hand in hand with a good Year 2000 project. For example, risk managers need to have a complete system inventory and risk assessment data. A good Year 2000 project will allow you to collect the data required for an effective risk management effort. You will also need Y2K project data for an ongoing assessment of the likelihood of Year 2000 system failures, both within and outside the organization.

It should be clear by now that you must put together a Y2K project and make your best effort in the time that remains. The rest of this chapter offers practical tips on how to establish a fast-track Year 2000 project.

Y2K Fast-Track Planning

Your first organizational step should be to create a fast-track Y2K project and a high-level strategy. The size of the project, the complexity of the technical problems, and interconnectedness of different systems will make this the most challenging project ever to face your organization. Add to this complexity shortages of staff and other resources, and you will find it even more difficult. First and fast, find the best project manager available and make Y2K his or her only priority. Develop a central focus and prepare a general plan for your Y2K efforts. Clear the decks by stopping work on other projects and pulling a dedicated team together. Construct an appropriate organizational structure with strong project oversight capabilities. Find a way to provide all the resources necessary to support the project.

Don't underestimate the resources and time a Y2K project will require. You need to make up for lost time, and you may need to redirect resources from other projects, defer current or planned initiatives, and establish multiple working shifts. While the size and make-up of the Y2K project office staff will vary based on your organization and systems portfolio, at a minimum, the team should consist of a program manager, a database administrator, a programmer for each major system, and a systems analyst. Larger efforts will benefit from administrative support including clerical, technical writers, contract administrators, and other administrative support personnel.

The Project Management Plan

The first objective should be to develop and publicize an overarching Y2K approach outlining the organization's high-level strategy. This approach will serve as the basis for the project management plan, which will define the organization's overall strategy in greater detail. The general approach should be included in the initial release of the plan. It is critical that the project management plan address Y2K goals and supporting objectives such as sizing the problem, identifying current efforts and solutions throughout the organization, informing and educating customers, identifying best practices, and establishing metrics for assessing project completion. Once this has been accomplished efforts should then shift immediately to drafting the contents of the plan, focusing on the *awareness* and *assessment* phases. Even though the first release of the project plan may be incomplete, it will still provide much needed guidance and direction throughout the organization.

The amount of detail included in a project management plan will depend on the organization's needs. Y2K is, above all else, a management problem. Attempting to prioritize and schedule systems, procure resources, and secure funding takes a team effort at every level. Those who attempt to accomplish these and countless other management tasks without a well-defined plan risk failure. The actual fixes will take place in the trenches, but obtaining resources for the repair team requires earnest planning at the highest level.

The project plan should make it clear that the success of the project will be measured by the degree to which things don't go wrong. It is not a project that is intended to improve technology but rather to prevent failure. A clear project plan can be used to prevent *scope creep*. The plan should make it clear that Year 2000 efforts can ill afford any unnecessary expansion of the project scope or any other additional burdens.

Select a Good Project Manager

To get a project started you need a great project manager. This person may or may not have technical experience. The person should be innovative, a strong leader with experience managing large projects, and comfortable with *systems thinking*. You may find the right person among your seasoned technical managers, or it could be an engineer or an executive. Whoever you choose, he or she should be the best person you can find. Eliminate all of their existing responsibilities and make Y2K project management their only task. If you have an established project but it has not made much headway, now is the time to put it in high gear; get a new manager if needed, or give the project the support and resources it needs. If you find yourself without a good project manager, don't despair. Many consulting firms are still offering project management services and can, for a price, establish a fast-track Year 2000 project for you.

Identify Technical and Management Representatives

Another area that is critical to successful Y2K resolution is the identification of all technical and management representatives or points-of-contact (POCs) beyond the groups described previously. These POCs will include system managers, budgeting and resource personnel, legal representatives, senior management, and, of course, contractors and other external contacts. Above all else, Year 2000 is a management nightmare that demands a tremendous coordinated effort. As a result, everyone who has a stake in its outcome must be made aware of his or her roles and responsibilities as quickly as possible. Just as important, each should know how other key players fit into the overall plan.

Identifying POCs will likely be a trying effort in the initial stages because many organizations are still trying to decide who is best suited to represent their needs. Nevertheless, the earlier permanent POCs are identified, the easier the overall effort should be. Post a listing on a dedicated Y2K project intranet site or on a shared network location to provide easy access to POC contact information.

Project Organization

Year 2000 projects should be organized in a way that facilitates rapid decision making. Whatever organizational structure is chosen, it should include close ties to senior management and as much delegation of authority as possible. You should avoid multiple layers of review and approval. Consider having a decision-making body that includes all the interested parties so that the review process can be minimized. This group can bring decisions directly to the top of the organization.

The Y2K project director must have easy access to the decision-making group as well as to the various program managers and other points of contact. Efforts under the project director should be organized along functional lines that provide as flat an organizational structure as possible but with suitable spans of control for both the project chief and the managers of each functional area. The final organizational structure will depend on the size and complexity of your organization's program. Make an effort to remove any unneeded layers. Figure 3.1 displays a typical project organization.

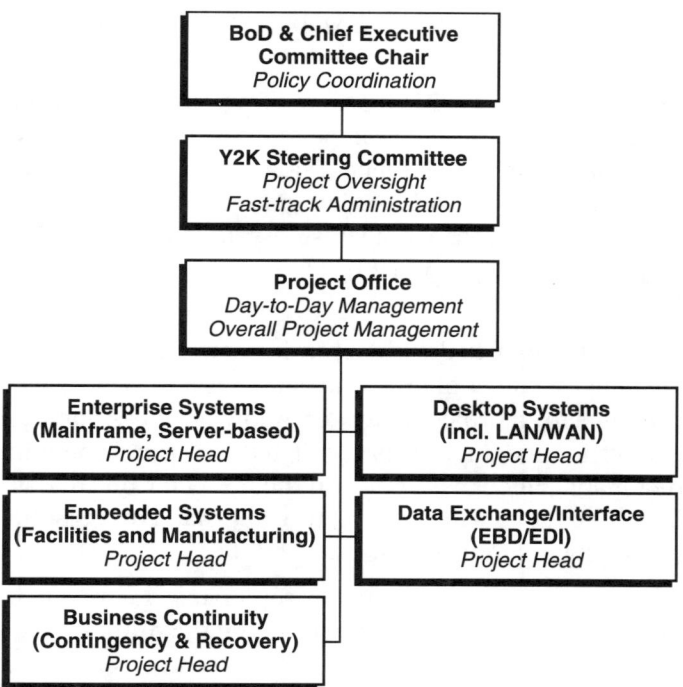

Figure 3.1 Typical Y2K program management organization chart.

Project Scoping and Triage

Given the precious little time that remains, you must realize that everything can't be fixed in time. In fact, if yours is a large and complex organization, it may be impossible to remediate and test the majority of your systems. Reasonable business judgment is a must in these cases. Determine which systems are critical to your continued business, which are at the most risk from Y2K-related failures, and which are the most likely to benefit from remediation efforts. This is why *triage*, as defined in Chapter 2, "Building an Effective Year 2000 Risk Management Program," is so important.

The Year 2000 project must sort through a battlefield littered with numerous systems. Some of these systems may be beyond hope, others may be easily fixed, while others may not need attention. In addition, some may be critical to business functions; others could be retired, and no one would notice. Like a field surgeon, your triage efforts must determine the severity of the individual problems, which ones can be saved, as well as which ones are the most critical to the mission of the organization. These are vital decisions for your business. You must use a clear and justifiable risk-rating methodology and assessment criteria. Once the risk assessment is made, top management must be briefed and given the final say in the decisions relating to which systems to remediate and how they are remediated as well as what level of resources are applied to the effort.

These decision steps represent a critical process for your organization. Not only will the decisions have a significant impact on the ultimate survival of your business; they will be later questioned if failures arise. Full documentation of the process and decision making is imperative. Later, when others are questioning whether you used reasonable business judgment (see Chapter 4, "Reducing Liability Exposure") you must be able to demonstrate that you made the best decisions possible.

The project manager will be tasked with preparing sound recommendations for senior management on a host of critical business issues. This is usually a new sphere of influence for a project manager. Allow business managers to participate in the decision making, either through the steering committee or by providing direct management assistance to the project. Consider assigning a seasoned business executive with a big-picture approach to assist the project manager in preparing recommendations.

The decisions that must ultimately be made by top management may include the risk rating and prioritization, the method of fixing the problem, as well as resource allocations. This latter issue includes the need to redirect scarce resources among the projects and decisions to forgo remediation of certain projects due to business judgments. Decisions that ultimately put one system or business unit in front of another are hard on project managers. It is quite likely that the project manager who attempts to fulfill this role will compromise his or her position with every customer who is not number one on the list. Because this activity is so sensitive and important, it should be developed based on criteria (such as that described in Chapter 2, "Building an Effective Year 2000 Risk Management Program") that are clear to everyone involved, and the final decisions should be made at the highest level possible. Senior management must make the difficult decisions, such as which systems to fix, which to abandon, or which ones will not get priority attention.

Other, similar decision-making issues parallel system remediation decision making. As discussed in Chapter 2, senior management should also prioritize contingency planning and other risk management efforts based on failure scenarios to determine how to plan for manual or alternative operations as well as for recovery.

Each organization's Y2K project manager should assist the steering committee in this decision-making effort by providing justification and supporting information, including all available assessment information, a customer survey, the inventory, the assessment, the renovation schedule, and perhaps a suggested list of core business processes that are critical to the organization. Beyond that, the steering committee should negotiate the position on the priority list with the customer. It is also imperative that the steering committee support the project manager in using the priority list and be open and flexible when new information is provided as the conversion effort moves forward.

Cost Estimates and Budgeting

Most organizations that started Year 2000 projects early performed an initial, rough cost estimate to inform decision makers of the potential fiscal impact of the Year 2000 work. Subsequent to the assessment of the problem, more detailed cost estimates and budgets were then constructed. Despite this process, according to a survey by Cap Gemini, only 3 percent of companies surveyed were on target with their estimates. Several U.S. companies are estimating repair costs in the hundreds of millions, with a few over a billion dollars. And, while the U.S. government's own cost estimates have doubled, analysts expect the true cost to exceed even recent estimates by a factor of 10.

Given that little time remains, you must immediately begin cost estimating to establish a project budget and to seek the financial resources necessary to carry out your mission. You will not have the time to complete assessments and to seek bids prior to requesting funding. You may have to rely on rough estimates and the experience of other organizations to develop your budget. You will need to convince your organization to be flexible in allocating resources; to be successful, the business must do whatever is necessary to bring resources to bear on Y2K. It is recommended that you work with your CFO or other finance officials to find innovative ways to accelerate the budget process. No time remains for an in-depth analysis of the costs associated with solving the problem. Although it is important to make the best cost estimates possible, it is even more important to begin working on the problem immediately. Initial assessment work, including pilot testing, does provide the best data for budget estimates, but you may need to use the experience of others (adjusting for complexity and inflation factors) in developing budget estimates. You should also consider using existing budget monies and redirecting other resources to fund the effort immediately.

We know from the experiences of others what the typical cost breakdown should look like. These breakdowns may be different for your project and may be affected by acceleration efforts, but they are nonetheless instructive. Figure 3.2 depicts a typical Y2K budget breakdown. *How to 2000* (IDG Books Worldwide, 1998) describes the typical breakdown as follows:

Planning and awareness. Approximately 5 percent of the overall schedule and up to 2 percent of the total budget.

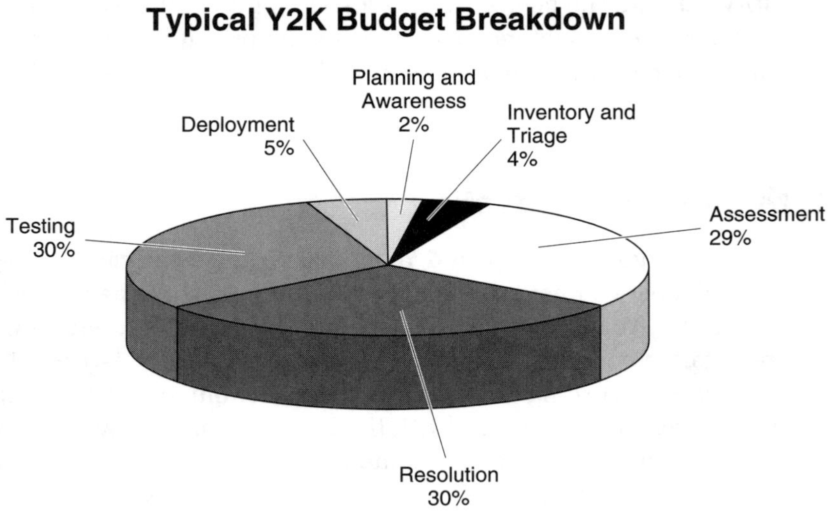

Typical Y2K Budget Breakdown

- Planning and Awareness 2%
- Inventory and Triage 4%
- Assessment 29%
- Resolution 30%
- Testing 30%
- Deployment 5%

Figure 3.2 Typical Y2K budget breakdown.

Inventory of systems and software. Approximately 5 percent of the overall schedule and up to 3 percent of the total budget.

Triage. Approximately 1 percent of the overall schedule and up to 1 percent of the total budget.

Detailed assessment. Approximately 35 percent of the overall schedule and up to 29 percent of the total budget.

Resolution. Approximately 10 percent of the overall schedule and up to 30 percent of the total budget.

Test planning and test execution. Up to 39 percent of the overall schedule and up to 30 percent of the total budget.

Deployment. Approximately 5 percent of the overall schedule and up to 5 percent of the total budget.

These types of metrics can be useful, along with the experience of others in building quick cost estimates. You will have to make adjustments for fast-tracking. You don't have time to waste; using the experience of others may be helpful in a quick and dirty cost estimate. You are not going to be able to project the cost accurately before a full assessment is done. What you can do is inform all of the decision makers of the magnitude of the problem and prepare to make rapid decisions on funding. If possible, set funding aside in anticipation of the expenditure requirements. Even better, ask for start-up funding now in anticipation of requests to come after the assessment.

It is important to remember that a number of other factors will influence the cost of making code Year 2000-compliant. Project estimators often overlook the following types of additional cost factors. These may vary greatly depending on your organization's current level of resources. These cost factors must be considered in estimating the total cost of your Year 2000 project:

- Building the test environment
- Buying testing and date aging tools
- Procuring contractual expertise
- Adding hardware and storage capacity (DASD—Direct Access Storage Device)
- Upgrading operating system software and commercial products
- Staff overtime
- Assessing embedded systems
- Conducting risk assessments

Develop Accelerated Administrative Processes

Due to the severe time constraints present in Year 2000 projects, your organization must develop procedures to accelerate the budget, human resources, and procurement processes. Here is where executive-level commitment will be key. Administrators in procurement, finance, and human resources must be made aware of the importance and the imperative of Year 2000 efforts by senior management. These administrators must be prepared to bend or change the rules as required to expedite Year 2000-related administrative processes. Your project manager must be able to move quickly to create and staff the project, to enter into contracts with vendors, to procure tools and software, and to take other actions where necessary.

Even if you are successful in winning the needed support, you may still run into roadblocks. In some cases, you will be asked first to justify expenditures by completing assessment work. Your cost estimates may be subjected to external audits. In normal circumstances, these situations would be reasonable and prudent. These, however, are not normal circumstances. Your project will need to proceed despite any administrative impediments. Your project manager will need to convince management that there is not enough time to go through normal channels and processes. Ask that the normal decision-making process be made more flexible and expedient. Ask that the steering committee be granted executive decision authority and that they exercise it quickly.

Budget	Procurement	Human Resources
Use emergency budget provisions	Use emergency procurement provisions	Use term, contract, or temporary positions
Reprogram existing budgets	Create special contract review process	Hire back retirees into temporary positions
Establish a set-aside fund balance	Bridge to existing contracts	Get special compensation and pay rates approved
Establish a contingency fund	Request sole-source contract approval if needed	Pay overtime freely; offer retention bonuses

Figure 3.3 Administrative process ideas.

Many more mundane administrative issues can slow your project down. It is a good idea to have special administrative privileges granted to your project from the start. Figure 3.3 offers some specific suggestions on how you can accelerate administrative processes.

Decision-Making and Reporting Structures

Because your Y2K project is expected to be one of singularly large proportions and significance, and because of the fixed deadline, having the best possible decision-making process in place is crucial. The process must be fundamentally sound and designed to be quick, responsive, and flexible. Broad-based input and coordination will be required to ensure the best possible outcome. This coordination must be constructed in a way that is not overly bureaucratic or burdensome. It is important that decisions can be made as quickly as possible. Crafting such a decision structure may be one of the most difficult of Y2K project management activities. Because the Year 2000 problem is more of a business problem than a technical one it must be dealt with as such. Rarely is there an application, network, system, or platform that is not perceived as critical to the user. End users may see the Year 2000 problem as an opportunity to replace systems that may have otherwise competed poorly for allocation of scarce resources.

Difficult decisions will have to be made about the priority of projects and among the various remediation alternatives. In addition, you must look for ways to accelerate the normal approval processes (like the accelerated administrative methods mentioned previously).

After an initial cost estimate is made, funds should be set aside for the effort. You should establish a rapid decision-making process and consider using high-level budget committees that can quickly review and approve budget requests. You may want to establish budgets that can be accessed through a quick administrative process. Emergency appropriation and procurement procedures are likely to already exist; use them to speed the budget and procurement processes.

Establishing a Y2K Plan

As with any large project, it is important to have a good plan. With Y2K, it is even more important to employ a best-practice approach to planning and to make sure that the basic framework is understood early on by all parties. Best-practice Y2K project plans are organized along the phases that make up a Y2K project life cycle, as described later in this chapter. For a late-starting plan, you need to think about how to conduct these phases as quickly as possible. Anyone starting this late may find it necessary to cut corners. Nonetheless, try to follow through on all of these steps, documenting everything you do or don't do. Although it will not be possible for all aspects of a Year 2000 project, you should consider using parallel processes and other ways to accelerate the life cycle.

Awareness

The awareness phase deals with the requirement for project buy-in and acceptance. You may think that it is far too late for awareness, but it seems that there will always be a need for it. For some reason, awareness has been one of the most difficult aspects of many Y2K projects. Perhaps it is because human nature prevents many people from accepting the reality of Year 2000 threats. Whatever the reason, many people have been slow to grasp the ramifications and gravity of Y2K and its related issues. Awareness and concern about Y2K issues are often hampered by denial, assumptions that others will take care of it, or a general feeling of helplessness. It is important that leaders and decision makers at every level of the organization understand the importance of achieving Y2K compliance.

To successfully promote awareness throughout an organization, it is essential that the project team provides oral presentations and background material to personnel at every level. This approach will offer credibility to your efforts and give everyone with questions a chance to ask them directly. As an example, the Y2K project team visits all major customers and presents its Y2K plan to both management and technical groups.

The project team will also have to establish communication avenues for promoting awareness and sharing information. Suggestions here include having articles published in organizational newsletters, developing a World Wide Web home page, creating a Year 2000 mailing list, attending industry Y2K conferences, conducting site visits, and holding video-teleconferences. Incorporating these suggestions into an overarching awareness strategy will go a long way in organizing awareness efforts. The Y2K page of Multnomah County at www.multnomah.lib.or.us/isd/Year2000/ is a good example of how to build awareness through a Web page (see Figure 3.4).

Assessment

The assessment phase deals with defining the scope of the problem and setting up the internal processes necessary to solve it. The primary purpose of the assessment phase is to gather and analyze systems inventory information to determine the size and scope of your Y2K problem. Only after the size and scope of the problem have been determined can you estimate the cost for budgeting purposes. The major issues encountered during this phase will concern inventory and assessment of systems, plus budgeting and scheduling issues.

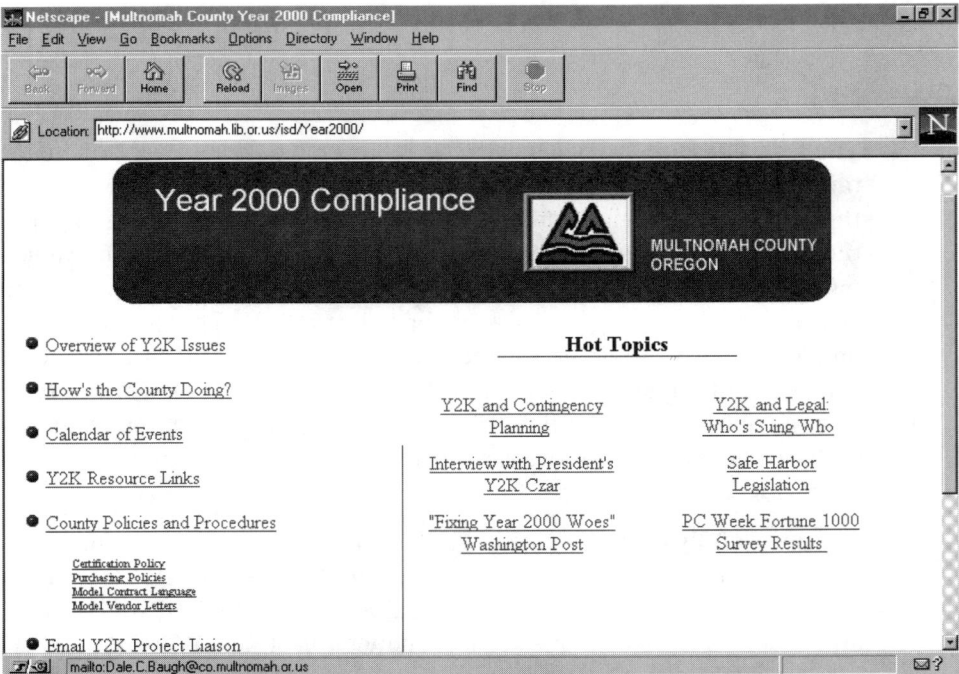

Figure 3.4 Multnomah County Year 2000 home page.

The primary deliverable from this phase is the project plan. Almost every industry consultant addressing the Year 2000 issue recommends that businesses first assess the impact of Y2K throughout their organization and follow up with a detailed analysis of each system to further identify Year 2000 costs and exposures. Most recommend that the first step in assessing the problem correctly is to inventory every system in the organization. We hope that you have complete and up-to-date inventories available. If not, you should work to develop them, but do not let the inventory process delay your other Y2K efforts.

Renovation

The renovation phase is the phase in which you make the actual repairs or modifications to your systems. During the renovation phase, and based on the assessment, final decisions must be made on how systems and processes will be made compliant. Additionally, risk-based decisions on conducting contingency remediations must also be considered. For instance, if a replacement strategy is chosen, you might consider encapsulating the old system as a backup should the replacement project fail to be completed on time. Once decisions are made, the actual work of fixing or replacing code begins. Computer systems, data applications, and processes can be made compliant in several ways:

System certification. Determining compliance through testing or vendor certification.

System retirement. Taking the system out of production.

System reengineering. Redesigning existing process by writing new software.

System modification. Correcting faulty code.

Expanded date fields. Switching from two- to four-digit years.

Windowing. Using a fixed or sliding *date window* to determine the correct century.

Procedural workaround. Working around the bad code.

Encapsulation. System converts input to past dates for processing, then converts to present for output.

Bridges/filters. May also be used for compliance.

Validation

Here is where the lion's share of the Year 2000 project efforts lie. Testing is estimated to account for 30 to 75 percent of the cost to correct the Year 2000 problem. The Y2K problem creates special considerations for validation of renovated systems, especially legacy systems. In such cases, test cases may not exist because the source code that produces the undesirable results may be unavailable, unreadable, impossible to recompile, undocumented, or legally inaccessible because of licensing issues. In other cases, Year 2000-compliant systems may be affected by data from other, noncompliant systems. Further, system problems may be aggravated by embedded systems and subsystems. Identifying the manipulation of date information to be tested can often be difficult. Date manipulations may span hundreds of lines of code within a given application. In some instances, these manipulations can occur across related programs or within or among supporting utilities. Often, year manipulations are embedded in controllers, firmware-based microcode, operating systems, real-time clocks, and other, less-than-obvious system-level resources. Thus, even if the application has no apparent date manipulation algorithms, it still may not be exempt from one of the Y2K-related problems.

Testing for Year 2000 compliance will be a difficult, sometimes highly technical, and time-consuming task. You will need to create a test environment that fully simulates Year 2000 dates at both the application and operating system level as well as in networking environments and interfaces. Even if a single application is compliant, its testing must be synchronized with other applications that may transmit date information to it to ensure the overall system compliance. Look at the automated testing tools now available as a way to accelerate testing. Also, as much as possible, use operations staff to design and run test scripts based on actual system use. Try to free up technical staff to work on remediation while your users do the testing.

Testing should never be done in the production environment because testing with the Year 2000 dates can create unexpected problems with existing production data. Using dedicated time machines (stand-alone CPUs) and independent test beds (stand-alone LANs) is a best practice. In some cases, though, a parallel system is cost-prohibitive. In these situations, you will have to look for alternatives such as dedicated LPARs (logical partitions) or use of a hot-site or leased resources. For a detailed treatment of testing, see William Perry's *Year 2000 Software Testing* (John Wiley & Sons, 1998).

Implementation

This phase involves the final implementation of tested systems. During this phase, decisions must be made on parallel processing, data conversion, file conversion, and backup/recovery. Although traditional implementation approaches may be taken, Year 2000 projects can expect this activity to occur under pressure to meet unusually short deadlines. This phase deals with software migration and control, data conversion, and the ultimate confirmation of both operational and procedural links to data exchange (for example, interfaces and access). These comments address special considerations above and beyond the typical activities an organization would perform to ensure that the production environment is protected from introducing inadequately tested or unauthorized software. It is important that you use structured implementation plans and schedules to ensure resource availability and that you minimize risk through continued testing after systems have been placed back into production.

Post-Implementation

This phase involves everything that needs to be done after the remediated systems or processes are implemented. Your project, as well as the rest of the information technology organization, must ensure a *clean management* approach to maintain the compliancy of the remediated applications and to protect the remediated systems from external factors. You will need to be extra diligent in managing updates, external data exchanges, maintenance, and other issues to mitigate the risks of contamination. Data exchanges are particularly threatening as business partners are beyond our control. Finally, during this phase you will need to focus on updating business continuity, business recovery, disaster recovery, and contingency plans.

Project Checklist

A Year 2000 project checklist is included at the end of this chapter to assist you in tracking the basic steps in this project life cycle process. Although we have attempted to address all of the important steps in the process, we are not offering technical advice on specific remediation and testing methodologies. You must ensure that appropriate staff or consultants are assigned to the project to ensure that the required technical expertise is applied to the project.

Establish Compliance Standards

The definition of compliance and the standards that deliver compliance are hotly debated issues, and they will be addressed in Chapter 4, "Reducing Liability Exposure." True enterprise-wide compliance requires an integrated approach to testing entire systems and their interfaces. In addition, the ability of critical suppliers and business partners is a factor in the organization's ability to function unimpeded. In other words, true compliance requires a holistic approach to Y2K certification and risk management. Given that you are starting late and that many of the suppliers and business partners will be beyond your control, however, total compliance certification may never be achieved.

Conclusion

We hope that by now you understand how important a Year 2000 project is and what you can accomplish at this late juncture. On the other hand, you may be thinking that you will never be able to complete a Y2K project in the time remaining. The truth is that you can still do a lot. The challenge is to make a good-faith effort to minimize the impact both before and after the date change.

Obviously, by starting late, you are extremely compromised by the short amount of time that remains. You do have the benefit of learning from the many Year 2000 projects that have been working over the past several years, and you will benefit from the many new analyzing, testing, and repair tools now available. We have discussed many ideas here on how you can be successful. Consultants are also available who will be able to bring a wealth of knowledge to your project.

Remember to follow the suggestions provided here and adhere as much as possible to industry best practices. Make sure that you and your organization see this effort as the number one priority for your business's survival. Everyone involved in the project will need to stop doing anything that is not directly related to fixing Year 2000 problems. Work to minimize unproductive use of time in meetings and conferences. If needed, pull staff in from other projects or from other departments. Work two or three shifts if necessary. Look for noncompliant systems that are not productive and kill them. Include nontechnical staff in the project; you may be surprised by how much they can offer.

Solving this problem is going to take a lot of effort and out-of-the-box thinking. Keep your mind open and flexible, and remember stress management techniques. Your project manager and project team are in for the challenge of their careers. Everyone should see this as an opportunity to grow and to gain valuable experience. Those who rise to the occasion are likely to be rewarded. Experience with successful Y2K projects will position project staff well for a successful career after 2000.

Alas, given even the best of Year 2000 remediation projects, risk management will loom large over the Y2K landscape. Your project will be competing for attention and resources with risk management issues throughout 1999. The remaining chapters deal with the many aspects of Year 2000 risk management.

Project Checklist

The project checklist is intended to give you a quick start to your Y2K project or to serve as a tool to assess existing project planning to determine if there are any gaps. The checklist has two parts. First, a *Project Initiation Checklist* provides a quick list of steps involved in getting your project started. Second, a *Project Life Cycle Checklist* offers a more detailed, step-by-step checklist to use in conducting the actual Year 2000 systems remediation project.

Project Initiation Checklist

Establish a Year 2000 Team

- ❏ Select a strong project manager.
- ❏ Establish a project management plan.
- ❏ Establish a Year 2000 program committee.
- ❏ Identify technical and management points-of-contact.
- ❏ Determine the project's organizational structure.
- ❏ Determine project scope.
- ❏ Conduct triage.
- ❏ Develop cost estimates and budgets.
- ❏ Establish a project office with sufficient staffing and space.
- ❏ Provide sufficient funding and resources.
- ❏ Provide risk management and audit resources to ensure that the team can quickly develop a risk-based Year 2000 project plan.
- ❏ Develop accelerated administrative processes.

Develop an Enterprise-Wide Year 2000 Plan

- ❏ Complete an inventory of all automated systems and processes including:
    - ❏ Computer operating systems
    - ❏ Computer hardware
    - ❏ Computer applications
    - ❏ Local and wide area networks
    - ❏ Telecommunications (PBX, ACD, voice mail, etc.)
    - ❏ Electronic data (databases)
    - ❏ Electronic manufacturing processes
    - ❏ Building systems (security systems, environmental controls, etc.)
    - ❏ Electronic interfaces

- ❑ Electronic data interchanges
- ❑ Infrastructure
- ❑ Perform triage to identify and prioritize applications and processes that are the most date-sensitive and most vulnerable.
- ❑ Determine whether systems, processes, and data should be modified, replaced, outsourced, or discontinued.
- ❑ Based on triage, determine if adequate funds and resources are available.

Year 2000 Plan Implementation

- ❑ Initiate projects to test solutions to identified problems.
- ❑ Implement Year 2000 remediation based on triage and in accordance with risk.
- ❑ Develop plans and timelines for each project.
- ❑ Begin monitoring and reporting of project progress.

Project Life Cycle Checklist

Awareness Phase Checklist

Goals and objectives: To raise awareness of executive and senior management, as well as the user community and external business partners, to the Year 2000 issue and its potential impact on company operations. Senior management and technology staff must be fully aware of the impact of Y2K and its potential consequences to operations. Management and the user community must establish a business case for providing the necessary level of resources to the Year 2000 project.

- ❑ Executive and senior management sponsors identified.
- ❑ Year 2000 project team established.
- ❑ Business impact identified.
- ❑ Awareness briefings for senior management conducted.
- ❑ Awareness campaigns for user community initiated.
- ❑ Year 2000 contacts with external business entities initiated.
- ❑ Working group for the Year 2000 established including representatives from management, business partners, users, and IT communities.
- ❑ Method for continued awareness building and distributing relevant Year 2000 information to other entities within company developed.

- ❏ Year 2000 compliance policy developed and approved.
- ❏ Year 2000 contract language developed and approved.

Assessment Phase Checklist

Goals and objectives: To estimate the scope and budget for the Year 2000 project. Develop a complete inventory of all hardware and software components for all IT systems. Collect compliance statements from hardware and software vendors and business partners. Categorize all identified systems based on the estimated level of impact to business functions. Complete an estimate for the scope of effort required for identifying, correcting, testing, and implementing changes to those systems deemed necessary to business functions. Identify and estimate resource needs to address the Year 2000 project, including personnel, office space, additional hardware, and supporting tools.

- ❏ Inventory methodology determined.
- ❏ Inventory of hardware completed.
- ❏ Inventory of software completed.
- ❏ Inventory of in-house application software (mainframe and desktop) completed.
- ❏ Identification of users and responsible support personnel conducted.
- ❏ Schedule for new development and/or replacement determined.
- ❏ Inventory of production control procedures conducted.
- ❏ Compliance information, including written communications received from hardware and software vendors, compiled.
- ❏ Compliance information, including written communications from outside business partners (that is, equipment and office suppliers, clients, financial institutions, etc.), compiled.
- ❏ Risk rating of all applications based on estimated level of impact to organization's business functions identified and performed.
- ❏ Estimate of required resources for correcting all high-risk applications made.
- ❏ Preliminary budget for the Year 2000 project execution developed.
- ❏ Senior management briefed on the results from the assessment phase.
- ❏ Senior management approval of preliminary budget and commitment of the required resources to execute the Year 2000 project achieved.

Renovation Phase Checklist

Goals and objectives: To perform a detailed analysis and develop detailed plans for correction, testing, and implementation of remediated applications.

Develop detailed plans and scripts for application correction, testing, and implementation. Identify all necessary applications and perform risk ratings. Determine a technical approach, and select tools to aid in the conversion of each application. Define a compliance test and procedures for each identified application. Develop a "time machine" testing environment containing Year 2000-compliant releases of the operating system and programming languages. Determine the appropriate level of contractual services to assist in-house staff. Identify where bridging solutions are needed. Procure necessary services, conversion, and testing tools.

- ❏ Year 2000 team has determined analysis methodology.
- ❏ Initial draft written for conversion sequence determined for identified applications.
- ❏ Detailed analysis of each application conducted and documented.
- ❏ Method of correction for each identified application selected.
- ❏ Preliminary conversion plan, including applicable bridging, for each application developed.
- ❏ Coding and naming standards for the conversion process developed.
- ❏ Resource requirements for correcting, testing, and implementing each at-risk application developed.
- ❏ Year 2000 compliance criteria and test plan for each application developed.
- ❏ Required external services identified and procured.
- ❏ Year 2000 budget adjusted as required.
- ❏ Senior management briefed on the results from the planning phase.
- ❏ Senior management approval of the budget adjustments obtained.
- ❏ Executive commitment to provide required resources secured.

Validation Phase Checklist

Goals and objectives: To correct, test, and implement all applications that were identified and remediated. By the end of this phase, the project should have converted all at-risk applications and have successfully completed all Year 2000 compliance testing and regression testing for each application. Where needed, you should have developed bridging solutions for the implementation of applications. Migration plans will have been developed and tested and procedures developed for each database associated with remediated applications. Finally, you will have developed a detailed implementation plan for each application.

- ❏ Application code and all associated data elements corrected (JCL, procs, datalibs, etc.).

- ❏ Software documentation updated.
- ❏ Corrected applications comply with coding and naming standards developed for the Year 2000 project.
- ❏ All unit, system, and acceptance tests successfully completed.
- ❏ Testing executed under system software releases that will be used in Year 2000.
- ❏ Testing executed using date simulation tool to represent dates (before, during and after 2000).
- ❏ Conversion phase schedule on time.
- ❏ Bridging solutions required for gradual implementation of specified applications developed.
- ❏ Data element migration plan and procedures for all data elements developed.
- ❏ Detailed implementation plan for each identified application developed.

Implementation Phase Checklist

Goals and objectives: To implement all corrected applications and data elements in the production environment. By the end of this phase, the project should have completed the conversion of all at-risk applications and placed them back into production. You will have implemented operational procedures associated with new or remediated applications and have completed user training. Finally, you will have developed contingency plans should any of the remediated applications fail.

- ❏ All converted applications moved into the production environment.
- ❏ All system and third-party software packages upgraded to meet Year 2000 compliance criteria as set forth in the Year 2000 compliance policy.
- ❏ All data elements associated with identified applications converted to acceptable Year 2000 compliance guidelines.
- ❏ All operational procedures associated with new or corrected applications implemented in the production environment.
- ❏ All users trained and ready to use the new or corrected applications as well as any upgraded third-party software systems.
- ❏ Fallback procedures to be implemented in case of application failure developed.

Post-Implementation Phase Checklist

Goals and objectives: To identify and correct any unpredictable malfunction of information systems caused by internal and external errors associated with the Year 2000 problem. By the end of this phase, your project should have developed safeguards to protect remediated systems and be ready to implement contingency plans and procedures required for continued system operation. You will have developed, and be ready to use, crisis management procedures to correct any system failures associated with the Year 2000 project execution. Users will have developed contingency plans and disaster recovery procedures including manual procedures for record keeping, report/document generation, data entry, and system recovery.

- Clean management procedures developed.
- Fallback procedures developed.
- Functional users prepared to conduct company business without automated systems for a specific period of time.
- Disaster recovery team assembled to deal with system failures.
- Procedures for manual record keeping and follow up data entry developed.
- Plans exercised.

CHAPTER 4

Reducing Y2K Liability Exposure

"Your Year 2000 project might be in trouble if . . . you finally get a meeting with corporate counsel after 15 phone calls [and] the first thing he asks is, "What exactly do you mean by the term 'Year 2000?'"

—MICHAEL COHN, COMPUTERWORLD, SEPTEMBER 21, 1998

This chapter examines the liability risks Year 2000 is likely to present and provides comprehensive strategies for managing those risks. Companies can avoid many disputes that would otherwise lead to lawsuits by exercising *Year 2000 due diligence*. We will also lay the groundwork for defending Y2K litigation and discuss the steps that should be taken to prepare for cost recovery suits.

Not Just for Lawyers

Year 2000 presents the unusual opportunity to anticipate legal problems long before they occur and to take steps to avoid them. Every thinking person is capable of understanding these legal risks. This chapter is written in plain English for lawyers and nonlawyers alike, to provide you with a basic understanding of the kinds of liability you might encounter and strategies for coping with a host of emerging legal risks. Of course, if you face a Y2K-related legal problem, or if you want to pursue any of the strategies that we recommend, you will need to consult a lawyer for advice that addresses your particular factual situation.

Executives, Managers, and IT Professionals

It should be obvious by now that Year 2000 could bring about many difficult changes in common business routines that would present significant legal risks. Your relationships with your customers and vendors could become adversarial if one or more links in the supply chain break without warning. Standard contract terms might fail to address important contingencies that no one considered at the time the transaction was negotiated. New contracts could become much more difficult to negotiate because the allocation of risks has become substantially more uncertain. Insurance coverage you thought you had might be denied or excluded by your carrier. Accounting and tax requirements are undergoing important changes that could affect your bottom line as you try to remediate your technology systems. There's a lot to think about.

Lawyers of Every Kind

For in-house and outside counsel, our objective is to provide a detailed roadmap of the changing legal landscape. Y2K is likely to cut across many practice areas, possibly for as long as a decade. It is by no means just for attorneys specializing in high technology or intellectual property matters. Consider the following situations in which Y2K issues could become routine considerations:

- Structuring business transactions for IT products and services, and among supply-chain and trading partners
- Advising clients about making disclosures to the SEC, working with independent auditors, and preparing corporate tax filings for technology investments required to achieve Year 2000 compliance
- Handling commercial litigation for direct and indirect Y2K failures and their ripple effects, in the form of breach of contract and warranty actions, and insurance coverage claims
- Handling tort cases involving malfunctioning traffic signals, defective electronic medical devices, or safety equipment that fails to operate as designed

For the most part, "Year 2000 law" applies well-established legal doctrines to novel and complex factual situations. Even experienced counsel, however, might not understand which rules of law apply to Y2K or how they are likely to come into play. This chapter will provide you with the understanding you need to spot the issues in virtually any practice area and help you advise your clients on effective strategies for staying out of harm's way.

Exercising Due Diligence

Most Y2K lawsuits will be precipitated by a date-related system or equipment failure involving your company or some third party with which you do business. Whether that failure becomes a lawsuit, and how well you can defend that suit, will depend in large part on whether you exercised *Year 2000 due diligence* to avoid that problem. Of course, due diligence is not a defense to some kinds of liability, such as simple claims for breach of contract. If your customer suffered monetary losses because your company failed to deliver an agreed quantity of goods by a certain date, you can be held liable no matter how hard you tried to honor your contract. In many other cases, however, the extent of your efforts to prevent harm to others could be the difference between being sued and avoiding suit, or between winning and losing.

What Due Diligence Means

There is no generally accepted definition of Year 2000 due diligence. In other contexts, due diligence is defined as follows:

> Such a measure of prudence, activity, or assiduity, as is properly to be expected from, and ordinarily exercised by, a reasonable and prudent man under the particular circumstances; not measured by any absolute standard, but depending on the relative facts of the special case (Nolan, 1979).

When we speak of Year 2000 due diligence, we mean an integrated collection of sound, well-documented practices that constitute a systematic effort to identify, evaluate, and mitigate business and legal risks that result directly or indirectly from date-related computer failures.

Year 2000 Due Diligence

Y2K due diligence will usually be measured in hindsight, after failures have occurred and lawsuits have been filed. In such cases, judges and juries will be asking one or more years from now whether the defendants made reasonable efforts before 2000 to protect the plaintiffs from harm. So, it is difficult to define the boundaries of Year 2000 due diligence now, particularly because few problems have occurred that have actually damaged others and no such cases have been decided yet. In those cases where good intentions and reasonable efforts are relevant to determining liability, however, a comprehensive risk management plan that is developed and managed aggressively along the following lines should put your company in a strong position to defend itself:

- Actively manage the technical remediation and testing of all internal IT and embedded systems to achieve Year 2000 compliance
- Track the compliance efforts of third parties upon which your business depends
- On a going-forward basis, develop Y2K contracting and purchasing policies that clearly allocate the risks and responsibilities of Year 2000 problems

- Prepare effective business continuity, contingency, and disaster recovery plans (because the likelihood of completely avoiding all Year 2000 disruptions is probably small)
- Disclose material Year 2000 risks as may be required by fiduciary relationships or regulatory and contractual requirements
- Provide timely notice to insurers of potential Y2K-related claims
- Document your Year 2000 compliance efforts
- Prepare now for future litigation by and against your company related to Year 2000 problems
- Provide directors and officers with information they need to comply with their fiduciary duties and other legal responsibilities

Legal Issues Checklist

Many attorneys will find that they have had long experience with the important legal doctrines that will govern Year 2000 disputes, but they don't yet know which ones will apply. As a foundation for exercising Year 2000 due diligence, let's take a high-level look at the range of legal issues that Y2K implicates. Lawyers advising business clients—either as in-house counsel or outside advisor—can use this list (and the explanations that follow) to make sure that no important area of Y2K liability exposure is overlooked and that appropriate attention is paid to those issues that present the greatest risks of liability to your organization.

RISK MANAGEMENT OF Y2K LIABILITY EXPOSURES

Business risk assessment	Y2K remediation contracts
Legal audit	Major corporate decisions
Directors and officers	Contingency and disaster recovery plans
Human resources policies	Documentation
Company compliance	Communication, privileges, and disclosures
Vendor compliance	
Customer compliance	Insurance and hold harmless agreements
Statutory/regulatory compliance	Claims management
Contracts and procurement	

Overview of Y2K Liability Risk Management Areas

As you can see, Y2K law covers a lot of territory. That's not surprising, given the many ways Year 2000 events can damage a business. Of course, many of these risk areas are not purely or even primarily legal issues, but each of them requires legal input: Attorneys need to be involved along the way so they can offer informed advice when needed.

Business risk assessment. As explained in Chapter 2, "Building an Effective Year 2000 Risk Management Program," a business risk assessment considers the business consequences of potential Year 2000 failures across the enterprise. Counsel should participate in the business risk assessment so they can become familiar with the financial, operational, and managerial risks the company faces. Otherwise, it will be difficult for the company's lawyers to provide legal advice later about a problem they don't really understand. Major tasks include the following:

- Define triage criteria
- Inventory risks in all departments relating to IT systems, embedded systems, third-party relationships, and data interfaces
- Identify business function impacts in terms of the likelihood and consequences of various types of business failures, how critical they are, and when they would be likely to occur (failure horizons)
- Prioritize risks

Legal audit. The purpose of a Y2K legal audit is to answer three questions: First, is someone else, such as a contract service provider or a value-added network (VAN), required to fix the organization's noncompliant IT systems or pay other remediation expenses, such as building EDI bridges? Second, does the company have legal obligations to others arising from Year 2000 issues? Third, what rights does the company have against others—such as its suppliers—in the event of a loss caused by Y2K failures? The legal audit is addressed in detail later in this chapter. There are three major steps:

- Inventory key legal documents
- Evaluate the organization's legal rights and duties
- Prepare a legal audit report for the Board of Directors or General Counsel

Directors and officers. Members of the Board of Directors and the CEO, CFO, and other senior officers must assume certain risk management responsibilities to protect the enterprise from Y2K problems and to protect themselves from personal liability. These duties include the following:

- Active sponsorship and oversight of the company's Y2K program
- Keeping informed about Y2K exposures
- Anticipating and mitigating Y2K consequences
- Complying with applicable disclosure requirements
- Producing accurate business records

- Establishing the Program Management Office (PMO) and enterprise-wide Year 2000 team
- Approving and funding a Y2K budget
- Developing Year 2000 human resource policies

Human resources policies. Year 2000 poses difficult HR challenges for most organizations because the compliance is labor-intensive, the work is often considered unattractive, and the IT labor market is extremely tight. Because these problems are widely known, companies that fail to make diligent efforts to assign, train, and retain qualified professionals to carry out the program successfully will face sharp attacks if lawsuits are filed later. Issues that should be considered include the following:

- Employee retention incentives
- Key employee contracts
- Employee indemnification policies
- Staffing and scheduling requirements and policies
- Employee awareness program

Company compliance. Organizations that sell noncompliant products and services must take affirmative steps to control their liability exposure. Counsel should advise their clients to carry out the following tasks, and where a legal judgment is needed, counsel should provide guidance:

- Inventory technology products and services sold that are still in the stream of commerce
- Determine their compliance status
- Evaluate compliance obligations under contract and warranty provisions
- Evaluate potential noncontractual liability, such as products liability
- Develop and implement policies for retrofitting or correcting Y2K impairments or recalling/replacing noncompliant versions
- Develop and implement policies for notifying customers and clients of the potential for Y2K noncompliance and the company's policies toward repair and remuneration

Compliance. Supply-chain risk management is covered in Chapter 5, "External Compliance Strategies." Counsel should ensure that the company is addressing the following issues:

- Inventory external business dependencies
- Develop triage criteria (consider: technical exposures, revenue exposure, liability exposure, regulatory exposure, personnel exposure, and/or good will exposure)

- Prioritize external business dependencies
- Develop and manage a vendor communications plan
- Verify compliance of critical vendors
- Develop contingency plans for supply-chain failures

Output dependency compliance. As we pointed out in Chapter 1, "Year 2000 Business and Legal Risks," companies can experience cash flow and revenue problems if important customers are unprepared for the century transition. Although we're certainly not suggesting that you turn customers away, you should find out whether key customers are likely to experience business disruptions that could affect your bottom line. Consider the following measures:

- Review credit policies concerning credit terms, outstanding balance limits, and acceptance of additional orders
- Review accounts receivable so you don't get overextended with vulnerable customers
- Audit key accounts where it would be appropriate to verify the customer's progress in carrying out its compliance plan
- Develop a communications plan to respond to customer inquiries and send inquiries to customers

Regulatory compliance. A host of statutes, regulations, and agency guidelines and directives have been adopted in response to the Y2K crisis. Some regulations apply across economic sectors, and others are industry-specific. Also, regulatory requirements that predate general awareness of Y2K and make no reference to it could still create important liability exposures. A coordinated compliance program should include the following tasks:

- Inventory applicable regulatory requirements
- Coordinate regulatory requirements and existing compliance programs
- Develop and manage a comprehensive compliance plan that ensures consistent disclosures and incorporates regulatory compliance into triage efforts

Contracts and procurement. Until 1998, very few business agreements mentioned Year 2000, and even fewer purchasing specifications included Y2K compliance among their requirements. But Year 2000 contract language is becoming as commonplace as warranty disclaimers and *force majeure* clauses, and there is really no excuse for failing to include appropriate provisions addressing date-related contingencies in contracts, requests for proposals, and purchase orders. There are three basic steps to ensure that your company no longer purchases noncompliant goods and services:

- Define Y2K compliance
- Draft appropriate contract provisions, including representations and warranties, remedies, and termination clauses
- Negotiate compliant contracts with your suppliers, vendors, and customers

Y2K remediation contracts. Contracts for Year 2000 remediation tools and services present special risks for both buyers and sellers. The greater risks of liability, increased importance of bargaining positions, short time horizon, limited market choices, and obstacles to successful performance all combine to make these contracts more difficult to draft and negotiate than ordinary commercial agreements. At this point, many Y2K *solutions providers* will offer their services subject only to one-sided boilerplate contracts on a take-it-or-leave-it basis. We will suggest strategies for structuring the engagement and managing the project in ways that acknowledge these new realities without turning Y2K remediation into a high wire act without a net.

Major corporate decisions. Strategic business transactions such as mergers and acquisitions, joint ventures, asset sales, and stock offerings can no longer be undertaken without first taking a hard look at each party's millennium preparations. Obviously, it would be irresponsible for one company to buy another without knowing what kind of shape the target is likely to be in come 2000. Thus, traditional due diligence activities—financial analysis, assets valuation, liability assessment, and so on—must now incorporate Year 2000 due diligence as well. As explained more fully in Chapter 7, "Major Corporate Decision Making," these activities should include the following:

- Add Y2K issues to due diligence checklists
- Investigate interoperability of systems to be integrated
- Adjust business valuations, as appropriate
- Exchange Y2K disclosures
- Draft representations and warranties
- Audit each party's compliance activities through closing and release of escrow funds

Contingency and disaster recovery plans. Chapter 6, "Contingency Planning," covers these important subjects in detail. For now, we will simply note that companies should involve their in-house or outside attorneys in formulating, documenting, and testing contingency and disaster recovery plans as an integral part of developing a sound due-diligence plan. Planning for failure is essential for every organization, but documenting foreseeable business risks and potential weak points in your compliance program could be used against you later in litigation if one of those failure scenarios actually happens and your contingency plan doesn't work as well as you'd hoped. You may need to make hard choices about the extent of emergency planning and the amount of backup resources and redundancies that should be put in place. Counsel need to understand what alternatives are available for consideration, who needs to be involved in the decision-making and approval process, and how to build a case to show that the client acted responsibly.

Documentation. Reliable and well-managed documentation is integral to an effective due-diligence process. Topics discussed further in Chapter 8, "Substantiating Due Diligence," include the following:

- Developing documentation guidelines
- Establishing records management systems (document repository)
- Protecting trade secrets and legally privileged communications

Communications, privileges, and disclosures. What you say about your Y2K preparations and how you say it can present substantial business and legal risks. Regulators, investors, auditors, trading partners, customers, and employees all may rely on your internal and external statements in ways that could create legal rights and impose legal obligations. Public companies face special risks in connection with Year 2000 disclosures; danger lies in saying too much or too little, or saying it too early or too late. In addition, inconsistent or unauthorized corporate communications could undermine your legal position in the event of litigation. Maintaining radio silence is not the answer, either. Companies need to educate their employees, work with their customers, exchange information with their suppliers, and keep regulators informed. Thoughtful planning and coordination with counsel will become increasingly important throughout 1999 and into 2000.

Insurance and hold harmless agreements. As we explain in Chapter 9, "Insurance Issues," the availability of insurance coverage for Y2K-related questions is already the subject of much consternation among insurers. Because insurance is such a fundamental component of managing business risks, it is essential that you thoroughly review your policies well before 2000 and make assessments about what can be done to protect your prospects for coverage. Companies may also have indemnification or hold harmless agreements with third parties that should be inventoried and evaluated to protect your rights. Basic actions every business should take include the following:

- Inventory all of the many different kinds of policies your company holds that might relate to the business risks you face
- Evaluate your coverage for Y2K applicability with experienced insurance professionals, risk managers, and legal counsel
- Identify and comply with any notification or other procedural requirements

- Prepare insurance claims in accordance with policy requirements
- Track renewal schedules and review renewal applications closely for new language that might affect both coverage for Year 2000 claims and the information you must provide to avoid claims by your carriers that you should be denied coverage for withholding information

Claims management. Not every customer dissatisfaction will become a lawsuit. In many cases, customers will simply exercise their legitimate rights to rescind a transaction, withhold payments, ask for their money back, or assert their warranty rights for repair or replacement. Companies that sell noncompliant IT products are likely to face substantial hits to their bottom line and may want to prepare efficient and consistent means of responding to and tracking these claims. Buyers should make sure they preserve and properly assert their contractual and statutory rights under the Uniform Commercial Code. In some cases, the UCC might enable buyers to rid themselves of noncompliant products before damaging failures occur by making proper notice and demand on the seller. Once claims have been asserted, both parties need to monitor their status as they proceed through the pipeline.

Causes of Action and Defenses

A *cause of action* is legalese for a type of a lawsuit, an *action* being a legal proceeding and its *cause* being the particular theory on which the claim is based, such as negligence or breach of warranty. Many different kinds of Year 2000 lawsuits are anticipated, and we will describe them shortly. We will also review the defenses that will likely be asserted in Y2K litigation. In this way, companies can take advantage of the opportunity that advanced knowledge about probable Year 2000 disputes affords.

The Elements of Legal Cases

You can think of the *elements* of a cause of action like the ingredients in a recipe. Recipes don't work without all of the required ingredients, and a lawsuit cannot be maintained without all of the necessary allegations. For example, the first class-action suit filed against Intuit, Inc., the maker of Quicken financial software, was dismissed because the court determined that the plaintiffs had failed to allege any injury, an essential element of most causes of action. Because the software had not yet failed to function properly, the court ruled that any claim of damage was too speculative at the time the suit was filed. Using more legalese, the case was not "ripe" for adjudication.

Because most suits require a legally cognizable injury, potential defendants have an opportunity to prevent lawsuits by taking appropriate steps to (1) negotiate modified contract provisions that contemplate Y2K; (2) prevent Y2K failures; and (3) mutually agree to alternative dispute resolution. (See Chapter 10, "Alternative Dispute Resolution.") For example, many software developers are offering their customers software "patches" or compliant upgrades free of charge or at a reduced price. Another approach vendors take is to charge a fee for the compliant software upgrade but include new features to justify its cost. This tactic is considered unfair and deceptive by many consumers, and it has spawned several class-action suits.

Dissecting Y2K Lawsuits

A survey of the different kinds of lawsuits that Year 2000 failures might engender should be helpful in understanding the legal risks companies face and what strategies can most effectively manage those risks. In this section, we first identify the likely parties to Y2K litigation and then discuss what causes of action and defenses can be anticipated. Note that there is no one-to-one correspondence between claims and defenses; instead, Y2K litigation will entail multiple theories of liability against which an array of defenses will be mounted. Also, as is often the case in business litigation, the suits will not merely involve one injured party suing another. Rather, several plaintiffs, such as the participants in a joint commercial venture, might file suit against several defendants that manufactured, sold, supplied, distributed, installed, customized, and maintained noncompliant software and hardware systems and their various components.

Whatever the theory of liability may be, however, plaintiffs are generally allowed only one recovery for a single injury. Alleging several causes of action arising from the same *transaction or occurrence* is a common way that plaintiffs try to improve their chances of success, not the amount of recovery. An exception would occur where one theory of recovery authorizes an award of special damages. Thus, a breach of contract claim for a nonfunctioning computer system would seek damages that would make the plaintiff whole, but a statutory unfair trade practices claim for the same defective system might result in the award of treble damages plus attorney's fees to punish the defendant for egregious conduct. Obviously, the latter claim would require more compelling evidence of wrongdoing than would the former.

Who's Likely to Sue Whom?

As we indicated in Chapter 1, "Year 2000 Legal and Business Risks," there are likely to be many kinds of parties to Year 2000 litigation:

- Business and consumer customers against companies that manufactured and sold them noncompliant information technology and embedded microprocessor systems

- Countersuits by IT manufacturers against customers that repaired noncompliant software in violation of copyright provisions in software license agreements
- Corporate customers against contract service agents that provide IT maintenance and support services, both for refusal to provide Y2K remediation services without additional cost and for any date-related failures that occur
- Business customers that experience Y2K problems against providers of Year 2000 repair services and software tools
- Shareholders against corporations and their directors and officers for Y2K-induced declines in stock prices
- Corporations against directors and officers responsible for the same falling stock prices
- *Intercompany liability* claims by "downstream" customers of "upstream" providers of goods and services that are disrupted because of Year 2000 supply-chain problems
- Policyholders against insurance companies and brokers that deny coverage for Y2K-related losses
- Citizens against federal and state government agencies for failing to provide entitlement checks and other legally mandated benefits and services as a result of Year 2000 disruptions

What Will the Suits Allege?

There are four main categories of possible Year 2000 litigation: (1) contract, (2) tort, (3) statutory/regulatory, and (4) fiduciary. These are not always mutually exclusive categories, as duplication and overlap exist among some of the elements that constitute the various causes of action. The four categories of suits can be differentiated by the source of the legal rights on which they rely: contract suits are based on agreements (usually written) between the parties; tort actions are generally based on judicially developed doctrines of the *common law*; statutory and regulatory suits and enforcement actions look to laws enacted by legislatures and administrative agencies; and fiduciary duties arise from special relationships of trust the law recognizes.

Table 4.1 lists the main causes of action in each of the four categories. An explanation of each entry in the table follows.

The Contract Claims

Contract-based claims are those that arise from the breach of a legally enforceable written agreement between two or more parties. After all, the purposes of business agreements are to define the respective rights and obliga-

Table 4.1 Classification of Probable Year 2000 Lawsuits

CONTRACT	TORT	STATUTORY/ REGULATORY	FIDUCIARY
Breach of contract	Negligence	Uniform Commercial Code	Corporate director and officer suits
Breach of warranty	Misrepresentation	Consumer protection laws	Shareholder derivative actions
	Fraud	Unfair business practices	
	Strict products liability	Securities law violations	
	Failure to warn after sale	State directors and officers laws	
	Professional malpractice	Copyright infringement	
	Trade secret violations	Patent infringement	
		ERISA violations	
		Criminal law violations	
		Tax code violations	
		Enforcement of industry-specific laws and regulations	

tions of the parties in a given transaction, including the terms and conditions for performance, and prescribe the remedies for nonperformance.

Contract law, like tort law, has been developed by the courts over the centuries in an evolutionary process known as the *common law*. Differing legal doctrines governing business dealings in different states and among different judges, however, can create inconsistencies and uncertainties that may undermine efficient and predictable transactions. Accordingly, the *Uniform Commercial Code* (UCC) has been adopted in virtually every state for the purpose of establishing standard rules for interpreting and enforcing contracts for the *sale of goods*.

There are likely to be two basic kinds of Year 2000 contract claims, breach of contract and breach of warranty, and both claims will often be alleged in the same complaint. Common law contract claims are often combined with UCC claims when that statute applies to the transaction. All courts interpret the UCC's definition of goods to include both computer hardware and combinations of hardware and software, and most courts consider COTS software to be goods as well. An agreement to develop custom software for one customer, such as a large corporate financial management or human resources system that does not include the sale of any hardware or equipment, is generally considered a contract exclusively for services and is therefore not covered by the UCC. Also, pure service contracts such as maintenance and support agreements generally do not fall within the UCC, but are governed instead by general contract law principles.

Breach of contract. As one would expect, breach of contract allegations assert that one party failed to fulfill one or more obligations under the agreement. Examples of probable Year 2000-related contract claims include hardware and software that fails to operate in accordance with its specifications, delays and errors in time-sensitive shipments, and inaccurate or uncompleted processing of financial transactions. This is likely to become the most common kind of Y2K suit, involving both IT-related breaches as well as intercompany suits along each link of a broken supply chain.

Breach of warranty. Under both the common law of contract and the UCC, statements by sellers of goods that become part of the basis of the bargain with the buyer—whether or not they are spelled out in a contract—assume special legal significance that courts can enforce. Statements that create *express warranties* can take the form of affirmations of fact, a description of the goods, or even samples or models. Even marketing materials or sales pitches can create warranties. The UCC also recognizes *implied warranties* that the product is suitable for its ordinary purpose (called the *implied warranty of merchantibility*) or, in cases where the seller knows that the buyer has a specific need for a product and that the buyer is relying on the seller's expertise to provide a product to fulfill that purpose, that the product is fit for that purpose (called the *implied warranty of fitness for a particular purpose*). In the Year 2000 context, design specifications or discussions between the parties about the purposes or life expectancy of IT hardware or software could give rise to both express and implied warranties. It is important to note, however, that the UCC also allows sellers to *disclaim* all implied warranties, which is almost universally done in both consumer and commercial contracts.

Because it may be too late for companies to wait until 2000 to find out whether their critical trading partners and customers will successfully traverse the millennium boundary, they should consider exercising their *right to adequate assurance of performance* under UCC section 2-609:

> A contract for sale imposes an obligation on each party that the other's expectation of receiving due performance will not be impaired. When reasonable grounds for insecurity arise with respect to the performance of either party the other may in writing demand adequate assurance of due performance and until he receives such assurance may if commercially reasonable suspend any performance for which he has not already received the agreed return.

In addition, UCC section 2-610 allows a party to sue another party for breach of contract "when either party repudiates the contract with respect to performance not yet due the loss of which will substantially impair the value of the contract to the other. . . ." Thus, there might be suits in 1999 claiming *anticipatory repudiation* by companies that refuse to provide compliant products and services that may be required by contract.

Tort Suits

A tort is an injury to one's person or property. Although most tort cases concern hazards like car accidents and medical mishaps, there has been a tremendous growth of business torts in recent years. These alternative theories of liability are attractive because they do not require an agreement between the parties and different types of damages might be recoverable. Many contracts attempt to disclaim tort suits and damages, but courts sometimes allow tort claims—such as fraud or strict products liability—even when contract causes of action have been foreclosed by the strict terms of the written agreement.

Negligence. Liability for negligence requires proof of four elements: (1) a duty to use due care to protect someone else, (2) a failure to conform to the standard of due care, and (3) damages that are (4) directly caused by the failure to exercise due care. The due care standard is measured by reference to what a "reasonable person" would do under similar circumstances. Negligence can arise in connection with the design, manufacture, testing, operation, and warnings of products and equipment. For example, a medical device manufacturer could be held liable for negligence if it failed to design a patient-monitoring system that was Year 2000 compliant, or if it failed to provide appropriate warnings of that fact, and a person was injured when the device malfunctioned.

Strict products liability. Strict liability is limited to certain areas that the law deems important enough that "fault" (that is, negligence) is not an element of the cause of action. It is generally limited to ultrahazardous activities and products liability. Claims for strict products liability are based on the defective condition of a product that physically injures a user or damages property when used in a foreseeable manner. As between the two distinct theories of products liability (design defect and production defect), Y2K-related products liability claims will more likely allege a design defect, that is, that the defective design of the product caused the injury. Thus, the manufacturer of a metal press might be held strictly liable for personal injury or property damage if its safety systems failed because it contained noncompliant embedded microprocessors.

Misrepresentation and fraud. False or misleading statements made for the purpose of inducing someone to buy a product or service could create liability for misrepresentation or fraud. Generally fraud requires the plaintiff to prove that the defendant intended to deceive the plaintiff and that the plaintiff detrimentally relied on the representation. Misrepresentation typically requires knowledge of the falsity of the representation, but not necessarily the intent to deceive. Some jurisdictions allow the tort of negligent misrepresentation, which requires only that the defendant should have known that the representation was false or misleading and that the plaintiff detrimentally relied on that statement. Allegations that IT vendors and consultants made false or misleading statements about Year 2000 compliance—rather than "mere puffing" or sales talk—upon which buyers reasonably relied to their detriment have already been common in Y2K suits filed to date, and they will become increasingly common as failures become more widespread. Misrepresentation and fraud are important theories to potential plaintiffs that otherwise would be limited to contract claims because they (1) carry different statutes of limitations, (2) allow for noneconomic damages, and (3) are more likely to be covered by corporate insurance policies (breach of contract is typically not insurable). Certain contract provisions, called merger or integration clauses, limit the contract to the document itself and therefore prevent the introduction of extraneous evidence such as sales representations. These are the most likely causes of action affected by the *Year 2000 Information and Readiness Disclosure Act* as it prevents the use of qualified "readiness disclosures" as the basis of litigation.

Failure to warn after sale. Many jurisdictions have held that sellers must warn buyers if they learn after the sale that a product is defective. This explains the widespread practice of product "recalls" that are common in the automotive and consumer electronics industries. IT sellers, VARs, and distributors that discover compliancy problems should consider carefully whether they have a duty to warn their customers of such defects, perhaps by posting information on their Web sites.

Professional liability. More commonly known as *malpractice*, the tort of professional negligence has long been recognized for such licensed practitioners as doctors, lawyers, and accountants. Very few courts have been willing to accept the notion of *computer malpractice*, although many such claims have been made in the past and they will likely increase with the advent of Y2K failures. Malpractice claims assert that the professional has a higher duty of care than ordinary persons because the comparatively unskilled client or customer relies on the professional's specialized expertise. Lawyers who fail to advise their clients to include Year 2000 clauses in contracts and accountants who fail to warn management or investors about Y2K vulnerabilities that could affect corporate financial statements may be exposed to malpractice claims.

Trade secret violations. State common law, and sometimes state statutes, protect trade secrets from unauthorized disclosure. A trade secret is "any formula, pattern, device or compilation of information which is used in one's business, and which gives him an opportunity to obtain an advantage over competitors who do not know or use it." [*Restatement of Torts* §757, *comment b* (1939).] A company or its consultant that repairs computer code in violation of the terms of its software license could be sued (or countersued) for violating trade secrets if the developer has not given permission to do so, which permission might be given only in exchange for a waiver of all Y2K liability.

Statutory and Regulatory Claims

There are far too many possible statutory and regulatory requirements that might form the basis for civil suits to provide a comprehensive list. We have already described the Uniform Commercial Code as an adjunct to common law contract claims. A brief overview should help counsel and their clients understand the kinds of issues to consider.

Consumer protection laws. Y2K suits alleging violations of state consumer protection laws will undoubtedly be an important weapon against sellers of noncompliant software products designed for home and small business use. These laws provide remedies for bad faith and deceptive and highly unreasonable conduct. The force of these statutes lies in the fact that they almost always authorize the award of treble damages and attorney's fees; this is why they are so often used in consumer class-action suits by enterprising plaintiffs' lawyers. Most of the Y2K suits filed to date complaining that software companies have failed to provide free upgrades include consumer protection counts.

Unfair business practices statutes. Many states have statutes similar to their consumer protection laws that protect businesses from unfair and deceptive trade practices. Although the standards of liability are generally higher than for consumer laws because business managers are assumed to be more sophisticated customers than ordinary purchasers of household goods, unfair trade statutes are still potent causes of action because they, too, authorize recovery of treble damages and legal fees.

Securities law violations. Federal and state securities laws generally allow investors to bring private civil suits against corporations and their directors and officers who provide inadequate or false and misleading information that a reasonable investor would consider *material* to making investment decisions. Year 2000 problems represent an obvious candidate for such litigation, particularly in light of the SEC's increasingly demanding requirements that publicly traded companies disclose meaningful information about their Y2K expenditures and risks.

State directors and officers liability laws. As we shall explain shortly, the fiduciary duties of directors and officers have been developed by state courts over many decades in ways that could expose them to personal liability in the event of serious Year 2000 failures. Some states, however, have codified those duties in their corporation laws, the violation of which can form an independent ground for liability. For example, many jurisdictions follow the Model Business Corporation Act, which includes the following provision in section 8.30:

A director shall discharge his duties as a director, including his duties as a member of a committee;

(1) In good faith;
(2) with the care an ordinary prudent person in a like position would exercise under similar circumstances; and
(3) in a manner he reasonably believes to be in the best interests of the corporation.

Copyright and patent infringement. Information technology is protected by federal copyright law, and the hardware and software licenses that entitle users to use that technology generally restrict the rights to copy and modify that technology. Although the federal statute contains certain exceptions that may apply to a limited extent to Year 2000 renovations, end users may be liable for copyright infringement if they modify software code, or allow Y2K solutions providers to do so, without the owners' permission. This issue is most likely to come up as a counterclaim by IT defendants in cases where their customers have sued them for providing noncompliant software under any of the causes of action discussed previously. Similar considerations apply in the more unusual case where the hardware or software is also covered by patents.

ERISA violations. The Employee Retirement Income Security Act is the federal statute that governs pensions and 401(k), health, and other employee benefit plans. Persons who administer those plans serve as trustees who owe fiduciary duties to their members to protect the trust funds and apply them in strict accordance with the plan agreements. U.S. Department of Labor guidelines have advised pension fund administrators that they must take appropriate steps to protect their beneficiaries' investments from Y2K problems. Although ERISA does not authorize the award of monetary damages, courts can issue sanctions for breaches of fiduciary duties.

Tax code violations. The IRS has issued Revenue Procedure 97-50, which requires companies to expense most expenditures for Year 2000 work. These guidelines could directly affect your bottom line and expose you to IRS penalties.

Criminal law violations. Criminal prosecutions arising from Year 2000 problems are likely to be extremely rare, but they cannot be ruled out entirely. For example, the False Claims Act and Medicare fraud and abuse regulations have been enforced aggressively to prosecute hospital administrators for failure to document the medical necessity of certain treatments paid for with federal funds. Y2K disruptions of hospital record-keeping systems could expose directors and officers to similar charges. One Delaware judge observed in a 1996 decision that there is "an increasing tendency, especially under federal law, to employ the criminal law to assure corporate compliance with external legal requirements, including environmental, financial, employee and product safety, as well as assorted other health and safety regulations." [*In re Caremark International Inc. Derivative Litigation* (Del. Ct. of Chancery 1996).] Other federal criminal laws that could be applied to Year 2000 failures include export control laws (for sending encryption software to offshore remediation facilities), the Clean Water Act (for unauthorized discharge of improperly treated effluent from malfunctioning wastewater treatment plants), federal securities laws (for failing to disclose material information to regulators and investors), and federal financial laws (for failing to properly manage funds and report certain funds transactions).

Enforcement of industry-specific laws and regulations. Finally, government agencies in numerous industries and economic sectors have adopted statutes, regulations, and other guidelines and directives that could create Y2K liabilities. These are discussed in the last section of this chapter.

Fiduciary Suits

Courts and legislatures have long recognized that certain relationships of trust give rise to special legal responsibilities to protect the interests of others. For present purposes, chief among these fiduciary duties is the legal obligations of corporate directors and officers to place the interests of the company and its stockholders before their own personal financial interests. Because fiduciaries exercise those duties in their *personal* capacity as trustees, and not in their *corporate* capacity as a representative of the organization, directors and officers who breach their fiduciary duties can and often do face lawsuits against them personally, which means their own private financial assets and possessions may be at risk.

Corporate suits against directors and officers. Corporations can file suit against directors and officers who fail to protect corporate assets, engage in conflicts of interest, or otherwise fail to fulfill their fiduciary duties to the enterprise. For example, a senior vice president assigned to manage a company's Year 2000 program could be sued by the corporation if he or she neglects the project and the company's operations and stock values suffer.

Shareholder derivative actions. Recognizing that corporations are often reluctant to enforce their rights against fellow officers and senior managers who may have engaged in errant conduct, investors can bring suits on behalf of the corporation, called *derivative actions*. The allegations are essentially the same as the corporation suits, except that the shareholders must prove that the corporation failed to take appropriate action to protect their interests. Recent pronouncements by the SEC concerning the obligations of corporations to disclose information about their Year 2000 preparations will likely serve as the basis for shareholder class action suits if Y2K disrupts operations and financial performance and stock prices suffer as a result. Law firms that specialize in filing suits alleging corporation mismanagement in other contexts are likely to be well prepared to handle cases relating to Year 2000 failures.

Some Important Liability Defenses

Before we consider strategies for reducing Year 2000 liability exposure, we will examine briefly some of the common defenses that can be raised in response to the anticipated lawsuits just discussed. In the *answer* to the complaint, the defendant admits or denies the factual allegations made by the plaintiff and presents its *affirmative defenses* (such as failure to file the suit within the time required by the applicable statute of limitations) and *counterclaims* (such as copyright infringement). Standard defenses include the following.

Warranty disclaimers and limitations of liability. Most commercial contracts, and virtually all IT contracts, exclude all warranties except those that are expressly provided in the agreement, which are usually limited to repair or replacement of the malfunctioning products. Such exclusions also block implied warranties of merchantability and fitness for a particular purpose. In response, buyers are likely to argue that the courts should refuse enforcement of these provisions on the ground that there has been a *failure of the essential purpose* of the warranty because vendors can't repair or replace noncompliant systems in time to do the customer any good.

Exclusions and limitations of remedies. Even companies that stand behind their products are reluctant to assume unlimited liability for any business losses that product failures might cause. Contracts typically provide that monetary damages are limited to the amount paid for the software, hardware, and services provided and exclude recovery of lost profits, special costs incurred to cope with operational disruptions, injury to business goodwill, and other *consequential damages*.

Impossibility (or impracticability) of performance. Some companies will take the position that catastrophic Year 2000 problems, such as supply-chain breakdowns or failed financial transactions, made it impossible for them to perform their contractual and warranty obligations.

Force majeure. A similar defense will be that events beyond the seller's control caused the Year 2000 problem that damaged the buyer. Note that most such clauses are not limited to "Acts of God," like floods and earthquakes, but include any unforeseeable event that the seller could not reasonably avoid. Even though Y2K events are foreseeable and preventable to some extent, the devil is in the details, and defendants may argue that the particular harm that the buyer suffered could not have been reasonably anticipated or avoided, notwithstanding the efforts the seller made to do so.

Statute of limitations. Under the UCC, lawsuits must be filed within four years after the cause of action "accrued," but the parties can agree in their contract to shorten the period for commencing litigation to as little as one year. In some cases, it can be difficult to determine when the clock starts ticking. For some Y2K defects, the right to sue may have begun when the contract was signed or the technology was installed, so the statute of limitations could expire even before the customer became aware of the problem. The right to sue could also be lost if a company learns it has noncompliant systems but waits to go to court until it has a problem serious enough to justify the expense of litigation.

Economic loss doctrine. Some causes of action and some insurance policies deny recovery for purely economic losses, absent some physical injury or damages. So, if a Y2K failure causes a company to lose sales without any property damage, it might not be able to recover.

Contributory and comparative negligence. These are defenses to tort suits that provide that plaintiffs who fail to exercise due care themselves to prevent their injuries should be denied recovery in part or in whole. It is unclear whether courts will be willing to allow these defenses in Y2K cases, but they will likely be asserted by IT vendors, systems integrators, and contract service providers that claim that their sophisticated business customers had advanced knowledge of the problem and share responsibility for addressing it.

Failure to mitigate damages. Even if companies are liable to their customers for remediation expenses and other business losses resulting from noncompliant technology, defendants will try to reduce their damages by showing that their customers failed to take appropriate measures—such as developing business continuity and contingency plans—to reduce those losses.

Directors and Officers Liability Exposure

Directors and officers have the responsibility to make many quick and vital decisions regarding Year 2000 based on voluminous information in a very short time frame. Corporate directors and officers face personal liability if they fail to carry out their fiduciary responsibilities in connection with Year 2000. The steps required to insulate corporate decision makers from litigation are consistent with diligent management practices. Directors and officers who actively lead their companies in a coordinated and systematic effort to prevent Y2K failures and aggressively manage their internal and external Year 2000 risks can effectively mitigate their personal legal exposures.

Fiduciary Duties

Board members and officers have several basic fiduciary duties, but only the duty of due care is an important consideration for avoiding Year 2000 liability. Corporate leaders are required to exercise reasonable diligence in carrying out their management responsibilities. This generally means they must act in a timely way with adequate information, and they must make business judgments that they believe in good faith are reasonable under the circumstances and in the best interests of the corporation. Directors and officers that assume the same managerial responsibilities for addressing Y2K as they do for other major corporate problems—obtaining periodic briefings about the nature of the problem the company faces, assigning qualified personnel to address those problems, allocating resources they believe are appropriate, and so on—are likely to satisfy the due-care requirement. Directors and officers that fail to supervise their organization's response to the Year 2000 crisis, however, are far more likely to become involved in lawsuits for their own inaction in the face of ample warnings about Y2K dangers.

Directors and Officers Legal Protections

Well-established legal doctrines and risk management mechanisms protect directors and officers from Year 2000 liability. As long as senior corporate officers don't ignore the problem altogether, they are likely to weather the storm, even if the company is buffeted by rough seas for which adequate preparations have not been made. In that event, the company may face litigation by its customers and trading partners, but those running the enterprise will be less likely to have to worry about their own legal exposures.

The Business Judgment Defense

The *business judgment rule* creates "a presumption that in making a business decision the directors of a corporation acted on an informed basis, in good faith and in the honest belief that the action taken was in the best interests of the corporation" [*Aronson v. Lewis*, 473 A.2d 805, 812 (Del. 1984)]. This is a powerful presumption, so much so that courts will not second-guess the decisions corporate officers and directors make absent a compelling showing that they acted in bad faith, without adequate information, or for their private financial interests. It is generally not sufficient for stockholders to argue that the board made a mistake or a poor decision. Instead, they must prove that the directors were grossly negligent in that they were "recklessly uninformed" or acted "outside the bounds of reason" [*Cincinnati Bell Cellular Systems Co. v. Ameritech Mobile Phone Services, Inc.*, 1996 Del. Ch. LEXIS 116, at *42-43 (Sept. 3, 1996)]. In other words, only if corporate leaders acted in a way that no conscientious board would act in the circumstances, will courts find that the business judgment defense has been overcome.

A complete failure to act, however, could expose corporate officers to liability. In that case, the officers must contend that they looked into Y2K and made a conscious decision in good faith to do nothing, and they honestly believed that the decision was in the best interests of the corporation. That will be a difficult position to maintain given the publicity of the business and legal risks that Year 2000 has engendered for the past year or two. Even more untenable would be the argument that the corporation decided not to even look into the problem. The "ostrich approach" needlessly invites judicial scrutiny and second-guessing that can be easily avoided.

We recognize that Year 2000 has been a hard sell for many CIOs and that general counsels often don't understand the problem well enough to feel comfortable advising directors and officers that the magnitude of the risk merits a substantial expenditure of funds just to keep the company's computers functioning as they do today. Y2K external risks often face considerable skepticism, with CEOs and CFOs understandably wondering how they can possibly control the actions of their suppliers and customers. From a liability perspective, however, it is quite difficult to mount a compelling case for the proposition that Y2K is not serious enough to justify active supervision by the board of directors. As but one example, consider this concise statement of the problem issued on October 1, 1997, by 11 international financial and technical organizations, including the American Institute of Certified Public Accountants, the International Federation of Accountants, the Institute of Internal Auditors, and the Information Technology Association of America:

> Mission-critical computer systems worldwide will perform inaccurate calculations or potentially crash if they have not been properly reviewed and updated to account for dates in the year 2000 and beyond. As a result, many organizations may suffer a financial loss, damage their reputation and credibility, and breach relations with customers, employees, investors, trading partners, regulators and other stakeholders.
>
> This is an action item for small, medium and large organizations as well as anyone using a personal computer. All senior managers, CIOs, software vendors, process owners, boards of directors, audit committees and world leaders in government bodies need to obtain assurance that the Y2K issue has been addressed internally and with external business and trading partners (American Institute of Certified Public Accountants, 1997).

Whether you or your directors ever became aware of this particular press release, similar statements were published in hundreds of articles and broadcast in scores of media stories in 1997 and 1998. Regardless of the source or the particular wording, the widespread availability of such information will make it difficult to argue in 1999 and 2000 that Y2K was not a problem that deserved senior management attention.

Moreover, directors and officers cannot fulfill their fiduciary duty of due care by holding one meeting to discuss Year 2000, delegating all responsibility to the CIO or other corporate manager, and never revisiting the issue again. Once a serious problem like Y2K has been identified, due care requires the board and senior management to exercise such oversight as they deem appropriate for problems of similar magnitude and gravity. The board needs to develop monitoring and reporting systems that will enable them to exercise sound judgment along the way. As the court observed in the seminal *Caremark* decision, "it is important that the board exercise a good faith judgment that the corporation's information and reporting system is in concept and design adequate to assure the board that appropriate information will come to its attention in a timely manner as a matter of ordinary operations" [*In re Caremark International Inc. Derivative Litigation*, 698 A.2d 959, 970 (Del. Ch. 1996)]. Thus, the fiduciary duty of care imposes a continuing responsibility to supervise company personnel to assess the organization's progress in achieving the compliance objectives articulated by the board and to order corrective measures as it deems appropriate.

Directors and Officers Liability Insurance

Even if directors and officers qualify for the business judgment defense, it is likely they will be named in lawsuits if their companies suffer serious Year 2000 problems. The first line of defense against such claims is directors and officers liability insurance, which (as discussed further in Chapter 9, "Insurance Issues") protects policyholders by "pay[ing] the Loss of each and every Director or Officer of the Company arising from a Claim first made against the Directors or Officers during the Policy Period . . . for any actual or alleged Wrongful Act in their respective capacities as Directors or Officers of the Company except when and to the extent that the Company has indemnified the Directors or Officers." The coverage is generally comprehensive, in that "'Wrongful Act' is often defined as any breach of duty, neglect, error, misstatement, misleading statement, omission or act by the directors or officers" (Paar, 1998). Unless insurers add Year 2000 exclusions or limitations to their policies at the time of renewal, the prospects appear good that director and officer policies will provide coverage for Y2K claims.

Corporate Indemnification Policies

Most states have statutes that authorize corporations to enact by-laws to indemnify their directors and officers for liabilities they incur in good faith during their tenure with the corporation. The following language is typical:

The Company may indemnify any present or past director, officer, employee or other agent against liability, costs and expenses, including legal fees, in connection with any actual or threatened proceeding, including any settlement thereof approved by vote of the Board of Directors at a meeting in which no Director participates against whom any suit or proceeding on the same or similar grounds is then pending or threatened, arising by reason of any act or omission within the scope of his duties or employment for the Company; provided, however, that no indemnification shall be provided to a person concerning a matter as to which such person is finally adjudicated to have acted either without the belief held in good faith that his conduct was in the best interests of the Company or with reason to understand that his conduct was unlawful.

Costs and expenses may be paid prior to a final disposition upon receipt of an undertaking, which the Company may accept without regard to the financial resources of the person indemnified, that the person receiving the benefit of payments will repay such payments if he shall be finally adjudicated not to be entitled to indemnification hereunder. The Company may purchase insurance on behalf of itself and any of its directors, officers, employees or agents against any liability arising out of his status as such, whether or not the Company would have the power to indemnify him against such liability.

The purpose of indemnification is to encourage directors and officers to exercise their best business judgment without concern about the possible personal legal consequences of their actions. It is an important way of assuring directors and officers that the company will stand behind them if a director or officer makes a decision in good faith that turns out to be a mistake or the subject of litigation. Counsel should ensure that the corporation's indemnification policies are effective for protecting directors and officers from Year 2000 risk.

Checklist for Directors and Officers Legal Risk Management

Directors and officers liability is one of the Year 2000 business risks that can be effectively managed by insuring that corporate leaders exercise the same level of supervision and control that they bring to other major corporate challenges. Documenting the actions of the board, including minutes, presentations, committee reports, and votes showing that directors and officers actively and continuously monitored the company's compliance efforts, is essential. Corporate counsel (whether in-house or outside) should establish and monitor a risk management program along the following lines.

Sponsorship and Oversight

- ❏ Executive briefings
- ❏ Y2K compliance, resolution, and program charter
- ❏ Steering committee

- ❑ Y2K program objectives
- ❑ Monitoring and reporting system
- ❑ Approve business risk assessment
- ❑ Approve program plan
- ❑ Approve contingency plans
- ❑ Assess nonessential projects
- ❑ Schedule update briefings
- ❑ Executive sign-off procedures
- ❑ Executive performance measures
- ❑ Internal audit support
- ❑ Independent compliance audit

Y2K Program Office
- ❑ Develop reporting structure
- ❑ Plan and schedule project
- ❑ Monthly work plans
- ❑ Assign departmental responsibilities
- ❑ Monitor planned versus actual progress
- ❑ Internal audit support

Corporate-Wide Team
- ❑ Managerial representatives
- ❑ Technical representatives
- ❑ End users
- ❑ Vendor/customer contacts

Budget and Finance
- ❑ Develop and control budget
- ❑ Accounting and tax compliance
- ❑ Identify "material" expenses
- ❑ External auditors

Human Resources
- ❑ Employee retention incentives
- ❑ Key employee contracts
- ❑ Indemnify key employees
- ❑ Staffing requirements

- Staffing policies
- Retain outside technical, accounting, project management, and legal experts and consultants
- Review employee manuals

Protection of Directors and Officers

- Business judgment defense
- Director and officer liability insurance
- Corporate indemnification policies

Protecting Technical Professionals

Although directors and officers can insulate themselves from personal Year 2000 liability, the situation is somewhat less clear for technology professionals. In the ongoing discussions about employee retention incentives for Year 2000 managers and technical professionals, one potentially important benefit appears to have been overlooked: protection against attorney's fees and litigation damage awards. If you are involved in a Y2K lawsuit a couple of years from now, you certainly do not want to be spending those hard-earned bonus dollars paying a lawyer to represent you, much less the substantially larger sums the plaintiff will be seeking in compensation for its business losses.

Errors and Omissions Insurance

As with directors and officers, the first line of defense for IT workers is professional malpractice insurance, more commonly known as errors and omissions or "E&O" insurance. Those policies, which virtually all but the smallest companies carry, require the insurer to "pay on behalf of the insured those sums which the insured becomes legally obligated to pay as damages because of a negligent act, error or omission in the performance of the insured's professional services" (Paar, 1998). E&O coverage is explained more fully in Chapter 9, "Insurance Issues."

Y2K Risks for IT Workers

The likelihood that company employees at the CIO level or below will actually be sued is fairly small precisely because, in crass legal slang, their pockets are just not deep enough. But even if middle managers and employees do not usually make very attractive defendants, they are often considered extremely important witnesses. When your company is sued and the company's lawyer informs you that the plaintiff wants to take your deposition (under oath, of course), you may feel as if you are faced with two unattractive alternatives: being blamed for your company's catastrophic Year 2000 failures that supposedly cost the plaintiff millions of dollars or pointing the finger at the good folks funding your 401(k) plan. The plaintiff hopes you will criticize the company for not listening to you in the years leading up to 2000. Not surprisingly, your employer will take a rather different view.

When you sit down in the opposing attorney's conference room for your deposition, to tell the truth, the whole truth and nothing but the truth, the other side will try to exploit those inherent tensions to prove that your employer acted irresponsibly. You need to understand that you have no moral, ethical, or legal obligation to sink your company just to prove you are not incompetent. In fact, you do not have to prove anything. But if you feel uncomfortable and unprepared, you might see the situation as a zero-sum game in which either you or your company must take the fall. Except in the rarest of cases, that just is not so.

What you need is a good lawyer to help guide you safely through unfriendly terrain. Your company will have a good lawyer, probably several from the same firm. Can they represent you?

Cooperating with Employers

In many, perhaps most, business cases, the company's lawyer can and should represent you and your employer. Generally, you and your employer have common interests in defending against the suit, the company's counsel may already be familiar with its business and Year 2000 program, and, by sharing the same lawyer, protecting all discussions about the case under the attorney-client privilege will be much easier.

But a Year 2000 failure serious enough to lead to litigation can sometimes be one of those situations where your interests and the interests of the company for which you have worked so hard might not be in precise alignment. Maybe you made recommendations—in writing, no less—that should have been followed but were not. Maybe you did not get all the resources you needed to do the job effectively. Perhaps too much turnover or inadequate planning or nonessential projects that were not postponed hindered your work. Those things happen in the best of companies. By itself, an honest difference of opinion among professionals does not mean your company is legally responsible for the damages another company claims it suffered as a result of problems you tried to avoid. It also does not mean that your professional reputation has to suffer to protect your job.

Indemnification

What you and your company both need is to find a way of reconciling your interests to present the best possible defense. One common way of doing that is having the company hire a separate lawyer for you. It is called indemnification: The company agrees to pay your legal bills and any monetary judgment that might be entered against you. Your lawyer's professional and ethical obligations, though, are to represent you, not the company. Of course, the corporation benefits as well by encouraging its directors, officers, and key employees to make difficult and sometimes risky decisions based on their best professional judgment, free from fear of adverse personal consequences if something goes wrong.

An important benefit of indemnification is that it enables you to get the personal legal advice you need and cooperate with your employer at the same time. You can tell your lawyer everything he or she needs to know to protect your interests, and your conversations will be protected by the attorney-client privilege. Maybe your company did not have the best Year 2000 program. Perhaps you could have done your job better in some respects, too. Your lawyer can prepare you to testify about such delicate subjects. Moreover, the atmosphere at work can become tense and awkward in the middle of litigation. When you and your company each have counsel, you can concentrate on your job and the lawyers can talk to each other (sometimes pursuant to a *joint defense agreement*) for the mutual benefit of both clients.

It's important to find a lawyer who understands that it is generally not in your best interest to be antagonistic toward your company during litigation. Except in a true whistle-blower situation, you and your employer are in the same boat. Row together and you'll both be less likely to sink. If serious differences about legal strategy or your job performance emerge, your attorney can probably negotiate more effectively with your employer than you can.

Common Law Indemnification

Note that an employer is free to indemnify its employees to the extent authorized by state law, and such laws are unlikely to prevent employers from hiring lawyers to represent employees when it is advisable for them to have separate counsel. Companies have a strong incentive to let their employees know that if they get into legal difficulty just for doing their jobs, the company will stand behind them.

Most companies also understand that it is not a good idea to have the same attorney represent the employer and the employee when their interests diverge, as they might in some Year 2000 lawsuits. There have been circumstances, however, in which employees have been made scapegoats and forced to incur substantial expense to hire their own attorney. To avoid such an uncomfortable situation, a written agreement to provide indemnification might serve both parties' interests.

Contractual Indemnification

As explained earlier in connection with directors and officers, most states have statutes that authorize corporations to provide indemnification within certain general parameters, and each company then adopts its own by-law that sets out the specific terms under which it will afford indemnification. A state law might allow companies to indemnify "employees," but your corporation's by-law might be limited to "directors and officers." CIOs take note: Just because your job title has the word "officer" in it doesn't necessarily qualify you for indemnification.

Most indemnification by-laws are limited to actions taken in good faith in the best interests of the corporation. You may have to agree in writing to pay the money back if a court decides later that you acted in bad faith, but that should not keep you from accepting indemnification. The by-law can be phrased in mandatory or discretionary language, or both, depending on the nature of the litigation (for example, civil versus criminal). The company might reserve the prerogative either to pay your legal bills in advance or to reimburse you later.

If you think this is just a clever scheme to multiply the number of lawyers hired to defend against Year 2000 suits, think again. Just as good doctors encourage their patients to get second opinions to give them peace of mind, good employers indemnify key employees so they can sleep at night without worrying about paying legal bills or damaging their careers if they make an honest mistake.

You and your company should think about this issue now to avoid any implication later on that it's buying your favorable testimony after a lawsuit has been filed. But don't overreact, either: Separate counsel is not always necessary or appropriate, especially if you are not likely to be a key witness. Also, indemnity deepens your pockets and potentially increases the chances that you'll be sued along with the company. In most cases, though, the protection of your professional reputation and the avoidance of legal expenses make indemnification worthwhile for CIOs and Year 2000 program and project managers who will find themselves in the thick of things when the lawsuits start to fly.

Conducting Y2K Legal Audits

The fact that Y2K problems are, to a substantial extent, foreseeable and preventable means that companies will have special legal duties to protect their customers, investors, employees, and other stakeholders from damage caused by Year 2000 failures. At the same time, our understanding of the problem does enable us to anticipate and mitigate the injury by exercising due diligence. A Y2K legal audit is an inventory and assessment of the liability risks your organization faces as we approach 2000.

Audit Objectives

Year 2000 legal audits have three overarching objectives. The first is to determine whether any third parties may be responsible for bearing some or all of the costs of IT remediation and related compliance costs. The second is to assess what legal rights and obligations your company may have to others so you can plan an appropriate course of action that will reduce your liability exposures. Third is to determine whether any existing contract partners may be responsible for damages your company suffers that are caused by a Y2K failure that they experience. Once you know where you stand from a legal perspective, then you can target your due-diligence efforts to the risks you've identified.

Responsibility for Compliance Work and Recovery of Compliance Costs

Third parties such as software and hardware vendors, systems developers and integrators, support and maintenance contractors, and providers of non-IT goods and services all may have contractual or warranty obligations to either help you become compliant or assume some of your compliance costs. Even when written agreements are silent on Y2K, the terms of the contract may be broad enough to shift the responsibility for achieving compliance. For example, a software vendor that has given an extended warranty that its product will perform in accordance with its specifications could be required to provide an upgrade that will achieve that result over the term of the warranty. Whether the vendor will honor its commitments is a question that can be answered only after you have identified that an obligation exists. IT vendors may have their own E&O policies that could apply to your claims.

Even suppliers of ordinary goods and services that are vital to your business may have enforceable obligations to alert you in advance if they will be unable to comply with their contractual responsibilities and compensate you for the costs of finding replacement suppliers and any increased costs (such as price differentials) you may incur. Again, legal obligations are just one of the factors that should inform your planning, but they should be considered as part of your risk management strategy.

We are not urging companies to find ways to sue each other. The objective of Y2K risk management is to help organizations maintain productive and profitable operations at a time of great uncertainty and risk. Understanding your legal rights does not mean that you will pursue them in court. But companies enter business agreements with the expectation that they can rely on the commitments that others have made, and they may have passed up opportunities with other companies that would have put them in a less vulnerable position. Once you understand your legal strengths and weaknesses, you can make whatever judgments you think are appropriate, taking all relevant factors into consideration. You might decide, for example, to forgo litigation that might be destructive to both parties and instead negotiate alternative arrangements that promote the survival of both businesses.

In other cases, cost recovery litigation may be an entirely appropriate strategy. A company that finds it has purchased and installed an expensive but substantially defective computer system cannot lightly overlook its losses. Indeed, directors and officers who fail to seek compensation from vendors who have caused the company to suffer significant monetary damages may themselves be liable for waste of corporate assets and other fiduciary breaches. A company in that situation that buys a replacement system from another vendor or patches its existing system to provide the minimum required functionality should seriously consider revoking any prior acceptance of the system (if that option is still available) and filing suit to recover not only the monies it has already paid, but also such other damages as it may have incurred because a functioning system was not delivered as promised.

Assessing Your Legal Rights and Duties to Others

Of course, virtually every company is both upstream and downstream of other businesses, so all companies need to consider whether Year 2000 problems could expose them to similar kinds of liability. Your investigation should focus on three broad groups.

Customers
- Have you sold products or provided services that are or may be noncompliant?
- Have you exercised due diligence by testing these products?
- How extensive are your obligations to your customers?
- How long do you support your noncompliant products?
- What recourse do your customers have against you if you fail to deliver the goods or services specified in your contract or purchase order on time?
- Can you provide reasonable assurances to your customers about your progress or product compliance status without assuming unreasonable liabilities at the same time?

Vendors and Trading Partners

- Do your agreements with your trading partners impose any legal obligations on you once you become aware of potential Y2K problems that could affect your business relationship?
- What rights do vendors and trading partners have if you inform them of delays in your compliance plan?
- Have you considered taking advantage of the protections under the *Year 2000 Information and Readiness Disclosure Act*?
- What steps could you take if they notified you of default?

Investors, Lenders, Insurers, and Regulators

- Who are the companies' stakeholders? Are their rights fiduciary in nature or just contractual?
- To whom do the board and senior managers owe fiduciary duties?
- What rights do they have, and what must you do to avoid breaching them?
- What procedures must you follow to preserve insurance coverage against Y2K liabilities?
- What information are you required to provide to banks and insurers when applying for loans or insurance policy renewals?
- Are there Y2K-related regulatory requirements or guidelines with which you must comply?
- Are you subject to loan covenants or other borrowing requirements that require you to disclose your compliance status to banks or investors?
- Has your board of directors complied with the requirements of insurance policies and its corporate charter and by-laws so that its directors, officers, and key employees are protected from litigation?

Conducting the Audit

A legal audit can be a substantial undertaking. You will need to collect every important document affecting your legal rights and conduct a thorough assessment of risk exposures.

Inventory Key Legal Documents

Some of the documents that should be reviewed as part of a comprehensive legal audit include the following:

- Hardware and software licenses
- Contracts, leases, requests for proposals, specifications, and purchase orders

- Contract amendments and change orders
- IT support and maintenance agreements
- Product manuals and documentation
- Agreements with consultants, distributors, value added resellers, database developers, systems integrators, and outsourced service providers
- Y2K remediation contracts
- Contracts and leases for non-IT goods and services
- Insurance policies and coverage and renewal applications
- Indemnification and hold harmless agreements
- Promotional literature, Web sites, and marketing materials that might create implied warranties
- Corporate charters, articles of organization, by-laws, and board of directors' votes
- Agreements for mergers, acquisitions, affiliations, purchase and sale of assets, and other major corporate transactions
- Loan applications, agreements and documentation
- Documents filed with regulatory agencies
- Any Year 2000 disclosures issued to date, including responses to inquiries

Evaluate Your Legal Rights and Duties

Once the relevant documentation is compiled, a systematic analysis should be undertaken by focusing on the following subject matters:

Scope of the obligations. What goods or services are to be provided? Is Y2K remediation beyond the scope of performance that the parties contemplated? What are the terms and conditions relating to date and manner of delivery, performance specifications, and quantities? Is date compliance expressed or implied? What representations have the buyer and seller made to each other that could relate to the resolution of Year 2000 problems? During what period of time are the obligations in effect?

Warranties. What warranties, express and implied, have been made? Are there specific Year 2000 warranty provisions? Are warranty disclaimers legally effective? Is it possible to assert anticipatory breach? Are there multiple or overlapping warranties provided by manufacturers, vendors, contract service providers, and others that have been involved in delivering the system? Are there gaps in the warranty coverage for some kinds of Y2K failures?

Remedies. What contractual remedies are provided, and which ones are excluded? Are the remedies sufficient to protect the buyer in the event of Year 2000 problems? Under what circumstances might a court find the remedy limitations and exclusions *unconscionable* so that they could be voided? What notification and other procedural requirements must be followed to invoke the remedies? Is there a dispute resolution clause that requires negotiation or other alternative dispute resolution (ADR) efforts before a suit can be filed? Does the contract require binding arbitration and foreclose litigation except for suits to enforce the arbitration award?

Force majeure. Is *force majeure* defined in a way that would include or exclude Y2K failures? What efforts must the seller make to comply with the contract in order to invoke the clause?

Statute of limitations. Does the contract specify a particular time within which legal actions to enforce the agreement must be commenced? Is the starting point specified?

Notification. Who must be provided with any notice of default, demand, recision, claim, or suit? Are those parties still in existence and located at the address specified in the contract? What timing and method of notice are prescribed?

Confidentiality. What information about the contract and the seller's products and performance can the buyer provide to others in order to renovate noncompliant systems? Is the buyer prevented from disclosing breaches, claims, or lawsuits to others? Would the seller expose itself to countersuit for breach of contract if it hired a third party to repair the seller's technology?

Intellectual property rights. What does the contract say about product ownership, license rights, copyright, access to source code, reverse engineering, use of outside consultants, and copying programs to rewrite the code?

Termination. Under what circumstances can either party terminate the contract? What procedures are required for an effective termination? What rights survive termination?

Insurance and indemnification. Has either party agreed to indemnify or obtain insurance for the other? What is the scope of any indemnification, hold harmless, or insurance obligation? Is the required insurance coverage sufficient protection against anticipated Year 2000 losses? Will the carrier dispute insurance coverage? Does the company have certificates of insurance, declarations pages, or other evidence of coverage? What obligation does the buyer have to mitigate Y2K damages?

Prepare a Legal Audit Report

Once the legal audit has been conducted, a report should be submitted to the board of directors or general counsel. Due to the inherently sensitive nature of this document, it should be prepared and submitted in a manner that qualifies it for protection under the attorney-client privilege and work-product doctrine.

Preserve Legal Privileges

When lawyers conduct an investigation of a business client's potential legal exposure in other contexts, they attempt to preserve the confidentiality of their inquiries and their analysis and recommendations. The attorney-client privilege and the attorney work-product doctrine may shield certain documents prepared by or for a lawyer. It can be more difficult to protect confidentiality when the attorneys are providing prophylactic advice to corporate clients about future legal and nonlegal (business) risks than when they are representing an individual client who is then or might soon be involved in actual litigation. For this reason it is sometimes preferable to retain outside counsel to conduct the audit because the dual roles of in-house attorneys as legal and business advisors sometimes cast doubt on the availability of legal privileges.

For the most part, companies will want to be able to share documents showing they exercised Year 2000 due diligence; indeed, that is the reason for preparing a "paper trail" of your compliance efforts (see Chapter 8, "Substantiating Due Diligence"). However, some conversations between the company's attorneys and its directors, officers, and key Y2K staff should be kept confidential. These include notes of interviews with employees who are dissatisfied with the company's compliance program, minutes of executive sessions of board meetings to discuss difficult triage decisions, and strategies for cost-recovery actions. In such cases, careful steps should be taken to preserve the confidentiality of privileged communications (Gergacz, 1990):

- A memorandum should be prepared explaining that the purpose of the investigation is to provide legal advice in connection with potential Year 2000 liabilities and setting forth the scope of the attorneys' responsibilities and identifying the corporate personnel who will be involved in the investigation.

- All documents should be maintained under the control of counsel in a locked and segregated file.

- Only final copies of attorney notes, legal memoranda, interviews, and other sensitive documents should be retained; photocopying and distribution should be limited to as few individuals as possible and should be imprinted with a stamp indicating that the document is confidential and privileged.

- Inform employees in writing that they will be interviewed by counsel in connection with the legal audit and instruct them to keep the conversation confidential.

- Any analysis or report prepared by counsel should present legal advice or discuss the legal dimensions of business decisions; purely business advice is not likely to be protected from disclosure in the event of subsequent litigation.

New Contracts—Stopping the Bleeding

Until 1998, few contracts mentioned Year 2000 at all. Given the wide range of potential liabilities associated with Y2K, it is imperative that new business agreements address the issue squarely.

Define Y2K Compliance

Not so long ago, the definition of *Year 2000 compliance* was the subject of vigorous debate. By the end of 1998, though, two definitional approaches have gained general acceptance, with some organizations even taking a "belt and suspenders" approach by combining the two.

The first approach is modeled after a definition originally adopted in the Federal Acquisition Regulations, section 39.002, and focuses on overall functionality:

> Year 2000 compliance shall mean that information technology shall accurately process date/time data (including but not limited to, calculating, comparing and sequencing) from, into and between the twentieth and twenty-first centuries, and the years 1999 and 2000 and leap year calculations. Furthermore, Year 2000 compliant technology, when used in combination with other information technology, shall accurately process date/time data if the other information technology properly exchanges date/time data with it (Commonwealth of Massachusetts, 1998a).

The second approach, which was developed by the British Standards Institution, provides a rules-based definition:

> Year 2000 conformity shall mean that neither performance nor functionality is affected by dates prior to, during and after the year 2000.
>
> In particular:
>
> Rule 1. No value for current date will cause any interruption in operation.
>
> Rule 2. Date-based functionality must behave consistently for dates prior to, during and after year 2000.
>
> Rule 3. In all interfaces and data storage, the century in any date must be specified either explicitly or by unambiguous algorithms or inferencing rules.
>
> Rule 4. Year 2000 must be recognized as a leap year (British Standards Institution, 1998).

It is important to note that the definition may or may not be used as part of a contractual requirement or warranty. For example, Microsoft's "Statement of Year 2000 Compliance" presents a modified version of the first approach but includes the following disclaimer:

Disclaimer: The Statement of Compliance refers to the Microsoft product as delivered by Microsoft. The Compliance Statement does not apply to user customizable features or third party add-on features or products, including items such as macros and custom programming and formatting features. The Microsoft Statement of Compliance does not constitute a warranty or extend the terms of any existing warranty. The warranties provided for Microsoft's products, if any, are set forth in the end user license agreements (EULAs) that accompany the products or the terms of the license agreement under which you make use of a Microsoft product. The information available from Microsoft concerning the Year 2000 is provided for the sole purpose of assisting our customers in their planning for the transition to the Year 2000 (Microsoft, 1998).

Year 2000 Warranties

Express warranties are an essential part of almost every commercial contract, and Year 2000 warranties should now become part of the standard terms and conditions of all business agreements, whether or not they directly involve the acquisition or use of technology. Several examples follow, starting with governmental warranty language, followed by private contractual provisions.

General Services Administration

The U.S. General Services Administration, which establishes procurement policies for the federal government, recommends that all agencies incorporate the following language in all acquisitions of technology products:

> The contractor warrants that each hardware, software, and firmware product delivered under this contract and listed below shall be able to accurately process date/time data (including, but not limited to, calculating, comparing, and sequencing) from, into, and between the twentieth and twenty-first centuries, and the years 1999 and 2000 and leap year calculations to the extent that other information technology, used in combination with the information technology being acquired, properly exchanges date/time data with it. If the contract requires that specific listed products must perform as a system in accordance with the foregoing warranty, then that warranty shall apply to those listed products as a system. The duration of this warranty and the remedies available to the Government for breach of this warranty shall be as defined in, and subject to, the terms and limitations of the contractor's standard commercial warranty or warranties contained in this contract, provided that notwithstanding any provision to the contrary in such commercial warranty or warranties, the remedies available to the Government under this warranty shall include repair or replacement of any listed product whose non-compliance is discovered and made known to the contractor in writing within ninety (90) days after acceptance. Nothing in this warranty shall be construed to limit any rights or remedies the Government may otherwise have under this contract with respect to defects other than Year 2000 performance (U.S. General Services Administration, 1997).

New York State is considered to have taken the most aggressive approach to incorporating strict Year 2000 requirements in its procurement contracts. The following language is mandated in all contracts:

> "Compliance" shall be defined in accordance with the following warranty statement:
>
> Vendor warrants that Product(s) furnished pursuant to this Agreement shall, when used in accordance with the Product documentation, be able to accurately process date/time data (including, but not limited to, calculating, comparing, and sequencing) from, into, and between the twentieth and twenty-first centuries, and the years 1999 and 2000, including leap year calculations. Where a purchase requires that specific Products must perform as a package or system, this warranty shall apply to the Products as a system.
>
> In the event of any breach of this warranty, Vendor shall restore the Product to the same level of performance as warranted herein, or repair or replace the Product with conforming Product so as to minimize interruption to Authorized User's ongoing business processes, time being of the essence, at Vendor's sole cost and expense. This warranty does not extend to correction of Authorized User's errors in data entry or data conversion.
>
> This warranty shall survive beyond termination or expiration of the Agreement.
>
> Nothing in this warranty shall be construed to limit any rights or remedies otherwise available under this Agreement (New York State, 1998).

The New York modifications of the GSA warranty are designed to overcome certain terms the state believes are unfairly favorable to vendors:

> The GSA language only provides a guaranty "to the extent that other information technology, used in combination with the information technology being acquired, properly exchanges date/time data with it." This allows the Vendor to void the warranty if the data supplied by one application does not use the same windowing solution as a second product. This particularly renders the "warranted as a system" coverage ineffective.
>
> The GSA warranty is limited in its duration and available remedies to whatever duration and remedy the Vendor's standard license offers, or to repair or replacement of the product if the defect is discovered within 90 days of acceptance, whichever is longer. This requires the agency to go immediately to Year 2000 testing in order to determine compliance within the warranty period.
>
> The GSA warranty limits remedies for Year 2000 breach to repair or replacement of the product. This does not permit the agency to impose additional liability on the Vendor elsewhere in the contract for associated damages (e.g., remediation of corrupted data) (1998).

Commercial Warranties

In theory, there is no obvious reason for the terms of commercial Y2K warranties to differ from the cognate provisions in public sector transactions. In practice, however, large government agencies may be able to offer more lucrative contracts or longer-term contracting opportunities than private companies making a one-time purchase. As a result, large agencies may be able to demand more stringent assurances than vendors would normally be willing to provide. Even for smaller contracts, individual agencies may be able to say to bidders that they are not authorized to vary the terms of standard procurement language. Whatever the case may be, here is a short-form and long-form Year 2000 warranty for commercial transactions.

Short-Form Warranty

Licensor represents and warrants that the [identify the software, firmware, equipment or system] is Year 2000 Compliant, is designed to be used prior to, during and after the calendar year 2000 A.D., will operate consistently, predictably and accurately, without interruption or manual intervention, and in accordance with all requirements of this Agreement, including without limitation any specifications and/or functionality and performance requirements, during each such time period, and the transitions between them, in relation to dates it encounters or processes (Ricci, 1997).

Long-Form Warranty

1. Licensor represents and warrants that the Software is designed to be used prior to, during, and after the calendar year 2000 A.D., and that the Software will operate during each such time period without error relating to date data, specifically including any error relating to, or the product of, date data which represents or references different centuries or more than one century.

2. Without limiting the generality of the foregoing, Licensor further represents and warrants:

    a. That the Software will not abnormally end or provide invalid or incorrect results as a result of date data, specifically including date data which represents or references different centuries or more than one century;

    b. That the Software has been designed to ensure year 2000 compatibility, including, but not limited to, date data century recognition, calculations which accommodate same century and multi-century formulas and date values, and date data interface values that reflect the century;

    c. That the software includes "year 2000 capabilities". For the purposes of this Agreement, "year 2000 capabilities" means the Software:

        (i) will manage and manipulate data involving dates, including single century formulas and multi-century formulas, and will not cause an abnormally ending scenario within the application or generate incorrect values or invalid results involving such dates; and

        (ii) provides that all date-related user interface functionalities and data fields include the indication of century; and

(iii) provides that all date-related data interface functionalities include the indication of century.

1. Definitions

Four Digit Year Format shall mean a format that allows entry or processing of a four digit year date: the first two digits will designate the century and the second two digits shall designate the year within the century. As an example, 1996 shall mean the 96th year of the 20th century.

Leap Year shall mean the year during which an extra day is added in February (February 29th). Leap Year occurs in all years divisible by 400 or evenly divisible by 4 and not evenly divisible by 100. For example, 1996 is a Leap Year since it is divisible by 4 and not evenly divisible by 100. 2000 is a Leap Year since it is divisible by 400.

Year 2000 Compliant shall mean that the data outside of the range 1990-1999 will be correctly processed in any level of computer hardware or software including, but not limited to, microcode, firmware, application programs, files and databases.

2. Year 2000 Compliance Performance Warranty. Licensor further warrants and represents that the Product is and will continue to be Year 2000 Compliant. All date processing by Product will include Four Digit Year Format and recognize and correctly process dates for Leap Year. Additionally, all date sorting by Product that includes a "year category" shall be done based on the Four Digit Year Format code.

3. Remedies for Non-Compliance of Warranty. Licensor agrees to pay liquidated damages in the amount of $ per day for each day the Product fails to maintain and uphold the Year 2000 Compliance Performance Warranty described in Section _ of this Agreement.

YEAR 2000 WARRANTIES.

Licensor represents and warrants that:

A. The Software will function without error or interruption related to Date Data, specifically including errors or interruptions from functions which may involve Date Data from more than one century;

B. The Software requires that all Date Data (whether received from users, systems, applications or other sources) include an indication of century in each instance;

C. All date output and results, in any form, shall include an indication of century in each instance.

When used in this Section _, the term "Date Data" shall mean any data or input which includes an indication of or reference to date. The foregoing is in addition to the other representations and warranties set forth herein (Feathers, 1998).

Interaction with Other Systems

As we have seen, compliance is often defined in terms of the product's performance in isolation, effectively excusing noncompliance that is caused by interconnections with noncompliant technology supplied by other parties. New York State is an exception. Here is an example of another clause that requires vendors to maintain compliance even when other integrated components are not compliant. Companies should anticipate that vendors will be unlikely to agree to such a provision unless they are in a singularly weak bargaining position for a contract they desperately want.

> To the extent that the [software, firmware, equipment or system] will accept data from other systems and sources that are not Year 2000 compliant, the [software, firmware, equipment or system] must properly recognize, calculate, sort, store, output, and otherwise process such data in a manner that eliminates any century ambiguity so that the [software, firmware, equipment or system] remains Year 2000 Compliant (Ricci, 1997).

New York State urges its agencies "to couple the warranty disclosure at the time of product quote with a demand that the Vendor simultaneously disclose their proposed Year 2000 solution by Product or Product Line (i.e., four digit year, windowing pivot point, etc.). This allows the agency to determine interoperability with existing systems and to make a determination on the desirability of the solution in view of available commercial alternatives" (New York State, 1998).

Other Y2K Contract Clauses

Other commercial contract provisions must also take Year 2000 into account. The following sections give examples of some of the most essential clauses that may be needed to address Y2K contingencies:

Representation of Timely Compliance Efforts

An *outcome-oriented* clause in the nature of a warranty that the other party will, by the time required, have computer applications that are Year 2000-compliant in all necessary respects can be useful to document due diligence:

> [Company] has (i) undertaken a detailed inventory, review, and assessment of all areas within its business and operations that could be adversely affected by the failure of [Company] to be Year 2000 compliant on a timely basis, (ii) developed a detailed plan and timeline for becoming Year 2000 compliant on a timely basis, and (iii) to date, implemented that plan in accordance with that timetable in all material respects. [Company] reasonably anticipates that it will be Year 2000 compliant on a timely basis (Harvey, 1998).

Here is an alternative formulation:

On the basis of a comprehensive inventory, review and assessment undertaken by [Company] of [Company's] computers and embedded microchips in non-computing devices, and upon inquiry made of [Company's] material suppliers, vendors and customers, [Company's] management is of the considered view that [Company] will be Year 2000 compliant before January 1, 2000 and that [Company] will suffer no material adverse effect due to the failure of any such supplier, vendor or customer to be Year 2000 compliant (Harvey, 1998).

Alternatively, a *process-oriented clause* could be used that "confirms that certain remedial steps are being undertaken by the [company] in order to become Year 2000 compliant on a timely basis."

[Company] has completed or accomplished or will complete or accomplish by the indicated dates, the following:

1. By [specify date], prepare a comprehensive, detailed inventory and assessment of the extent to which [Company] is not Year 2000 compliant;

2. By [specify date], make detailed inquiry of all material suppliers, vendors and customers of [Company] to ascertain whether such entities are aware of the need to be Year 2000 compliant and are taking all appropriate steps to become Year 2000 compliant on a timely basis;

3. By [specify date], prepare a detailed project plan and timetable for ensuring that [Company] is Year 2000 compliant on a timely basis;

4. By [specify date], renovate all systems and equipment to cause them to be Year 2000 compliant, or replace them with technology that is Year 2000 compliant, and commence testing thereof; and

5. By [specify date], complete testing and installation of all material systems and equipment such that [Company] is Year 2000 compliant (Harvey, 1998).

Representation of Supply Chain Compliance

[Company] has made written inquiry of each of its key suppliers, vendors, and customers as to whether such persons will, on a timely basis, be Year 2000 compliant in all material respects and on the basis of such inquiry believes that all such persons will be so compliant, or [Company] has developed a feasible contingency plan to avoid any material adverse effect as a result thereof. For purposes hereof, "key suppliers, vendors, and customers" refers to those suppliers, vendors, and customers of [Company] whose business failure would, with reasonable probability, result in a material adverse change in the business, properties, condition (financial or otherwise), or prospects of [Company] (Harvey, 1998).

Indemnification by Vendor

Vendor hereby indemnifies Purchaser and agrees to hold Purchaser harmless from and against any and all losses, costs, expenses, claims, obligations, and liabilities of every name and nature, including, without limitation, court costs and reasonable attorneys' fees, incurred by Purchaser and arising from or in connection with, or resulting directly or indirectly from, any failure of Vendor's computer hardware (including hardware owned by, leased to, or otherwise operated by Vendor), software (including software owned by, licensed to, or otherwise operated by Vendor), or other computer or information systems to be Year 2000 Compliant (as defined herein) (Rosenthal, 1997).

Termination Rights

Notwithstanding any provision herein to the contrary, Purchaser shall have the right to terminate this agreement (by giving written termination notice to Vendor) if at any time Purchaser determines, in Purchaser's good faith judgment, that Vendor is not Year 2000 Compliant (as defined herein) or that there is a significant possibility that Vendor will not be Year 2000 Compliant (Rosenthal, 1997).

No Disclaimers

The Year 2000 warranties set forth herein shall not be subject to any disclaimer or exclusion of warranties or to any limitation of Licensor's liability under this Agreement (Ricci, 1997).

Force Majeure

Neither party shall be responsible for failure of performance due to causes beyond its reasonable control (excluding Year 2000 problems), including, without limitation, accidents, acts of God, labor disputes, actions of any government agency, or shortage of materials. The party claiming exclusion hereunder shall promptly notify the other of the particulars giving rise to the excuse, and shall to the best of its ability minimize the extent and duration of such circumstances (Ricci, 1997).

Year 2000 Remediation Contracts

Contracts with Year 2000 solutions providers present special business and legal risks, particularly at this late date, for several reasons. Although the IT industry is well known for failing to complete projects on time, in accordance with specifications and within approved budget parameters, Y2K projects often have insufficient time, hastily developed specifications, and poorly planned budgets. Further, some Y2K consultants and contractors have more work than they can handle and are therefore unwilling to agree to standard terms and conditions designed to protect the owner, such as liquidated damages, and repair or replace warranties might not be worth much if the customer is effectively unable to conduct operations during the additional time necessary to correct the defective work. Thus, although Year 2000 remediation agreements are high-stakes contracts, they often lack many of the basic provisions that are considered essential to commercial risk management.

Manage Remediation Contracts Closely

Because owners often lack their usual economic leverage when it comes to Y2K remediation contracts, Gregory P. Cirillo, a leading technology and Year 2000 attorney at Williams, Mullen, Christian & Dobbins, has proposed a unique solution. Rather than focusing the contract on the end *product*—a compliant system—Mr. Cirillo suggests companies develop contractual arrangements along the following lines that enable them to exert control over the compliance *process* and to manage that process closely (Cirillo, 1998).

Personnel

The professionals assigned to the contract are essential, so the contract should specify the following:

- The number of dedicated personnel, including their qualifications and, for key personnel, their names
- The time they will commit to the project, including overtime, if needed
- Controls on turnover and reassignment, and notice and preapproval of new staff

Termination

In case the project runs into such serious trouble that the owner needs to change contractors, the agreement must contain sufficient *portability provisions* to minimize disruptions and recover the benefit of the work performed to date:

- All *work in process*, including logs and records, are the owner's property and remain on site
- The contractor provides a license to use the contractor's tools and techniques (perhaps subject to further payment if the license is exercised)
- The contractor's personnel will remain on site or available for consultation for a post-termination transition period

Contract Management

Once the foregoing contracting tools are in place, the owner must closely audit and monitor contractor performance based on the following additional contract provisions:

- Mandatory contractor status reports, covering staffing, progress, and project benchmarks
- Audit rights, including access to the contractor's books and records and the right to interview project personnel
- Personnel attendance logs
- A defined procedure for promptly and efficiently resolving any of the process-oriented contract provisions, including change order and alternative dispute resolution procedures

Other Contract Provisions

In addition to the process-oriented approach just described, some of the more garden-variety contract provisions can be particularly important in Y2K remediation contracts:

- Insurance
- Project schedules and milestones
- Budget control measures
- Quality assurance/quality control measures (including internal audit review)
- Confidentiality
- Trade secret protection
- Predefined corrective actions for breach of contract
- Performance incentives and penalties
- Source code licenses

Independent Verification and Validation Contracts

Independent verification and validation (IV&V) is a process by which an independent third party determines whether the previously defined assessment, remediation, testing, and deployment requirements for a Year 2000 project have been implemented successfully. Given the difficulty of testing renovated systems and the complex external environment with which companies must interact, IV&V is expected to become an important final check on enterprise compliance during 1999. Responsibilities of the IV&V contractor should include the following elements (Commonwealth of Massachusetts, 1998b):

- An independent verification and validation of project plans, work products, and deliverables for the owner

- Performance of the tasks necessary to ensure that project plans, work products, and deliverables are of the highest quality consistent with the project requirements and goals
- Identification as early as possible of project risks and anomalies in project plans, work products, and deliverables to allow for effective and timely resolution
- Identification, documentation, and communication of steps required for correcting anomalies and mitigating risks in a timely manner so as to reduce the negative impact of such anomalies and risks on the success of the overall project

Protecting Y2K Vendors and Consultants

Many companies providing Y2K remediation services and tools expect that they will face lawsuits by customers that experience date-related system failures. Year 2000 contracts may be lucrative, but they also entail higher degrees of risk for which there is no track record for making difficult risk allocation and pricing decisions. If customers come to believe that they have been taken advantage of and their businesses suffer despite glowing assurances by vendors' marketing representatives, the post-2000 environment could be a tumultuous one for solutions providers in which they give back in legal fees, settlements, and damage awards what they gained in premium pricing and overbooked engagements before 2000. Perhaps a more realistic business strategy is in order.

Contractual Risks

IT contractors have a plethora of liability and warranty limitations, remedy exclusions and disclaimers, license restrictions, notice requirements, acceptance provisions, cancellation rights, and other contractual terms that negate or limit their liability for nonperformance and poor performance. In the context of Year 2000 contracts, solutions providers often have greater leverage to insist on the inclusion of these one-sided protections. Such provisions have generally been upheld by the courts on the premise that commercial customers understood the risks they were assuming and the contract price fairly allocates those risks among the parties. Whether the courts will regard suits against Y2K remediation contractors differently if widespread failures occur may depend on several factors.

Unknown risks. Customers will be likely to argue that they did not fully appreciate the risks associated with Year 2000, including complex networking and embedded microprocessor frailties, and that they depended on contractors to provide an effective solution, not merely to "devote their best efforts," as many contracts provide. Contractors that jumped on the Y2K bandwagon without understanding the technical complexities or the difficult project management demands will be particularly vulnerable to such charges.

Misrepresentations. Customers will surely claim that contractors misled them about their capabilities, experience, and capacity in the scramble to line up companies with the scarce technical and personnel resources to meet the Y2K challenge. In many cases, the courts will tell those business customers that they simply failed to look out for themselves to the same extent they do in other commercial contexts. But tort claims of fraud or misrepresentation can, if proved, overcome contractual limitations of liability and remedy exclusions, opening the door to potentially unlimited liability. Y2K contractors should control what their salespeople say about their services and capabilities and be prepared to back up with sound documentation the claims they make before the contract is signed. They should also provide clients with accurate and complete status reports, even—or perhaps especially—if the news is not good. Most project managers will accommodate and work with contractors who give bad news while there is still time to take corrective action, but they will understandably try to "nuke" contractors that hide the truth until it is no longer possible to recover from excessive schedule slippage or abysmal test results.

Unconscionability. Under section 2-302 of the UCC, "If the court as a matter of law finds the contract or any clause of the contract to have been unconscionable at the time it was made the court may refuse to enforce the contract, or it may enforce the remainder of the contract without the unconscionable clause, or it may so limit the application of any unconscionable clause as to avoid any unconscionable result." Unconscionability includes "an absence of meaningful choice on the part of one of the parties to a contract together with contract terms which are unreasonably favorable to the other party" (Nolan, 1979). Although unconscionability is not easily proved, particularly among commercial parties, Year 2000 contractors should recognize there may be risks associated with taking unreasonable advantage of their superior bargaining power, particularly with new engagements undertaken in 1999 for clients that did not understand the problem sufficiently to get started earlier.

Failure of essential purpose. When a limited warranty fails to provide a meaningful remedy for its breach, a court may, in unusual cases, effectively void the limitation and enforce the standard UCC implied warranties and remedies. For example, IT vendors typically promise, as the exclusive remedy under the contract, to repair programming defects within a "reasonable" period of time. If the vendor has been unable or unwilling to fix serious errors for an extended period of time, the buyer might seek to avoid the warranty limitation by filing suit and alleging that the warranty has *failed of its essential purpose*. For Year 2000 contracts, buyers are likely to argue for shortened repair periods and claim that the warranty has failed if the viability of their business has been put at risk or business losses have been suffered that far exceed the purchase price of the system or the vendor's services.

A New Approach

The last year before 2000 is probably going to be a hectic time for Y2K contractors and their clients. Although many solutions providers signed up less business in 1998 than they had hoped and there was a fair amount of excess capacity in the industry, it stands to reason that 1999 will see more intense interest by small and medium-sized companies that became aware of the problem late in the game and have more limited in-house resources to renovate their own systems. Solutions providers that have missed their financial targets in the past, as well as those that may have exceeded them, will be hard pressed not to pursue these contracting opportunities with a vengeance. At the same time, they will be in a superior position to exact favorable contract terms, thinking with some justification that they must do so to protect themselves from lawsuits caused by failures that might be someone else's fault, in whole or in part.

Our advice is to proceed with caution. With all of the external factors and interdependencies that affect compliance, it is difficult to say with confidence at this point whether Y2K repairs will be successful, especially in low-budget projects that started late. Clients that have system failures and are sued by their customers will surely look to share the blame—and the liability—with their Year 2000 contractors. Consultants and solutions providers that overreach by insisting on unreasonable contract terms, taking on more work than they can competently handle, reassigning key personnel to more lucrative contracts, and failing to keep owners advised of the true status of the project are giving ammunition to the other side and inviting uncomfortably close judicial scrutiny. Here are some suggestions for staying out of harm's way.

Don't make promises you can't keep. There should be plenty of work in 1999 for which customers will be willing to pay premium rates, so don't get greedy and become a fatter litigation target. Tell prospects what your real areas of expertise and capabilities are, and tell them straight up what, when, and how you can perform. Salesmanship is one thing; misrepresentation is another.

Accept provisions that manage the contract process. Greg Cirillo's suggestions for incorporating process-oriented terms into Y2K remediation contracts are just as beneficial to contractors as they are to owners. Define the scope of work carefully, negotiate personnel requirements you can satisfy, establish interim performance milestones, provide timely and accurate status reports, and work with your client to correct problems along the way. But don't leave out the usual limitations of liability, warranty disclaimers, and all the rest. If the contract is even-handed as a result, it's more likely to be left intact by the courts.

Honor your commitments. There's a lot of talk that solutions providers will accept better jobs and leave their existing customers in the lurch or assign less experienced personnel that may or may not be up to the task. Whatever business judgments might lead a company to consider such a course of action, it should factor into the equation the fact that litigation can be an extremely costly, protracted, and painful process.

Don't hide bad news. Avoid fraud and misrepresentation claims by keeping your client informed on a regular basis about how the contract is going and what needs to happen to get back on track. Work with the owner to reach pragmatic solutions to short-term problems and carefully document any midcourse corrections to which the parties agreed. State clearly that any accommodations you make do not modify the warranty, remedy, or other terms of the contract.

Verify your E&O insurance coverage. Get a coverage opinion from your lawyer and your insurance broker or agent, and make sure you comply with any policy requirements to preserve the opportunity for coverage.

Avoiding Liability from Selling Noncompliant Products and Services

It is too early to say how the current crop of suits seeking free compliant upgrades will turn out, but more software products are likely to experience actual Y2K failures in 1999 if they process forward-looking date information. If so, customers will be able to clear the hurdle that led to the dismissal of one of the suits on the ground that the plaintiffs had failed to allege that they had suffered any actual injury. At this point, little time remains for jockeying with customers over who is responsible for replacing or upgrading noncompliant products. Just as doctors with good bedside manners face fewer malpractice claims, technology companies might reduce their Y2K liability exposure by extending themselves to their customers before an adversarial situation develops.

Take Stock of Your Compliance Status

The first step, of course, is to understand the specific compliance problems of your products and services. Which versions are affected, whether you no longer support certain older versions, the nature and seriousness of the defects and the potential business consequences for your customers, when you knew or reasonably should have known about them, what it will take to correct them, and the financial exposure to your company are all considerations that should be evaluated as part of your business risk assessment. Don't overlook embedded chip problems.

Assess Your Legal Obligations to Customers

Next, your lawyer should take a hard look at the strength of your legal position. Do your warranty limitations and other contract terms sufficiently protect you from liability? Will the courts enforce those clauses? What remedies are available to your customers if you don't work something out with them? Do you have a duty to notify your customers of problems you've discovered? What are the chances they will take you to court? How damaging and expensive would a class-action or other lawsuit be? How large would the class be? Even if you might prevail, do you have other business reasons for wanting to avoid litigation? Would litigation put your intellectual property at risk? What are the prospects for settlement? What would it cost to placate the activist customers? If you reached a settlement with some customers, would they honor an agreement to keep its terms confidential, or would everyone want the same deal? Keep in mind that more than 90 percent of lawsuits eventually settle, so try to develop realistic strategies for avoiding the expense, distraction, bad publicity, and opportunity costs of litigation by offering sound business-based solutions to your customers' problems.

Communicating with Customers Under The Year 2000 Information and Readiness Disclosure Act

Once you've staked out a position on what assistance you will offer your customers and on what terms, you need to get the word out in ways that don't expose you to liability. The safest course to follow is set forth in The Year 2000 Information and Readiness Disclosure Act, which was signed into law on October 19, 1998. A summary of the law follows, but the full text of the act must be reviewed to fully understand its terms.

Purpose of the Act

The act recognizes that "[c]oncern about the potential for legal liability associated with the disclosure and exchange of Year 2000 compliance information is impeding the disclosure and exchange of such information." To mitigate that concern, the purposes of the law include "to promote the free disclosure and exchange of information related to Year 2000 readiness [and] to lessen burdens on interstate commerce by establishing certain uniform legal principles in connection with the disclosure and exchange of information related to Year 2000 readiness." The act establishes a number of defenses against civil actions claiming injury from erroneous Year 2000-related statements.

The Honest Mistake Defense

First, in any federal or state civil suit (except a regulatory, supervisory, or enforcement action brought by a public agency) alleging that a Y2K statement was false, inaccurate, or misleading, the person or company that made the statement "shall not be liable under Federal or State law" unless the statement was material and made as follows:

- "with actual knowledge that the Year 2000 statement was false, inaccurate, or misleading"
- "with an intent to mislead or deceive; or"
- "with a reckless disregard as to the accuracy of the Year 2000 statement."

As defined in the act, a "Year 2000 statement" includes any statement concerning an assessment, projection, estimate, plan, objective, timetable, and test plan and result concerning Y2K processing capabilities of an entity, product, or service.

The Republication Defense

In the case of a republication of an allegedly false, inaccurate, or misleading statement, there would be no liability if, in addition to the foregoing requirements, the republication discloses that "the maker [of the republished statement] has not verified the statement" and "the maker is not the source of the republished year 2000 statement, the republished statement is based on information supplied by another person or entity, and the notice or republished statement identifies the source of the republished statement." Thus, the statute standardizes legally authorized disclaimers that will be effective in avoiding liability.

The Defamation Defense

The third defense relating to allegedly damaging Y2K statements in civil litigation concerns claims for defamation or trade disparagement. Here, the legislation adopts the standard the Supreme Court developed in *New York Times v. Sullivan* for defamation suits against public figures. Thus, someone accused of making a written or oral defamatory Year 2000 statement "shall not be liable

... unless the claimant establishes by clear and convincing evidence ... that the statement was made with knowledge that the statement was false or with reckless disregard as to its truth or falsity." This standard is difficult to meet, so the defamation provision might promote reporting of product compliance information by third parties.

The Web Site Defense

Another area of serious concern has been potential liability exposure from posting compliance information on Internet Web sites. The act affords limited protection for the company supplying compliance information about its own products and services on the Internet. It provides that, in cases where "the adequacy of notice about Year 2000 processing is at issue, the posting in a commercially reasonable manner and for a commercially reasonable duration, of a notice by the entity charged with giving such notice on the year 2000 Internet Web site of that entity shall be deemed to be an adequate mechanism for providing that notice." Here, counsel will have to exercise somewhat more caution in advising their clients. The legislation creates several exceptions that the Internet posting was an adequate method for providing notice, and future plaintiffs may well dispute whether some other method of notice was required.

If these concerns can be overcome—which they should be in the case of large corporations, utilities, public agencies, and others that are being bombarded with hundreds or even thousands of letters from customers asking detailed and often redundant questions about their compliance efforts—the Web site defense could provide useful protections that would encourage broad dissemination of compliance information over the Internet. Note that this defense does not relate to the sufficiency of the *content* of any information posted on a Web site or the *duty* to post such information. But it would enable product manufacturers to more effectively manage the logistical burdens of disseminating Y2K information.

Disclaimers

The legislation also provides, in the absence of an agreement by the parties, that "no Year 2000 statement shall be interpreted or construed as an amendment to or alteration of a contract or warranty." That is, unless contract negotiations establish a contrary indication, the provision of Y2K compliance information, by itself, would not create any contractual rights or warranties that could form the basis for a lawsuit. In effect, the act would establish an implied disclaimer by operation of law. This provision, like the rest of the act, would apply only to compliance statements made after the date the law went into effect (October 19, 1998). Although careful counsel are likely to advise their clients to make explicit disclaimers in any event, and the act expressly provides that it does not "preclude any party from making or providing any additional disclaimer," the law would address many of the questions that are likely to be litigated in the future about what legal effect, if any, should be attached to voluntary compliance statements.

The Use Immunity Provision

An interesting provision of the act authorizes federal agencies to "expressly designate requests for the voluntary provision of information relating to year 2000 processing . . . as special year 2000 data gathering request." Any information provided in response to such a request would be exempt from the Freedom of Information Act and could not be used in any civil action by the government or any third party. The information, however, could be used in government lawsuits if it were obtained from an independent source. This device could be useful in cases where the federal government has expressed concerns about not being able to obtain important information about compliance efforts in key industries (such as telecommunications) that affect Year 2000 preparations in other dependent industries (such as banking and securities, which must perform "end-to-end" testing using compliant telecommunications systems).

Regulatory Compliance

Lawsuits by private parties (and government agencies procuring goods and services from the private sector) are not the only kinds of legal actions that Year 2000 problems will engender. Regulatory and law enforcement agencies have become aware that Y2K poses financial, health, and public safety risks over which they have jurisdiction. Effective risk management strategies must take these players into account as well.

The Evolving Year 2000 Regulatory Landscape

Many federal agencies have been so preoccupied with their own Y2K compliance problems that they have devoted little or no attention to worrying about the compliance efforts of the institutions and industries they regulate. There are exceptions, however, and regulatory activity is likely to increase during 1999.

The financial and securities regulators have been particularly aggressive in directing and auditing the compliance programs of banks, savings associations, credit unions, mortgage lenders, securities dealers, and investment advisors. In addition, the Federal Financial Institutions Examination Council (FFIEC), which comprises the Federal Reserve Bank (FRB), the Office of the Comptroller of the Currency, the Federal Deposit Insurance Company, the Office of Thrift Supervision, and the National Credit Union Administration, has adopted compliance guidelines that apply to the customers—particularly borrowers—and service providers and software vendors of financial institutions. Inasmuch as the FFIEC guidelines, together with those announced by the Securities and Exchange Commission (see Chapter 8, "Substantiating Due Diligence"), are referenced by other organizations such as the American Institute of Certified Public Accountants, they might have broader standard-setting significance. The following documents are available from the FFIEC Web site at www.ffiec.gov/y2k.

Bank Awareness and Business Risk

FFIEC Interagency Statement (IS), June 1996. The Effect of Year 2000 on Computer Systems.

FRB Supplemental Release (SR) 96-16, July 3, 1996. Re: The Effect of Year 2000 on Computer Systems.

FFIEC Press Release, May 5, 1997. Federal Bank Regulators Outline Year 2000 Project Management Goals.

FFIEC IS, May 5, 1997. Year 2000 Project Management Awareness.

FFIEC IS, December 17, 1997. Safety and Soundness Guidelines Concerning the Year 2000 Business Risk.

FRB SR 97-34, December 22, 1997. Safety and Soundness Guidelines Concerning the Year 2000 Business Risk.

Federal Supervision of Year 2000 Programs

FRB SR 97-16, May 6, 1997. Re: Year 2000 Supervision Program.

FDIC Financial Institution Letter, May 9, 1997. Re: Year 2000 Project Management Awareness.

FRB SR 97-29, December 12, 1997. Re: Year 2000 Supervision Program and Follow Up Actions.

FRB SR 98-3, March 4, 1998. Re: The FRB's Intensified Year 2000 Compliance Efforts.

FFIEC Year 2000 Examination Procedures.

FFIEC Year 2000 Examiner Questionnaire.

Testing of Software

FFIEC Press Release, April 10, 1998. FFIEC Issues Year 2000 Guidance on Testing.

FFIEC IS, April 10, 1998. Guidance Concerning Testing for Year 2000 Readiness.

FRB SR 98-8, April 16, 1998. Guidance Concerning Testing for Year 2000 Readiness.

Contingency Planning and Customer Awareness (Disclosures)

FFIEC IS, May 13, 1998. Guidance Concerning Contingency Planning in Connection with Year 2000 Readiness.

FFIEC IS, May 13, 1998. Guidance on Year 2000 Customer Awareness Programs.

FFIEC Press Release, May 13, 1998. FFIEC Issues Year 2000 Guidance on Contingency Planning and Customer Awareness.

FRB SR 98-11, May 14, 1998. Guidance on Year 2000 Contingency Planning, and Customer Awareness Programs External Exposures (Customer & Vendor Preparedness).

FFIEC Press Release, March 17, 1998. FFIEC Issues Guidance on Vendors and Customers' Year 2000 Risk.

FFIEC IS, March 17, 1998. Guidance Concerning Institution Due Diligence in Connection with Service Provider and Software Vendor Year 2000 Readiness.

FFIEC IS, March 17, 1998. Guidance Concerning the Year 2000 Impact on Customers.

FRB SR 98-4, March 19, 1998. Year 2000 Impact on Customers, and Due Diligence in Connection with Service Provider and Software Vendor Year 2000 Readiness.

In addition, as of the fall of 1998, all of the following governmental bodies have issued Y2K directives or guidance documents:

- Freddie Mac
- Government National Mortgage Association (Ginnie Mae)
- Bank for International Settlements, Joint Year 2000 Council
    - Basle Committee on Banking Supervision
    - Committee on Payment and Settlement Systems
    - International Association of Insurance Supervisors
    - International Organization of Securities Commissions

- Food and Drug Administration, Center for Devices and Radiological Health
- Health Care Financing Administration
- Veterans Health Administration
- Federal Aviation Administration
- Internal Revenue Service
- Department of Labor (pension funds and health care plans)
- Financial Accounting Standards Board (an influential nongovernmental body)
- Governmental Accounting Standards Board (same)
- Nuclear Regulatory Commission
- Federal Communications Commission

Any company, association, or other organization whose activities are regulated directly or indirectly by any of these entities should monitor what these agencies are saying about Year 2000 compliance and develop appropriate action plans to avoid becoming targets of regulatory enforcement action. Indeed, all regulated entities should keep a watchful eye on the agencies with which they deal on a regular basis for new Y2K directives.

Note that many preexisting statutes and regulations could come into play before and after 2000, even if they don't explicitly mention Y2K. For example, the Center for Devices and Radiological Health of the U.S. Food and Drug Administration has advised medical device manufacturers that provisions of the Food, Drug and Cosmetics Act, the Quality System Regulation, and the Safe Medical Devices Act will apply to the approval, manufacture, and sale of certain kinds of biomedical devices and equipment that may have Y2K problems. The Nuclear Regulatory Commission has informed licensees that "existing reporting requirements under 10 CFR Part 21 provide for notification to NRC of deficiencies, non-conformances, and failures, such as the Y2K problem in safety-related systems." The Department of Labor has instructed trustees and administrators of pension and retirement plans that they have fiduciary duties to safeguard their participants' investments and to ensure that their contracted providers are taking appropriate steps to become compliant.

In addition, many private and nonprofit associations, as shown in the list that follows, have issued guidance documents to their members concerning Year 2000 issues. Although such advisory statements do not constitute legally enforceable mandates, failure to follow industry standards will be fair game in most Year 2000 litigation.

- National Association of Securities Dealers
- New York Stock Exchange

- American Stock Exchange
- American Institute of Certified Public Accountants
- Credit Union National Association
- National Association of Federal Credit Unions
- American Hospital Association
- American Medical Association

Although many states have been working hard to bring their own systems and external business dependencies into compliance, state governments have been less active to the point of virtual silence about Y2K in a regulatory sense. Many industries, however, are regulated primarily or jointly at the state level, including insurance, banking, securities, healthcare, utilities, telecommunications, environmental compliance, public safety, and education. As public awareness of Year 2000 risks increases in 1999, it is safe to assume that citizen and political pressure for state agencies to get into the act will increase.

Developing a Y2K Regulatory Compliance Program

Businesses need to inventory the potential regulatory consequences of Year 2000 failures and develop compliance programs that demonstrate due diligence. Economic, health, and safety regulations have become so pervasive that it is not possible to catalogue them in detail, but a systematic approach can be outlined.

What Regulators Want

Of course, regulatory agencies expect that the organizations subject to their jurisdictions will comply with applicable legal requirements. But Year 2000 problems are just as likely to interfere with regulatory compliance as they are to cause business disruptions and contractual breaches. If regulatory violations should occur, most enforcement agencies will take the existence of effective programs to prevent and detect violations into account as mitigating circumstances that will avoid or reduce the penalties to be imposed. To qualify for such favorable consideration, agencies are looking for evidence that violators intended to comply with the law, developed systematic compliance programs, and voluntarily disclosed violations before they were caught.

Compliance Program Components

The Office of Inspector General (OIG) of the Department of Health and Human Services has developed a model compliance program for hospitals and clinical laboratories that draws on earlier guidelines of the U.S. Sentencing Commission. These guidelines were developed to prevent, detect, and correct incidents of fraud in healthcare facilities, but applying them to Y2K-related regulatory violations undoubtedly would be viewed favorably by other enforcement agencies, particularly those that have not provided specific guidance for Year 2000 preparations.

At a minimum, comprehensive compliance programs should include the following seven elements:

(1) the development and distribution of written standards of conduct, as well as written policies and procedures that promote the [organization's] commitment to compliance (e.g., by including adherence to compliance as an element in evaluating managers and employees) and that address specific areas of potential fraud . . .;

(2) the designation of a chief compliance officer and other appropriate bodies (e.g., a corporate compliance committee) charged with the responsibility of operating and monitoring the compliance program, and who report directly to the CEO and the governing body;

(3) the development and implementation of regular, effective education and training program for all affected employees;

(4) the maintenance of a process, such as a hotline, to receive complaints, and the adoption of procedures to protect the anonymity of complainants and to protect whistleblowers from retaliation;

(5) the development of a system to respond to allegations of improper/illegal activities and the enforcement of appropriate disciplinary action against employees who have violated internal compliance policies, [or] applicable statutes, regulations . . .

(6) the use of audits and/or other evaluation techniques to monitor compliance and assist in the reduction of identified problem areas; and

(7) the investigation and remediation of identified systemic problems and the developments of policies addressing the non-employment or retention of sanctioned individuals (Office of Inspector General, Department of Health and Human Services, 1998).

Conclusion

Year 2000 due diligence encompasses a broad array of project management, risk management, and liability mitigation measures that reach across many different areas of legal practice. Effective control of Year 2000 legal risks requires a programmatic approach to protecting directors and officers, technical professionals, and other corporate stakeholders, using comprehensive legal audits to identify and evaluate the organization's rights and responsibilities. Appropriate Y2K clauses must be incorporated into all new business agreements, including Year 2000 remediation and IV&V contracts, and a regulatory compliance program must be developed that can adapt to evolving requirements established by a host of federal and state agencies. Particular attention should be paid to the directives of the FFIEC and the SEC, the *Year 2000 Information and Readiness Disclosure Act*, and any industry-specific guidelines that may be issued by regulatory bodies with jurisdiction over your company's affairs. The establishment of a systematic program to reduce Year 2000 liabilities is an important predicate to formulating external compliance strategies, to which we turn in the next chapter.

CHAPTER 5

External Compliance Strategies

"Crashing computers could foul up air traffic, communications, business deliveries, credit card sales, financial accounts, benefit payments, tax refunds, electricity and even some medical treatments. Deutsche Morgan Grenfell Bank's chief economist fears the bug could cause a worldwide recession. In an increasingly interconnected world, an unfixed system at one company can recontaminate repaired systems at others. Private surveys show health care, retail stores, local governments and education are woefully behind. If the government doesn't know who isn't ready, it can't protect those who are. And 00 hour is almost here, ready or not."

—USA TODAY, APRIL 6, 1998

No business operates in a vacuum. Every corporation, partnership, organization, or association has its customers, clients, or constituents. Each utilizes resources in the form of information, raw materials, component parts, or other goods or services. Each relies on at least one financial institution, an electric company, and multiple telecommunications providers. Understanding the full scope of Year 2000 implications on an organization requires an understanding of the world we live in and the relationships among businesses.

Understanding Business Dependencies

Often referred to as the *supply chain* or *food chain*, external business dependencies (EBDs) are those entities required for the successful operation of a business and the fulfillment of its mission. They are sometimes obvious (the supplier of motherboards to a CPU manufacturer) and sometimes more obscure (the clearinghouse that processes securities transactions). They include government agencies and financial institutions. This chapter addresses the nature of business dependencies, planning for breaks in the supply chain, and anticipating how this changed business landscape will affect the way organizations do business.

The best example of EBDs comes from General Motors, the world's largest corporation. In 1995, General Motors had 87,000 vendors. Some of these vendors supplied services used in the manufacturing process. Others supplied goods in various forms (raw materials, components, and so on). For decades the process of building cars has shifted away from warehousing toward "just in time" delivery of component parts and raw materials. Then, in 1995, a GM-owned Canadian brake manufacturer went on strike unexpectedly. Because the brakes were made to specification, no alternative suppliers were readily available. Within four days, General Motors had exhausted its supply of brake systems and had to shut down production. This raised a red flag among senior management, who promptly commissioned a study of their 87,000 vendors to determine which were mission-critical (defined as providers of goods and services that would shut down production). The internal audit department identified 1000 such mission-critical vendors. Given the importance of this issue to General Motors' operations, the company retained an external auditing firm to confirm this information. This engagement revealed not only that General Motors had 1000 mission-critical suppliers, but that the level of risk went nine layers deep. In other words, each mission-critical supplier had mission-critical suppliers, which had mission-critical suppliers, and so on.

Presumptions about Resource Dependencies

Organizations large and small depend to varying degrees on suppliers, subcontractors, vendors, service providers, government agencies, and/or utilities. Without such resources no business can obtain permits, operate computers, turn on the lights, or purchase raw materials, machinery and equipment, office supplies, or essential services. Organizations spend considerable time and effort evaluating, ordering, procuring, and paying for new and improved resources. The world, it seems, is full of alternative resources—a virtual cornucopia of business options to choose from. In the Year 2000 context, assuming that plentiful alternatives exist creates a sense of false confidence that essential resources can be obtained readily and easily. This undue comfort is predicated on several myths.

Myth 1: Resource Capacity Is Unlimited

Capacity within an industry is always an issue. Those responsible for contingency planning and EBD management must understand capacity issues and that while alternative resources may be readily available today, they may not be after January 1, 2000. Although marketers would have us believe that capacity is unlimited and businesses would love to take on all prospective clients, there is a point at which their ability to deliver goods and services on time, with consistent quality, becomes inadequate. Such was the case in the United Parcel Service (UPS) strike. Entities that relied on UPS to deliver their critical packages were blissfully ignorant that workers would strike in 1997 or that alternative overnight delivery carriers would exceed their capacity to handle new business. Within hours of the strike, Federal Express, Airborne Express, and other carriers quickly were inundated with additional business and applications for new corporate clients. Unfortunately for many businesses, these alternative overnight transporters became unable to accept new large clients and could no longer guarantee next-day delivery. Nearly all businesses were affected at some level. The entire mail-order industry took a financial loss during that quarter, and some businesses were so severely damaged that they went bankrupt. This example highlights capacity issues that exist even under normal business conditions.

Year 2000 is a universal phenomenon that may compound capacity limitations. If Gartner Group's estimate that 50 percent of all organizations will not achieve compliance within mission-critical systems is accurate, an organization's resource dependencies may experience internal system failures, as may their suppliers. In other words, normal rules of capacity limitations may not apply in the Year 2000 context. Multiple company failures are expected to occur, and this may hold true within an industry. Applying Y2K-type universality to the UPS example, the analogy would be if multiple overnight air cargo companies simultaneously went on strike.

Moreover, Y2K events may be more likely to afflict an entire industry because of industry-standard systems architecture, applications, operating systems, or data-entry procedures. For example, in June 1998, American Airlines experienced delays of up to four hours in flight schedules because of errors that occurred during Y2K remediation efforts of its SABRE reservation system. SABRE is a standard in the airline industry. Even though remediation efforts for SABRE systems may well be successful for most airlines, this example illustrates the concept of commonality among industry systems. If undiscovered date dependencies exist in SABRE applications, capacity for the airline industry can be diminished significantly beyond normal limitations.

Myth 2: Changing Alternative Suppliers Requires Minimal Time and Will Not Affect Operations

Few resource transitions are instantaneous or automatic. Selecting an alternative online travel reservation service may be simple and quick, but changing banks, component part manufacturers, service agents, billing companies, and so on, require careful consideration and time. Significant decisions such as changing accounting firms may also require approval of the board of directors. Delays caused by changing resource dependencies can pose a significant threat to operations. Failure to anticipate such delays is an unnecessary risk to the organization. Mission-critical resources should have at least one viable alternative. If none exists, some other solution should be considered.

Myth 3: Goods and Services Are Essentially Fungible

Few goods or services are identical. Fungible goods, such as lumber, gasoline, and flour, pose less risk of inconsistency. Some substitutes require modification in the good or service itself or in the implementation process. For example, retraining of data-entry personnel may be required to implement a new inventory application. Changing resource dependencies can require time and expense to make modifications or adjustments. When determining the feasibility of alternative resources, contingency planners should factor in time requirements and expenses.

Other goods or services have no feasible substitute due to incompatibility, uniqueness, or prohibitive price. Custom-made and sole-source products may be impossible to substitute without substantial preparation. Specialized expertise may be required for certain services. In other instances, a product or service may be impossible to substitute because of its universal acceptance in a given industry. For example, consumer preference for a particular component (such as a specific name brand of microprocessors) may prevent manufacturers from marketing an alternative.

Myth 4: Procurement Procedures Are Relatively Consistent

Often the logistics of procurement can be unique to an enterprise. Proprietary ordering systems and customized procedures can be difficult to change. Unforeseen time and expense may be required to complete a transition to a new resource. One aspect of Y2K that often goes overlooked is the human intervention component. Data-entry personnel need to be retrained, and those who rely on or make decisions based on date data must be watchful for Y2K errors. This holds true for any procurement software utilized by the corporation. Switching to a new resource's procurement software or procedures requires time and training. Here again, a replacement procurement software application can have its own Y2K problems.

Multilevel Dependencies

Figure 5.1 shows that organizations have multiple levels of external business dependencies, both with respect to resources and output dependencies. Identifying the outer limits of multilevel dependencies can be difficult, requiring exor-

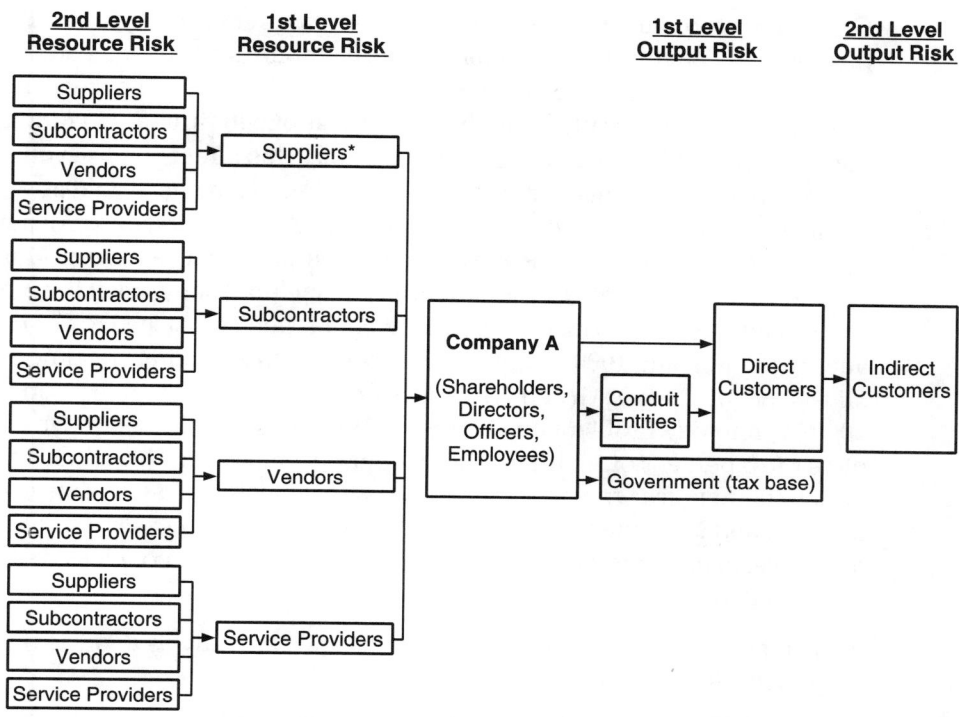

Figure 5.1 Overview of external business dependencies.

bitant time and resources. General Motors had nine levels of resource risk among its mission-critical vendors. Given that resource dependencies have their own resource dependencies, we can quickly see how interdependent our economy is. For this reason, organizations must see themselves as an integral part of an interconnected chain of private and public entities. Failure of any business will directly affect its customers and indirectly affect higher-level output dependencies and ultimately consumers or end users. Even the GM brake manufacturer affected far more entities than just General Motors. Trucking companies, auto dealerships, and ultimately fleet and individual car buyers were all affected. In addition, every other supplier of materials and components that facilitated the production of the stalled cars was affected, in that new purchases were put on hold and production schedules were altered until the strike ended.

One important lesson can be gleaned from this analysis: Y2K failure within any organization affects both directions of the supply chain. It affects output dependencies by failing to supply timely or accurate goods or services. It affects resource dependencies by triggering a change in demand for the purchase of new goods and services, and it can cause a delay or discrepancy in the payment of outstanding accounts.

Given the interconnectivity of industries and market sectors, Year 2000 progress reports from any segment of the economy should be a concern to everyone. On September 8, 1998, VNU Newswire cited a recent report by International Data Corporation that noted that one in three U.S. companies had yet to begin internal systems remediation. This affects multilevel output dependencies including customers, shareholders, employees, and governments (relying on corporate taxes), as well as multilevel resource dependencies that rely on them for the purchase of their goods and services. Multilevel resource dependencies for the Fortune 1000 include many small businesses. Hence small business owners should be concerned about the lack of progress among the Fortune 1000. Conversely, according to the expert testimony of Lou Marcoccio of Gartner Group to the U.S. Senate Special Committee on the Year 2000 Technology Problem on October 7, 1998, small businesses have completed 0–5 percent of their internal systems remediation. This should be a concern to companies who provide resources to small businesses, as well as mid-size and large businesses that depend on small businesses within their multilevel supply chains. This discussion leads us to two conclusions about external dependencies:

- Y2K assurances from external dependencies are only as good as the Y2K preparedness of their external dependencies.//
- Organizational Year 2000 compliance (as opposed to product compliance) is virtually impossible to state with certainty.

This second conclusion was reached in June 1997 by the Securities and Exchange Commission when it stated in its report to Congress, "It is not, and will not, be possible for any single entity or collective enterprise to represent that it has achieved complete Year 2000 compliance, and thus to guarantee its remediation efforts. The problem is simply too complex for such a claim to have legitimacy" (Securities and Exchange Commission, 1997).

Output Dependency Risks

Equally important and often neglected are the risks to *output dependencies* (customers, wholesalers, middlemen, value-added resellers, etc.) posed by the Year 2000 problem. The fact is that output dependencies frequently inconvenience their suppliers by canceling or changing orders, disputing invoices, or delaying payments. While these bumps in the road are often considered the cost of doing business, they can be significant. In the Year 2000 context, output dependencies negatively affected by Y2K may take similar actions, and the potential exists for simultaneous problems among different output dependencies. The impact posed by output dependencies was acknowledged by the Federal Financial Institutions Examination Council (FFIEC) when it issued the March 16, 1998 *Interagency Statement: Guidance Concerning the Year*

2000 Impact on Customers. This interagency statement notes the exposure that funds providers, funds takers (borrowers), and capital market/asset management counterparties pose to financial institutions. For this reason FFIEC requires banks to assess dependency exposure and mitigate it to the extent possible. The result of this requirement has been a series of Y2K preparedness questionnaires by federally supervised financial institutions to their customers. In addition to insurance renewal questionnaires, bank questionnaires are among the most commonly generated.

Sole-Source and Affiliated Suppliers

A *sole-source* provider is one for which an alternative is not readily available. Such resources pose a special risk to their customers. Alternative resources do not exist and typically these relationships have existed for long periods of time, and the futures of the organizations are inextricably intertwined. For this reason, organizations relying on sole-source providers must scrutinize the Year 2000 program and progress of the provider, paying special attention to external dependencies that support the provider.

Affiliated suppliers (those companies whose products or services are necessary parts of a customer's completed product or service) must also recognize their increased external exposure to Y2K. Simply put, affiliated suppliers are dependencies of one another. Failure of one business causes negative repercussions for all the others. For example, the GM Canadian brake manufacturer strike additionally affected those who produced the cars' chassis, wheels, glass, and so on, because GM temporarily stopped purchasing these products until production was restored.

Electronic Trading Partners

In addition to general Y2K failures among EBDs (internal systems, embedded systems, and multilevel external risks), there are unique areas of concern for electronic trading partners. Continuous and accurate data transmissions are vital to many businesses, such as securities, financial institutions, insurance, health care, and so on.

One issue will be problems in the transmission access itself. Successful transmissions are dependent on the successful operation of telecommunications switches, hubs, routers, internal systems (mainframes, client/servers, networks, PCs, and all the operating software and applications that run on them) as well as the electricity and facilities that power and house them. In other words, there are numerous critical failure points in any electronic data transmission.

The data itself can be incompatible as it travels from one system to another, causing misinterpretations or miscalculations. In this context, incompatible data is a more complete description than noncompliant data. Data transmission between one company that has successfully remediated, integrated, and tested its date data and one that has not, can cause errors—this is not the end of the analysis. The question of data compatibility requires further analysis.

Because *compliance* has no commonly accepted definition programmers, solutions providers, and consultants have used the term in many ways. In general, systems are commonly considered compliant where they correctly interpret and calculate date data and correctly account for leap years and days of the week. Some maintain that no *Year 99* problems should reside in the program or database records before a system can be deemed compliant. In this context, *compliance* is not synonymous with *compatibility* because there are numerous and inherently different methods of achieving compliance. Methods of correctly interpreting date data include field expansion, sliding or fixed windowing, encapsulation, hexadecimal, data compression, and so on. Each method is inherently incompatible with the other. Encapsulated data will be misinterpreted by a system using a fixed window without the existence of a bridge. So, companies that will be "compliant" before 2000 may nonetheless experience data transmission errors with their electronic trading partners because of incompatibilities between compliance methodologies.

A related aggravating circumstance is the issue of timing. When a company goes live with its newly converted date data, it affects all who exchange date data with the remediated system. Communication between electronic trading partners is understandably critical.

Responsibilities Within the Organization

As with most corporate challenges, success depends on organizational commitment and participation from all relevant personnel. The most effective way of ensuring a successful external compliance program is through *ownership*, *accountability*, and *monitoring progress*. This is the same rationale behind organizing Year 2000 steering committees and task forces in general. To address external exposures be sure the chief information officer, chief operating officer, chief financial officer, general counsel, and senior manager of sales/purchasing are members of the Year 2000 steering committee, and perhaps the Year 2000 task force as well.

Initiating an external compliance program and keeping it on track requires dedication and proper incentives. Year 2000 projects are burdensome and complex and will become disorganized without ownership, accountability, and progress monitoring. Identifying each EBD in and of itself can be a challenge. Department heads typically have the authority to procure their own supplies, maintain their own marketing channels, communicate directly with regulatory agencies, and interface electronically with customers and suppliers.

Each department must participate in the identification process at the managerial level. Often an initial vendor listing can be produced from the corporate accounting package. A chart of business partner categories should be distributed as a guide to each manager. Figure 5.2 is a suggested template of EBDs.

The business dependency template should be filled out by every department head and reviewed by the Y2K task force for overlap and comprehensiveness. As with all Y2K documentation, the collection of worksheets (or a summary thereof) should be kept within the organization's central repository. Whoever is assigned external Year 2000 risk management responsibilities should be familiar with the impacts of Y2K and the risks posed to the organization and have a demonstrated ability to accomplish difficult tasks.

Assessing and Managing External Business Dependencies

This section addresses the "how to" of managing EBDs. In risk management vernacular, it represents the risk analysis and risk control phases of the process. This section specifically treats resource dependencies and output dependencies as substantially similar. Even though suppliers generally have not demanded Y2K assurances from customers, this section presumes that they should as customer failures greatly impact upstream entities. For this reason, the term EBD is used intentionally to encompass both resource and output dependencies.

Once the inventory of resource dependencies is complete, organizations must assess and manage these risks. The most common questions asked regarding EBDs are, "How far should I go to verify external Year 2000 preparedness? What constitutes due diligence?" Unfortunately, there is no simple answer except "It depends." Your answer will correspond to the level of reliance on the particular dependency. With the benefit of 20/20 hindsight, legal counselors will be answering the due diligence question in Y2K negotiations, mediation, arbitration, and litigation. Considering the estimated cost of Year 2000 projects and anticipated operational failures, you should consider the post-2000 legal landscape. Organizations should make every effort to help their Y2K lawyers and arbitrators understand decision-making processes related to the Y2K project. Determining the relative level of dependence requires a consis-

138 Y2K RISK MANAGEMENT

Category	Business Dependency	Company X Y2K Compliance Contact
Resource Dependencies		
Raw Material Suppliers		
Consumer Products Suppliers		
Component Part Suppliers		
Office Supplies		
Information Suppliers		
Marketing Entities		
Service Providers		
Financial Institutions		
Output Dependencies		
Customers		
Clearinghouses/Conduits		
Financial Institutions		
Infrastructure Dependencies		
Transportation:		
Air Cargo		
Ground Transportation		
Maritime		
Rail Transportation		
Electric Power Supplier		
Telecommunications		
Gas Supplier		
Oil Supplier		
Water Supplier		
Other Dependencies		
Subcontractors		
Outsourcers		
Professional Services Firm		
Government Agencies		

Figure 5.2 Business dependency template.

tent and meaningful methodology. Again, looking at the problem from a corporate law perspective, directors and officers need not make correct business decisions. They must, however, make decisions that are well informed, in the best interest of the corporation, and that reasonable directors and officers would make. How an organization determines dependence and thereby identifies mission-critical dependencies can vary, but the process must be well documented.

One efficient method of prioritizing EBDs is to associate them with core business processes. This method is efficient because the same core business processes (once prioritized) can drive the triage for internal and embedded systems. A core business process is a set of functions or tasks essential to an enterprise's business operations. Examples include sales, business development, production, distribution, and customer service. Core business processes are not universal, and they vary with each organization. Other methods can include prioritizing business dependencies by products or services that generate maximum revenue or liability, support the most personnel, and so on.

Communications Program (Disclosure)

After resource dependencies have been prioritized, inquiries as to their Year 2000 preparedness must be made. To ensure consistent and germane responses from the resource dependencies, a communications program should be implemented. This program should include outgoing inquiries to resource dependencies, collection and interpretation of responses as well as the organization's responses to incoming inquiries. The importance of implementing a communications program cannot be overstated. These communications are forms of disclosure that may be the basis of significant Year 2000 litigation. For this reason, general counsel, outside counsel, or a qualified legal consultant should be a member of the Year 2000 task force. Communications programs should include three components.

Step 1: Initial Inquiries

Much has been discussed about the paper blizzard taking place throughout American businesses. Sending requests for information has become the *de facto* standard of care for addressing external compliance issues. These inquiries range from rudimentary to exhaustive. For some external exposures, it is not enough to send blind inquiries and wait for responses. The more critical the external dependency, the more detailed the inquiry and the more aggressive the follow-up must be. This process is *triage* applied.

The content of these inquiries is very important. External dependencies are generally reluctant to complete questionnaires. Sending unnecessary follow-up inquiries because of poorly developed or managed inquiries only decreases the chances of forthright and complete responses. Inquiries should delve into the subjects that are pertinent to your organization. For example, a software vendor not only provides the software but may also provide technical support, maintenance, upgrades, and/or fixes. For such vendors, asking about product compliance is not enough. Equally important is organizational compliance, which includes embedded systems remediation, external business dependency exposure mitigation, electronic trading partners coordination, and contingency plan construction and implementation.

The scope of the inquiry and level of detail vary tremendously. Some questionnaires are as simple as, "Are you compliant? If not, when do you plan to be?" Others require pages of information that take hours to complete. The following sidebar is a sample survey letter intended for the most basic of EBDs. It is provided as a base-line guide and is not intended as a guide for critical business dependencies. More detailed questionnaires should be commensurate with the level of risk and developed in conjunction with qualified consultants.

Sample Vendor Survey Letter

[Name/Address]
Re: The Year 2000 Computer Problem
Dear [Vendor]:

We are writing to request your assistance in addressing an important issue confronting all businesses that rely on information technology. As you may be aware, many computer systems that abbreviate date codes to two digits (e.g., 1998 as "98") will not be able to accurately process date information for years after 1999 (e.g., "00"). The Year 2000 problem is not limited to computers themselves but extends to computer-generated data that includes dates or date-sensitive calculations, as well as many kinds of automated equipment with embedded microprocessors that contain date logic, such as systems for fire safety, security, telecommunications, and building operations.

Because [Company] depends on [vendor] for services that are vital to our business operations, it is important that we communicate with you directly to ensure that your services will continue to be provided without interruption or malfunction throughout the century date change. Also, we need to obtain this information promptly because some Year 2000-related problems are likely to occur before the end of 1999 and the process of achieving compliance is lengthy and difficult.

In order to conduct this project as efficiently as possible, we have enclosed a one-page questionnaire, which will provide us with some basic information about your Year 2000 compliance efforts to date. Please return the questionnaire in the enclosed business reply envelope by [date]. We have also attached [Company's] definition of Year 2000 compliance to make sure that we are speaking the same language.

[Company's] goals in this effort are, first, to ensure that we can continue to provide the highest-quality services to our customers and, second, to maintain the productive business relationships we have enjoyed with our business partners, vendors, and suppliers. If you have any questions, please contact [name/title/phone], who is coordinating [Company's] Year 2000 vendor compliance program.

Thank you for your support.

[Signatures]

cc: [Vendor's contact person for Company]
    [Company's contact person for Vendor]

Certified Mail/Return Receipt Requested

Sample Year 2000 Questionnaire

1. Company name: _____

2. Please identify the person we should contact for business and technical information about your Year 2000 preparations and attach his or her business card:

   Name: _____
   Title: _____
   Company: _____
   Address: _____
   City, State, Zip: _____
   Telephone: _____
   Fax: _____
   E-mail: _____

3. Has your company developed a plan to address issues relating to the Year 2000?
   ❏ Yes ❏ No ❏ In process

4. When do you intend to complete your preparations to achieve Year 2000 compliance for your company's information technology systems? Date: _____

5. Has your company developed plans to address Year 2000 issues relating to:
   Other companies with which you do business?   ❏ Yes ❏ No ❏ In process

continues

(Continued)

Exchanging data with other companies? ☐ Yes ☐ No ☐ In process

Embedded microprocessors (e.g., in phones, security systems, heating/air conditioning)? ☐ Yes ☐ No ☐ In process

6. Are you aware at this time of any Year 2000-related problems that are likely to occur in connection with the services you provide to [Company]?
  ☐ Yes ☐ No ☐ Don't know

If so, please briefly describe the problems and when you anticipate they might start to occur:

_____

_____

Please return this questionnaire by [date] to: [name/address]

Thank you for your assistance. Please contact [name/title/phone] if you have any questions.

Sample Definition of Year 2000 Compliance

Year 2000 compliance means that neither the performance nor functionality of computer products, equipment containing embedded microprocessors, or other information systems is affected by dates prior to, during, or after the calendar year 2000 A.D. Year 2000-compliant products, equipment, and other information systems:

1. Will operate during each such time period without error of any nature relating to date data that includes, represents, or references the year 2000 or later years, or resulting from the passage of time from the year 1999 to the year 2000;

2. Will not terminate ordinary operations nor produce invalid or incorrect results as a result of date data that includes, represents, or references the year 2000 or later years, or the passage of time from the year 1999 to the year 2000;

3. Will specify the year in any date data either explicitly or by unambiguous implication in all interfaces and data storage; and

4. Will recognize and correctly process year 2000 date data as a leap year.

Step 2: Tracking and Analysis of Responses

From informal conversations among Year 2000 program directors, initial survey response rates are consistently between 10 and 30 percent. (The insurance and financial services industries generally report higher response rates, presumably because of their greater leverage.) For this reason follow-up may be warranted, either by repeated written inquiries, phone calls, e-mail, certified mail, site visits, or otherwise. Send copies of the compliance survey to the relationship manager for your company and the vendor so they can follow up with each other. Again, the greater the dependence, the more diligent the follow-up should be. Despite the cost of administering these surveys and persistent follow-ups, this is now the *de facto* standard of care for external compliance tracking.

Given the number of external dependencies and the importance of ensuring external compliance, an organized tracking system is recommended. Figure 5.3 is a suggested spreadsheet for tracking compliance statements from EBDs. This is yet another area that requires unusually diligent documentation efforts. Consistency in external dependency treatment is extremely important because of the liability implications. For example, company X tracks its suppliers diligently except for supplier Y. Supplier Y not only had not addressed its Year 2000 exposures, but it also had trouble spelling "Y2K." As it turns out supplier Y's shipping system was date dependent and wreaked havoc on supplier Y's distribution of its products for several weeks. Company X had not lined up an alternative supplier, breached numerous contracts with its customers, and lost bids it had been working on for months. Its earnings suffered, and the shareholders filed suit against the directors and officers for Y2K mismanagement. Because company X had been diligent in tracking a majority of its suppliers, attorneys for the shareholders could argue that company X created its own standard of care, which it failed to meet with regards to supplier Y. Such a case may be simpler to litigate than one that requires establishing an industry-wide or universal standard of care.

Step 3: Responding to Inquiries (Disclosures)

Another function of a Year 2000 communications committee (or any appropriate subcommittee of the Year 2000 task force) is to respond to inquiries from external dependencies. These inquiries generally come from insurers, financial institutions, and customers. Increasingly, suppliers and other resource dependencies are inquiring about customers' abilities to continue purchasing goods and services after January 1, 2000. Responding to these inquiries is a form of disclosure. For this reason in-house counsel, general counsel, or a

Number	External Business Dependency (EBD)	Date Inquiry Sent to EBD	Date Response Received	Completed Survey (S) or Form Letter (F)	Response Adequate (Yes/No)	Date of Inadequate Response Follow Up	Date of Second Follow Up	Date of Third Follow Up	Date of Fourth Follow Up
1									
2									
3									
4									
5									
6									
7									
8									
9									
10									
11									
12									
13									
14									
15									
16									
17									
18									
19									
20									
21									
22									
23									
24									
25									
26									
27									

Figure 5.3 External business dependency tracking spreadsheet.

qualified legal consultant should be a member of the Year 2000 communications committee.

The Year 2000 Information and Readiness Disclosure Act

As explained in Chapter 4, "Reducing Y2K Liability Exposures," *The Year 2000 Information and Readiness Disclosure Act* is designed to encourage businesses to voluntarily share Year 2000-related information including strategies, solutions, status, and tools with their contract partners, customers, and the public at large. There is a belief that the discoverability of these statements in the event of litigation has hampered such disclosures. The act renders unintentionally misleading and properly marked written statements inadmissible to prove the underlying facts contained within the statement. For Year 2000 statements generally (oral or written) the act prohibits all federal and state causes of action that are based on those statements, except to prove fraud by "clear and convincing evidence." This raises the bar for potential plaintiffs. It is hoped that companies will provide important and helpful information in the short time remaining before January 1, 2000. This evidentiary privilege protects only the documents themselves. It does not prevent companies and their attorneys from investigating underlying facts independently. The extent to which this act will quell liability concerns and encourage open and honest disclosures is yet to be seen.

Standardized Responses

Many companies refuse to complete questionnaires and instead forward standardized, preapproved compliance statements. This policy has multiple benefits. It allows for more expeditious responses compared to obtaining approval from the communications committee in each case. It ensures consistent disclosures, avoiding the risks of inconsistent disclosure-based litigation. It also provides a vehicle to uniformly disclose progress status updates. Updates or improvements in program status can be sent to entities that have previously been sent statements.

Some entities refuse to accept standardized responses and instead insist on the completion of their particular questionnaire. One of the primary reasons for such insistence is the definition of compliance. There is no accepted standard definition of Year 2000 compliance. Accordingly most questionnaires include a definition that the inquiring entity subscribes to (see the *Sample Survey Letter* sidebar). If the entity receiving the questionnaire adheres to the same or a substantially similar definition of Year 2000 compliance, there may be less concern about completing the questionnaire as asked.

Because of the prevalence of standardized disclosure statements, Year 2000 communications committees must reconcile these statements against their own questionnaires to determine if all their concerns were addressed. This can be an incredibly burdensome process, requiring money and allocation of limited intellectual capital.

As with outward investigation of external exposures, responses to inquiries received should be tracked and copies of each retained as part of the documentation repository. A tracking system should be developed and diligently maintained. Figure 5.4 is a suggested tracking system spreadsheet.

Quid Pro Quo Inquiries and Statements

A discretionary tactic to consider is the offering of compliance statements as part of a request for information (*quid pro quo statement*) or the inclusion of an inquiry as part of a disclosure statement (*quid pro quo inquiry*). Quid pro quo ("this for that") inquiries can be an effective means of obtaining valuable information. Insurers, banks, and other companies that routinely send inquiries have a vested interest in obtaining information about their clients' exposures and project status. Immediately upon receipt of a request for information, companies may want to send an inquiry of their own to these organizations. While a prudent communications program should encompass sending these inquiries regardless, the timing of simultaneous requests for information may improve the likelihood of receiving meaningful responses for both organizations.

Quid pro quo statements encourage forthright responses by offering information, showing a gesture of good faith, and demonstrating the type of information and level of detail sought. Some attorneys caution against offering any information beyond that which is absolutely necessary. Companies that have acted diligently and made reasonable progress should be encouraged to offer disclosures. Particularly in light of *The Year 2000 Information and Readiness Disclosure Act*, companies may want to consider offering this type of information if they hope to receive meaningful information from their external dependencies. Public companies that face disclosure requirements from the Securities and Exchange Commission may already be making their program status a matter of public record. Consistent disclosures pose no additional risk when included as part of a request for information.

A Note on SEC Disclosure Requirements

The SEC Interpretation, *Statement of the Commission Regarding Disclosure of Year 2000 Issues and Consequences by Public Companies, Investment Advisers, Investment Companies, and Municipal Securities Issuers*, dated August 4, 1998, is an onerous document. It all but chastises the securities

Number	External Business Dependency (EBD) requesting statement	Relationship- Vendor, Supplier, Customer, Other	Date Statement Sent to EBD	Survey (S) or Form Letter (F)	Was Follow Up Requested (Y/N)	Statement Authorized by	Quid Pro Quo Inquiry Sent?
1							
2							
3							
4							
5							
6							
7							
8							
9							
10							
11							
12							
13							
14							
15							
16							
17							
18							
19							
20							
21							
22							
23							
24							
25							
26							
27							

Figure 5.4 Disclosure tracking system.

industry for inadequate Year 2000 disclosures. It states that, "[W]hile the number of companies disclosing Year 2000 issues has increased dramatically [since the release of Revised Legal Bulletin No. 5], the task force surveys show that many companies are not providing the quality of disclosure that we believe investors expect." The statement goes on to liberally define *materiality*, the trigger for disclosure, to include those that have not yet completed impact assessments and those for whom the Year 2000 would be a material event despite efforts to prevent or mitigate it. This *worst-case* analysis is new, and the SEC makes expressly clear that, "[It] expect[s] that for the vast majority of companies Year 2000 issues are likely to be material, and therefore disclosure would be required." Once deemed material, public companies must disclose: (1) the company's state of readiness; (2) the costs to address the company's Year 2000 issues; (3) the risks of the company's Year 2000 issues; and (4) the company's contingency plans. The Year 2000 communications committee should approve all disclosures to ensure consistency, including SEC disclosures—yet another reason why counsel should serve an active role in the committee. The SEC Interpretation is discussed further in Chapter 8, "Major Corporate Decision Making."

Consideration of Alternative Resource Dependencies

Tracking external dependencies' compliance is only the first step. Incorporating the results into strategic planning is the next step. While preparing for external dependency failures overlaps somewhat with *contingency planning* in Chapter 6, it warrants discussion here. Armed with the information about its external dependencies' exposures and status, organizations now face the task of deciding what action to take, if any. A corporate policy on treatment of EBDs would ensure consistent treatment. Two general factors should guide this policy: (1) *confidence* in EBD preparedness and (2) *criticality*. Confidence is the net result of the compliance tracking system implemented above. Criticality ratings (or *triage*) are the net result of a business impact study of all EBDs. These two factors offset each other to some degree. Figure 5.5 highlights the conflicting nature of criticality and confidence.

The operative question is, for which EBDs should an organization arrange an alternative? If anyone had a crystal ball, making these decisions would be simple. Unfortunately it is not. Table 5.1 is a useful guide to follow in making these decisions. In this chart, "Replace" refers to a situation where an alternative EBD should be secured prior to 2000. "Arrange" refers to a situation where an alternative EBD should be located and arrangements made whereby a transition would pose minimal disruption. "Neither" refers to acceptable risk situations where no alternative EBD need be secured.

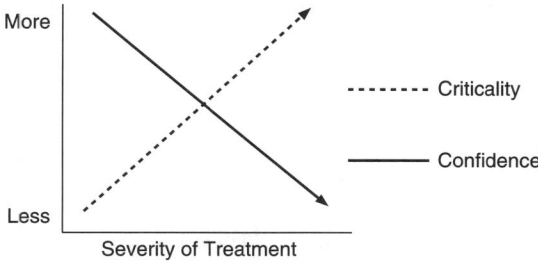

Figure 5.5 Importance of tracking.

Embracing Sole-Source Dependencies

The discussion so far has dealt with situations where alternative EBDs are available and a transition is feasible. Earlier discussions dispelled the myth that such circumstances exist as a matter of course. For circumstances where alternatives do not exist, a different approach is required. Where appropriate, an organization may choose to (or be forced to) embrace its sole-source supplier or most significant customer. Y2K is often called the greatest exercise in business management. Ultimately it is a business decision whether to expend resources to assist an EBD with its Year 2000 endeavors. Especially in circumstances where arranging for an alternative is not realistic, organizations may want to loan money, loan expertise, assume oversight responsibilities, or even assume control of the EBD's Year 2000 program. Despite the concern over assuming liability, a less adversarial, more cooperative approach may make good business sense.

Anticipating Marketplace Changes

Corporate Year 2000 strategy need not be completely defensive. Opportunities exist for organizations that can anticipate marketplace changes. Tracking marketplace changes can include the following:

Table 5.1 Guidelines for Securing Alternative External Business Dependencies

	LOW CONFIDENCE	MODERATE CONFIDENCE	HIGH CONFIDENCE
High Criticality	Replace	Arrange	Arrange
Moderate Criticality	Arrange	Arrange	Neither
Low Criticality	Arrange	Neither	Neither

- Identifying entities that may or may not survive the millennium bug unscathed
- Identifying entire industries that look likely to be affected by the millennium bug
- Identifying entire countries that look likely to be affected by the millennium bug
- Predicting consumer behavior before and shortly after January 1, 2000 as well as long-term implications
- Predicting future dependence upon or skepticism of technology generally

These endeavors can guide investment strategy and aid in long-term corporate strategy formation. Companies that suffer insurmountable Year 2000 problems will lose qualified personnel, lose customer base, become targets for acquisition, file for bankruptcy, or fail outright. The prototype company most at risk: a publicly traded corporation, heavily dependent on older information technology, with numerous multilevel dependencies (many of whom are themselves heavily dependent on older information technology), in a highly litigious industry, that has largely dismissed Y2K as a legitimate threat to its survival.

Conclusion

The Year 2000 is an unprecedented phenomenon. Never before has an event simultaneously threatened every business, large and small, core infrastructure, and government. The largest percentage of Year 2000 efforts have been focused on internal systems, but external exposures posed by this insidious problem are equally as significant.

Upon implementing an EBD program, we hope that you have now developed a sense of confidence as to which dependencies are critical to the organization, which are of particular concern because of their nonresponsiveness or lack of Year 2000 preparedness, and therefore which require incorporation to the organization's contingency plan. Chapter 6 deals with contingency planning directly, a significant portion of which is preparing for critical EBD failures.

CHAPTER 6

Contingency Planning

"The problem's going to be pretty bad."

—ANDREW S. GROVE, CHIEF EXECUTIVE OF INTEL,
WASHINGTON POST, APRIL 24, 1998

Giving your full attention to Year 2000 contingency planning is not giving up on fixing your systems—it's just good business. No matter how early you started on your Year 2000 remediation project, you can not guarantee that every system, interface, and business partner will be compliant. Despite your organization's and your business partners' best efforts at Year 2000 remediation, you must make contingency plans for your potential system failures as well as disruptions in utilities, in communications, and with business partners. Planning should include a range of scenarios, from worst case to best.

Overview

Simply put, contingency planning involves the proactive preparation of alternative work processes in the event of possible system or process failures. Year 2000 contingency planning is very different from planning for traditional information systems failures because of the increased likelihood of Year 2000-related disruptions. There are no guarantees that everyone's remediation efforts will be successful, so various failure scenarios must be assumed. The traditional model of information systems contingency planning is based on off-site data storage and computer *hot sites*. The idea has always been that if you have a data problem you recover your data from your backup or off-site archives. If you have a system problem that an IPL (initial program loading or restart) does not correct, then you go to your hot-site, where copies of your software reside on a different system. These solutions will not work if the data format, the application, or the operating system is the problem.

Y2K contingency planning needs to be performed for both your Y2K remediation projects and for your critical business operations. You should assume that system failures can occur as the result of incorrect date data or calculations or that they may occur due to external problems with power, telecommunications, or other business dependencies. Computer specialists have typically dealt with traditional disaster recovery relating to critical applications, systems, and data. Contingency planning for noninformation system disasters similar to those for floods, tornadoes, fires, explosions, and other calamities has normally been left to safety officials. Among these safety officials, plans are less common for the types of simultaneous and widespread (internal and external) problems that may result from Y2K. The possibility of extended electrical, gas, water, or phone outages, transportation disruptions, and supply-chain failures affecting critical resources such as food, raw materials, and consumer goods, presents a new challenge to contingency planners. For these reasons, many organizations will need to significantly increase efforts to develop contingency plans.

How Bad Will It Be?

It is impossible to predict just how bad Year 2000 problems will be. There is clearly *potential* for simultaneous and widespread disruptions and, therefore, the *potential* for some of the gloomier worst-case scenarios, but no one can accurately determine the *probability* of these disruptions given the current state of global risk assessments. Capers Jones, chairman of Software Productivity Research, Inc., in a paper titled "Probabilities of Year 2000 Damages" (February 27, 1998) estimates that there is a 55 percent probability of electrical service loss in excess of one day. He admits a large margin of error and stresses that it is impossible to determine the exact probability. Obviously, the level of remediation efforts in the remaining months will have a direct impact on the level of disruptions.

Contingency planners must assume the possibility of some service disruptions occurring. Disruptions include electricity outages that may exceed normal battery or generator operating times and telecommunications failures that will have secondary impacts on other systems. Other possibilities include failures that affect transportation (of both supplies and employees), failures of building environmental and security systems, failures of other electrical equipment including manufacturing and safety equipment, and general disruptions in the supply of goods and services.

Everyone will be watching business and government leaders for information on the likelihood and consequences of these types of failures occurring. Given the propensity of officials to be overly optimistic, it is prudent to assume problems will be more likely than leaders tell us. Even if the news appears generally optimistic, planning for disruptions is wise. Reasonable business judgment concepts will apply to the level of contingency planning that your firm conducts.

Why You Need Contingency Plans

As we've already noted, even the best project plan cannot eliminate all risks to your organization. This is particularly true in the case of the Year 2000 problem, which simply involves too many unknowns and external issues for anyone to feel secure about their state of readiness. Despite your best efforts, you may not have enough time or resources to guarantee Y2K compliance in time. Even if you have prepared thoroughly, you may experience sudden disruptions due to circumstances entirely beyond your control.

In a report provided to the U.S. Senate Special Committee on the Year 2000 Technology Problem (October 7, 1998), the Gartner Group disclosed that its research indicates that 30–50 percent of companies and government agencies worldwide will experience at least one mission-critical system failure through the first quarter of 2000. This figure is estimated at 15 percent in the United States. Ten percent of these failures are expected to last longer than three days. For small organizations, Gartner sets this figure as high as 50–60 percent (0.8 probability) (Marcoccio, 1998).

Given the possibilities for Y2K-related disruptions, preparing contingency plans is simply good business. These plans will allow you to continue business and minimize the negative impact on your business, your employees, and your customers. As noted earlier, given the limited time remaining, your Y2K efforts should be focused on ensuring that your most critical services remain operable into the new century. For this reason, contingency planning must be an integral part of your project—to avoid disruptions, to prepare for potential disruptions, and to guide you toward a permanent solution at the earliest time possible.

Essentially, contingency plans set your course if and when critical systems fail by providing backup plans to address unforeseen problems resulting from Y2K. Additionally, contingency plans can be employed when it becomes apparent that current remediation efforts might fail. In this case, contingency plans are implemented before an actual failure occurs and limit or minimize damages that might result. In constructing these plans, it is important to realize that Y2K contingency plans require a careful analysis to determine whether any of the usual alternatives will be available. This is one of the unique factors that make the Y2K contingency plans different from previous plans developed in the IT sector.

Your organization should have a contingency plan in place for each of its most important functions, systems, and equipment to ensure that your basic business functions can continue without disruption. Your contingency planning effort should consider your organization's hardware, software, and electronic equipment as well as the systems and infrastructure of external organizations and services that affect your operations.

The remainder of this chapter is organized along the contingency project planning phases and will provide to you a general understanding of contingency planning concepts. It is important to realize that each business unit will have to customize the planning approach to its particular circumstances.

Contingency Planning Project Phases

As shown in Figure 6.1, the contingency planning process involves four phases of activity:

Assessment. Organizing the planning team, defining the scope, prioritizing the risks, and developing failure scenarios.

Planning. Building contingency plans, identifying trigger events (criteria under which the plans will be used), testing plans, and training staff on the plan.

Plan Execution. Based on a trigger event, implementing the plan (either preemptively or reactively).

Recovery. Disengaging from contingent operations mode and restarting primary processes of normal operations by moving from contingency operations to a permanent solution as soon as possible.

Assessment Phase

The risk assessment process was covered in detail in Chapter 2, "Building an Effective Year 2000 Risk Management Program." During the assessment phase of contingency planning, you will organize and staff a contingency planning team. This phase includes scope definition, scenario development, and contingency planning prioritization. Information gathered can be used to set the agenda for your contingency planning effort. You should look at the current status of your risk management efforts and the products of the risk assessment efforts so far. Use this information to identify any additional areas that need attention. You should be able to quickly determine what systems or processes are the most important to your organization and which are most at risk. Critical systems information will be essential in prioritizing your contingency planning efforts.

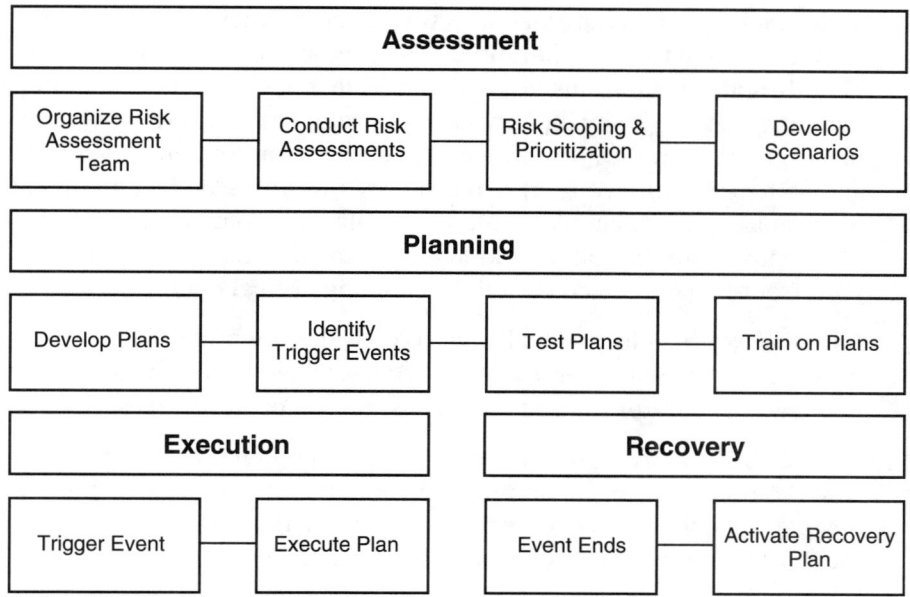

Figure 6.1 Contingency planning phases.

Organizing the Planning Team

Year 2000 contingency planning requires the same broad-based participation and support as described for the overall risk management effort in Chapter 2. You will need risk management and information technology professionals in addition to subject matter experts. People throughout the organization will need to understand the contingency plans, so include as many functional area staff as possible. Because these plans may involve the shutdown of some processes, the affected staff must be involved in the planning process. You will need to include staff from functional and line-of-business areas both for expertise and staff resource purposes. A good cross-section of your business is necessary to conduct a thorough risk assessment and to develop the scenarios that contingency planning requires. Consider selecting individuals who are known for having a "big picture" or "systems" way of thinking as well as those with hands-on operational expertise.

Developing Failure Scenarios

Failure scenarios can be of infinite number and variety. Even though there is no need to develop every conceivable failure scenario, you will want to consider as many as possible to choose the best ones to plan for. This effort should include not only day-to-day operations but also include key suppliers and business and data partners, as well as infrastructure components that are deemed critical to your operations. The primary objective of this step is to identify and prioritize business processes that are candidates for contingency planning. Begin by consulting your Y2K project plan and the inventory/assessment information that you have collected for your computer systems. This should help identify your critical processes, systems, and equipment. If you are preparing a project plan simultaneously with your contingency plans, simply identify your critical operations for both efforts. It's important to consult your front-line employees when determining critical operations.

As much as possible, you will want to consider the probability of various failures. Currently it is generally assumed that widespread power and telecommunications failures may occur, at least on a short-term basis.

If these failures occur, many other downstream failures are likely to follow. Have your contingency planning team conduct brainstorming exercises to develop as many scenarios as possible, and then decide which ones are the most prudent for your organization to plan for.

This is where the "big picture" and "system" thinkers will come in handy. It will take some effort to realize how interconnected your various systems may be or what the effects of extended outages will be. You will likely start with "what if" discussions like "what if the payroll system crashes?". You may then move on to consider the ramifications of multiple system failures. Additionally you will want to consider failures of different durations. For instance, if power outages exceed eight hours, most telecommunication systems' battery backups will be drained. If there is no alternative power source, telecommunications may fail. Longer outages may exceed the run time of generators due to fuel capacity issues. The secondary or "ripple effects" of these failures will need to be explored in developing your various failure scenarios.

Prioritizing Contingency Plans

Just as with system remediation and other risk management activities, you will need to prioritize contingency planning efforts. To prioritize you must first look at the risk associated with the system or process failure and then look at the time of expected failure. The first topic was covered earlier; use your risk rating to help prioritize your efforts. The second issue is one of timing; you need to identify each system's date-event horizon (DEH), the date at which that system might begin to fail. The DEH represents the absolute deadline before which contingency plans must be executed to prevent Y2K disruptions. Still, there will be situations where contingency plans should be implemented in advance of a system failure, not at the last possible minute.

Also consider the potential duration of the malfunction. If a systems failure will occur only on date rollover and can be easily reset then the need for contingencies for this failure is minimal. If, however, you are planning for malfunctions that will last until new systems are implemented, it is all the more important to have a good, workable plan in place that you can live with for an extended period of time.

You should develop a prioritization methodology that you are comfortable with. Typically this involves weighted criteria similar to the risk rating methodology discussed in Chapter 3, "Fast-Tracking a Year 2000 Project." David Myrick (1998) recommends a documented standardized methodology such as one where the priority is determined by the weight assigned to a particular characteristic multiplied by the value associated with that characteristic summed for all of the identified characteristics, as shown in this formula.

$$\text{Priority} = \sum_{i=1}^{n} W_i V_i$$

Defining the Scope of the Project

Once you have reviewed the failure scenarios and prioritized areas needing contingency plans it is time to define the scope of the project. It is important that you define a controllable scope before beginning the next phase of your contingency planning effort. The output of your triage and prioritization will be useful in defining the scope of your overall contingency planning effort. You should have previously completed the process of evaluating electronic and infrastructure risk at every location, identifying all the key components, their interdependencies, and their relative importance, and then developing failure scenarios. You will now need to use this information to draw a box around your contingency efforts—what risks will you address and which will your ignore? These will be critical business decisions and will require careful consideration.

It is important to realize that you can cover only a limited number of issues in the time available. The prioritization and risk rating will be critical to this process, but the difficult decisions will be in determining where to draw the line on contingency planning. It will be important to set achievable goals and not to dilute the effort by casting too wide a net. The idea here is to protect the *most critical* processes from failure.

Planning Phase

The planning phase is where you will actually develop contingency plans and define the events that will trigger their implementation. Additionally, testing and training are included in this phase. Developing the plans will involve an exercise to identify and evaluate various contingency alternatives based on scenarios developed in the preceding phase. As with the failure scenario effort, building the list of alternatives will require a careful analysis to determine whether the alternatives are likely to be available. Backup systems will not work when the data, the application, or the operating system is the problem.

Identifying Alternatives

Like failure scenarios, alternatives can be endless. Nonetheless, you must identify alternatives to be able to identify the best contingency options. Begin with the risks that were identified as top priorities; these should be the risks that would have the greatest negative impact on your organization's critical services and functions. A good starting point could be to review the alternatives contained in your existing emergency management or disaster recovery plans. You will want to use brain-storming techniques to maximize the list of identified alternatives.

It is important to consider all of your contingency options. Some contingency plans may be as simple as identifying a vendor that can quickly replace a critical piece of equipment. Other plans may involve outlining a series of manual steps to perform activities that normally are automated. Manual alternatives often require hiring and training additional staff and developing detailed procedures. Replacement automation, using a combination of in-house developed spreadsheets, databases, and compliant off-the-shelf applications, is an option. Some business processes may be fully supported by compliant off-the-shelf application packages that can be purchased and installed rapidly. Your plans may involve a technical solution (involving hardware, software, or equipment replacement), a business solution (such as manual procedures for your employees to follow), a quick fix (such as using generators for emergency electricity), or combinations of all three. In any case, your plans should identify dependencies and impacts, and the time and resources required to implement each contingency alternative.

Table 6.1 displays the array of choices that you may consider.

Table 6.1 Contingency Planning Matrix

OPTIONS	MANUAL OPERATION	REPLACEMENT	OUTSOURCING
Quick-and-dirty fix			
Partial fix			
Full fix			

Table 6.2 Contingency Planning Matrix Examples

OPTIONS	MANUAL OPERATION	REPLACEMENT	OUTSOURCING
QUICK-AND-DIRTY FIX	Go to manual process for priority customers only.	Have spare (compliant) hardware available.	Have temporary staff to fill the breach.
PARTIAL FIX	Use spreadsheet or database to provide some of the original system's functionality (capture data).	Use database or COTS package to replace system functionality.	Have contractor process payments off-site.
FULL FIX	Provide fully functional operations through manual process using additional staff as needed.	Abort repair effort and quickly implement a fully functional commercial system.	Move entire payroll operation to a commercial firm.

Your contingency planning team should develop numerous alternative responses for contingencies. A large number of alternatives may be developed during scenario brain-storming exercises—make sure that they are recorded and cataloged. (See Table 6.2.) Identifying good alternatives may require you to look at many. No workaround is too silly or preposterous to consider. Once a good list is established, you can then go back and decide which alternatives are best for your organization.

Workaround Alternatives

As we mentioned earlier, a good starting point for identifying alternatives is to review existing emergency management or disaster recovery plans. The following are some good examples of alternatives that may help you start the thinking process. Have *SWAT* (Special Wits and Technologies) teams standing by during the rollover to respond to system problems.

- Schedule additional personnel to handle problems that may occur.
- Schedule an additional New Year's holiday to permit system checking.
- Use emergency telephone systems, radios, or runners if public telecommunications services fail.
- Use manual processing (of invoices, orders, checks, etc.) if automated systems fail.
- Plan for shutdown and progressive restart of devices and systems that are considered at risk.

- Install generators in case the local power grid is not available.
- Preposition additional supply of fuel for generators in the event of extended power failures.
- Procure manual fuel pumps in case of electronic pump failures.
- Install wells or water tanks in case water utility is not available.
- Print two sets of payroll and/or vendor payments on the last run of the calendar year in the event that automated processing fails on January 1.
- Finish key projects or deliverables prior to January 1, 2000.
- Run end-of-month or first-of-month processing early (prior to January 1, 2000).
- Stockpile critical supplies prior to January 1, 2000.
- Shut down process, operation, or buildings on December 31 with controlled and phased-in startup after January 1, 2000.
- Put a moratorium on vacations for essential personnel and required leave periods for nonessential personnel before and after the rollover period.
- Do nothing and see what happens—sometimes called *fix-on-failure*.

Evaluating Alternatives

After establishing a complete list of alternatives, you will begin to weigh your options. In evaluating workaround options it is important to compare the costs, benefits, and risks of each. The alternative chosen for each system or process should be practical as well as cost-effective. It is important to consider both the financial costs and the difficulty involved in developing service delivery alternatives. In some cases, limited resources may force you to plan that important services may not be available or may be delayed because of the Year 2000 problem. While all alternatives, including "do nothing," should be considered, less active solutions may prove not to be desirable ones. The more practical alternatives are those that can be implemented with a reasonable level of assuredness that the functionality of the process will be maintained.

The most important factors to consider in the selection process are the following:

Functionality. The degree to which the contingency plan provides an acceptable level of service. Contingency plans may provide limited, partial, or full levels of functionality and will affect service levels accordingly. Also, a plan can be built in phases, so that manual workarounds are used to restore limited service or production for one or two weeks before converting to outsourcing to resume full operation if the contingency lasts longer.

Practicality. The degree to which it is reasonable in terms of the time and resources needed to acquire, test, and implement the plan. The plan must be final before the date-event horizon (DEH) is reached. Remember to consider the time needed for budget, procurement, and personnel processes.

Cost-Benefit. The degree to which the cost is justified by the benefit to be derived from the plan. This will be affected by the estimated time for operating in contingency mode and will include acquisition cost, testing, training, staffing, communications, and hardware/software costs.

Identifying Trigger Events

Once the planning team selects the best contingency alternative, it must then define triggers that will cause implementation of the plan. Trigger events are those events that will make you say, "OK, it is time to go to plan B." These events will include system failures or other events that make it apparent that you need to implement the contingency plan. Many trigger events, however, will be predefined "go/no-go" decision points. Given the time horizon of a system, the event that will trigger the decision to pull the plug on existing systems or processes may be a date set in advance of the anticipated failure or at a certain juncture or milestone in the remediation process. For example, if testing identifies that a system will begin to malfunction on September 30, 1999, and if repairs are not completed and tested by September 15, then an alternative process is implemented to prevent data corruption.

The information needed to define the triggers for each system or process will come from both the implementation schedule for the renovated or replaced mission-critical systems and the deployment time requirements for each contingency plan.

Examples of Trigger Events

Following are some examples of the types of events that can serve as triggers for your contingency plans:

- Word from vendor that software patch will be delivered late or will not be available
- Late discovery that an interface has serious problems
- Early (unanticipated) system failures—remediation/replacement not ready to substitute
- Year 2000 system failure (for example, bad data on reports or screens, lost transactions, etc.)
- Interface failures—noncompliant data exchanges

- Regional infrastructure failure (power, communications, financial systems, etc.)
- Implementation problems (for example, no more time or money)
- Erroneous or falsified claims of compliance discovered too late to initiate compliance action
- Your remediation project falling significantly behind schedule or having one or more team members quit

Developing Contingency Plans

Once alternatives have been chosen and trigger events identified, it is time to develop your plans. The actual contingency plan may be short and simple (as in the case of buy and install the latest version) or lengthy and complex (such as in a scripted manual process). Plans should be documented well enough that anyone can pick up the plan and understand what needs to be done to implement it. The contingency planning team or Y2K project office should maintain a master set of plans along with a schedule of trigger dates, resource information, and a complete contact list.

There is no one way to prepare contingency plans. The issues involved in Year 2000 contingency planning are new enough that best practices have not really emerged yet. Common sense is your best guide in making plans. Contingency plans must be custom made for your particular system or process as well as for your own situation and risk factors. An outline is presented next to give you an idea of how a contingency plan should be structured. For examples of working contingency plans, visit one of the Web resources listed at the end of this chapter. Your planning team, working with users and other personnel, must develop the specific details of your individual Year 2000 contingency plans.

The contingency plan should at a minimum include the following:

- A clear objective of the plan
- Implementation criteria or trigger events for invoking the plan along with procedures for implementing the plan
- Criteria for returning to normal operations
- Roles, responsibilities, and authority for all participants
- Resource requirements for operating the contingency plan
- Procedures for training on and testing the plan

Contingency Planning Outline

Contingency plans will vary with each system, process, and intended purpose. We have developed a generic outline to help you visualize what a contingency plan should include. As noted earlier, plans can range from very simple to very complex. The difficulty is in identifying the best plan or alternative process to best address the potential failure.

I. **Contingency Plan Title.** Use a fully descriptive title for the system or process that the contingency plan addresses. It should be clear in an emergency exactly what the plan covers.

   A. *System Mission Description.* Describe the basic functions and outputs of the system or process. Differentiate from complete or partial systems such as human resources or payroll.

   B. *System Specifics.* Describe in detail the system or process specifics. This can be as detailed as you like; it may not be necessary to go into great detail if specifics are not needed for the particular plan.

      1. *Current Platform or Technology.* Describe what technology the current system uses. Include hardware, software, and networking information.

      2. *Interfaces with Other Systems.* List all known interfaces. Information on data formats and bridge programs should be included if applicable.

      3. *Critical Processes and Outputs.* Describe exactly what the system does in terms of specific processes and outputs. Include reports and other outputs on which the business unit may rely.

      4. *Key Contact Information.* List key personnel that have responsibility for the system or process. Include those personnel that have a good working knowledge of the system.

II. **Objectives of the Contingency Plan.**

   A. *Risks of Failure.* What was determined to be the risk of failure? Include a copy of the risk rating form or other risk evaluation documentation. Describe the risk and how it would impact the business.

   B. *Risk of Contingency Plan.* Describe what risks are involved with using the chosen contingency plan alternative. How might they affect the business?

   C. *Desired Outcomes.* What are the desired outcomes in terms of output and level of service? How long do you intend to operate under the contingency mode?

   D. *Potential Impact.* What is the anticipated effect on the business or organizational unit in lower service or functional levels? This should include descriptions of potential impact in terms of financial, market share, and good will costs.

III. **Resource Requirements.**
   A. *Time Estimates*. Describe the estimated time required to implement the plan. Remember the approval processing time for necessary spending authorization and procurement processing.
   B. *Cost Estimates*. Determine the plan's budget for the cost of equipment, supplies, services, staff overtime, and so on.
   C. *Source of Funding*. Where will the money come from?

IV. **Implementing the Plan.**
   A. *Implementation Criteria*. Describe the basic criteria for implementing the plan. What will be the situation that prompts the decision to implement?
   B. *Trigger Events*. Describe the date or specific failure that will trigger implementation of the plan. You may want to describe the various scenarios that could lead to a trigger event.
   C. *Responsibilities*. Detail who is responsible for making implementation decisions. If you have a clearly documented trigger event this could be whoever is on duty at the time the event happens.
   D. *Duration*. What is the estimated length of time that contingency operations will cover? Are there different phases of the plan to restore differing levels of service?

V. **Operation and Management.**
   A. *Management Structure*. To the degree necessary, describe the management structure that will be used to ensure smooth operations under the contingency plan.
      1. *Decision Makers*. Who will be making the decisions to implement, change, and discontinue the contingent operations?
      2. *Support Personnel*. What support personnel will be used to implement and operate processes under the plan.
   B. *Assigned Roles and Responsibilities*. Provide details on who will do what under the plan.
      1. *Emergency Response or SWAT Teams*. Here you should describe the teams that will be used to respond to emergencies or breakdowns. These may be the same teams that are used to implement the plan in the event of premature or unanticipated failures.
      2. *Contingency Operations Team*. Provide detailed information on the team that will run the process or system
   C. *Personnel Notification Procedures*. Describe how you plan to notify staff that the plan is being implemented. Given the possibility of

telecommunication disruptions, you may want to have an automatic response (in the event the phones go dead or the power goes out) or have teams standing by at critical times and dates.

D. *Records Management Procedures.* Describe how you plan to manage records issues. Consider reports and data dumps that will be useful in the recovery phase.

E. *Data Security Procedures.* Describe the processes to be employed to ensure data security, recovery, integrity, and confidentiality. Contingency plans may open the door to significant security issues. Review systems security and access rights, data integrity assurance procedures, and records confidentiality procedures.

VI. **Criteria for Returning to Normal.** Here you will describe how you will determine that it is time to discontinue the contingency mode and return to the normal operation mode.

A. *Criteria.* Describe the conditions or events that would lead to returning to normal operating mode. The criteria should include certification that the system or process is functioning normally.

B. *Procedures.* Describe the detailed procedures required to return to normal operating mode.

C. *Points of Contact/Notifications.* List key personnel who have responsibility for returning the system or process to its normal operating mode.

1. *Decision-Makers.* Who will be making the decisions to discontinue the contingent operations and begin the recovery process?

2. *Operational Personnel.* List the key operational resource personnel who will be needed to return to normal operations.

3. *Business Recovery Team.* Include detailed information on the team that will run the process of resuming normal operations after the contingency period.

4. *Business Partners.* List any business partner relationships (internal and external) that will be involved in resuming normal operations.

VII. **Training and Testing Requirements.** Describe the training and testing requirements that are required to prepare for implementing the contingency plan. Training may include desktop exercises and rehearsals to ensure smooth implementation of the plan. Testing is used to validate the plan's capabilities.

A. *Contingency Team Training.* What training will be required for the contingency operations team? Will they need to be trained on new or different processes? Will they need to practice manual operation scripts? Will you include a drill?

B. *Recovery Team Training.* What training is required for the team that will bring processes back online?

C. *Testing Requirements and Procedures.* Describe the plans and requirements for testing the contingency plan. Testing is required to validate the plan and ensure its completeness. Include test scripts and other detailed testing procedures.

D. *Training and Testing Schedules.* Document the timeline for training and testing that will ensure readiness of both staff and the plan prior to the DEH of the system or process.

Testing Contingency Plans

Testing contingency plans is necessary to validate the effectiveness, feasibility, and capacity of the chosen alternative. Once the plan has been developed, the planning team should immediately develop test plans and test scripts for the new plan. You may want to consider having a different team develop and conduct the test or using outside consultants to get a fresh and independent look at your planning assumptions.

This effort is needed to validate the assumptions behind your plan. Complete integration testing and dress rehearsals are the best way to validate your plan's capacity to support your operations. You may determine, however, that full-scale testing is cost-prohibitive. In that event, you may want to test only key components or processes. The highest level of assurance would come from using outside experts to perform independent validation and verification (IV&V) of the plan.

If testing results in the discovery of problems, you will need to cycle back through the development process and revise and retest the plan as needed. As a part of this process, you should also document the final test results and update plans as required. This step will include final determination of the resource and time requirements for implementing the plan. Once revisions are completed, you should obtain management approval for the final plan.

Training for Contingency Plan Execution

Once the plan is finalized, training on the contingency plan is necessary to ensure its smooth and successful implementation. The documentation in the plan should be detailed enough to provide the step-by-step guidance needed. You can not expect staff to pick up a plan during a crisis and read about what they should do. All parties involved will need to be trained on all of the new procedures or practices envisioned under the plan as well as on what their assigned roles will be.

Some of the best training practices include walk-throughs and desktop exercises. For the most critical planning areas, full dress rehearsals will be required to ensure that everyone knows what they are supposed to do and how to do it. This process will also uncover any flawed assumptions in the plan.

Plan Execution

The contingency plan should be implemented when a trigger event occurs or when management decides to reduce risks. Contingency plans may be put into effect anytime to prevent a service disruption. The objective of the plan execution step is to manage the operation of the contingency plan as smoothly and efficiently as possible.

The training and testing that should have previously occurred will go a long way to ensure the successful implementation of your plan. Strong communication and management, however, will also be key. You must make sure that everyone in the organization knows that the contingency plan is being put into effect. Notification of key personnel and emergency response teams should be followed by communication to all staff and customers. You should let anyone affected by the plan know that the plan has been activated and the expected duration of the contingency mode.

Strong management oversight will likely be needed during these periods of contingency operations. If warranted, emergency operations centers should be established to ensure that oversight and rapid decision making can occur. Training and rehearsing the management team in emergency operations concepts and drilling this team are good ideas.

Recovery

Your contingency plan will need to include business resumption and recovery planning. It is important to have a plan for "standing down" from the contingency mode and for the resumption of normal business activities after the contingency has ended. You may choose to organize separate business resumption teams to develop these specific plans.

Disengaging from Contingent Operations

As you did with the preparations for implementation of the plan, you will need to determine trigger events for ending the contingency mode of operations. What events will be required to determine that it is safe to "stand down" and to begin the recovery phase? You will want to conduct post-2000 testing of the primary systems and process to ensure that they are operating appropriately. Test plans and scripts for these tests should be predetermined.

Once the organization is confident that it is safe to disengage from the contingency mode, staff will need to have step-by-step instructions for stopping the contingency process and transitioning to the primary process. Depending on the situation, these instructions may need to cover data transfer and archival as well as various data management and table maintenance issues.

Restarting Primary Processes

Restarting primary processes leads your organization from its contingency operations to a stable, permanent solution. If you are returning to the original process or system, you will need to make sure that it is tested and operating smoothly. Data captured in the contingency mode will need to be transferred to the new system. Staff will need to transition out of the contingency mode and back into the normal operating processes. Restarting will be simple for many applications, but it could be quite complex for manufacturing or other integrated processes. Supplies of raw materials will need to be reestablished and production lines brought back up to speed.

In the event that the primary system is fatally affected and the contingency plan provides a sufficient level of service, you may decide to make your contingency solution permanent. In this case, your reinstatement activities may already be complete. If your Y2K remediation efforts were under way but incomplete at the January 1, 2000 deadline, resumption would simply require you to complete your organization's transition to its converted systems.

Emergency Management

Emergency management is a type of contingency planning for which most governments and businesses routinely plan. It includes responses to potential emergencies such as fires and tornadoes. The Y2K problem is such a potential emergency, and, like a hurricane, we know it is coming. The good news is that, unlike a hurricane, we have time to prepare.

Businesses need to be aware of the added risks from some of the worst Y2K scenarios. Retail operations can be affected if panic buying or looting occurs. Property damage can result from extended power outages. Manufacturing processes can be severely affected when liquid product cools in the pipes.

Recently we have seen several local governments announce plans to conduct Y2K disaster drills. Emergency management officials are now developing scenarios and plans to respond to them in light of the potential for long-term and widespread infrastructure failures. Your safety officials should work to review and revise existing disaster plans and look for new areas that need disaster plans.

Chuck Lanza, the Director of the Miami-Dade (Florida) Office of Emergency Management (Lanza, 1998, used with permission) has prepared an emergency response plan that identifies and prioritizes functions and services as follows:

1. Food and water
2. Utilities (electric, natural gas, water, and sewer)
3. Energy (fuel)
4. Protective services (police, fire, and EMS)
5. Transportation
6. Health care
7. Communications
8. Information dissemination
9. Government
10. Education
11. Economy

For each function and service, Mr. Lanza suggests that you take the following actions:

- Identify threats.
- Develop threat monitoring procedures.
- Identify actions that may eliminate the threat in advance.
- Identify actions that may be taken to minimize the impact of the threats if they materialize.

As an example, Mr. Lanza suggests that the food and water function might have the following plan:

I. Identify threats
   A. Pre-event hoarding
   B. Post-event shortages
   C. Run on markets and food distribution centers
II. Develop threat-monitoring procedures
   A. Pre-event hoarding
      - Establish liaison with major grocery chains for early warning of hoarding

B. Post-event shortages
- Establish liaison with major food distributors to obtain periodic inventory of local food supply

C. Run on markets and food distribution centers
- Establish liaison with major supermarkets for early warning of runs on markets and distributors

III. Identify actions that may eliminate risks in advance

A. Pre-event hoarding
- Public education
- Voluntary rationing plan
- Mandatory rationing plan

B. Post-event shortage
- Establish liaison with food producers in local area to gain control of local food inventory if necessary

C. Run on markets and food distribution centers
- Develop a market protection plan with local law enforcement agencies
- Inform public of market protection plan

IV. Identify actions that may be taken to minimize the impact of risks that may materialize

A. Pre-event hoarding
- Public education
- Voluntary rationing plan
- Mandatory rationing plan

B. Post-event shortage
- Establish liaison with food producers in local area in order to gain control of local food inventory if necessary

C. Run on markets and food distribution centers
- Develop a market protection plan with local law enforcement agencies
- Inform public of market protection plan

Mr. Lanza notes that even if Y2K turns out to be a nonevent, the effort put into high-level planning and training will improve response capabilities for other threats.

Year 2000 Contingency Planning Resources

Dealing with the Year 2000 Problem. Author Steven Davis' site has information on risk management, contingency planning, and emergency management.
www.erols.com/steve451/impact.htm

Journal of Business Continuity. This site provides information and news on business continuity.
www.business-continuity.com/business_continuity.html

ZDY2K Web site. This site has several good articles on contingency planning and community preparedness, including "Contingency Planning Step by Step"
www.zdnet.com/zdy2k/1998/09/4796.html.

Social Security Administration—Business Continuity and Contingency Plan.
www.gsa.gov/gsacio/ssay2kb1.htm

For planning matrices, a link from the SSA site points to a PDF document.
www.gsa.gov/gsacio/ssamatr3.pdf

Y2K Contingency Management Plans—Provided by Electronic Systems Center and The MITRE Corporation.
www.mitre.org/research/y2k/docs/CONTINGENCY_PLAN.html

Guidelines for Contingency Plan Development—The U.S. Fish and Wildlife Service.
www.fws.gov/pullenl/security/contpln.html

FDIC—Guidance Concerning Contingency Planning.
www.fdic.gov/banknews/fils/1998/fil9851b.html

State of Texas—Guidelines for Contingency Planning.
www.dir.state.tx.us/y2k/resources/guidebook2000.

Disaster Recovery Institute of Canada—Professional Practices for Business Continuity Planners.
www.dr.org/ppover.htm

Year 2000 Journal Articles. This publication specializes in technical Year 2000 issues but has had several excellent articles on Y2K contingency planning
www.y2kjournal.com/hot/contingency.htm

California Energy Shortage Contingency Plan—A good example of a complete contingency plan.
www.energy.ca.gov/contingency/introduction.html

General Accounting Office—Year 2000 Computing Crisis: Business Continuity and Contingency Planning.
www.gao.gov/special.pubs/bcpguide.pdf

Conclusion

By now you should realize that good contingency planning requires substantial effort. This effort is needed to protect your organization from the disruptions that may occur as well as the loss of business that would result from the potential Y2K disruptions. Reasonable business judgment can be expected to require that you make sufficient efforts to prepare contingency plans. This does not mean that you should stop remediation efforts and do nothing but contingency planning. It means that you must determine where contingency plans are needed and make sure that a "plan B" will be available for the most critical systems should remediation efforts fail or, despite your best efforts, the systems themselves fail.

Contingency planning must be seen as part of the overall approach to risk management. It is not a substitute for any of the other components of the overall risk management effort. Contingency plans are an important backstop for the most critical and at-risk systems.

Chapter 7, "Major Corporate Decision Making," extends our analysis beyond maintaining current systems and operations. The discussion considers ways in which enterprises should include Year 2000 risk management into strategic corporate initiatives.

CHAPTER 7

Major Corporate Decision Making

"The typical organization is like an enormous mass on a frictionless surface."

—DANIEL S. APPELTON

The Year 2000 problem has broad, sweeping implications. Most companies consider the year 2000 as a target for corporate achievement or a symbolic transition point toward future projects and goals, but the millennium bug could scuttle many of those plans. This chapter deals with proactively incorporating Y2K thinking into making major corporate decisions and reassessing strategic goals. Incorporating Y2K considerations into primary business initiatives has two important and interdependent dimensions: avoiding short-sighted mistakes and capitalizing on new opportunities.

Disclosures and Communications

Chapter 5, "External Compliance Strategies," dealt with external exposures and specifically addressed establishing and administering a corporate communications plan that both proactively sought assurances of compliance among, and reactively responded to, inquiries from external business dependencies. This section focuses on the process of deciding whether to volunteer information about your organization's Year 2000 status or the status of IT products currently for sale or previously sold.

Organizations are beginning to incorporate Y2K into strategic marketing. More and more, advertisements are appearing for products and services that the providers believe are fully compliant. For example, companies such as ADP,

Lexis-Nexis, Abacus Law, and IBM have all advertised that their products, services, or enterprises are Y2K compliant.

But for some companies, the decision whether to disclose information about organizational or product Year 2000 capabilities is a major corporate decision. Publicly traded companies in volatile industries or those in highly competitive markets should consider the impact disclosure will have on market capital and the functional repercussions that can cause.

So far Wall Street has had mixed reactions to various Year 2000 disclosures. Most large organizations that have announced substantial expenditures to address Y2K issues have not experienced instantaneous drops in stock value. Examples include General Electric ($500 million) and Citicorp ($300 million), among others.

Wall Street, however, did react negatively to Moody's downgrading of Executive Risk Management Associates (ERMA) because of concerns about Year 2000 claims filed against its Director & Officer's insurance portfolio. Almost overnight, ERMA's stock went from $75.00 per share to $32.00.

One conclusion may be that Wall Street reacts well to announcements perceived as positive steps toward remediation and negatively to announcements of potential liabilities or disruptions. By the time this book is printed, the first round of SEC 10Q forms under the new, more stringent disclosure guidelines will have been filed, and we will have a better sense of precisely how investors react to certain types of Year 2000 disclosures.

Decisions about communications to customers and resource dependencies can also be a major corporate decision. Revealing that a mission-critical system has been identified as noncompliant may give customers and trading partners concerns about the future of the business relationship. Customers may even abandon the relationship in favor of suppliers that state that they are fully compliant or remain elusively silent on the issue. These business pressures are very real and could inhibit forthright disclosures about Y2K.

As Year 2000 becomes a mainstream issue, corporate America and Wall Street may come to understand the problem well enough to change their attitudes toward Y2K disclosures. One truism about Year 2000 is that all companies have Y2K exposures. Those willing to disclose their exposures and risk management program may, in fact, make better business partners than those viewed as having something to hide. With less than one year remaining before January 1, 2000, the short-term concern over losing a customer should be weighed against the liability that may stem from false, misleading, or inaccurate business communications.

Mergers and Acquisitions

Few corporate decisions are as major as whether to merge, acquire, or be acquired. Since 1996 we have seen unprecedented frequency of corporate restructuring. Y2K is likely to slow some of these transactions in 1999, but others will surely continue. Year 2000 will add significant risk management consideration to the M&A calculus.

Year 2000 Mergers and Acquisitions Due Diligence

Mergers and acquisitions are perhaps the best example of functional due diligence, inasmuch as legal, business, and accounting due diligence have long been standard practices. The greater the corporate decision, the greater the deliberation of Year 2000 issues should be. Unfortunately, although Year 2000 is both universal and pervasive, Y2K due diligence is not yet common practice. The need for such a due-diligence check should be obvious. Reasons to perform Y2K M&A due diligence follow.

Overvaluation

The correct valuation of the target entity is of paramount concern throughout the M&A due-diligence process. Incorrect valuations can lead to incorrect profit projections and, if the discrepancy is significant, shareholder derivative suits. Y2K can affect the functional value of a corporation in fundamental ways.

Underestimation of Expenses

Establishing cost estimates in light of Y2K remains a difficult issue. The American Institute of Certified Public Accountants (AICPA) and the Federal Accounting Standards Board (FASB) have addressed accounting for the costs associated with Y2K repairs and replacement of computers. Other hidden Y2K costs may exist as well, such as increased inventory and interest charges and other contingency planning expenses.

Cost of Y2K Remediation and Risk Management

Cost estimates of Year 2000 risk management efforts (including remediation, contingency planning, new purchases, etc.) on a national scale are quite substantial. Cap Gemini estimates that total spending for Y2K may amount to 8 percent of the total $1.5 billion IT spending for the United States, or $120,000,000. The Gartner Group's estimates are significantly higher at 5 percent of IT budgets in 1997, 21 percent in 1998, and 44 percent in 1999, or $1.05 billion over the 3-year period. Not surprisingly, corporations have struggled to budget for Y2K, with both over- and under-budgeting. Clearly, incorrect budgeting of Y2K corrective measures can affect the accuracy of the purchase price of the target company.

Costs Resulting from Y2K-Caused Business Failures

The costs an organization will incur as a result of Y2K events is much harder to predict. As a general rule, however, organizations making greater progress on their Year 2000 efforts should experience fewer Y2K events and those with effective contingency plans should experience less severe disruptions and costs. Short-term spending on emergency repairs of systems, substitute procurements, or stockpiling as part of a contingency plan all will negatively affect the accuracy of the purchase price. These costs are predictable on a relative basis.

Overestimation of Revenue

Year 2000 is expected to affect customers and clients just as much as suppliers and vendors. Increased disruptions and expense among customers may result in temporary delays in payment or discrepancies in monies owed. An example of this type of disruption is the impact Y2K can have on an accounts payable or check production system. For these reasons, M&A due diligence should include an evaluation of customers and clients and their ability to continue to pay for services rendered or goods supplied.

Effect on Net Income and Profitability

Both increased expenses and decreased revenue affect net income and hence profitability. One of the keys to an accounting due diligence is a pragmatic review of the accuracy of net income projections. Y2K can also affect profitability by causing operational disruptions, delays, damaged goods, and service errors. These, too, can be evaluated by investigating the overall Year 2000 program against best-practice standards.

Effect on Taxes

Errors in net income can result in increased tax obligations at both the federal and state levels. Tax penalties are not the only risk to the organization. Errors in tax estimates are a red flag for plaintiff's attorneys and shareholders, potentially triggering shareholder derivative suits and other complaints by corporate stakeholders.

Oversight of Discoverable Potential Liabilities

The legal due-diligence process is intended to uncover contingent liabilities by reviewing corporate documents, business plans, and contracts, as well as business operations generally. Year 2000 should be part of legal due diligence to establish that best-practice standards are employed, deadlines are met, and program goals are attainable and receiving sufficient resources. The following are categories of M&A legal due diligence that can be affected by Y2K:

- Strategic issues
- Property (tangible)
- Patents, trade secrets, trademarks, copyrights, and other intellectual properties
- Environmental and safety
- Contingent liabilities, including guarantees, contractual indemnities, and warranties
- Pension plans (defined benefits)
- Management
- Manufacturing
- Transportation
- Research and development
- Insurance
- Product liability exposures

Because each of these categories can be affected by Y2K, either the legal due-diligence process should be amended to include Year 2000, or a separate Y2K investigation is in order.

M&A Disclosure Requirements

Just as the SEC requires disclosure of material information as part of various corporate filings, disclosures during the M&A process are equally required if deemed "material." In Chapter 8, "Substantiating Due Diligence," we discuss in detail the SEC guidelines and the test for materiality.

Technical and Business Risks

Several technical and business risks are associated with merging with or acquiring another entity. Some of these are described next.

Systems Integration

Integrating computer systems is a complex process, requiring substantial time, personnel, and financial resources. The ITAA estimates that only 17 percent of all IT projects are completed on time and on budget. Large systems integration projects are among the most complex and often encounter significant problems. In the Y2K context, integrating a compliant system with a noncompliant system poses obvious problems where date data is merged and processed.

Incompatible Compliance

Besides the issue of compliant versus noncompliant systems, CIOs involved in corporate restructuring must also be concerned with incompatible compliance. There are several accepted methods of code conversion or other solutions to date data processing. Unfortunately, these methods are inherently incompatible, and remediation projects may have to be altered midstream or bridges might have to be built to integrate corporate systems successfully. Obviously, time is short, and alternatives, such as waiting to integrate certain systems until after 2000, must be considered. The cost of altering Y2K programs, building bridges, operating and maintaining separate systems, and building appropriate firewalls should be incorporated into the due-diligence process.

Operational Disruptions

Projections, estimates, and synergies between organizations can all turn out to be false assumptions if Year 2000 failures impair operations. Operational disruptions can occur in an infinite variety if Y2K affects internal systems, embedded systems, external business dependencies, or electronic trading partners.

In evaluating synergies between corporations as part of the M&A process, the integration team looks to improve overall efficiency by modifying methodologies, processes, and management structures. This business process improvement can also occur within one organization apart from an M&A situation.

Business Process Improvement

Over the course of the last decade, enterprises of all types have examined their business operations with an eye toward increasing efficiency. The theory behind this trend has been to increase efficiencies that would translate into a healthier bottom line. Some methods used to realize this goal include corporate reorganization, quality improvement, outsourcing, and business process reengineering, to name a few. For purposes of this discussion, we will classify all of these efforts as *business improvements*. The decision to take an enterprise through the ambitious exercise of business improvement is one of the most significant decisions management will make. Among the other issues raised by business improvement, Year 2000 challenges should also be considered.

The types and effects of business improvements vary to a significant degree. *Corporate reorganizations* focus on reshaping the organizational aspects of an enterprise. For example, an enterprise may "flatten" its organization by removing layers of middle management or certain operational departments. A *quality improvement* exercise uses an enterprise's existing corporate framework and focuses on incremental improvement of the business processes. *Business process reengineering*, or BPR, is the most extreme of business improvements. In the seminal text, *Reengineering the Corporation: A Manifesto for Business Revolution*, Michael Hammer and James Champy defined business process reengineering as "the fundamental rethinking and radical redesign of the business processes to achieve dramatic improvements in critical contemporary measures of performance, such as cost, quality, service, and speed" (Hammer, 1994). In essence, BPR means starting from the beginning. No consideration is given to incremental improvement of past processes.

A common element in most types of business improvement is the use of information technology to support the effort. Although IT should not be the driving force behind a business improvement effort, it is an integral part of its overall success. The decision of what type and to what extent IT is used to support a business improvement effort is likely to create Year 2000 concerns. These issues include compliance and interoperability of IT systems (including embedded systems) within the enterprise, a mission-critical business process's reliance on potentially noncompliant IT systems, and the ability of external business partners to continue trading information with noncompliant IT systems. The role of IT and the potential for Year 2000 disruptions are inextricably linked.

Role of the Decision Maker

Business improvements, though quite disparate, share a common element. Each such effort requires leadership at different levels of the organization, from the CEO to senior managers. To be effective, the leader must be able to focus on the overall goals of the business improvement and overcome resistance from those charged with implementing the required changes.

The business improvement leader must consider all Year 2000 implications of the business improvement for it to be successful. Failure to do so will jeopardize not only the effort, but the viability of the enterprise. In other words, if the enterprise experiences Y2K-related disruption, not only will the company fail to get ahead of its competition, but the enterprise may very well fall *behind* its competition. To communicate the importance of Year 2000 to the business improvement initiative, the leader (or leaders) should be part of the

Y2K project team to ensure that Year 2000 issues are identified and addressed throughout the enterprise. Clearly, any decision that involves the enterprise's business processes will have Y2K implications. Communication among the members of the Year 2000 task force and the change leader is necessary to identify potential risks early in the effort and to mitigate problems early in the project.

The Y2K Factor (Internal Systems, Embedded Systems, EBDs)

The effect of internal systems disruption on the business improvement effort is perhaps the single greatest threat to its success. For example, the acquisition of software to improve business processes is a significant aspect of most business improvement efforts. This software is extensive enough to affect several mission-critical business processes. If the software is not compliant, the enterprise could virtually shut down. Thus, the business process leader should plan to assess and test all software for Year 2000 compliance, and incorporate that work into the business improvement plan timeline, particularly for business improvement projects that are well underway. Analyzing Year 2000 readiness is a time- and resource-consuming process that deserves special resource allocations so that it is performed correctly and in concert with the business improvement plan. An outside consultant specializing in Year 2000 should be brought in to discuss the effects of noncompliant IT systems on the success of the improvement plan.

One specific IT business improvement decision is whether to move to an *enterprise system*. These systems, which are also known as *enterprise resource planning* (ERP) systems, are designed to provide seamless integration of all enterprise information. Enterprise systems are typically massive commercial products that require a significant commitment in terms of time, effort, and money. The decision to go the enterprise system route is not one that should be made lightly. Obviously, the decision maker should consider whether the system will be Year 2000 compliant. A written inquiry should be made to the manufacturer of the enterprise systems as to the compliance status of the product as well as the compliance status of the company (for maintenance issues). Further, if consultants are used to implement or manage the enterprise system, a written inquiry about their Y2K readiness is appropriate.

Apart from the acquisition of new software, the consolidation or elimination of certain business processes has Year 2000 considerations. For example, risk assessment and contingency planning focus on core business processes (CBPs). CBPs are those business processes that directly affect the enterprise's ability to execute its mission. If an organization is planning to add, remove, or re-designate certain groups of activities as CBPs, the Y2K effects must also be analyzed.

Another aspect to business improvement is outsourcing of some business processes. Corporate decision makers, as a method to cut costs, are hiring consulting firms to take over the operation of discrete business processes; hence, outsourcing. The outsourcing entity should be treated as an EBD and analyzed accordingly. Questions raised by outsourcing include what will be the effects on the enterprise's operations if the outsourcing entity is not fully prepared for Year 2000, with effective business continuity, contingency planning, and disaster recovery strategies.

Business Improvement Programs

Generally, decision makers and management should look at the processes and the supporting IT, embedded systems, and EBD that will be affected by the change. With reorganization, it is important to reconcile the Year 2000 project with personnel changes. For example, an enterprise-wide Y2K contingency plan requires that certain personnel execute certain tasks. Thus, the proper personnel with knowledge of the steps for implementing the plan must be in appropriate roles within the organization. In terms of business improvement initiatives, it is important to understand the nexus between the organizational changes and Year 2000. The leader of the business improvement project should ask the consultants about the potential Year 2000 implications of planned changes and communicate the changes and the project's status to the rest of the Y2K task force.

If core business processes are being outsourced, or if there is a plan to outsource, the Year 2000 project team should work with the outsourcing decision maker to ensure that the outsourcing agreement contains provisions outlining the Y2K-related responsibilities. The outsourcing entity should receive Year 2000 preparedness inquiries and have its responses tracked in the same manner as other mission-critical EBDs. In the case of the ERP implementation, the leader should secure appropriate Year 2000 representations and warranties from both the software provider and the consultant responsible for implementation.

The problems raised by Year 2000 disruptions and determining how to address them are as important as any other strategic decision made during the business improvement effort; they must not be overlooked. Regarding the effects of not addressing Y2K concerns, a parallel can be drawn between the rush to implement an enterprise system and the failure to include Year 2000 in business improvement systems generally. In the July–August 1998 issue of *Harvard Business Review*, Thomas H. Davenport noted that "If a company rushes to install an enterprise system without first having a clear understanding of the business implications, the dream of integration can quickly turn into a nightmare."

The analogy to Y2K is simple. If a company makes the decision to pursue a business improvement strategy without taking all Year 2000 issues into account, the choice may hurt the enterprise more than it helps.

Conclusion

Many ongoing business initiatives cannot stop for Y2K. But neither can they proceed oblivious to Year 2000 risks. Executives need to consider the strategic aspects of Y2K in relation to public and private communications, and coordinate major corporate decisions with Year 2000 planning, assessment, and testing.

The significant risks inherent in mergers and acquisitions, business improvements, and Y2K remediation projects make it imperative to substantiate Year 2000 due diligence, which is the subject of Chapter 8.

CHAPTER 8

Substantiating Due Diligence

"It's not enough that we do our best; sometimes we have to do what's required."

—WINSTON CHURCHILL

By now it should be clear that effective Year 2000 risk management programs must address a wide range of issues in order to mitigate exposures and minimize disruptions and liability. If a claim is made based on a negative Y2K outcome, or if accusations of faulty decision making arise, an organization usually can defend itself by showing that it exercised due diligence in each area of Y2K risk. To make that showing, you will have to document the extensive information gathering, decision making, implementation, and monitoring for each Y2K program area (internal systems, external dependencies, insurance review, and so on).

Due diligence is not limited to Year 2000 project documents you generate internally. It also includes official and unofficial communications you have with regulatory agencies, banks, insurers, and others on whom your business depends. Those third parties will hold you legally accountable for the statements and disclosures you make about your Y2K preparations. It is important to consider what guidelines have been established for Year 2000 disclosures and communications by such important entities as securities regulators and the accounting profession.

Reasons to Substantiate Due Diligence

The Y2K problem has been characterized by widely varying levels of understanding, commitment of resources, and start dates of remediation. Because there is no established standard of care regarding Year 2000, the question of whether organizations exercised due diligence or, conversely, mismanaged their compliance programs will be answered in hindsight. More importantly, even companies that have, by all measures, met or exceeded whatever threshold may be deemed reasonable, could nonetheless be found to have mismanaged Y2K if they experience serious failures and cannot substantiate their efforts. Consider the following reasons for substantiating Y2K due diligence.

Directors and officers. Directors and officers could face liability for breach of the duty of care with regards to Year 2000, as we discussed in Chapter 4, "Reducing Y2K Liability Exposure." Both the legal presumption of good business decisions (the business judgment rule) and the substantive defense of satisfying the duty of care require documented proof, that is, substantiation of due diligence.

Negligence and professional liability. All claims based on negligence, including professional liability, require four factors to be shown: duty, breach, causation, and harm. In the Y2K context, many negligence-based claims may turn on the second element, breach of the duty of due care. To determine whether a defendant fell below the standard of care, the plaintiff must establish the applicable standard of care and show that the defendant did less than what was required. Here again, even if the defendant company acted reasonably, it may be held liable for want of sufficient proof.

Insurance claims. Insurers are expected to deny commercial property insurance claims on the basis of a lack of fortuity (that the loss was nonaccidental, foreseeable, or otherwise preventable) and to deny liability insurance claims on the basis that the loss was not "unexpected or unintended." Both of these bases for claim denials put the burden on policyholders to establish that the loss was, in fact, fortuitous, unexpected, or unintended. That would be the case if the policyholder took all reasonable steps to prevent Y2K-related losses, but they still occurred. Insurance precedents include overcoming the arguments that policyholders expect that storefront windows in Manhattan will be vandalized by pulling down "insurance shutters" and that homeowners expect that Florida storms will break unprotected glass by putting protective tape across them prior to a storm. Insureds with well-substantiated evidence of due diligence should fare better in collecting insurance claims and overcoming claim denials based on policyholder omissions or insufficient preventive actions. We discuss insurance in more detail in Chapter 9, "Insurance Issues."

Qualified liability immunity protection. Discussions on Capitol Hill and in state governments have focused on effectively and fairly limiting lawsuits relating to Year 2000. The *Year 2000 Information and Readiness Disclosure Act* was an attempt to prevent claims based on disclosures; further discussions have focused on how to protect "good corporate citizens" that have made good-faith efforts to address their Y2K exposures. Many believe that the only acceptable approach is a qualified liability immunity statute that would protect those deemed to have exercised due diligence. Precisely how to fashion and administer such a bill is a difficult task. Should such a law be enacted, it will be doubly important for entities to substantiate due diligence.

Documentation

It is impossible to give you an all-purpose list of documents that "should" be retained as part of managing Year 2000 risks. Instead, the objectives of building a Y2K *paper trail* are (1) to help you manage the project effectively and (2) to show that you exercised due diligence. Don't lose sight of the first reason and fall into the trap of thinking that project documentation is just makework that your lawyers force you to do. Irene Dec, the renowned Year 2000 Program Manager for Prudential Insurance, made the point succinctly when she advised, "reduce Year 2000 business risks by implementing a structured reporting process" (Dec, 1997).

You may recall that we previously defined Year 2000 due diligence as an integrated collection of sound, well-documented practices that constitute a systematic effort to identify, evaluate, and mitigate business and legal risks that result directly or indirectly from date-related computer failures. Should problems arise, you're going to want to be able to show that you did your best to prevent them. What are some of the main points you need to be able to establish?

- How management exercised effective oversight
- What compliance efforts were made
- How priorities were established and enforced
- What alternatives were considered and how and why certain choices were made
- How tasks were assigned and monitored

Table 8.1 provides examples of the kinds of documents most organizations should maintain for effective project management and showing due diligence.

Just as there is no universal rule about what documents you should keep, there also is no fixed standard governing how long to keep them. We recommend that you consider three factors. First, how long is the longest statute of limitations for suits that could be filed against your company? Second, are there any applicable statutory or regulatory requirements for how long you must keep certain kinds of documents, such as tax or financial records? Third,

Table 8.1 Examples of Y2K Documentation

Board and steering committee minutes	Project planning, organization, and staffing
Cost estimates and budgets	Contractor and consultant selection and oversight
Inventory and assessment reports	Triage and prioritization decisions
Change control procedures	Schedules, status reports, and planned vs. actuals
Renovations made	Testing plans and results
Independent verification and validation	Disclosures made and notices given
Contingency plans	Disaster recovery plans
Communications with external business dependencies	Privileged communications

has your company established documentation retention policies for other kinds of documents? If so, do not discard your Y2K documents sooner than you would throw out similar non-Y2K documents.

Obviously, maintaining a well-organized and centralized document repository is essential. If your organization does not have documentation retention policies and procedures, consider adopting some now to establish consistent practices and to avoid having to make *ad hoc* decisions about one set of documents or another. The policy should include the following elements:

- Definitions of what documents are covered, including electronic data
- Retention periods for various kinds of records
- Computer backup and retention policy
- E-mail retention
- Document storage and disposal practices
- Access to data and privacy controls

In the event of litigation, your adversaries will have access to virtually all of your project documents, so your attorney should be closely involved in deciding what records to maintain and developing guidelines for avoiding the creation of "smoking gun" documents. Here are some useful principles to keep in mind:

> Those working on Year 2000 compliance projects should be instructed to be objective in documenting problems and issues. Attributions of blame or responsibility for the existence of problems can and should be avoided. Similarly, subjective assessments of the magnitude of problems, gloom and doom comments, jokes and the like serve no useful purpose in Year 2000 project documentation,

but they can be used to devastating, out-of-proportion results when used by skillful plaintiffs' counsel in the court room (Gross, 1998).

In the remainder of this chapter, we will look closely at disclosures you may be required to provide to the SEC and to independent auditors for assessing your due diligence. We will also discuss how internal auditors can help monitor your compliance efforts and substantiate due diligence.

Disclosures to the Securities and Exchange Commission

On July 28, 1998, the Securities and Exchange Commission (SEC) issued an interpretation entitled *Statement of the Commission Regarding Disclosure of Year 2000 Issues and Consequences by Public Companies, Investment Advisers, Investment Companies, and Municipal Securities Issuers*. The statement is essential reading for those who participate in the preparation of the disclosures and reports of the entities identified in its title, including auditors, financial and tax advisers, and legal counsel. We will summarize the statement here, but our analysis cannot take the place of a detailed review of the full text by persons with legal and fiduciary responsibilities to comply with its mandates.

The statement, which can be found at www.sec.gov/rules/concept/33-7558.htm, addresses the following matters:

> This release provides guidance to public companies so they can determine whether their Year 2000 issues are known material events, trends, or uncertainties that should be disclosed in the Management's Discussion and Analysis of Financial Condition and Results of Operations ("MD&A") section of their disclosure documents. This release also sets forth our guidance regarding specific matters for companies to address in their MD&A Year 2000 disclosure. In addition, we address the need for companies to consider the Year 2000 issue in connection with other rules and regulations and when they prepare financial statements. Finally, we remind municipal securities issuers, as well as public companies, investment advisers, and investment companies, that the anti-fraud provisions of the federal securities laws apply to disclosure about the Year 2000 issue.

The SEC issued the interpretation because "many companies are not providing the quality of disclosure that we believe investors expect." The commission makes clear that "[w]e intend to intensify our efforts to elicit meaningful disclosure from companies about their Year 2000 issues," including "possible referrals to our Division of Enforcement." It supersedes an earlier guidance document issued and subsequently revised, known as *Staff Legal Bulletin No. 5*, which was apparently ineffective in inducing disclosures of satisfactory quantity and quality.

The unmistakable purpose of the statement is to strongly encourage public companies and the other designated entities to exert strenuous efforts to become internally and externally compliant. Companies that fail to make diligent efforts to achieve compliance will either have to disclose that fact and risk capital flight or violate the disclosure requirements and expose themselves to enforcement actions by the commission and shareholders' lawsuits.

In this section, we will examine the SEC's interpretation of the disclosure obligations of public companies concerning Year 2000 issues. The following additional subjects are discussed in the SEC interpretive document but are not covered here: accounting and disclosure in financial statements; responsibilities of independent auditors; other regulations concerning Y2K disclosures; and disclosures by investment advisers, investment companies, and municipal issuers.

Effective Date

The SEC interpretive guidance became effective after August 4, 1998. Companies with June 30th or July 31st fiscal year ends were required to follow the guidance document when they filed their next annual reports, as were companies with quarter ends after the effective date of the release. Companies with quarters that end on June 30th or July 31st were encouraged to consider this guidance in their quarterly reports.

Required Disclosures by Public Companies

The guidance document addresses two important MD&A issues: "whether companies are required to provide Year 2000 disclosure and the type of Year 2000 disclosure that is required." The SEC answers both questions as follows:

[A] company must provide Year 2000 disclosure if:

(1) its *assessment* of its Year 2000 issues is not complete, or

(2) management determines that the consequences of its Year 2000 issues would have a material effect on the company's business, results of operations, or financial condition, *without taking into account the company's efforts to avoid those consequences* [emphasis added].

We expect that for the vast majority of companies Year 2000 issues are likely to be material, and therefore disclosure would be required. When a company has a Year 2000 disclosure obligation, we believe that full and fair disclosure includes:

(1) the company's state of readiness;

(2) the costs to address the company's Year 2000 issues;

(3) the risks of the company's Year 2000 issues; and

(4) the company's contingency plans.

Whether Disclosure Is Required

Under the SEC's stringent guidelines, it is difficult to imagine circumstances under which *any* public company would not be required to issue Year 2000 disclosures. As the italicized language in the preceding quotation shows, disclosure is required (1) whenever the company has not completed its "assessment" *or* (2) when the consequences of Y2K issues would be material "without taking into account the company's efforts to avoid those consequences." It is important to understand the significance of each of these tests for triggering the duty to disclose.

Assessment Includes External Business Dependencies

Assessment is not limited to the company's own IT and non-IT systems. Instead, "a company's assessment should take into account whether third parties with whom a company has *material* relationships are Year 2000 compliant" (emphasis added). Third parties include vendors, suppliers, and customers, and the company is required to consider its "potential liability to third parties if its systems are not Year 2000 compliant, resulting in possible legal actions for breach of contract or other harm." Moreover, completing the assessment requires the company to verify the compliance status of material third parties:

> In our view, a company's Year 2000 assessment is not complete until it considers these third party issues *and takes reasonable steps to verify the Year 2000 readiness of any third party that could cause a material impact on the company*. We understand that this is often done by analyzing the responses to questionnaires sent to these third parties. In the absence of receiving responses to questionnaires, there may be other means to assess third party readiness [emphasis added].

Taken together, these requirements suggest a public company must provide disclosures unless it has done all of the following:

- Completed an assessment of its own IT and non-IT systems
- Completed an assessment of its material vendors, suppliers, trading partners, and customers
- Verified the compliance of its material third parties, either by receiving responses to compliance questionnaires or by other means
- Conducted a legal audit to determine its potential liability exposure to its material third parties

The SEC considers a vendor, supplier, or customer to be *material* "if there would be a material effect on the company's business, results of operations, or financial condition if they do not timely become Year 2000 compliant." As this circular definition suggests, the SEC construes the concept of materiality broadly. Indeed, materiality is a moving target that gets closer all the time:

As the end of the century draws near, the Year 2000 technical and legal issues become increasingly material to investors. We are concerned that some companies may not be meeting their Year 2000 disclosure obligations. With each passing month, the extent of the Year 2000 risks becomes more evident and companies' obligations to disclose their Year 2000 issues becomes clearer.

At this stage, it would appear doubtful that any public company could satisfy all of the above requirements for a complete assessment, so it is likely that virtually every such company is required to provide Year 2000 disclosures. Moreover, "[i]n almost all cases, companies will have material events and changes requiring updated Year 2000 disclosures in each quarterly and annual report filed with" the SEC.

Noncompliance Must Be Assumed

Under the second test for deciding when disclosures must be made, companies must evaluate whether the consequences of their Year 2000 issues would be material "without taking into account the company's efforts to avoid those consequences." In other words, "in the absence of clear evidence of readiness, a company must assume that it will not be Year 2000 compliant and weigh the likely results of this unpreparedness." Companies must make the same assumption for their material third parties, "unless these third parties have delivered written assurances to the company that they expect to be Year 2000 compliant in time." Because very few companies can justifiably claim "clear evidence of readiness" of themselves and all of their material third parties, disclosure is almost always required under the second test, as it is under the first.

What Must Be Disclosed

The touchstone of the SEC's disclosure requirement under the Securities Act of 1933 and the Securities Exchange Act of 1934 is the dissemination of "material information that enables investors to make informed investment decisions." The Year 2000 Statement is highly unusual because the commission rarely provides specific guidance concerning MD&A disclosure requirements on any particular issue. Although "each company has to consider its own circumstances in drafting its MD&A," certain general considerations apply:

- Disclosures should be quantified to the extent practicable.
- Some companies may have to disclose by business segment or subdivision.
- Companies should avoid generalities and boilerplate language.

The Company's State of Readiness

The first required disclosure concerns the company's own state of Year 2000 preparedness:

A company should describe its Year 2000 issues in sufficient detail to allow investors to fully understand the challenges that it faces. We suggest that the description be similar to that provided to a company's board of directors—which typically is non-technical plain English and answers the important questions—such as "will we be ready?" and "how far along are we?" So far, most companies have provided only a cursory description of their Year 2000 issues.

At least three elements must be disclosed:

- The status of IT and non-IT systems, including embedded microprocessors.
- The status of the company's progress, identified by phase, including the estimated schedule for completing each remaining phase and for remediating multiple computer systems.
- The compliance status of material third parties, including the nature and level of importance of these relationships and the status of third-party risk assessment.

The Costs to Address the Company's Year 2000 Issues

The SEC requires companies to disclose material historical and estimated costs of remediation, including costs directly related to fixing Year 2000 issues, such as modifying software and hiring Y2K solution providers. The replacement cost of a noncompliant IT system generally should be disclosed as an estimated Year 2000 cost, even if the company had planned to replace the system and merely accelerated the replacement date.

The Risks of the Company's Year 2000 Issues

Disclosures must contain "a reasonable description of their most reasonably likely worst case Year 2000 scenarios" to enable investors to understand whether the consequences of a known event, trend, or uncertainty are likely to have a material effect on the company's results of operations, liquidity, or financial condition. "If a company does not know the answer, this uncertainty must be disclosed, as well as the efforts made to analyze the uncertainty and how the company intends to handle this uncertainty. For example, companies must disclose estimated material lost revenue due to Year 2000 issues, if known."

The Company's Contingency Plans

Companies must describe their contingency plans for handling the most reasonably likely worst-case scenarios to answer the question, "What will the company do if it is not ready?" The commission recognizes that many companies have not yet established contingency plans, in which case that fact should be disclosed and whether and when they intend to do so.

Specific Disclosures Suggested by the SEC

Although the statement recognizes that the particular circumstances of each company—such as personnel turnover, foreign risks, special litigation risks facing IT manufacturers, and the applicability of other regulatory requirements—will necessarily shape what disclosures must be made, the commission offers the following "suggestions" that "all companies should consider":

1. Disclose historical and estimated costs related to their Year 2000 issues, even if disclosure of the dollar amounts is not required because these amounts are not material.

2. As of the end of each reporting period, disclose how much of the total estimated Year 2000 project costs have already been incurred.

3. Identify the source of funds for Year 2000 costs, including the percentage of the IT budget used for remediation. This allows investors to determine whether Year 2000 funds will be deducted from the company's income.

4. Explain if other IT projects have been deferred due to the Year 2000 efforts, and the effects of this delay on financial condition and results of operations.

5. Describe the use of any independent verification and validation processes to assure the reliability of their risk and cost estimates. The use of independent verification may be particularly important in the testing phase.

6. Use a chart to provide Year 2000 disclosure. The chart may help investors track a company's progress over time, as it is updated, and make peer comparisons based on the same data. In addition, a chart can reduce lengthy Year 2000 disclosure that otherwise may overwhelm other disclosure.

7. Include a breakdown of the costs, such as disclosure of costs to repair software problems, and costs to replace problem systems and equipment.

Statutory Safe Harbors

The federal securities laws provide protections from civil liability known as *safe harbors* for certain kinds of *forward-looking statements*. A forward-looking statement includes "(A) a statement containing a projection of revenues, income, earnings, capital expenditures, or other financial items; (B) a statement of the plans and objectives of management for future operations; (C) a statement of future economic performance; [and] (D) any statement of the assumptions underlying or relating to any statement described in subparagraph (A), (B), or (C)." The SEC document provides interpretive guidance regarding the application of the safe harbors to forward-looking Year 2000 information.

Forward-Looking Statements

Although virtually all Year 2000 disclosures will include forward-looking statements that are protected under the statutory safe harbors, some statements of *historical fact* are not protected. Table 8.2 lists examples the SEC has provided of each kind of statement.

Other Safe Harbor Requirements

Even as to forward-looking statements, the safe harbor provisions apply only to the following:

- Statements that are accompanied by "meaningful cautionary statements," that is, boilerplate language is not sufficient
- Statements that were not knowingly false when made
- Private lawsuits filed in federal court (but not federal agency enforcement actions or criminal prosecutions)

Disclosures by Private Companies

Companies that are not subject to SEC jurisdiction do not have a single set of disclosure rules with which they must comply. Instead, they face a patchwork

Table 8.2 SEC Examples of Forward-Looking and Historical Fact Statements

FORWARD-LOOKING STATEMENT	HISTORICAL FACT STATEMENT
Projection of capital expenditures and other financial items such as the estimated cost of remediation and testing	Historical costs
Estimated future costs due to business disruption	Whether a company has a contingency plan
Assumptions concerning estimated costs or plans for future operations	Whether a company has performed an assessment
Contingency plans that assess which scenarios are most likely	Inventory of hardware, software and embedded chips
A description of the problems that the company anticipates	Identification of the remediation phase that a company is currently in
Timetables for implementation of future phases	
Estimates of how long internal and third-party testing phases will take	

quilt of disclosure requests from insurance companies considering renewal applications, banks reviewing requests for loans, customers trying to find out whether their external business dependencies are prepared for Y2K, and the like. Responses to many of these inquiries may have legal consequences. For example, most applications for loans and insurance coverage are likely to contain statements such as, "The applicant represents that the above statements and facts made in this application are true and that no material facts have been suppressed, omitted, or misstated." In the event of a Y2K problem, the information provided at the time the representation was made will be closely scrutinized and could lead to denial of coverage or declaration of a default. In addition, information about your company's Year 2000 preparedness may well affect its upstream and downstream business relationships, as enterprises look for vulnerabilities in their supply chain.

The first line of defense for all nonpublic entities providing information about their Y2K status is the protections from liability afforded by *The Year 2000 Information and Readiness Disclosure Act*. Keep in mind, however, that the act does provide that the parties can essentially agree to waive their rights by contract. Depending on your bargaining strength with your customers and business partners, you might find yourself in the position of having to accept written contractual waivers as a condition of continued business.

In addition, many nonpublic organizations are required to obtain audited financial statements for a variety of reasons, and independent auditors now have professional obligations that extend to privately held companies in connection with Year 2000 issues. CFOs will need to understand many of the issues discussed in the section entitled, *Working with External Auditors*.

Internal and External Audits

Auditors play a unique role in substantiating business information. Many business transactions require independent verification, and corporate boards of directors need a source of information that is independent of management to be able to carry out their fiduciary duties. The business and legal risks of Year 2000 are sufficiently serious that inside and outside auditors can be expected to bear weighty responsibilities during 1999 and 2000 that must be taken into account as we confront "the first economic disaster to arrive on a schedule" (Mandel, 1998).

Y2K Role of Internal Auditors

Given the scope, complexity, and risks of Year 2000 projects, every organization that has internal audit capabilities should direct those resources to supporting the effort. As Wynne Carvill, a leading Y2K lawyer, has observed, "internal audit staff . . . know the company, frequently have access to all its departments, typically have some degree of independence, and thus provide a means of testing an entity's Y2K readiness" (Carvill, 1998). The definitive paper on the role of internal auditors in Year 2000 projects is "Year 2000 Programme: The Audit Contribution," by Steve Wakeland, a Y2K consultant in England, which is available at www.jks.co.uk/y2ki/recent/index.htm. He identifies three principal responsibilities:

- Identify and monitor the risks which the organization faces in dealing with the problem and ensure that actions are planned to reduce or eliminate the risks
- Provide advice on any control issues arising
- Provide regular audit opinion on the adequacy of the management action to resolve the problem

The following sections from "Assessing the Risks" to "Third Parties" are generously contributed by Mr. Wakeland, who has identified multiple phases of Year 2000 internal audit work and offers the recommendations that follow.

Assessing the Risks

- Tailor the Year 2000 risk matrix to your organization/part of the organization and adjust the likelihood and impact scores to suit the circumstances.
- Amend the suggested risk management activities to the actual processes adopted, ensuring that these are appropriate to minimize or eliminate the risks.
- Establish a process by which all of the risk management activities will be regularly reviewed with any deviations being reported to an appropriate level of management.

The Project Structure

- Obtain details of the project structure and the responsibilities of the individuals concerned.
- Report on any areas of the business that are not represented within the program structure.
- Ensure that responsibilities are allocated at appropriate status levels and to individuals with relevant experience/expertise.
- Ensure that the Year 2000 program is being appropriately prioritized within the present list of business initiatives (assess the impact on the business of the failure of each project—I would be surprised if any are higher than Year 2000).
- Review the mechanisms for reporting information through the structure ensuring that the information is sufficient for monitoring and control purposes.

- Ensure that appropriate action is taken on the information provided at an appropriate level of seniority.
- Ensure that Internal Audit has appropriate representation within the program structure and is prepared to offer regular independent reports.
- Ensure that there is a means of challenging any actions that threaten to undermine the Year 2000 project plan.

Documentation

- Obtain all of the above documentation, ensuring that Internal Audit appears on the circulation lists for those produced at regular intervals.
- Respond, with a minimum of delay, to the originators of the documentation with any concerns (if possible try to obtain the documents at the draft stage to ensure that your comments can be incorporated into the final version).

Communications Strategy

- Ensure that an effective strategy is developed for communicating to all levels within the organization.
- Ask to review the communications at the draft stage to ensure that the details are factual and relevant for the intended audience.
- Ensure that a policy is developed for communicating with third parties (e.g., customers and other stake holders).
- Ensure that a process is developed to ensure compliance with the policy for the delivery of any messages outside of the organization.
- Ensure that systems developers are warned not to introduce noncompliant code after renovation has taken place.

Systems Inventory

- Perform a broad assessment of the quality of the inventory with reference to the business systems subject to routine audit.
- Perform substantive tests of the detailed inventory using program library or catalog information.
- Ensure that the inventory includes an assessment of each system's criticality for prioritization purposes. This should include the value of the system to the organization and the critical date horizon by which time remediation must be effected.
- Ensure that the inventory includes details of interdependencies between systems and calls to common subroutines that may affect the order of renovation.
- Examine the processes by which the inventory information was gathered. Ensure that the process was sufficiently robust to avoid inaccuracies, omission, or duplication.

Change Management

- Ensure that there is an effective mechanism for freezing any other development work while the renovation is performed.
- Ensure that an appropriate centralized control is applied to any renovation work being performed (thus ensuring adherence to the plan).
- If the code is to be renovated in a factory environment or by a third party, ensure that reconciliation controls are applied that make sure the number of programs/modules out and in agree.

The Renovation Process

- Examine the configuration for renovation/testing environment ensuring that it mirrors, as far as possible, the production environment in which the systems will eventually run.
- Ensure that the operating system and other systems software is at the same version/release levels in the renovation and production environments.
- Review any proposals for and subsequent decisions made relative to the renovation method. Ensure that such decisions take account of the risks, the cost, the criticality of the system, the time remaining to the critical horizon, and the resources required (most of which are interrelated).

The QA Process

- Examine the proposals for sign-off at various stages of the renovation process, ensuring that these give appropriate control.
- Ensure that the QA processes are incorporated into the contractual documentation where appropriate.
- Examine the information available to those applying QA checks and ensure that it is appropriate for the purpose.

Testing

- Obtain details of the organization's overall testing strategy and review it to ensure that it forms a realistic framework.
- A test policy will be required for each application as it is renovated; again, this should be reviewed by Internal Audit.
- Testing must be effected using appropriate test data. Internal Audit should check the quality and validity of the test data to be used (taking account of the fact that there will be a number of standard dates to be used in conjunction with some which may be more system specific).
- Ensure that there is a means of comparing the test outputs before and after renovation (based on present dated transactions), thus proving that the system functionality has not been altered by the renovation process.

- Review the methods for performing testing for future dated transactions (particularly after 1/1/2000).
- Ensure that tests are performed using an environment with a future date (i.e. Year 2000 system date), which may be accomplished through the use of date simulators/interceptors.
- Review the details of tests performed ensuring that any errors/faults are logged and followed through to conclusion.
- Where automated testing methods are used, the Auditor should be able to form an opinion on the tools used and their integrity.

Third Parties

- Review the list of third parties with whom the organization transacts and perform some substantive testing to other primary records (e.g., Accounts Payable section).
- Ensure that the criticality of the third parties is identified to ensure that formal responses are received from those organizations on which your organization most depends.
- Review the process by which all third parties have been contacted and ensure that it is appropriate.
- Ensure that follow-up action has been taken to process any nonresponse, in an appropriate time scale.

Y2K Risks Facing External Auditors

The Gartner Group includes "accounting firm auditors," along with institutional fund managers, credit rating agencies, and insurers, as one of the "catalysts [that] have emerged that will radically heighten the level of interest that the [Y2K] crisis attracts and catapult it to the top of financial management agendas" (Kyte, 1998). CPAs face extremely serious liability risks as they audit the books of companies that are vulnerable to Year 2000 problems. Because outside auditors must conduct their work in ways that reduce their own risks, companies undergoing audits in 1999 and 2000 must understand the institutional pressures that will come into play in these unusual times.

Two recent developments bear on Year 2000 liability exposures for independent accountants and auditors. First, a guidance document issued by the American Institute of Certified Public Accountants (AICPA) points out the professional risks inherent in traditional accounting functions arising from Y2K business disruptions. Second, the Year 2000 problem could invigorate suits against auditors for failing to warn investors about the prospects for adverse business impacts from widespread computer, infrastructure, and supply-chain failures.

AICPA Year 2000 Accounting Guidance

On October 19, 1998, the AICPA issued a revision of "The Year 2000 Issue—Current Accounting and Auditing Guidance," which it first released on October 31, 1997. The guidance document describes "the responsibilities of various parties, clarifies the auditor's role, provides guidance on communications with clients, and describes disclosure considerations and certain practice management matters that auditors may wish to consider in connection with the Year 2000 issue" (AICPA, 1998). The SEC's interpretive document on Y2K disclosures by public corporations endorses the AICPA guidance.

Auditing Current Financial Statements

The AICPA guidance is confined to the impact of Year 2000 on the accountant's role in connection with traditional audits of *current year* financial statements. For example, the interpretation states that "[a]n auditor does not have a responsibility to detect current or future effects of the Year 2000 Issue on operational matters that do not affect the entity's ability to prepare financial statements in accordance with generally accepted accounting principles." Although "the auditor may determine that it is necessary to consider whether data processing errors caused by the Year 2000 Issue could result in a material misstatement of the financial statements under audit," a GAAP audit does not contemplate that the auditor would need to assess the prospect for such misstatements "in periods subsequent to the period being audited." Moreover, for current accounting purposes, the existence of Y2K problems that could "adversely affect the organization's ability to record, process, summarize, and report financial data consistent with the assertions of management in the financial statements" in some later period is not a reportable condition now, even if the auditor has actual knowledge of an impending technical failure.

Given the short time remaining for businesses to prepare for Year 2000, the liability risks for accountants and auditors are self-evident. According to the AICPA interpretation, an accountant who has actual knowledge that a client's IT systems will likely produce inaccurate financial statements if date information for years 2000 and beyond is entered during the very next reporting year has no current obligation to report that circumstance to his client. However, "the auditor also *may* identify matters that, *in his or her judgment*, are not reportable conditions but that the auditor nonetheless *may choose to communicate . . . for the benefit of management*" (emphasis added). It may well be that auditors will face considerable client pressure not to volunteer such unwelcome news. In the event of Year 2000–related litigation against accountants and auditors, the questions "What did you know?", "When did you know it?", and "Whom did you tell?" will surely become paramount.

AICPA acknowledges that "[m]anagements and audit committees may not understand that the auditor is not required to report potential future internal control problems as 'reportable conditions' if such problems do not affect the period under audit." CPA firms would be well advised to inform the client as clearly as words allow that management's Year 2000 preparedness is being considered only for two limited and very different purposes: first, to avoid material misstatements about the accuracy of *current year* financial statements as the result of *existing* Y2K problems and, second, to provide helpful information to the client solely for management's benefit about potential *future* date-related problems that are not part of the current engagement or any compensated services for which the accountant may be held professionally liable. "An audit of financial statements conducted in accordance with generally accepted auditing standards is not designed to detect whether a company's systems are year 2000 compliant" (AICPA, 1998).

Going Concern Issues

Auditors do have limited duties for making assessments about the client's future prospects: "The auditor has a responsibility to evaluate whether there is substantial doubt about the entity's ability to continue as a going concern for a reasonable period of time, not to exceed one year beyond the date of the financial statements being audited." The auditor is required to consider whether there is evidence of "conditions and events that, when considered in the aggregate, indicate there could be substantial doubt about the entity's ability to continue as a going concern for a reasonable period of time."

Four familiar categories could constitute *conditions and events* that could raise going-concern issues: (1) noncompliant computerized systems; (2) actions of others affecting the entity; (3) problems of customers, vendors, and service providers; and (4) related costs. If substantial doubts arise that create going-concern issues, the auditor "should consider the effect on the auditor's report." A *qualified* audit report that casts doubt on the client's continuing viability as a going concern is likely to have very serious business repercussions, including the loss or denial of insurance coverage, the calling in of loans, the downgrading of securities, and the loss of important customers.

However, "the auditor does not have a responsibility to plan and perform procedures solely to identify conditions and events relating to the Year 2000 issue." Instead, the auditor merely considers other information it has collected during the regular course of its audit. Because the main focus of an audit is on the accuracy of the financial statements, "[t]he auditor is less likely to identify conditions and events relating to the Year 2000 Issue in its systems and information affecting operations and compliance objectives because these generally do not come to his or her attention during the audit."

If the auditor identifies issues that raise going-concern questions, he or she can resolve them by obtaining written management representations on matters such as the following:

- Management's intent and ability to commit the necessary resources to complete the Year 2000 remediation plan on a timely basis.

- Management's assertion that the Year 2000 remediation plan addresses all mission-critical systems.

- Management has not been notified by a regulator that it must achieve Year 2000 compliance thresholds by a specified date or significant regulatory action will be taken.

- Management has no information that indicates that a significant vendor may be unable to sell to the entity; a significant customer may be unable to purchase from the entity; or a significant service provider may be unable to provide services to the entity, in each case because of Year 2000 compliance problems.

Auditors are likely to require such representations in order to transfer the responsibility and risk for Y2K deficiencies from themselves back to management. Although caution must be exercised before making legally-significant statements, providing such representations may be a welcome alternative to an audit opinion expressing going concern reservations (AICPA, 1998).

Liability to Third Parties for Negligent Nondisclosure of Y2K Information

As discussed earlier in this chapter, the issue of disclosure of Year 2000 risks and expenditures has been the subject of recent attention by the SEC. But such concerns are by no means limited to securities regulators. As the AICPA Year 2000 Guidance observed, "[g]iven the significant nature of the Year 2000 Issue and the publicity and attention it has received, investors, creditors, customers, vendors, regulators, and other users of financial statements will probably be interested in matters relating to this Issue"(1998). A recent Massachusetts case brings into focus the circumstances under which accountants may be held liable for negligently supplying information for the guidance of persons with whom they have no contractual relationship. In *Nycal Corp. v. KPMG Peat Marwick LLP*, the Supreme Judicial Court rejected a suit against an accounting firm that audited a company (Gulf) in which the plaintiff wished to invest. Nycal alleged that KPMG's audit report materially misrepresented Gulf's financial condition and should have included a going-concern qualification. The undisputed facts, however, showed that at the time the audit was being prepared, "the plaintiff was an unknown, unidentified potential future investor" and KPMG became aware of the stock purchase transaction between the plaintiff and Gulf only after the agreement had been signed and just days before the completion of the sale. Further, KPMG did not intend to influence the investment transaction and did not know that Gulf intended to use the audit report to influence the investment transaction (Mass., 1998).

In reaching its decision, the Court adopted §552(1) of the Restatement (Second) of Torts (1977), which "describes the tort of negligent misrepresentation committed in the process of supplying information for the guidance of others." Under the Restatement test,

> [O]ne who, in the course of his business, profession or employment, ... supplies false information for the guidance of others in their business transactions, is subject to liability for pecuniary loss caused to them by their justifiable reliance upon the information, if he fails to exercise reasonable care or competence in obtaining or communicating the information.

But the Restatement limits liability to

> loss suffered (a) by the person or one of a *limited group of persons* for whose benefit and guidance he intends to supply the information or knows that the recipient intends to supply it; and (b) through reliance upon it in a transaction that he intends the information to influence or knows that the recipient so intends or in a substantially similar transaction [emphasis added].

Thus, "one who relies upon the information in connection with a commercial transaction may reasonably expect to hold the maker [of the report] to a duty of care only in circumstances in which the maker was manifestly aware of the use to which the information was to be put and intended to supply it for that purpose." Because the duty arises only in the context of identifiable business transactions "an auditor retained to conduct an annual audit and to furnish an opinion for no particular purpose generally undertakes no duty to third parties." The "limited group of persons" requirement protects accountants from liability exposure "in an indeterminate amount for an indeterminate time to an indeterminate class."

All this being said, it takes little imagination to conceive of circumstances likely to occur during the next two years in which auditors will perform accounting services that could expose them to liability under the Restatement standard for failing to disclose material Year 2000 information. For example, had KPMG come into the picture earlier, it might well have been aware of Nycal's planned stock purchase and Gulf's probable intention to supply the audit information in connection with that deal.

Given the prospects for investor litigation challenging the adequacy of Year 2000 disclosures, auditors must develop a clear understanding with their clients about the objectives of the audit and the persons to whom audit information may be provided. As the Year 2000 vulnerabilities of corporate computer systems and supply chains become increasingly apparent, disappointed investors will ask whether the independent auditors sent out the right early warning signals. The attendant pressures on accountants and auditors will directly affect the way audits are conducted as the millennium approaches.

Working with External Auditors

Independent auditors will confront new and difficult challenges in 1999 and 2000, and auditors and their clients may find themselves sparring over what questions are asked, what information is provided, and what statements the auditor puts in writing that could adversely affect the client's business. For public companies, audit reports could become an important source of information in shareholder lawsuits. Private companies may find themselves unable to borrow funds or to engage in certain transactions in which a "clean" audit opinion is required. At this point, we know little about how strictly CPAs will follow the admonitions of the SEC and the AICPA. Here are some points to have in mind for the upcoming audit seasons:

The AICPA Guidance requires auditors to express an opinion about the company's Year 2000 MD&A disclosures by "considering whether such disclosures . . . have been accurately derived . . ." Audit clients should expect to be asked for documentation supporting disclosures on such matters as amounts expended to date for Y2K remediation, the state of Year 2000 readiness, and management's view of whether the entity will be compliant in time (AICPA, 1998). Auditors will also look for inconsistencies between the financial statements and the MD&A disclosures relating to Y2K.

Auditors have several methods by which they can communicate with management concerning Year 2000 matters, including audit engagement letters, management letters and other direct correspondence, and discussions with management and the audit committee. Companies should strive to obtain that form of communication that is the least problematic for its financial operations and future litigation.

Carefully evaluate any written representations the auditor requests management to provide about Y2K. For understandable reasons, the auditor will want to shift the liability risks from his or her firm to yours. Try to negotiate language that you both can live with and that fairly allocates the risk.

Clients who wish to rely on the advice of their auditor to decide what Y2K reports to make and to whom should be sure to inform the auditor that the report will be shared with an identified "limited group" of third parties in connection with particular transactions. The auditor would then have fair notice of his or her professional obligations and the client could reasonably expect a report tailored to its intended uses.

For purposes of deciding going-concern issues, auditors are required to consider all relevant circumstances, including management's plans

for addressing Year 2000 and the process used by management to control its adverse effects. Clients facing "qualified" audit opinions must be prepared to make the case, supported by appropriate documentation, that Y2K should not create "substantial doubt about the entity's ability to continue as a going concern for a reasonable period of time" (AICPA, 1998). Elements of Year 2000 remediation that the AICPA says may be "particularly significant" for making such judgments include the following (AICPA, 1998):

- Identification of mission-critical systems (including related hardware and software) that are not year 2000 compliant.
- Identification of products being sold that contain noncompliant components (hardware or software) or services being provided with noncompliant resources.
- The dates on which mission-critical systems are expected to fail.
- The dates by which mission-critical systems are expected to be year 2000 compliant.
- Plans for replacing or remediating and testing mission-critical systems (including affected hardware and software).
- Plans for addressing situations where mission-critical systems are not expected to be year 2000 compliant before failure.
- Procedures for identifying and responding to hardware or software failures that may occur.
- Plans for identifying significant customers, vendors, and service providers that may be unable to purchase from, supply, or provide service to the entity as a result of their year 2000 compliance problems and plans for minimizing the effects on the entity.
- Identification of regulatory requirements for reporting on year 2000 compliance efforts.
- Procedures for monitoring and evaluating the progress of the remediation efforts (including timetables and resource requirements) and for taking any necessary corrective action if established schedules are not met.

Conclusion

Substantiating due diligence must be looked at from several different angles. First, each organization must develop systematic documentation procedures that will improve project management and demonstrate due diligence in the event that Y2K failures occur. Second, internal auditors should be used to verify that the organization has followed through with its chosen compliance strategy and provide the board of directors with an independent assessment of the company's Year 2000 readiness. Third, publicly traded companies must carefully comply with SEC disclosure requirements. Finally, any company that faces an external audit in 1999 and beyond must be mindful of the professional obligations imposed on accountants in connection with audits of financial statements that may be impaired by Y2K events.

CHAPTER 9

Insurance Issues

"Standard business policies are not designed to cover the risks associated with the century date change problem."

—ASSOCIATION OF BRITISH INSURERS

Now that we have shown you how to identify, analyze, and mitigate Year 2000 risks, we will cover alternative means of addressing *residual risk* (including *risk finance* and *risk transfer*). According to the SEC, "[e]fforts to solve Year 2000 problems are best described as *risk mitigation*" (SEC, 1997a). We agree that no Year 2000 program can *eliminate* risk exposures. The SEC, however, fell one step short in its analysis by ignoring the need for risk transfer. This chapter discusses the nature of Year 2000 residual risks and risk finance alternatives and focuses heavily on risk transfer, that is, the insurance industry and coverage potential.

Year 2000 Residual Risks

Residual risks are those that cannot be eliminated or those that remain after risk control. Despite safety precautions, procedural policy changes, and, in the Year 2000 context, despite remediation and contingency planning, there remains the potential for loss that should be addressed. This section describes examples of Year 2000 residual risks that may exist for a corporation.

Unknown Exposures

The first concern voiced among Year 2000 program directors is: "Have we missed something?" In most circumstances, you can be confident that your efforts to address *identified* exposures have been successful. It is the fear of the unknown application, programmable logic controller, systems interface, or the forgotten vendor that keeps risk managers and CIOs awake at night. Even an internal or external audit cannot guarantee the inclusion of all Year 2000 exposures. This is the insidious nature of Y2K.

Conversion Errors and Incomplete Testing

Across all information technology sectors, programming errors consistently run at approximately 10 percent. Early testing reports from Y2K conversion projects confirm this error rate. While automated conversion tools are becoming more accurate, date modification for Y2K is a relatively new technology. It was for this reason that Gartner Group recommended between 12 and 18 months for complete testing of fully remediated systems. Similarly, it recommended that testing be allocated over 50 percent of the project life cycle (Gartner Group, 1996). One of the rationales was to allow for at least one complete accounting cycle. Most organizations (for one reason or another) have not allowed for such robust testing. Because of conversion errors, incomplete testing, and other risk factors, it is highly plausible that errors will occur, that is, residual risk remains.

External Exposures

Even when your Year 2000 project encompasses a thorough external exposure mitigation program that includes primarily positive survey responses, comprehensive intercompany systems testing, and so on, external exposures remain. In Chapter 5, "External Compliance Strategies," we discussed how General Motors had nine levels of exposure among its mission-critical vendors. A statement of organizational compliance is only as reliable as the preparedness of every external business dependency (EBD) that supports that organization. This is not to say that efforts of EBD monitoring will not reap dividends, but rather that a legally sufficient external exposure program does not guarantee timely receipt of adequate goods or services.

Problems of Remediation Itself

Systems remediation, like all technology projects, comes with its own risks. Some examples should clarify this point. In mid-1996, a major New York bank discovered an error in its daily balance of accounts. Its MIS department had been remediating code using field expansion. Fortunately for efficiency's sake, the YY/MM/DD format the bank was using lent itself well to field expansion, as simple addition of the number 19 million to every existing date field was required (for example, 990115 + 19000000 = 19990115). Unfortunately for this large institution, however, its programmers did not stop with date fields, but inadvertently added $19 million to every customer's account with a six-digit balance.

In another less spectacular example, according to the October 18, 1998 edition of *Business Today*, the city of Amesbury, Connecticut recently could not generate water bills to more than 100 properties because the newly remediated billing system read the current year as 2008, instead of 1998. Although this error occurred during remediation, apparently from a keystroke error, it was better than the alternative. Had the system not been brought into compliance it would have read the due date as 1908 and billed the residents $11 million. These examples demonstrate that having a remediation program does not eliminate systems exposures. In fact, it can create new ones.

No Litigated Standards of Care

One of the non-precedential elements of Year 2000 is a lack of established *standards of care*. Lessons can be learned from issues such as asbestos, toxic torts, and so on, but until the courts rule on what is (or was) due diligence, Year 2000 standards of care remain an uncertainty and a residual risk. For example, if it turns out in hindsight that due diligence required full EDI systems testing with each and every electronic trading partner and nothing less will suffice, many companies' current efforts could be deemed legally insufficient. On the one hand, it is easy to dismiss such stringent requirements because a true *industry standard* for Year 2000 preparedness may, in fact, be low (and this *is* the opinion of some Year 2000 experts). It would seem unlikely for the courts to adhere to a supposed standard that very few companies actually met. On the other hand, hypothetically, it would be hard to absolve certain companies, such as hospitals, that rely on an industry-wide standard of care that allowed for incomplete remediation efforts that could put lives at risk. Accordingly, while Year 2000 programs are built to perceived best-practice standards, the possibility of unforeseen high standards of care leaves another form of residual risk to be addressed.

Risk Finance Techniques

Risk finance techniques are those methods used by organizations to fund uninsured residual risks. The most common uninsured residual risk in need of a risk financing technique is a self-insured retention (or deductible). Deductibles range from hundreds to millions of dollars, and claim frequency varies as well. For organizations that assume a significant portion of the risk, either by design or because of a lack of available insurance, it is often up to the board of directors to decide which risk financing technique best suits the stakeholders. In the Y2K context, deciding among risk financing techniques requires sufficient information about what residual risks remain uninsured, a reasonable estimation of expected claim frequency and severity, and an overall cost estimate. Unfortunately, this information is necessarily speculative because no actuarial data or claim history exists to draw on. The following are the four basic types of risk financing techniques. (We have intentionally omitted discussion of captive insurance programs—those established by an entity or group of entities strictly for insuring the members, that is, no third-party financing is used—because organizations do not have sufficient time to create a captive strictly for Y2K purposes.)

Current Expensing of Loss. In much the same fashion that some companies intend to deal with Y2K problems as they occur (the antithesis of risk management), residual risks can be left to occur with the intention that corporate funds are sufficient to pay for recovery expenses as they are required. Conversely, companies may expect that losses will be few or insubstantial. Companies that make no other risk financing or risk transfer provisions, by default, will be expensing losses as they are incurred.

Unfunded Reserves. CFOs can establish reserve estimates to pay for anticipated and uninsured Y2K losses. These reserves are expensed in the year the reserves are established, and the expense is reflected as a liability on the balance sheet that would reduce owner's equity.

Funded Reserves. CFOs can additionally set aside or earmark easily liquidated investments or other corporate assets. The anticipated losses are then said to be "funded." One potential problem in the Year 2000 context is that the funding for reserves may likely become a target for Y2K or other corporate projects.

Use of Borrowed Funds. Another risk financing technique is the borrowing of funds from outside sources. Pre-loss borrowing is typically in the form of a line of credit. Most organizations have lines of credit already established for general liquidity issues. Lines of credit are prudent to obtain or extend in light of Year 2000 for two reasons. First, losses can be substantial. Second, previous liquidity exposure analysis used to establish lines of credit should be reevaluated in light of how Y2K can impact customers' ability to pay and potential problems with access to corporate assets (as a result of Y2K problems within financial institutions). Obviously every Year 2000 risk management program should include evaluation of Y2K preparedness among those financial institutions issuing lines of credit. Post-loss borrowing is the most frequent of traditional corporate loans. An advantage of this strategy is that you do not have to estimate Y2K losses, but the disadvantage is that you must rely on the ability of banks to issue loans. Banks may be unable to issue corporate loans during the months that follow New Years

2000 for several reasons. First, the banks may find their own systems Y2K impaired. Second, Y2K may create unprecedented demand for such loans. Third, banks may experience a credit crunch if borrowers default on outstanding loans because of Y2K. Fourth, financial underwriters may be untrained to evaluate Y2K preparedness and therefore unable to determine which applicants may be so severely affected by Y2K that they cannot ensure repayment of the loans.

Risk Transfer: Insurance

The final step in the risk management process is perhaps the most unsettled and perplexing. Risk transfer includes contractual agreements such as *hold harmless* and *indemnification* agreements, but most frequently risk transfer is in the form of commercial insurance. Insurance as a risk transfer vehicle for Y2K risks is dubious and directly dependent on the Year 2000 exposures facing the insurance industry itself. This section addresses the specific coverage issues within common commercial insurance policy forms, arguments for and against coverage, treatment of Y2K by the insurance industry, the problems insurers will likely experience, and specific Year 2000 insurance policies.

Insurer Alternatives

Because cost estimates for Year 2000 range from 300 billion dollars up to trillions, liability estimates are similarly in the trillions of dollars (Capers Jones, 1997).[1] Insurers will likely be called on to bear a significant portion of this enormous estimate. The insurance industry has gradually broadened policy offerings to insureds to the point where most business insurance policies today are written as *all risk* policies. The construction of an all risk policy has important implications for Y2K perils. An all risk insurance policy is a contract that contains a broad affirmative grant of coverage limited only by exclusions and other conditions expressed in the policy. One important result of this form of contract construction is the presumption of coverage and the burden on the part of insurers to prove that coverage does *not* apply. Insureds prefer the all risk approach to the prior standard of *named peril* policies where only specific risks are covered by virtue of affirmatively naming each type of peril to be covered by the policy. Most existing insurance policies remain silent regarding Y2K. Without any specific Year 2000 exclusionary language, an all risk policy form theoretically provides coverage for Y2K-related losses subject

---

[1] Gartner Group estimates that 40 percent of 1998 aggregate United States IT budgets is being spent on Year 2000 projects. Total IT spending is reported as $1.5 trillion. That percentage is expected to increase to 50 percent in 1999.

to the rest of the policy terms and conditions. Conversely, existing named peril policies theoretically do not grant coverage for Y2K related losses unless the loss is otherwise covered under another named peril. The insurance industry has not adopted and is not expected to adopt a unified stance on Y2K coverage issues. Insurers may do one of three things in response to Year 2000 risks: remain silent, add exclusions, or specifically grant coverage.

Silence

How silence will be interpreted regarding Year 2000 claims is uncertain. Due to the expected magnitude of Year 2000 losses, it may be that silence from your insurer means there is no coverage. Alternatively, silence may predominate due to a general apathy or lack of understanding on the part of insurers. Using silence as a means of avoiding coverage, insurers will rely on the factual assumption that Y2K was not anticipated, not an underwriting criteria, and not a basis of actuarial calculation, nor were premiums collected specifically for this exposure. This follows a fundamental maxim of contract construction: "that which is not included is, by design, excluded." There are several problems with this approach. First, as previously mentioned, most contemporary policies are written on an *all risk* basis, where silence may mean inclusion. Second, insurance is a matter of state law. Therefore there will likely be inconsistent interpretation among 50 states, 14 federal circuits, and other court systems. In general, large-scale actuarial unpredictability is contrary to insurance principals, as would be coverage for nonfortuitous (or expected) losses. Third, the cost of litigation to determine coverage alone may become quite significant. Fourth, silence within the policy may turn greater scrutiny to the words and actions of insurers' agents. This is a problem for insurers that do not have a standardized and sound policy on Y2K representations by agents and those lacking confidence in their agents' adherence to such policies. Finally, from a public policy perspective, courts may be reluctant to leave insureds without a viable means of cost recovery.

Year 2000 Exclusions

Some insurers are adding specific Y2K exclusions across many policy lines. This opens a great debate. Are such exclusions mere clarifications as to the intent of the original policy or substantive changes in terms and conditions? If courts determine the latter is true, prior policies may *de facto* be determined to cover year 2000. Prior policies are a great concern to the industry in part because of its experience with asbestos and other environmental risks. Using an *installation* theory of occurrence, courts found Commercial General Liability (CGL) carriers liable for each policy in existence between installation and remediation. The analogy, though, is not without flaws; because Year 2000 problems are only now materializing, its true impact remains largely unpredictable, and third-party bodily injury is only one narrow component of the complete Y2K risk montage. Because of the asbestos cases, nearly all CGL policies in effect today have an annual policy aggregate limit to prevent unlimited *stacking* of limits on a temporal basis. The insurance industry is noticeably quiet on this issue, but attorneys are quick to point out similarities that may exist between the two.

Fashioning exclusions is an imperfect science for two reasons. First, defining the Year 2000 problem is no small task. Second, insurance policies are typically contracts of adhesion, and therefore ambiguities are generally interpreted in favor of the insured. The Insurance Services Office (ISO) recently released Y2K exclusions for several standard policy lines. ISO's influence should not be lightly regarded because many insurers utilize ISO standard policy forms. An example of one ISO exclusion for Commercial General Liability reads as follows (ISO, 1997):

> This insurance does not apply to "bodily injury", "property damage", "personal injury" or "advertising injury" arising directly or indirectly out of:
>
> A. Any actual or alleged failure, malfunction or inadequacy of
>
>   (1) Any of the following, whether belonging to any insured or to others:
>
>   a. Computer hardware, including microprocessors;
>
>   b. Computer application software;
>
>   c. Computer operating systems and related software;
>
>   d. Computer networks;
>
>   e. Microprocessors (computer chips) not part of any computer system; or
>
>   f. Any other computerized or electronic equipment or component or components; or
>
>   (2) Any other products, and any services, data or functions that directly or indirectly use or rely upon, in any manner, any of the items listed in Paragraph 2.a.(1) of this endorsement due to the inability to correctly recognize, process, distinguish, interpret or accept the year 2000 and beyond.
>
> B. Any advice, consultation, design, evaluation, inspection, installation, maintenance, repair, replacement or supervision provided or done by you or for you to determine, rectify or test for, any potential or actual problems described in Paragraph 2.a of this endorsement.

This exclusion does little to define the Year 2000 problem. It is unclear how courts will interpret this definition. Does "the inability to correctly recognize, process, distinguish, interpret or accept the year 2000 and beyond" encompass many expected time/date calculation errors including year miscalculations, day-of-the-week miscalculations, leap-year miscalculations, the *year 99 problem* (the intentional use of 99 as a default or placeholder date for all years after 2000), and/or human interpretive errors? Does it exclude otherwise-covered-losses exacerbated by Y2K? What becomes clear is that incomplete or poorly worded exclusions may fail to achieve the desired objective, engender declaratory judgment lawsuits to determine whether coverage exists, and adversely clarify coverage within prior policies.

Express Coverage Grant

Insurers can expressly underwrite policy provisions specifically designed for Year 2000. Coverage grants allow insurers to collect premiums for Y2K coverage (for which they may be held liable, in any event), include sublimits, define what they want to cover, and monitor insureds' compliance programs. A sample broad-form coverage grant for a Directors and Officers liability insurance policy might look like the following:

> The coverage provided by this Policy shall specifically include, but not be limited to Claims based upon or arising out of any computer program software, computer system or network, computer or computer chip that fails or is alleged to fail to perform a function involving: (i) any time or date on or after midnight on December 31, 1999; (ii) any time or date data representing or referring to different centuries or more than one century, or (iii) the change in millennium occurring when the year 1999 changes to the year 2000; provided, always that such Claims include allegations of Wrongful Acts by one or more Assureds for which coverage is not otherwise excluded by this Policy.

Coverage grants, as exclusions, open the debate of clarification versus substantive change in terms and conditions. Here, if the courts deem coverage grants to be substantive changes, this would favor the industry as prior policies that are silent on Year 2000 may be deemed to have excluded coverage for Y2K-related losses.

State of the Industry

Although the insurance industry is not unified in its approach, most companies remain silent on Y2K. There is a growing trend toward requiring Y2K questionnaires to be completed at renewal, particularly for E&O and D&O policy lines. There appear to be three purposes for this practice. First, D&O carriers are putting insureds on record for potential disclosure-based derivative actions. Second, some carriers look to provide insureds the opportunity to *buy back* Y2K exclusions. Third, some insurers are effectively accepting coverage and attempting to underwrite Y2K exposures based on the answers to the questionnaire. A few insurers are excluding Y2K for specific industry segments, such as software developers, on a wholesale basis. The language and prevalence of exclusions vary by policy line and carrier. Only a few select carriers and certain policy lines expressly cover Y2K, and the extent of the coverage provided varies greatly.

Applicability of Existing Coverage

One of the most frequently asked questions is, "Am I covered for Y2K losses?" While this is a simple question, the answer is very much unsettled and complex. This section attempts to describe some of the key areas of contention that exist within the various forms of commercial insurance. No discussion of insurance can be complete because specific wording varies by policy and may be interpreted differently in different states. Therefore, this section should be used as a guide to spot issues and a demonstration of just how complex the Year 2000 insurance question truly is. Similarly, this section does not include a discussion of personal lines of insurance (homeowners and automobile) or life and health insurance because this book is focused on corporate risk management. Problems may exist in these coverage forms as well, and individual readers may want to investigate further.

Property Insurance

Property insurance coverage is likely to be the subject of a variety of Y2K-related claims. Whether the property coverage form will respond to these claims is a subject of debate that will certainly continue into the next millennium. Many variations of property insurance coverage are in effect at the current time. For the purposes of this discussion we will address the standard commercial property form.

Direct Damage Requirement

Property insurance is generally written on an all risk basis subject to exclusions in the coverage form. There are no exclusions that expressly limit recovery of Y2K-related losses under this form; the property must suffer some type of covered direct physical loss. Many insurers maintain that Y2K events are not direct physical damage, but rather programming errors, and therefore they maintain that property policies do not apply to Y2K. This view may be short-sighted because *consequential losses* can be tangible losses for many Y2K scenarios. For example, a Y2K failure in an environmental monitoring system may not be covered *per se*, but the resulting freeze and pipe burst may be.

The Fortuity Requirement

The aleatory nature (dependence on an uncertain event) of insurance contracts requires that losses be fortuitous (unplanned and accidental) in nature for coverage to remain in effect. This may be the single greatest burden for insureds because proving fortuitousness may require an explanation of steps taken to prevent the loss. As a practical matter, claims denied on the basis of lack of fortuity call into question those steps taken by insurers to address their own internal Y2K exposures. This is due to the nature of litigation. The standard for reasonableness in terms of steps taken to prevent the loss will be a question of fact for the judge or jury. An insurer's own inaction will clearly be explored at trial in an attempt to lower the standard of reasonableness to a point that the insured did, in fact, meet.

Business Income/Extra Expense

Where applicable, *business income* (BI) provides coverage for losses incurred due to a necessary suspension of operations. The suspension may be due to internal failures (direct business interruption) or external failures (contingent business interruption). BI is intrinsically related to the property coverage forms on which it is written. In other words, BI claims require a covered property loss. It is a common misconception to consider Y2K-related BI claims without first determining coverage under the property policy on which BI was written (be it general property, electronic data processing, boiler and machinery, and so on).

Operating under many insurers' belief that Year 2000 will not cause direct physical damage, BI coverage should not lie. As discussed above, however, many Y2K loss scenarios have potential for significant physical damage. If these losses are otherwise covered by the underlying property policy, insureds can legitimately claim BI losses.

Electronic Data Processing Insurance

Electronic data processing (EDP) insurance is an inland marine form of property insurance that provides coverage for many types of computer-related equipment, data, and media. It is similar to the *all risk* (special) property coverage form with additional provisions that contemplate unique EDP exposures. One such exposure is the cost to recreate lost data, a form of intangible property not normally covered by property insurance.

Errors in machine instruction exclusion. Some attention has been given to an exclusion that exists in most EDP coverage forms. This exclusion eliminates coverage for errors in machine instruction and processing. It is uncertain whether intended two-digit date fields can be considered an error.

Business income/extra expense. As with the property coverage form, business income under the EDP policy is linked to coverage being triggered by some form of covered direct damage to the subject property.

Boiler and Machinery (Machinery and Equipment)

Boiler and machinery or machinery and equipment (*B&M*) coverage is another special form of property insurance that contemplates unique exposures, typically excluded under standard forms, most notably electrical arcing, explosion, and mechanical breakdown. Typically this coverage is provided to large facilities and manufacturing and processing entities. B&M has tremendous potential exposure from embedded systems, which are suspected to experience widespread failures. This is particularly worrisome for process controls of all types.

Analogous to EDP, most B&M insurers may seek to avoid coverage for Y2K by noting the exclusion of breakdown of an *electronic computer or electronic data processing equipment* from the definition of an *accident*, which is the coverage trigger. As with other property forms, any BI claim under a B&M policy is predicated on a covered loss to the subject property.

Commercial General Liability Insurance

Commercial General Liability (CGL) insurance is a form of casualty insurance primarily concerned with the insured's legal liability for third-party physical harm or property damage. Either can result from Y2K events. Examples include water damage and consequential losses from frozen pipes caused by a malfunctioning heating system and the product liability of insureds caused by traffic light failures. CGL has historically been a significant cost-recovery vehicle, as it was for asbestos, silicone implants, and pollution contribution suits. It is likely that property insurers seeking restitution for Y2K-related property losses will subrogate against CGL policies. Often insurers provide both lines of coverage. This explains why ISO first introduced Y2K exclusions for property and CGL simultaneously.

Property Damage Defined

The definition of property damage in a standard CGL policy omits coverage for intangible property claims and nonphysical injuries. This effectively eliminates coverage for data and other software as well as programming errors or glitches, as in machinery or equipment. An example of an ISO CGL form definition is as follows (ISO, 1984):

> "Property damage" means:
> (a) Physical injury to tangible property including all resulting loss of use of that property; or
> (b) Loss of use of tangible property that is not physically injured.

This basis of denying coverage would also exclude any claims for consequential losses that resulted from the Y2K event. It is interesting to note that insurers added the term "physical injury" to their policies only in 1973.

Expected or Intended Injury or Damage Exclusion

Expected or intended bodily injury or property damage are generally excluded from CGL coverage. What is expected or intended is judged subjectively from the insured's point of view. As with the fortuity requirement in property coverage, determining expected or intended losses requires an analysis of steps taken to prevent the loss. Lack of Y2K diligence on the part of the insured may effectively void coverage.

Arguably, because Y2K risks have been greatly publicized, insureds should expect bodily injuries or property damage to occur in the absence of timely and adequate correction. This argument may be very persuasive in denying coverage to computer manufacturers and software programmers that continued to design noncompliant computer systems, even after they were well aware of the risks.

Impaired Property Exclusion

The *impaired property* exclusion is the means CGL carriers use to exclude claims for losses resulting from the failure of a product or completed operation to perform as intended, as well as purely contractual issues. Some insurers are relying on this provision as the primary basis for excluding Y2K claims. It is admittedly a complex area of policy construction, but the intent seems to be to prevent recovery for property damage to products sold or completed operations resulting from factors within the insured's control. Impaired property is defined by the ISO as follows (ISO, 1985):

> "Impaired property" means tangible property, other than "your product" or "your work" that cannot be used or is less useful because:
>
> A. It incorporates "your product" or "your work" that is known or thought to be defective, deficient, inadequate or dangerous; or
>
> B. You have failed to fulfill the terms of a contract or agreement; if such property can be restored to use by:
>
> (1) The repair, replacement, adjustment or removal of "your product" or "your work;" or
>
> (2) Your fulfilling the terms of the contract or agreement.

Certain losses to impaired property are then excluded from coverage, such as:

"Property damage" to "impaired property" or property that has not been physically injured, arising out of:

A. A defect, deficiency, inadequacy or dangerous condition in "your product" or "your work;" or

B. A delay or failure by you or anyone acting on your behalf to perform a contract or agreement in accordance with its terms.

This exclusion does not apply to the loss of use of other property arising out of sudden and accidental physical injury to "your product" or "your work" after it has been put to its intended use.

The last sentence raises the issue of consequential losses caused by *impaired property*, which in the Y2K context can be quite significant. While many insurers and authors maintain that the impaired property exclusion effectively eliminates all Y2K-CGL exposures, they may have overlooked this *loss of use* provision. An additional hurdle an insured must therefore overcome is establishing that the loss was due to *sudden and accidental physical injury*. It is unclear at best whether Y2K fits this prerequisite.

Directors and Officers Liability Insurance

Y2K can generate liability for directors and officers (D&O) for a myriad of reasons. D&Os can breach their fiduciary duty by not controlling costs associated with Year 2000 remediation, preventing Y2K business losses or litigation, or by failing to maintain accurate business records. In addition, they can breach their duty of diligence[2] by failing to become sufficiently informed, supervise Y2K projects, allocate resources, or adequately disclose Y2K impacts to relevant parties. D&Os who discharge their duties with regards to the Year 2000 problem using good business judgment[3] will be successful in defending suits from shareholders, business partners, and third parties, except where duties are statutorily imposed.[4]

---

[2] The "duty of diligence" requires the discharge of duties (1) in good faith; (2) with the care that an ordinarily prudent person in a like position would exercise under similar circumstances; and (3) in a manner he reasonably believes to be in the best interest of the corporation. REVISED MODEL BUS. CORP. ACT § 8.30.]

[3] Directors and Officers are protected by what is commonly known as the business judgment rule. The American Law Institute's formulation is as follows: "A director or officer who makes a business judgment in good faith fulfills the duty under this Section if the director or officer: (1) is not interested in the subject of the business judgment; (2) is informed with respect to the subject of the business judgment to the extent the director or officer reasonably believes to be appropriate under the circumstances; and (3) rationally believes that the business judgment is in the best interest of the corporation." ALI Proposed Final Draft § 4.01(c)(1)–(3).

[4] The business judgment rule will not insulate directors whose decisions breach their fiduciary obligations imposed by statutes or public policy (Knepper, 1993).

One important component for all liability insurance policies is the duty to defend. Even diligent D&Os may find themselves mired in litigation and need to call on their D&O insurance policies to defend against allegations that they were not diligent. With all this potential for liability, D&O insurance coverage becomes one of the most important and scrutinized policy lines (and ultimately one of the most active coverage lines related to Y2K claims). Most D&O insurers have adopted the first alternative for dealing with Y2K exposures discussed at the beginning of this chapter, that is, silence. The D&O coverage issues for various Y2K-related scenarios are particularly complicated. Following are some of the coverage issues.

Claims-Made Policies

D&O policies are written on a claims-made basis, that is, they respond to claims for covered acts or omissions filed or noticed within the policy period. Occurrence-based policies (such as CGL and commercial property), on the other hand, respond to the occurrence that gives rise to claims. The prospect of not having coverage for past occurrences makes each claims-made renewal a tenuous process. The claims-made nature of D&O insurance is exceptionally important with regards to Y2K because most claims are not expected to be filed until after January 1, 2000, when widespread problems begin to occur. That gives the D&O insurance marketplace another annual policy cycle to become better educated, more organized, and more deliberate in their treatment of Y2K risks.

Extended Reporting Periods

Often claims-made policies include an option for an extended reporting period (*ERP* or *tail*) that lasts for a specified time beyond the life of the policy. ERPs generally range from one to three years and may give policyholders a certain comfort level that one difficult renewal process will not leave them completely without coverage. Some ways insurers can limit their D&O exposure is to shorten ERPs at renewal, limit the ability of the insured to purchase the ERP, or charge the maximum premium if the ERP is purchased. It is important to note that the purchase of an extended reporting period will not provide coverage on a going-forward basis. In other words, claims reported during the ERP must be based on losses that occurred during the policy period.

Retroactive Dates

To limit exposure, insurers often impose a retroactive date, which precludes all coverage for losses arising out of circumstances occurring prior to the retroactive date. Due to an extremely competitive D&O liability insurance market, retroactive dates on contemporary D&O policies are generally set back to the date of the insureds' incorporation or omitted entirely. Insurers consider coverage of these *past acts* somewhat of a risk. In the face of significant Y2K litigation, one avenue some insurers might pursue to limit their exposure is advancing the retroactive date, thereby eliminating D&O coverage for older Y2K-related acts or omissions.

For example, if a CEO mismanages Y2K efforts in 1998 and stock prices tumble in 2000, the resulting derivative suits brought by shareholders may be uninsured if the Year 2000 renewal advanced the retroactive date to 1999.

Prior Acts and Later Exclusions

During the underwriting process itself, underwriters can exclude specific circumstances that they believe create a substantial risk for claims. Year 2000-related losses might qualify for such specific exclusionary treatment. Many D&O insurers have Y2K exclusions drafted, ready for use. Some insurers are already using their exclusions when the underwriter determines the insured has significant exposures or the insured has not recognized and is not effectively addressing Y2K risk factors.

Underwriting Criteria

Essentially, underwriters evaluate D&O exposure based on type of business, demonstrated management control, financial strength and stability, and foreseeable liabilities. Each criterion can be affected by Year 2000. Certain industries are more likely to experience Y2K-related losses than others, both from direct impact and resulting third-party liability and litigation. Financial services, healthcare, information technology, and even the insurance industry itself are particularly prone to Year 2000 problems because of the prevalence of and dependence on technology and the competitive pressures that prevent adequate resource allocations to fully remediate the problem.

Management's ability to control the organization is directly related to its ability to be informed. Much of management's information comes in the form of financial and other automated data reports produced from Y2K-impacted systems. Errors are expected to occur in information collection, interpretation, or display. An example of erroneous information collection is inventory control problems. Many companies with goods that expire in the year "00" have already experienced erroneous expiration notices because the system interprets "00" as numerically inferior to the current date, such as "98," and therefore determines that the goods expired 98 years ago.

Companies with financial strength and stability are less likely to generate D&O liability, not only because sound financial management demonstrates good business judgment, but also because potential plaintiffs are generally content. Y2K will alter many companies' financial landscape by affecting supply chains, internal operations, financial controls, and ultimately cash flow and credit ratings. As Year 2000 events begin to occur with more frequency, underwriters will find it more difficult to assess financial strength and stability.

Underwriting for foreseeable liabilities is generally based on experience as well as expected results from new business ventures or relationships. Y2K poses a special problem in that there is no experience to draw from, and seemingly stable business ventures and relationships can change literally overnight. It is foreseeable that D&Os can mismanage their organization's Year 2000 program. Standards of care are being publicized and legislated for the securities and banking industries and are otherwise developing for all industries[5] (SEC, 1998; FFIEC, 1997). These standards include the duty to be fully informed, to directly supervise projects, and to assess, mitigate, and disclose Y2K impacts. Currently D&O underwriters are not rating for Y2K program management, *per se*. Year 2000 questions on new and renewal applications are discussed below.

Errors and Omissions Insurance

Errors and omissions insurance (E&O), also known as professional liability, provides coverage of damages arising from negligence, omissions, mistakes, and errors made by the insured in the course of providing professional services. Accountants that fail to adequately inquire about Y2K problems while auditing a company's financial statements, attorneys that miss court filing deadlines because their internal systems are noncompliant, remediation vendors that fail to properly convert code, and so on, all will rely on E&O insurance for incurred losses. Technology providers, electronic hardware manufacturers, software developers, and those who integrate these assets into their own business may face some of the most serious Y2K E&O liability exposures.

Similar to D&O insurance, E&O insurance is written on a *claims-made* basis. Purchasers of E&O should carefully review the policy because terms vary dramatically among policies.[6] Unlike D&O, most E&O insurance policies have a retroactive date that provides coverage only for claims arising out of covered acts dating back to the first time the E&O policy was purchased. As with CGL, E&O policies generally exclude *expected or intended* losses. Moreover, companies that are successfully sued for fraudulently misrepresenting that items were compliant will find such actions excluded from E&O coverage.

[5] Best practice standards for Year 2000 management have been developed by Gartner Group, Giga Information Group, and the Society for Information Management Year 2000 Working Group.

[6] E&O insurance varies greatly in terms because it is based on manuscript form, as opposed to common policy form. Manuscript form is tailored, whereas common policy forms are standardized forms used throughout the industry.

Fiduciary Liability Insurance

Fiduciaries of employee benefit plans retain personal liability for the management of many types of ERISA-qualified plans. This personal exposure may be likened to the personal exposures of a corporate director or officer for the management of corporate issues. The duty a fiduciary has to safeguard the assets with which he or she is entrusted should not be taken lightly. Failure of a fiduciary to anticipate Y2K-related problems in the viability and appropriateness of plan investments could trigger claims, exposing the fiduciary's personal assets. Fiduciary liability insurers are beginning to ask questions related to the Y2K preparedness of plan investments. A bill is currently before the United States Senate that would codify the responsibility and liability of fiduciaries for Y2K-related plan losses.[7] Care should be taken when negotiating fiduciary liability insurance renewals to make certain that coverage extends to new legislation that, if made into law, could alter the way the insurance policy responds to a loss. For example, if the new bill before the Senate becomes law and makes fiduciaries criminally responsible for not accounting for Y2K problems, the fiduciary liability insurance policy may exclude coverage based on a criminal acts exclusion.

Y2K Questions on New or Renewal Applications

Many underwriters are now requiring some form of Year 2000 disclosure from insureds to gain an understanding of how the problem may affect the insured and how the company is preparing for Y2K-related situations. This is particularly true of D&O, fiduciary, and E&O liability policies. Some of these Y2K information-gathering tools come in the form of questionnaires; others are more formal supplemental applications. It is important to note that some of these supplements contain warranty language, which requires the signatory to warrant the accuracy of each answer. In the D&O context the warranting officer is likely to be the first to lose coverage for inaccuracies. Another important consideration for public companies is potential discoverability of these completed applications in subsequent litigation. For this reason, it is important to ensure insurance disclosures are consistent with other disclosures, such as SEC filings. If possible, insureds should request a conference with the underwriters as the preferable means of satisfying their concerns.

[7] S. 2000. "A Bill to ensure that businesses, financial markets, and the Federal Government are taking adequate steps to resolve the year 2000 computer problem" was introduced to the Committee on Governmental Affairs on April 29, 1998 by Senator Bennett.

Grounds for Voiding Coverage

Insurance companies have a number of ways to avoid providing insurance coverage based on a variety of issues.

False or Misleading Statements on Applications

Companies seeking D&O and E&O insurance must submit applications and supplemental material to insurers. This information is relied upon by the insurer and constitutes representations and warranties by the applicant. Applications of this type typically become a part of the insurance policy when it is issued. To avoid claims coverage, insurers can argue that the application and supporting materials were misleading, incomplete, or otherwise incorrect, and therefore the policy was void from the beginning (*ab initio*) or that a particular claim is excluded from coverage. The accuracy of submitted financial reports, such as SEC Forms 10K or 10Q, will be crucial in the context of Y2K D&O coverage. Companies that fail to provide accurate and timely Year 2000 information in their financial reports may find D&O coverage void. In fact, the SEC's disclosure interpretation reinforces the need to disclose material Y2K information, such as the costs of remediation and the consequences of incomplete or untimely resolution of year 2000, in their 10Ks and 10Qs.

Moreover, the strength of the SEC statement makes nondisclosures the exception. Failure to comply with this SEC interpretation can translate into loss of D&O coverage. The foreseeability of Y2K claims will be heavily litigated. D&O policies generally exclude coverage of claims for periods prior to the inception date of the policy if the D&O knew or could have reasonably foreseen the *wrongful acts* that might be the basis of a claim. It follows that D&O insurance might not cover actions or inactions surrounding Y2K occurring after the insured knew or should have known of its potential effects. Some experts cite 1996 as the year of generalized awareness, but some executives may not have been aware of the serious nature of the problem until 1997 or even 1998. With information about the Year 2000 problem prominent in the media, including articles in *Business Week*, *The Wall Street Journal*, and *The New York Times*, as well as hundreds of millions of dollars being spent to correct the problem, it will be nearly impossible for D&Os to successfully hide behind the business judgment rule, absent well-documented, aggressive, and proactive efforts. The business judgment rule requires D&O to make reasonable and informed decisions based on all material information that is reasonably available. Because of the foreseeability exclusion, D&Os that fail to qualify for protection under the business judgment rule may simultaneously be left unprotected by D&O insurance for claims based on actions or omissions that occurred in the mid-to-late 1990s.

The Year 2000 Information and Readiness Disclosure Act might play an interesting role in the use of Year 2000 insurance questionnaires. Some attorneys think that, under what they believe to be a plausible reading of the provisions of the act, an insurance company may be prevented from denying claims based on allegedly false or misleading information contained in the application. While this was not necessarily an intended purpose of the act, it may generate significant activity in the legal departments of many carriers.

However, there are two reasons why the act may not apply in this context. First, Year 2000 statements "made in conjunction with the formation of the contract" may "alter or amend the contract." If the questionnaire is deemed part of the contract, then the tort-based protections of the act would be irrelevant. Often the stated purpose of the carrier is not to incorporate the questionnaire into the contract, but rather simply to assess the company's preparedness as a means of underwriting. Still other times the carriers merely want to keep a record of the insureds' position in the event of a disclosure-based claim, such as a shareholder derivative suit. These latter uses for the questionnaires may not qualify for the exception. Second, the act immunizes makers of Year 2000 statements against *civil actions*. Procedurally, it would be the insured that brings an action for wrongful denial of insurance coverage and the carrier that defends its decision on the basis of false or misleading underwriting application information. A defense to a civil action might not be a civil action for purposes of the act. If it is not, carriers are free to deny claims without hindrance from the act.

Breach of Warranty Clauses

Most applications for D&O liability insurance contain significant warranty language related to the completeness of required disclosures and accuracy of the answers to insurer underwriting questions. The application becomes part of the coverage form, so that less than forthright answers or incorrect or incomplete facts can have serious consequences related to the insurers' responsibility to cover claims later. A recent trend in D&O renewal applications actually favors insureds. D&O insurers generally do not require the same warranty statements at renewal as they do for a new coverage application. These disparate applications are intended to ease the renewal process, and insurers rely on the continued accuracy of the original warranties. Historically a *main-form* renewal application containing warranties was required to protect the underwriter by getting new disclosures of important facts. The competitive D&O insurance market has significantly eroded this standard practice to the point where most insurers are willing to accept renewal applications without warranties. This trend may limit insurers' ability to deny Y2K claims on the basis of breach of application warranty, especially for long-time policyholders.

Criminal Acts

In addition to false or misleading statements on the application, any act found to be intentionally fraudulent or criminal will always be excluded on all coverage forms. As a matter of public policy such acts typically cannot be covered by insurance. *Severability of covered persons* can therefore become an important coverage feature when these issues arise. If the insurance contract features severability, those covered persons who are innocent of the excluded act may still find themselves protected by the insurance coverage.

Failure to Notify Insurer of a Material Change in Risk

Most policies require insureds to notify their insurers of *material changes in risk*. This obligation may be a basis for avoiding coverage. The argument is that had insurers been notified of the increased risk due to Y2K, they may have charged additional premiums, sought additional information, instituted exclusions, or canceled the policy.

Failure to Preserve Insurers Right of Subrogation

One fundamental principal of insurance is the *right of subrogation*, or transfer of all legal rights of the insureds to the insurer. Failure to preserve insurers' right to recover claim payments from third parties can void the carriers' obligation to pay on the claim. In the Y2K arena, these risks are omnipresent. One example is the elimination of the warranty of merchantability under a software license by modifying, tampering with, or otherwise attempting to view the source code. This can occur during remediation and preserving the warranty for software and systems requires proper legal counseling.

Risks for Insurers

The insurance industry is faced with perhaps greater Year 2000 exposures than any other industry. Insurers face the same exposures addressed throughout this book (internal systems, embedded systems, external business dependencies, electronic data interchange, etc.) and utilize systems that are particularly date-dependent. Unique to the insurance industry are the financial dependence on the stock and bond markets and the tremendous claims exposure not felt by any other industry. This section addresses the risks unique to the insurance industry.

Bad Faith Claims

Because of the historical differential in power between insurers and insureds, policyholders are entitled by statute and common law to bring bad faith claims against insurers for various forms of malfeasance. In the Y2K context there is an increased likelihood of such claims being filed and won. As discussed previously, determining whether a given policy extends or excludes coverage to Y2K-related losses is not a simple matter. In addition, proving the ultimate cause of a given loss may be extremely difficult, if not impossible. Adjusters will have a difficult time dealing with the complexity of these cases, not to mention the increased volume that may be expected in the months and years to follow. Insureds will experience delays in claim processing and perhaps wrongful denials. These are the typical bases for bad faith claims. Successful bad faith claims often result in treble damages, which in the Y2K context could be quite onerous for insurers.

Collusion

One of the factors contributing to the astronomical cost associated with Y2K is the threat of sanctions or penalties associated with federal antitrust laws and state commercial codes preventing *collusion* (agreements between insurers intended to deceive or defraud policyholders). Even though sharing research and compliance information would reduce the overall cost of Y2K and benefit the business community tremendously, fear of allegations of collusion (as well as liability concerns for disseminating incorrect information) prevents this form of cost sharing. In the insurance context, insurers might be prevented from establishing a unified approach to Y2K risks. Although policies vary, a unified approach from the industry would give clarity and serve to prevent future bad faith litigation. For example, industry standards for the definition of Year 2000 and Y2K-related losses would benefit policyholders and insurers alike. Such attempts by industry, however, may bring allegations of collusion by consumer groups and large insureds.

The *Year 2000 Readiness and Disclosure Act* exempts from the antitrust laws "conduct engaged in . . . solely for the purpose of . . . communicating or disclosing information to help correct or avoid the effects of year 2000 processing failure." It is unclear, however, whether the exemption would apply to conduct designed to protect insurers from excludable losses, particularly in view of the statutory language stating that "the exemption granted by this section shall be construed narrowly."

Reinsurance

All insurers have a limited capacity for risk and depend on the reinsurance market to limit their exposure by specific policy or policy line (facultative reinsurance) or by annual aggregate exposure (treaty reinsurance). Until recently, the reinsurance market has not addressed the issue of Y2K. Given the substantial sums and the litigious nature of Year 2000, it should be a paramount issue for reinsurers. To give the issue some perspective, the current capacity for all liability insurance (and reinsurance) for North America is approximately $290 billion. The $300 billion remediation cost estimates alone dwarfs this total capacity, not to mention the $1 trillion litigation estimate discussed previously. If the actual expense is even one-tenth of these estimates, Y2K losses, if covered by insurance, will bankrupt the industry.

One reinsurer has recently added a Y2K exclusion to some of its facultative policies. This may mark a trend that others will follow. If treaty reinsurance excludes Y2K, there will be no choice for primary carriers but to follow suit. It is also likely that the policy language adopted by reinsurers will be mirrored in those policies held by primary insureds.

Subrogation

It is a basic tenet of insurance coverage that insurers may stand in the place of the policyholder to recover claims paid against the ultimately responsible party. This ability to *subrogate* allows insurers to recover billions of dollars of claims paid every year. Often the ultimately responsible party has insurance coverage of its own, and insurers often find themselves recovering from one another. Y2K-related claims will come in many forms. Many such claims, if paid by insurers, will be subrogated.

Even though such phenomena do occur regardless of year 2000, the sheer number of similar situations insurers may face resulting from Y2K may be

Example of a Subrogated Y2K Claim

A control circuit overheats due to a Y2K failure that results in a fire. The fire destroys an automobile plant. The automaker files a property damage and business interruption claim with its property insurer (insurer A). Although insurer A denies coverage for the failed circuit, it pays for the resulting property and business income loss. As expected, insurer A subrogates against the manufacturer of the control circuit. The manufacturer, upon receiving the complaint, files a products liability claim with its CGL carrier (insurer B). After extensive coverage review (and a declaratory judgment action), insurer B pays insurer A for the consequential losses suffered by the automaker. We can easily imagine a scenario where insurer A and insurer B are one and the same.

overwhelming. Each stage of subrogation creates additional expense that may be born by the party left standing at the end. It is easily imaginable that a single loss could be subrogated four or five times until the final ultimately responsible party is held accountable, and that party may be the initial insurer that sought subrogation. These are the types of issues insurers must consider today before substantial resources are wasted.

Loss Adjustment

Insurers face at least five problems with adjusting Y2K-related claims. First, adjusters have never dealt with year 2000 and lack practical experience in assessing related losses. Second, the nature of Y2K in many cases makes determining the ultimate cause of loss extremely difficult. Third, as discussed throughout this chapter, issues of coverage determination for Y2K-related losses are complex and require information unavailable to adjusters. Fourth, the pervasiveness and acute timing of year 2000 will create an unprecedented number of claims being filed in a relatively short period of time. Fifth, at precisely the same time when volume is at its highest, adjusting claim tracking systems (insurance company computers, Internet, telephony, etc.) might become impaired by Y2K. In short, insurers face the daunting task of making many rapid decisions of a complex nature, with potentially volatile implications, relying on hampered technology and untrained, undirected, and overwhelmed adjusters.

Disclosure of Y2K Insurance Coverage

There are many reasons to assess the applicability of existing coverages to the millennium bug. Aside from the obvious benefits of knowing whether your organization is insured for Y2K losses and satisfying senior management's duties to be informed and mitigate known risks, another reason to review your policies is to be able to disclose this information. Several disclosure requirements are associated with year 2000; insurance is one of them.

FFIEC Disclosures

The Federal Financial Institutions Examination Council has required all federally supervised banks to assess the impacts of Y2K on their borrower's ability to repay their loans (1997):

> The approach of the Year 2000 creates potentially adverse effects on the creditworthiness of borrowers. Corporate customers who have not considered Year 2000 issues may experience a disruption in business, resulting in potential financial difficulties affecting their creditworthiness. Financial institutions should

develop processes to identify, assess, and control the potential Year 2000 credit risk in their lending and investment portfolios.

Most banks are developing disclosure criteria to request from their borrowers. It is expected that many banks will include requests for insurance information.

Mergers and Acquisitions

Y2K is not a routine due-diligence investigation as part of a merger or acquisition, but it should be. Because insurance programs are typically evaluated as part of the overall liability profile, and because Y2K is now on the front pages of most legal and business periodicals, Year 2000 insurance will likely become a standard disclosure requirement during most corporate restructuring.

Y2K Specialty Policies

Insurance is currently available for risks associated with the Year 2000 computer problem. In general, the policies tend to be very expensive and require the would-be insured to undergo a lengthy approval process. The insurers take an appropriate comprehensive risk management approach by blending insurance with Y2K consulting services.

With prohibitive costs, however, such policies are aimed at larger companies and do not address the needs of millions of small and medium-sized businesses. Moreover, Y2K insurance does not provide a panacea for Year 2000 problems. Companies will qualify for policies only if they are diligent in addressing Y2K issues. Specialized Y2K policies are or have been available from Aon, AIG, and J&H Marsh & McLennan.

Aon's ARM2000

Aon Risk Services and AM-Re Managers, Inc. created the ARM2000 program, which is now closed to new business. ARM2000 is intended to help achieve compliance in *best-practice* fashion, while providing risk management, insurance, validation, and business continuation strategies. Best-practice methodology separates compliance efforts into five phases: awareness, assessment, renovation, validation, and implementation. During the awareness and assessment phases, Aon evaluates the prospect's overall Y2K risks. The prospect may purchase the Twenty-First Century Insurance Policy if it passes the first two phases. Once insured, the company must undergo periodic Y2K evaluations throughout the life of the policy.

With a policy period from inception to March 1, 2001, the Twenty-First Century Insurance Policy includes direct and contingent business interruption, extra expense coverage, general liability, and E&O and D&O liability insurance. Self-insured retention can be as low as $250,000 and policy limits as high as $1 billion. Premiums are 3 to 6 percent per annum on the first $100 million, and excess limits of $900 million are available at market rates.

J&H Marsh & McLennan's 2000 SECURE

J&H Marsh & McLennan's (J&H) Y2K insurance product is dubbed *2000 SECURE*. Similar to Aon, J&H blends advisory services with insurance coverage. The product is intended for companies with the financial capability to accept retention and premiums ranging from $1 million to $10 million. Coverage is offered after a successful, thorough review of the prospect's Y2K correction plan. The insurance covers wrongful acts, business interruption, and hot site expenses.

Several important exclusions exist in 2000 SECURE, and may exist in other policies as well. First, unless specifically added to the policy, Y2K problems relating to embedded microprocessors in noncomputing equipment are not covered. Second, increases in Year 2000 hazards subsequent to the effective date of the policy are not covered if they are not accounted for in the Y2K corrective plan and are within the control of the insured. Last, copyright infringement that may result from remediation efforts is not covered.

Several other brokers are currently working on products to compete with AON and J&H Marsh & McLennan offerings.

American International Group

American International Group (AIG) is the largest commerical insurer in North America. AIG has produced two policies that address Year 2000 that are important because of their professed coverage of Year 2000 and because AIG is a driving force behind many insurance trends.

Millennium Insurance Policy

AIG Risk Finance, a division of American International Group, Inc., has marketed a Year 2000 insurance product called *Millennium Insurance*. Unlike Aon's and J&H Marsh & McLennan's, AIG's policy is closer to risk financing than risk transfer. Similar to Aon and J&H, AIG makes underwriting subject to an audit of the applicant's Y2K conversion plans, as well as an ongoing requirement that the insured refrain from materially altering or intentionally failing to execute the conversion plan. This program is now closed to new business.

Millennium Insurance covers direct business interruption, contingent business interruptions, E&O, D&O, and the insureds' legal liability resulting from its own or a third party's conversion efforts. The policy period is from inception to January 1, 2001 and provides aggregate coverage limits up to $100 million. Premiums range from 65 to 85 percent of the purchased limit and are paid in quarterly installments to the year 2000. A significant portion of premium funds may be returned to the insured in the event of good loss experience. The initial audit is expected to take two weeks to complete and cost $50,000. Subsequent audits are estimated at $25,000 each.

AIG D&O Gold

In addition to offering its Millennium Insurance risk financing package, AIG has taken a unique approach to its D&O portfolio. *AIG D&O Gold* is the first substantial revision to its primary D&O product since May 1995, also known as the 5/95 form. D&O Gold incorporates some new coverage features unrelated to Y2K, which reflect the current practice in the market of continuing to offer broader, more favorable terms to its insureds. What is interesting about the product is the treatment of year 2000.

AIG Gold departs from the rest of the industry by attempting to define and grant limited coverage for Year 2000 rather than remain silent. Those who acquire and negotiate D&O policies have received it with mixed reviews. Some have expressed the concern that AIG, as the market's leading D&O insurer, is attempting to put Y2K in a box. By offering an alternative policy with specific coverage grants and higher premiums, AIG may be laying the groundwork to deny Y2K-related claims for policies other than the AIG Gold product.

Other Policies

There are rumored to be new specific Year 2000 insurance coverage forms released after the publication of this book. Four in particular are Globex Insurance, Monitor Insurance, CNA, and the Year 2000 Residual Risk Insurance Policy.

Commentary on Available Insurance Coverages

Upon examining the exposures facing insureds and insurers alike, the only certainty is uncertainty. This phenomenon alone is contrary to underwriting principles and the principles of the entire insurance industry. Although the Y2K-specific insurance programs provide a certain degree of comfort to those organizations that participate, they require replacement of the existing policy lines that have been negotiated and shaped over years of insurance relationships. In addition, Y2K policy pricing makes insurance unattainable to all but the Fortune 250.

The insurance industry, like most industries, has not effectively addressed year 2000 by tackling it head on. Instead, with less than a year remaining, insureds are left with few options for insurance protection. This is particularly troublesome for proactive entities that have effectively addressed their exposures, but may nonetheless experience losses.

Conclusion

The landscape for the insurance market is as uneven as for Y2K in general. The interaction of established insurance policies and the multitude of claim scenarios that will occur create complex coverage questions. The centuries-old insurance industry has never before faced an exposure like year 2000. Perhaps this is why it has responded so slowly and inconsistently.

The complexity and diversity of insurance issues is testament to the very nature of Year 2000 and its pervasiveness. Every Y2K-related liability, every Y2K-related property loss, and every cost-recovery effort may implicate insurance coverage. Because billions of dollars are at stake, insureds and insurers alike will exhaust substantial resources to collect or prevent claims. Likewise, the ultimate question of coverage will be very much fact-dependent, and each case will involve difficult questions of coverage interpretation and proof of loss.

Suffice it to say, insurers and insureds face a very uncertain future. For centuries, of course, uncertainties were the basis for insurance. Ironically, insurers have effectively balked at year 2000. Today, the greatest uncertainty is the size of the impact of Y2K on insureds, insurers, and the economy. Congress may have to consider measures to avoid a collapse of the insurance industry, widespread bankruptcies of insureds, or a flood of litigation overwhelming the nation's court dockets. To forestall widespread insurance coverage litigation, the industry should also consider alternative forms of dispute resolution, which we discuss next in Chapter 10.

CHAPTER 10

Alternative Dispute Resolution

"Litigation—A popular, efficient, quick, inexpensive and enjoyable means of resolving business disputes without disrupting productive activities and with predictable, rational and gratifying results every time."

—THE WISHFUL THINKER'S LAW DICTIONARY
 (HOCK, 1997)

In the Year 2000 context, *alternative dispute resolution* (ADR) can represent the last clear chance to maintain business operations and resolve conflicts among trading partners without lawsuits that may be destructive to all concerned. Organizations should work with their external business dependencies to put written ADR agreements in place before disputes arise. In this chapter, we will explain what types of Y2K disputes are best suited to ADR, the various types of ADR available, and steps for developing an ADR program that can serve as a legal contingency plan to resolve disputes without litigation. We begin by looking more closely at potential Year 2000 disputes and the hard realities of litigation that make ADR such an attractive alternative.

Examples of Year 2000 Disputes

Businesses are likely to face a broad array of disruptions that range from annoying, to aggravating, to incapacitating. Shipping delays, personnel turnover, late payments, missed deadlines, unsuccessful remediation work, poor test results, consultant and contractor defaults, insurance disputes, and customer complaints are likely to become commonplace in 1999 and 2000. Let's consider a couple of possible Y2K scenarios that might crop up in the next two years as a way of better understanding the need for efficient, nonadversarial mechanisms for resolving conflicts in the real world.

A Difficult Remediation Project

Medicinal Compounds, Inc. is a corporation with sales of $500 million that distributes generic pharmaceutical chemicals to wholesale drug manufacturers. In 1995, it hired Tech Services Corp. to upgrade its midrange computer and storage capacity, expand its client/server network, and develop a customized turnkey system to automate its financial management, order placement and fulfillment, and warehouse management systems for $3.5 million. After some delays and performance problems, which Tech worked diligently to address without additional cost to Medicinal, the project was substantially completed in late 1996, at which time Medicinal signed a maintenance and support agreement with Tech at an annual cost of $50,000. Neither the original project specifications nor the 1996 agreement mentioned Year 2000.

In 1998, Medicinal heard about Y2K and asked Tech to certify that the system was compliant. Tech refused, saying that the system conformed to all contract specifications and that the system could not be made compliant without upgrading the operating system and network hardware at a cost of $250,000. When Medicinal demanded that Tech provide the upgrades and additional services under the maintenance and support agreement, Tech again refused, stating that the inability to process twenty-first century dates was not a "defect" or "program error" and was therefore beyond the scope of the contract.

Medicinal reluctantly agreed to pay Tech to perform the work necessary to make the system Y2K compliant because it would have cost substantially more to hire a new contractor that was unfamiliar with the system architecture to start from scratch. Tech had started a new Year 2000 remediation practice in early 1998 to serve its existing customers and found that it was able to attract many new clients throughout 1998. Tech prepared a project plan for Medicinal that called for the hardware upgrades to be installed by May 1999, the noncompliant software code to be rewritten by June, and testing to be completed by October.

The project was plagued with problems from its inception. Medicinal was not one of Tech's larger clients and Medicinal believed that Tech had not assigned its best people to the task. The first two project managers were reassigned to other projects on more lucrative contracts, and the third manager left to take a higher-paying position with another company. In April, the manufacturer of the network hardware informed Tech that the delivery of routers, hubs, and other necessary components would be delayed by two months, so Tech proposed to suspend work and reassign its team until the equipment arrived. It promised to assign additional personnel to the project and assured Medicinal that it would complete the "mission-critical" work in time. When Medicinal asked Tech for access to the source code so Medicinal's own IS staff could begin remediation, Tech informed Medicinal that it was prohibited from doing such work under the terms of its license agreement.

To no one's surprise, Tech did not complete Medicinal's mission-critical systems in time. The automated warehouse system rejected perishable chemicals because the "00" expiration dates had apparently passed. Electronically placed orders were not logged or filled in sequence, and customers were erroneously notified that their accounts were substantially past due. Tech informed Medicinal that it would be necessary to suspend operations for two weeks in order to restore reliable operations. Medicinal's insurance agent informed Medicinal that its business interruption policy would not provide coverage for any financial losses resulting from the shutdown since no "physical loss of use" had occurred, as required by the policy. Customer inquiries and threats to curtail business began to mount, and the bank providing Medicinal's line of credit was calling for an independent audit of its books. Medicinal has threatened to sue Tech, which would have serious repercussions for Tech's other Y2K work.

An Unreliable Supply Chain

Household Goods & Supply has operated a chain of six department stores throughout the Midwest since the 1950s, selling clothing, household appliances, and consumer electronics. It started its internal Y2K remediation project in 1996, rewriting and testing the code its IS department had developed and refined for over 20 years. That project was in good shape, with all work scheduled for completion and testing by March, 1999.

The compliance status of its external business dependencies, however, was another matter entirely. In 1998, Household compiled a list of 1500 suppliers, 25 distributors, and 150 service providers from its schedule of accounts payable. It sent out a detailed questionnaire to all 1675 vendors requiring an authorized officer of the company to certify that it would be compliant no later than June 1999. Fewer than 10 percent responded, none signed the certification, and most of the responses were form letters that simply stated that the vendor was aware of the problem and was "confident" that it would be compliant in time. Follow-up phone calls increased the response rate marginally. Its value-added network provider would not certify EDI compliance unless Household installed an expensive software upgrade.

Household began to encounter serious problems starting in late 1999. EDI transactions failed or were inaccurate. Many staple items such as jeans, CD players and washing machines were not delivered on time, and its shelves became depleted. When it tried to buy replacement goods from other suppliers, it found them backlogged by other retailers having similar problems. The delivery company it had used for many years went out of business when its payroll company was unable to process paychecks for its employees.

The Moral of Both Stories

In 1999, Medicinal and Household missed opportunities to work with key business partners to avoid later problems. In 2000, they both need expeditious ways to restore operations and forestall further losses. Thus, the kinds of dispute resolution mechanisms that businesses need include resolving disagreements with Y2K contractors to successfully complete remediation projects, fairly allocating the unanticipated costs of Year 2000 repairs, enabling work to get done in the face of multilevel business dependencies, accelerating mission-critical work, eliciting cooperation among suppliers fearful of liability, protecting cash flow and credit, maintaining customer support, and controlling losses through insurance coverage. How could they accomplish these objectives in times of crisis?

Differing Perspectives on Y2K Failures

To evaluate dispute resolution options it is important to understand that trading partners come into Y2K conflicts from divergent points of view. How companies perceive their economic and legal self-interests will affect their orientation toward Y2K disputes.

Buyers

Companies that purchase IT and other products and services that are damaged by their own Y2K failures and those of their trading partners are likely to view Year 2000 problems along the following lines:

- A trivial technical problem—two measly digits—threatens the viability of their business.
- IT vendors are responsible for the problem because they should have foreseen it and known that their customers relied on their technical expertise.
- Buyers are forced to repair, replace, or upgrade their technology systems much sooner than they had expected.
- The IT industry has a terrible record of project mismanagement and bug-ridden systems.
- Enormous remediation expenditures are required just to enable businesses to continue operating as they are today.
- IT customers need a functioning system now, not just monetary compensation.
- If their businesses are disrupted, IT customers want to be made whole for all of their losses, including additional direct expenditures they incurred to keep

operating, such as temporary staffing, overtime costs, and increased inventory charges, as well as lost profits and damage to their business goodwill.
- They don't see litigation as an effective solution to their immediate problems.
- They expect insurance coverage for their Y2K losses.

Sellers

Companies selling goods and services that are affected by Y2K failures—including but not limited to IT companies—see things quite differently:

- Six-digit dates have been a standard programming design parameter for decades that saved customers millions of dollars in storage and processing costs.
- Sellers cannot afford to assume unlimited liability for all of the business consequences of technical failures.
- IT companies must protect their valuable intellectual property rights from infringement.
- The problem is just too big to fix without charging clients for the additional services they need to become compliant.
- Otherwise thriving companies could face severe financial losses and even bankruptcy.
- Companies that don't sell information technology products or services feel that they should not be liable to third parties due to IT failures that are beyond their control.
- The IT industry could take a huge public relations hit that will damage goodwill with customers and invite federal and state regulatory oversight.
- Companies cannot afford the time, expense, and other transaction costs of litigation.
- Companies expect liability insurance coverage if they are sued due to Y2K problems.

What active steps can companies take in 1999 to reconcile these differing interests and ameliorate the business and legal risks from Y2K disputes? We will look first at what litigation has to offer before considering ADR.

The Burdens of Y2K Litigation

Few "civilians" who have never sued anyone or been sued themselves understand how excruciatingly difficult and frustrating lawsuits can actually be. The General Counsel of Netscape Communications Corporation speaks critically of "a civil justice system reduced to an ugly mix of lottery, gladiatorial combat, and farce" (Katz, 1997). Even for cases that do not become acrimonious—as they all too often do—litigation is almost always a black hole that sucks up time, energy, and money. In many cases, there might not be any choice but to file suit. But before you decide to sit back and just wait to see if you'll be sued for Y2K problems, consider the limitations and costs of uncontrolled litigation.

Judicial Relief

Litigation is a very blunt instrument. It is designed primarily to compensate a party whose legal rights have been violated by awarding them monetary damages. But financial compensation is an incomplete remedy at best for many of the business risks we discussed in Chapter 1, "Year 2000 Business and Legal Risks." Even a monetary judgment for financial losses incurred often fails to fully compensate the plaintiff, particularly when the considerable transactions costs of commercial litigation are taken into account.

Although courts can provide *equitable remedies*—judicial orders to do or refrain from doing something in violation of someone else's rights—those powers are exercised sparingly and require very compelling evidence of wrongdoing and imminent and unavoidable injury. By and large, courts are not in the business of telling companies how they must deal with each other or protecting them from harm. Rather, the court's primary job is to enforce pre-existing contractual agreements to adjust the monetary gains and losses after the damage has been done. Thus, courts will often be the appropriate forum for Y2K cost recovery actions, but judicial remedies are generally not the stuff of which risk management is made.

Lawsuits do sometimes produce settlements in which the parties agree on certain acts of further performance, but placing a gun to your vendors' head is not a very sound basis for a productive business relationship, and the process is likely to be slow. Litigation is far more likely to generate antagonism than serve as an instrument of behavior modification.

Preparing the Case

Everyone knows that litigation is too expensive and takes too long, but few understand why. The most common reason is *discovery*: the fact-finding process that consumes most of the time, money, and energy in civil litigation. Modern discovery rules were enacted to reform the litigation process, but they have become a frequent subject of abuse responsible for many of the inefficiencies of litigation. It is not unusual for the discovery phase to take more than a year or even two or three, depending on the size of the case. The principal discovery devices are document requests, interrogatories, and depositions, and they can become civilized instruments of torture.

Document requests. The discovery rules allow each party to request copies of all documents in its opponents' "possession, custody, or control" that are even remotely relevant to the case. It is not unusual in a large commercial dispute for parties to request roomfuls of documents from each other, all of which must be reviewed, indexed, abstracted, checked for privileged communications, copied, and produced, as part of a tremendously time-consuming exercise. All litigators have reams of standardized document requests in their word processors, ready to cut and paste for each new case. A typical document request—of which there might be 30 or more served by each party, depending on the rules of the particular jurisdiction—might look this:

> Please produce a copy of every document evidencing, referring, or relating to each and every defect removal and remediation test you performed or caused to be performed, including but not limited to (a) subroutine testing, unit testing, new function testing, regression testing, integration testing, capacity testing, system testing, and acceptance testing, and (b) for each such test, the original and nonidentical copy of every test assessment, plan, script, library, bed, data, creation, execution, report, certification, validation, and acceptance.

Interrogatories. These are written questions that opposing parties are required to answer under oath. Again, word processors generate them in no time at all, but it can take many hours to answer them. A typical interrogatory—again, one of two or three dozen—might read as follows:

> Please separately identify each and every action you took or directed others to take to prevent the occurrence of Year 2000 problems, stating for each such action:
>
> a) The date the action was taken;
>
> b) A full and complete description of the action that was taken;
>
> c) The name, job title, business address, and phone number of each person who was involved in taking the action;
>
> d) The instructions you gave to, and the responsibilities of each such person;
>
> e) How you determined that such action was necessary and sufficient;
>
> f) The human, financial, technical, and other resources you caused to be provided to support the action taken;
>
> g) Your role in supervising or monitoring each such person to ensure that the action was properly performed;
>
> h) The results that were achieved by taking the action; and
>
> i) The steps taken to verify that the action would be successful in preventing the occurrence of Year 2000 problems.

Depositions. Depositions are examinations of a party or a witness under oath before trial. The deposition is transcribed by a court stenographer. Given that more than 90 percent of cases settle, a deposition is likely to be the only live testimony in most cases, so lawyers treat them seriously as the best opportunity to force their client's adversaries to directly answer question after question about every detail of the circumstances giving rise to the dispute. It is not unusual for a deposition to last more than a full day for a key witness and, in cases with many parties, the lawyer for each party can conduct his or her own examination. As in the case of interrogatories and document requests, the relevancy standard is extremely broad, so counsel can ask many invasive questions about the witness's salary and other compensation, employment history, job performance on the current and past positions, and everything he or she did or—more importantly—failed to do to avert the Year 2000 failures that led to the lawsuit. Not surprisingly, a great deal of time is required to prepare for the deposition, both for the attorney conducting the examination and for the witness who is being deposed.

The Court's View

Judges serve many roles in the judicial process: managing crowded dockets, finding the facts in bench trials decided without a jury, ruling on motions, and instructing juries on the legal principles that govern their deliberations. Although it is dangerous to generalize, most judges believe that they are burdened with many unnecessary matters that attorneys and their clients should resolve by agreement, and they often encourage and sometimes pressure parties to settle cases. They tend to be an independent-minded lot with strong opinions about the merits of the cases before them that often translate into priorities about the processing of cases through the system. The trial of criminal cases take precedence over civil cases (for constitutional and statutory reasons), older cases come before newer ones, shorter before longer, and so on. Cases that judges think should be settled and that involve difficult technical questions that judges and juries might not understand and find tedious may take longer to see their day in court. Complex Year 2000 cases that involve a lot of dry testimony and technical documents about programming code, project management schedules, and compliance testing will probably take years to reach trial. This is especially likely to be so if the courts become clogged with thousands of Y2K cases, as they did with asbestos suits in the 1980s.

In addition, the lack of precedents for problems like Y2K present significant uncertainties about how courts will treat the novel legal issues they raise. How will courts enforce "repair or replace" warranties when plaintiffs contend that their IT vendors misled them about the capabilities of the system? Will judges find that such warranties are unconscionable or failed of their essential purpose with respect to intractable Year 2000 problems? Will cases against suppliers of older, noncompliant computers be dismissed for missing statutes of limitations, even when the buyers were unaware of latent Y2K defects? Will courts finally recognize the tort of computer malpractice? Will judges instruct possibly unsympathetic juries that they may find that directors and officers were grossly negligent—and therefore unprotected by the business judgment rule—if they failed to tackle Year 2000 risks more aggressively? Even experienced attorneys don't yet know the answers to these questions and dozens more like them, so there is likely to be greater uncertainty in bringing a Year 2000 dispute to court.

How Will Juries Regard Y2K?

Conventional wisdom holds that technical cases bore and confuse juries. Even though awareness of Y2K has increased among businesses and the public and will surely continue to do so through the century transition, many jurors will find it hard to understand how corporate managers—be they plaintiffs or defendants—could have allowed this trivial problem to get so far out of hand. Add project mismanagement on both sides, and you have an unpredictable mix that could cut against either side of the case.

Businesses should also recognize that plaintiffs' attorneys understand the need to entertain juries with a compelling and even lurid reason for awarding substantial damages to their clients. IT companies can expect to see themselves depicted as callous, indifferent, sloppy, and incompetent—hardly an ideal marketing image to read about in the newspaper.

Special Risks for IT Companies

Indeed, when it comes to far-reaching Y2K failures, the IT industry has much more at stake than just potentially massive financial losses, as if that weren't enough. *Computerworld* columnist Peter G.W. Keen has written that IT will soon be "as popular as air pollution," with Year 2000 being just one of several reasons he cites for an imminent IT backlash (Keen, 1998). If our dependence on computers becomes the catalyst for cascading business disruptions and bankruptcies, worsening recession, and lawsuits seeking hundreds of billions of dollars in damages, customers are likely to become increasingly hostile to poorly planned and executed technology projects.

Both the industry as a whole and the tens of thousands of companies that constitute it have vital reputational interests that acrimonious lawsuits by angry customers will severely damage. Technology projects could become harder to sell, and procurements could be reduced in scope by companies that have been badly burned by Y2K. At a minimum, corporate customers will undoubtedly insist on stronger project management controls and tighter contract specifications, further eroding the razor-thin margins under which many hardware and software firms now operate. Prices of overvalued technology stocks could deflate dramatically. Forced retirements, resignations, and turnover of directors, officers, and CIOs are widely expected.

The point is both simple and obvious: Getting sued by your customers is not good for business. It is understandable that IT companies would be reluctant to make the first move toward negotiated resolution of Y2K disputes before they materialize. But hoping in vain that inevitable problems aren't going to happen will probably make it more likely that you'll end up in court, caught up in a process in which both sides lose control and decisions are generally not business-based. Technology companies therefore have special incentives to initiate discussions about ADR during 1999 as a way of maintaining confidence in the industry and forestalling time-consuming and corrosive litigation.

The ADR initiative sponsored by the Information Technology Association of America (ITAA) represents a worthy beginning:

> When an IT/Y2K dispute arises, the use of ADR will enable businesses to:
> - Save time and money
> - Promote and facilitate productive communications
> - Encourage sharing of crucial information
> - Maintain and preserve important on-going business relationships
> - Continue business operations with minimal disruptions through the century date change and beyond
> - Resolve issues in a private and confidential setting
> - Take charge of the result
> - Create practical and fair solutions (ITAA, 1998a).

Objectives of Year 2000 ADR

We hope that the preceding discussion demonstrates convincingly that there are many inherent limitations in resorting to lawsuits to resolve Year 2000 disputes. Let's now look at the benefits that ADR offers in their place. ADR can serve three important purposes to which litigation is poorly suited: (1) promoting information exchange, (2) working out incipient supply-chain disputes, and (3) resolving Year 2000 failures without destroying business relationships.

Sharing Compliance Information Safely

The *Year 2000 Information and Readiness Disclosure Act* helps companies avoid liability from disclosing compliance information, but it does not protect them from losing customers or taking hits in the press if their preparedness is not what it should be. It is likely that timely and accurate information about vendor compliance will continue to be difficult to obtain. But companies need to assure themselves and their stakeholders that they are exercising due diligence by investigating the compliance status of their external business dependencies. A neutral third party can help business partners safely exchange and rationally evaluate compliance information, and hammer out confidentiality agreements that will prevent unauthorized dissemination of sensitive information.

Preventing Supply-Chain Breakdowns

Trading partners must do more than simply exchange information; they must also cooperate in taking concurrent action to face the millennium transition. Shared interests include providing timely alerts of early failure horizons and coordinating testing protocols, contingency planning, and disaster recovery. ADR can help vertical market participants and industry groups work together to allocate risks, responsibilities, and costs of joint compliance efforts and to develop contract terms to account for Y2K contingencies that were not considered when relationships were first developed. For example, a mediator could help large retailers negotiate agreements with all of their suppliers to stockpile designated items of inventory in exchange for the retailer agreeing to pay additional storage and finance charges. By negotiating a mix of payments, services, and accommodations consistent with each side's interests, the parties can avert problems that might otherwise expose them to liability.

Settling Disputes and Avoiding Lawsuits

When failures occur, companies need to recoup their losses *and* get back to business. Incorporating ADR agreements into new and existing contracts before Year 2000 problems emerge will give both parties a clear path to an efficient and nonadversarial mechanism for settling claims. With the prospect of massive litigation looming on the horizon, it makes little sense for corporations to simply wait and see whether they get caught in the storm before they adopt ADR contingency plans.

Types of ADR

There are four main categories of alternative dispute resolution: (1) negotiation, (2) case evaluation, (3) mediation, and (4) arbitration. Typically, ADR agreements provide for sequential steps of negotiation, mediation, and arbitration until a resolution is achieved. Negotiation and mediation are consensual, while arbitration can be either binding or nonbinding, depending on the preferences of the parties. In addition, it is becoming increasingly common for courts to require the parties to go through an ADR screening process before proceeding further with civil litigation once a case has been filed.

Negotiation

Businesses engage in negotiations with other companies all the time. By simply agreeing in advance to engage in negotiations as a first step to addressing Y2K problems, the parties can put in place a structured arrangement that requires them to explore a nonadversarial resolution of the dispute. Good faith negotiation provides the parties with an opportunity to explain their respective points of view to see if there are common interests that can enable them to continue working together rather than suing each other.

Case Evaluation

Sometimes, it is important for the parties to a current or prospective dispute to take a reality test. If one or both sides have an exaggerated sense of their chances for prevailing in court or unrealistic expectations about the amount of monetary damages they are likely to recover or be forced to pay, the prospects for settling the case sooner rather than later could be diminished, to the detriment of all. Lawyers try to give their clients their own assessment of how the case looks, but it is hard to be objective when you are working hard to develop winning legal arguments and compelling evidence to support your side and defeat your opponent. Becoming convinced of the merits of your client's cause is an integral part of preparing the strongest possible case. Lawyers often think they should have won cases they lost; it is far less common for them to believe they should have lost a case they won.

ADR offers various methods for evaluating cases, including *neutral evaluation*, *mini-trials*, *conciliation*, and *summary jury trials*. In each case, an experienced neutral or panel of neutrals, usually senior lawyers or retired judges, hears an abbreviated presentation of evidence and legal arguments by their attorneys and then gives the parties a confidential appraisal of the case and a prediction of the probable outcome.

Mediation

Mediation involves the use of a neutral skilled in facilitating negotiations to promote a mutually agreeable settlement of some or all of the issues in dispute. The process usually begins with the submission of position papers by each party to the neutral. At the first meeting, all parties meet with the neutral and each party summarizes its position and discusses its approach to settlement. This is a good opportunity for the clients to hear the evidence, arguments, and settlement rationale of the other side. The parties then separate and meet privately with the neutral so he or she can learn each side's position, areas of common and disputed ground, the flexibility of the respective positions, and the interests of the parties. If successful, the neutral will be able to bring the parties closer through hours, and sometimes days, of shuttle diplomacy.

Arbitration

Arbitration is a private version of litigation that can be significantly more cost-efficient. In this process, the parties select an odd number of neutral panel members whose role is to conduct hearings, accept evidence, and render a summary decision and award based on the evidence. The arbitrators are typically individuals with experience in the relevant industry and with the legal and factual issues to be resolved, which reduces the need to educate the fact finder about things such as industry custom and practice. The parties control the hearing dates and the amount of evidence introduced, and arbitrators are typically required to render a decision within a short amount of time, usually 30 days after the last hearing date. A binding arbitration award can be enforced in court in an expedited proceeding in which only limited issues are considered.

The main advantages of arbitration are speed, confidentiality, and finality. The disadvantages are that, in binding arbitration at least, the parties must accept the arbitrator's decision with only very narrow rights of appeal.

Court-Ordered ADR

Legislators and the judiciary have recognized that the court system cannot efficiently handle all of the disputes presented to it. Increasingly, the judicial system is requiring some form of ADR before the parties proceed too far down the litigation path. Most state and federal trial courts and certain state agencies have instituted early settlement conferences or referrals to mediation or conciliation. Parties that are already involved in lawsuits can use ADR to reduce the scope of disputed issues, thereby reducing the cost and time required to reach a final disposition.

Building Corporate Y2K ADR Programs

Every business that might become entangled in Year 2000 litigation should make ADR a purposeful and strategic risk management initiative. Such programs provide a vehicle for preventing many identifiable Y2K failures and amicably resolving those that do occur. The planning process should follow other risk management models we have presented elsewhere in this book: enlisting management support, assigning program management responsibility, and identifying and prioritizing risks that ADR could ameliorate.

Gaining Management Support

Management might not leap at the suggestion that the company should contact its major customers and suppliers and propose that they agree to mediate disputes that have not occurred as a result of Y2K failures that have not yet happened. But there are strong selling points to be made in support of such a proactive program:

> Management's complaints about the litigation budget, the outrageous decision by a rogue jury, the interruption of business activity caused by seemingly meaningless depositions, the demands for endless document discovery, and the inability of courts to conclude an important case even after years of litigation, signal an opportunity for corporate counsel to introduce the possibility of switching to arbitration and mediation to resolve external and internal disputes (Baum, 1998).

Make the business case that in the course of discussions the company is already having with its customers, suppliers, and other external business dependencies about Year 2000 compliance, there is no incremental disadvantage in raising the subject of avoiding litigation if problems should occur. Present quantitative and qualitative assessments of the effects of a single lawsuit with measures that directors and officers can understand:

- The amount of time required for each of two or three directors, as well as the CEO, the CFO, the CIO, and the Y2K project manager to spend one day preparing to testify (including reviewing all relevant documents and being trained in the dos and don'ts of answering questions under oath) and one day giving deposition testimony.

- The impact of litigation on other ongoing business initiatives, such as mergers, expansions, marketing campaigns, or new product development.

- The customers and revenues that would be lost, either temporarily or permanently, if critical failures identified in the business risk assessment remained unresolved for two days, one week, or one month.

- The transaction costs that would be associated with a two-year Y2K suit, including attorneys' fees, expert witness fees, and other direct expenses.

- The specific technical, business, and liability risks facing your company (using the legal audit, if available), including any issues, notices, or cautions raised by the company's outside auditors, financial institutions, rating agencies, investment advisors, insurers, regulators, and attorneys, together with examples of actual Y2K failures that have already occurred in your company and your industry.

- A description of the Year 2000 ADR programs organized by the ITAA, the American Arbitration Association, private ADR providers, and state and local bar associations (see the sidebar entitled *Year 2000 ADR Resources*).

Program Development

The development of a corporate Year 2000 ADR program need not be an onerous undertaking. Once the organization examines its external business dependencies and conducts a business risk assessment, it should designate an ADR coordinator to draft and negotiate written ADR agreements with those third parties and screen cases that should be directed into the program.

Drafting Effective Year 2000 ADR Clauses

It is quite common for business contracts to include boilerplate dispute resolution clauses, such as the following:

> In the event of any dispute, claim, question, or disagreement arising from or relating to this agreement or the breach thereof, the parties hereto shall use their best efforts to settle the dispute, claim, question, or disagreement. To this effect, they shall consult and negotiate with each other in good faith and, recognizing their mutual interests, attempt to reach a just and equitable solution satisfactory to both parties. If they do not reach such solution within a period of 60 days, then, upon notice by either party to the other, all disputes, claims, questions, or differences shall be finally settled by arbitration administered by the American Arbitration Association in accordance with the provisions of its Commercial Arbitration Rules (American Arbitration Association, 1994a).

For purposes of resolving Year 2000 disputes, this standard form clause has several shortcomings. If one of the parties finds itself in a crisis situation as a result of serious Y2K failures, 60 days of unsuccessful negotiations could prove fatal. The clause does not provide for the parties to go to court to seek immediate *equitable relief*, such as a preliminary injunction, that might be essential if a case can be made that expedited judicial intervention is necessary to keep systems running, protect data, assist in recovery, or provide immediate access to escrowed source code.

In addition, the prescribed procedure jumps abruptly from negotiation conducted by the parties themselves—which might be ineffective without the participation of a skilled mediator—to arbitration, which can be the most time-consuming form of ADR (albeit much quicker than litigation). Moreover, arbitration is often better suited to settling monetary disputes than resolving ongoing operational emergencies. A phased approach of negotiation and mediation, followed by arbitration if the parties choose to go that route, is recommended.

> ### Year 2000 ADR Resources
>
> **Information Technology Association of America.** Provides information on its Web site to "assist your organization to build ADR clauses into your current and future contracts with vendors, suppliers, customers, risk managers, and others—and, if a dispute arises, help parties access expert ADR services."
> www.itaa.org/y2kadr.htm
>
> **American Arbitration Association.** A well-known nonprofit organization with offices and neutrals nationwide.
> www.adr.org
>
> **CPR Institute for Dispute Resolution.** A nonprofit alliance of 500 global corporations, leading law firms, and legal academics at the forefront of new alternatives to litigation. CPR announced the formation of a panel of Year 2000 neutrals in March 1998.
> www.cpradr.org/year2000.htm
>
> **JAMS/Endispute.** A large national private firm working with ITAA on a nonexclusive basis to establish a Y2K ADR program.
> www.jams-endispute.com
>
> **Dispute Resolution 2000.** A private ADR provider specializing in Year 2000 mediation and arbitration services provided by neutrals expert in Y2K law and technology.
> www.dr2000.com
>
> **Y2K-LAW.** Sponsored by U.K. solicitor Graham Ross, the Y2K Compliance Co-Operation Protocol (CCP) is designed to overcome suppliers' concerns about sharing compliance information with their customers.
> www.cybermetrix.co.uk/ccpindex.html

Finally, although ADR clauses are often drafted to expressly name the American Arbitration Association (AAA) as the organization that will conduct the dispute resolution process, parties might consider simply designating "a mutually agreeable provider of dispute resolution services experienced in Year 2000 matters" in order to afford flexibility in choosing an organization that is best suited to handling the particular dispute that comes to pass. AAA has recognized that ADR "can play an effective role in resolving many of these [Y2K] disputes" (Halket, 1998), but there are other ADR providers that also offer specialized expertise in addressing Y2K disputes (see sidebar, *Year 2000 ADR Resources*).

Here are examples of two Year 2000 ADR clauses. The first, prepared by the ITAA, prescribes a two-phase process of negotiation and mediation and includes an equitable relief provision. The second clause, developed by the State of Minnesota, adds a case evaluation component and sets forth detailed procedures for conducting the negotiations.

Information Technology Association of America

The parties will attempt in good faith to resolve through negotiation any dispute, claim or controversy arising out of or relating to this agreement. Either party may initiate Negotiations by providing written notice in a letter to the other party, setting forth the subject of the dispute and the relief requested. The recipient of such notice will respond in writing within five days with a statement of its position on and recommended solution to the dispute. If the dispute is not resolved by this exchange of correspondence, then representatives of each party with full settlement authority will meet at a mutually agreeable time and place within ten days of the date of the initial notice to exchange relevant information and perspectives, and to attempt to resolve the dispute. If the dispute is not resolved by these negotiations, the matter will be submitted to [designation of the ADR provider of parties' choosing], or its successor, for mediation.

Except as provided herein, no civil action related to any dispute, claim or controversy arising out of or relating to this agreement may be commenced until the matter has been submitted to the ADR provider, or its successor, for Mediation. Either party may commence Mediation [under specific rules of the ADR provider] by providing to the ADR provider of their choosing and the other party a written request for Mediation. A written request for Mediation shall set forth the subject of the dispute and the relief requested. The parties will cooperate with the ADR provider and with one another in selecting a Mediator from that ADR provider's panel of neutrals, and in scheduling the mediation proceedings.

The parties covenant that they will participate in the Mediation in good faith, and that they will share equally in its costs. All offers, promises, conduct and statements, whether oral or written, made in the course of the Mediation by any of the parties, their agents, employees, experts and attorneys, and by the mediator and any employees of the ADR provider of their choosing, are confidential and inadmissible for any purpose, including impeachment, in any litigation or other proceeding involving the parties. Notwithstanding this, that evidence that is otherwise admissible or discoverable shall not be rendered inadmissible or non-discoverable as a result of its use in the Mediation.

Either party may seek equitable relief prior to the Mediation to preserve the status quo pending the completion of that process. Except for such an action to obtain equitable relief, neither party may commence a civil action with respect to the matters submitted to mediation until after the completion of the initial mediation session, or 45 days after the date of filing the written request for mediation, whichever occurs first. Mediation may continue after the commencement of a civil action, if the parties so desire. The provisions of this Clause may be enforced by any court of competent jurisdiction, and the party seeking enforcement shall be entitled to an award of all costs, fees and expenses, including attorneys fees, to be paid by the party against whom enforcement is ordered (ITAA, 1998b).

State of Minnesota

In the event of a dispute between the Parties arising out of, or related to, the Year 2000 warranty of this Agreement (the "Dispute"), the Parties agree to utilize the procedures specified in this Section (the "Procedure") unless otherwise modified by agreement of the Parties at the time the dispute arises.

A party seeking to initiate the Procedure (the "Initiating Party") shall give written notice to the other party, describing briefly the nature of the dispute and identifying an individual with authority to settle the dispute on its behalf. The party receiving such notice (the "Responding Party") shall have five (5) days to provide the Initiating Party with a written response identifying an individual with authority to settle the Dispute on its behalf. (The individuals so designated are the "Authorized Individuals.")

The Authorized Individuals shall make investigation as they deem appropriate and thereafter promptly (but in no event later than fifteen (15) days from the date of the Initiating Party's notice) shall commence discussions concerning resolution of the Dispute. If the Dispute has not been resolved within fifteen (15) days from the commencement of discussions (such fifteenth day being the Submission Date) it shall be submitted to alternative dispute resolution ("ADR Process") in accordance with the following procedure.

The parties shall have five (5) days from the Submission Date to agree upon a mutually acceptable neutral person not affiliated with either of the parties (the "Neutral"). If no neutral has been selected within such time, the parties agree to jointly request the American Arbitration Association to supply within five (5) days a list of potential neutrals with qualifications as specified by the parties in the joint request. Within five (5) days of receipt of the list, the parties shall independently rank the proposed candidates, shall simultaneously exchange rankings and shall select as the Neutral the individual receiving the highest combined ranking who is available to serve.

In consultation with the Neutral, the parties shall promptly designate a mutually convenient time and place for the ADR Process (and unless circumstances require otherwise, such time to be not later than ten (10) days after selection of the Neutral).

In the event either of the parties has substantial need for information in the possession of the other party in order to prepare for the ADR Process, the parties shall attempt in good faith to agree on procedures for the expeditious exchange of information, with the help of the Neutral if required.

One week prior to the first scheduled session of the ADR Process, each party shall deliver to the neutral and to the other party a concise written summary of its view as to the facts, law and conclusions in connection with the matter in dispute.

In the ADR Process each party shall be represented by their respective Authorized Individuals and by counsel. In addition, each party may bring such additional persons as needed to respond to questions, contribute, inform and participate in the negotiations, the number of such additional persons to be agreed upon by the parties in advance, with assistance of the Neutral if necessary.

The parties, in consultation with the Neutral, will agree upon a format for meetings, designed to assure that both the Neutral and the Authorized Individuals have an opportunity to hear the oral presentation of each party's view on the matter in dispute. The Authorized Individual will attempt to negotiate a resolution of the matter in dispute, with or without assistance of counsel or others, but with assistance of the Neutral. To this end, the Neutral is authorized to conduct both joint meetings and separate private caucuses with the parties. During the ADR Process, the Neutral will be free to divulge to the disclosing party all information learned in private caucus with either party unless specifically requested by a disclosing party to keep such information confidential as to the other party.

The Neutral, if no agreement has been reached between the parties, and not later than thirty (30) days after the first scheduled session of ADR Process, (i) shall provide his or her opinion to both parties on probable outcomes should the matter be litigated, and (ii) shall make one or more recommendations as to the terms of a possible settlement, upon any conditions imposed by the parties (including but not limited to, a minimum and maximum amount). The Neutral should base his or her opinions and recommendations on information then requested by the parties to be kept confidential. The opinions and recommendations of the Neutral shall not be binding on the parties.

The parties agree to participate in the ADR Process to its conclusion (as designated by the Neutral) and not to terminate negotiations concerning resolution of the matter in dispute until at least ten (10) days thereafter. Unless requested by the State to stop work, the vendor agrees to continue working to resolve the performance problem during the ADR Process. Vendor shall raise any and all claims for additional compensation vendor believes due and owing for such work during the ADR Process.

The fees of the Neutral shall be shared equally by the parties. The Neutral shall be disqualified as a witness, consultant, expert or counsel for either party with respect to the matters in dispute and any related matters.

The ADR Process procedure is a compromise negotiation for purposes of applicable State and Federal rules of evidence. To the extent allowed by the Minnesota Data Practices Act, the entire process is confidential, and no stenographic, visual or audio record shall be made. To the extent allowed by the Minnesota Data Practices Act, all conduct, statements, promises, offers, views and opinions, whether oral or written, made in the course of the ADR Process by either of the parties, their agents, employees, representatives or other invitees and by the Neutral (who will be the parties joint agent for purposes of these compromise negotiations) are confidential and shall, in addition and where appropriate, be deemed work product and privileged. Such conduct, statements, promises, offers, views and opinions shall not be discoverable or admissible for any purposes, including impeachment, in any litigation or other proceedings involving the parties, and shall not be disclosed to anyone not an agent, employee, expert, witness or representative of any of the parties; provided however, that evidence otherwise discoverable or admissible is not excluded from discovery or admission as a result of its use in the ADR Process (Minnesota Department of Administration, 1997).

AAA Arbitration Clause

Neither of the above ADR clauses contains an arbitration provision. AAA recommends the following language, which could be added to either of the other two clauses, perhaps introduced with a phrase such as, "In the event that negotiation or mediation fail to resolve the dispute . . ." Again, the clause could be modified to leave open the choice of ADR provider to negotiation at the time an actual dispute arises.

> Any controversy or claim arising out of or relating to this contract, or the breach thereof, shall be settled by arbitration administered by the American Arbitration Association in accordance with its Commercial Arbitration Rules, and judgment on the award rendered by the arbitrator(s) may be entered in any court having jurisdiction thereof (American Arbitration Association, 1994b).

Getting the Parties to the Table

In cases where you have an agreement to take Year 2000 disputes to ADR, the method for invoking the process is usually spelled out in the clause. But perhaps you couldn't convince your company to establish ADR agreements with its external business dependencies, or the particular party wouldn't sign an ADR clause, or you did not anticipate a dispute with that party. There are still several ways you can steer the dispute resolution process to ADR:

- The best technique is to ask the neutral to invite the other party to negotiate. They are experienced in bringing parties to the bargaining table (as it is in their economic interest to do so), and it will not seem as if you are eager to settle a weak case.
- Even if the dispute has not reached the point where the parties are dealing with each other through their respective attorneys, your lawyer can still act as your agent to broach the subject of ADR with their lawyer without putting either side's professional pride at risk.
- Propose nonbinding mediation as a first step that might not seem disadvantageous to a party that feels it has the upper hand by going to court, even if you hope to end up in binding arbitration. If necessary, agree to *toll* (extend) the applicable statute of limitations so the other side won't give up any rights by deferring litigation.
- If a suit has already been filed, counsel can call the clerk and request a referral to mediation. If the parties have not agreed to mediate, raising the issue might induce the judge to call the parties in for a status conference and urge

them to pursue ADR. Most lawyers will counsel their clients to accept the judge's recommendation, unless it would clearly be a waste of time.

- Once litigation begins in earnest, suggest evaluative ADR to the other side so you can each gain an early assessment of the relative strengths and weaknesses of your case, which might lead one or both parties to consider settlement more seriously once the legal bills start to add up. You can also propose ADR at pivotal points in the case, such as before a dispositive motion or conference with the judge, or after discovery has been completed.

Screening Cases

ADR is not the answer to every Y2K disagreement. To be successful, it requires a genuine willingness to compromise by all parties, reasonably comparable bargaining power around the table, and, in most cases, something to exchange in addition to money (which is one reason why shareholder suits are generally poor candidates for ADR). The Massachusetts Standing Committee on Dispute Resolution has concisely summarized some of the considerations that make disputes suitable for ADR:

> . . . many students of ADR believe that ADR processes should not be used when there is a need for public sanctioning of conduct, a public declaration of rights, or the establishment of precedent; when repetitive violations need to be dealt with collectively and uniformly; or when a party or parties are not able to negotiate effectively because of a power imbalance or for any other reason . . .
>
> On the other hand, ADR is often more appropriate in litigation in cases involving a conflict in an ongoing relationship (such as cases involving . . . business associates). Moreover, parties often choose ADR because it gives them greater control over the outcome of the dispute and find that outcomes of ADR are uniquely satisfactory because they are tailored to the complex interests underlying the dispute. In addition, parties often find that agreements reached through consensual ADR processes (such as mediation, conciliation and case evaluation) are more durable and result in greater compliance than agreements imposed by a judge. Other reasons for choosing ADR are that the process itself is more private and less confrontational than litigation (Supreme Judicial Court, 1998).

Understanding what kinds of cases are amenable to ADR can help you bring parties to the table before lawsuits are filed or positions become entrenched. Decision tree analysis can be useful in systematically evaluating the relative risks and outcomes associated with different litigation and settlement strategies (Victor, 1990). Additional factors that are conducive to ADR include the following:

- The decision makers have authority to settle, a mature understanding of the issues, and a sincere desire to reach a sensible result quickly and cost-effectively.

- The parties have not developed rigidly antagonistic views toward each other.
- Neither party believes that delay or publicity is to its benefit in resolving the dispute.
- Neither party insists on conducting extensive discovery.
- The litigation is likely to be protracted and the outcome is uncertain (CPR Institute for Dispute Resolution, 1998).

Conclusion

The risk of Year 2000 litigation should be faced head on like other Y2K perils. An affirmative strategy to develop ADR agreements with your critical customers and suppliers can help your company exchange compliance information, prevent supply-chain disruptions, and resolve disputes without embarrassing and expensive legal actions. Such an activist approach is likely to promote intercompany compliance, minimize operational disruptions from date-related failures, and maintain advantageous business relationships that would otherwise be impaired, if not destroyed, by litigation.

Of course, not every dispute is suited to ADR, so enterprises should take the opportunity now to begin planning for the wave of litigation that Y2K is expected to produce. It is to that important subject that we turn next.

CHAPTER 11

Litigation Planning and Management

"While a favorable end result in a single case is important, a fiscally sound litigation plan, applicable to several cases, is exponentially more important."

—RANDY L. DECKER,
  ITT FINANCIAL CORP. (DECKER, 1998a)

So far, we have presented strategies for reducing business and legal risks and, in the process, avoiding litigation. There will be circumstances, though, in which litigation is both unavoidable and appropriate. The clearest and most common example is likely to be *cost recovery* lawsuits that seek monetary compensation for financial losses incurred as a result of Y2K failures. Of course, any time your company is sued, it has no choice but to defend itself.

Two types of risks are associated with litigation: the risk of an unfavorable outcome and the risk of excessive legal transaction costs. Litigation planning that can improve your chances of success and reduce the expense of legal representation is an essential part of Year 2000 risk management.

Selecting and Managing Litigation Counsel

Predicting what the legal market will look like in 1999 and 2000 is difficult. In 1998, the supply of attorneys offering Y2K legal advice far outstripped the demand for their services. 1999 is likely to see a substantially higher incidence of actual Year 2000 failures. Companies that find themselves running out of time to complete remediation and testing and becoming increasingly concerned about the preparedness of their external business dependencies should consider bringing counsel on board to prepare for potentially severe dislocations throughout the national and global economy.

At the same time, active management of Year 2000 counsel is essential to control costs. The declining economic outlook in Asia and Latin America has already begun to fuel a U.S. recession in late 1998. In combination with the disruptive effects of anticipated Y2K events on transportation, communication, finance, and commerce, many companies will find the expense of cascading Year 2000 litigation an onerous burden. Business should take advantage of the opportunity to make considered decisions about hiring outside litigation counsel during 1999 in anticipation of the fallout in 2000.

Qualifications

Lawyers are not fungible. They are differentiated not only by skill and experience, but also by temperament, aptitude, and personality. Most companies have experience in hiring outside litigation counsel, and many have long-standing relationships with one or more law firms that provide whatever service may be needed at any particular time. As companies find themselves in need of Y2K counsel, it will be natural for them to turn to lawyers in whom they already have confidence. Starting in 1997 and increasing sharply in 1998, the legal profession has geared itself up for the anticipated wave of Year 2000 lawsuits, and clients may find that their existing lawyers are well suited to the task.

Whether you simply want to intelligently assess your current counsel's capability to handle Y2K litigation or you need to start from scratch, you should consider three general areas when hiring a Year 2000 lawyer: expertise in Y2K law, technical knowledge, and historical understanding.

Year 2000 Legal Expertise

In the last couple of years, a burgeoning body of Y2K law has developed at a remarkable pace. Dozens of legal conferences, seminars, and continuing education workshops have been conducted around the country in which an extremely wide range of issues has been discussed, debated, and written about, including vendor liability, due diligence, regulatory liability, disclosures, causes of action and defenses, directors' and officers' liability, and insurance coverage. More than 20 lawsuits have been filed, and the pleadings and motions filed in those cases are widely available. Several leading legal publishers, including LEXIS, BNA, and Mealey's, have published monthly newsletters and reports of significant Y2K developments. Although most litigators are generalists who are accustomed to getting up to speed quickly in new areas of the law, it would certainly be an advantage—other things being equal—to engage counsel who have been following these trends as they have developed.

For example, in the area of Year 2000 preparedness disclosures, the Securities and Exchange Commission issued an important interpretive document that took effect on August 4, 1998, that every lawyer advising publicly traded corporations must understand thoroughly. That document was issued after the SEC's legal staff issued a much shorter and less commanding directive, known as SEC Staff Legal Bulletin No. 5, on October 8, 1997. By all accounts, Legal Bulletin No. 5 was ineffective in helping companies understand their reporting obligations or inducing them to make meaningful disclosures. As a result, the original bulletin was revised on January 12, 1998, with slightly more forceful guidance. But the revised bulletin proved no more effective than the original. The SEC essentially started over again by issuing the official interpretive statement by the commission itself that is about eight times as long as the legal bulletin and contains significantly more explicit directives. Understanding the course of development of the final interpretation may be vital in representing defendants in shareholder derivative suits or SEC enforcement actions, inasmuch as the regulatory and fiduciary duties of corporations and their directors and officers may have changed over time, and figuring out the meaning of the final document might require comparison to the earlier bulletins.

Familiarity with the development and progress of Y2K insurance exclusions, FFIEC credit risk policies, and Year 2000 legislation and lawsuits can offer similar advantages to lawyers handling Y2K litigation. Attorneys who were "present at the creation" of the legal doctrines that will shape lawsuits over supply-chain failures and other Year 2000 events are likely to have a richer and more nuanced understanding of this new area of practice than their colleagues who are just getting up to speed as the cases come in the door. Organizations that already have confidence in lawyers and firms with whom they have worked for many years might consider adding a Year 2000 legal specialist to their litigation team to add a broader and deeper perspective that general commercial litigators might lack.

Technical Knowledge

Competent lawyers know that they cannot effectively represent clients in litigation unless they have a solid understanding of the business transaction at the center of the dispute. Legal expertise is not something that can be applied in a vacuum or tacked on as something separate and distinct from the activity underlying the client's business. Construction litigators need to understand how buildings are erected, malpractice lawyers must have a working knowledge of the standards of appropriate medical treatment, and Year 2000 lawyers must have a basic understanding of information technology. Without such knowledge, an attorney cannot form independent judgments about the merits of the case or make informed decisions about formulating strategy, conducting discovery, preparing for trial, or negotiating a settlement.

The kinds of technical issues a Year 2000 lawyer should understand in at least a general sense include the following:

- The different types of operating systems, platforms, languages, and computing environments
- How electronic data interchange works and who uses it for which kinds of transactions
- Differing skills and responsibilities of CIOs, systems and network specialists, programmers, and technical consultants
- How organizations procure, develop, and integrate IT systems
- The ways in which hardware, software, and embedded microchips process date information
- Alternative methods and tools for Year 2000 remediation and testing
- The management and organization of Y2K projects

Although Y2K attorneys don't need to be IT professionals, having such knowledge will enable them to talk with their client's technical employees at more than a rudimentary level, ask the hard questions and understand the answers, and assess the strengths and weaknesses of the case and deal with each. Moreover, Y2K litigation is likely to involve expert testimony, so the lawyers need to be able to see through weak credentials, expose shortcomings in the expert's analysis, and tell the difference between good and bad Year 2000 solutions providers and consultants.

Historical Context

In every lawsuit, it is imperative for counsel to keep an eye on the big picture. Because the judge and jury must be able to grasp the contours of each party's case, good lawyers identify three or four overarching themes to which every witness, document, and argument relate. You can't persuade a jury to find in your favor if they don't understand your position, and the disjointed presentation of evidence that occurs at trial requires counsel to reduce the case to its most salient points, even in complex suits.

At the same time, both plaintiffs and defendants must contend with issues and arguments that might seem counterintuitive to the average person called for jury duty. How could IT companies have been so shortsighted about using six-digit dates? Why isn't there a linear relationship between the number of lines of code that contain dates and the cost to repair them? Why didn't companies start compliance projects sooner and devote more resources to them? Why have businesses tolerated IT projects, products, and services that are late, full of bugs, and so much more expensive than planned? Why are some industries—such as banking and securities—so much better prepared than others—such as health care? Why did the Social Security Administration start to address the problem in the 1980s but the Health Care Financing Administration didn't get started until nearly a decade later?

Thus, Y2K litigation counsel must be able to see not only the forest and the trees, but also how they came to be planted there in the first place and grew over time. The complex matrix of compliance decisions, technical challenges, risk management, due diligence, fiduciary responsibilities, and cost must be placed in a manageable context that is both comprehensible and compelling to the average person. Understanding how this seemingly trivial technical oversight was allowed to become a crisis of unprecedented proportions will be crucial in most Year 2000 cases. Counsel who are familiar with the complex origins of the problem—technological, social, financial, managerial, and commercial—will be better equipped to deal with the larger questions that will be asked as this historical transformation plays itself out in court.

Litigation Guidelines

Organizations that have not already adopted guidelines for outside law firms representing them in litigation should do so before major Y2K lawsuits arrive. Litigation guidelines provide counsel with clear expectations about how cases should be handled, how legal services are to be provided, and how bills will be submitted, reviewed, and paid. As the Greater New York Chapter of the American Corporate Counsel Association observed recently:

> A corporation's bargaining position in relation to a law firm is never stronger than at the moment the corporation is deciding whether to select the firm to represent it. We believe that corporations should more fully utilize their bargaining position during the selection process. One way to do so is to request that the law firm agree to the corporation's engagement letter or corporate policies and procedures before the law firm is selected (American Corporate Counsel Association, 1997).

Topics covered in corporate litigation guidelines often include some or all of the following:

- The identification by name of the attorneys who will work on the matter, with prior approval by corporate counsel required for additions or substitutions
- Any expectations or corporate philosophy concerning such matters as the relationship between in-house counsel and the law firm (including what kinds of matters require consultation and what tasks will be performed directly by in-house attorneys and other corporate employees), the importance of cost control, interest in ADR and early settlement discussions, and limitations on discovery
- Identification of the corporate employees to whom bills should be sent and who will serve as the principal and secondary contacts for the law firm, including all persons who have authority to act on the corporation's behalf in directing the activities of the law firm

- The fee arrangement for the engagement; if hourly rates are used, the rate for each identified partner and associate, as well as the rates for law clerks, paralegals, and nonlegal personnel
- The preparation, approval, and modification of litigation budgets
- Requirements for using the attorney charging the lowest rate who is capable of competently providing the particular service rendered (for example, conducting legal research, reviewing documents, and drafting pleadings)
- Restrictions on the involvement of multiple attorneys at depositions, court appearances, and case conferences, without prior approval
- Restrictions on billing for time devoted to educating inexperienced attorneys in general matters of law or getting lawyers newly assigned to the case "up to speed"
- Restrictions on using legal personnel to perform nonlegal services
- Required billing formats, including the level of detail required and the use of task-based billing categories
- Rules governing reimbursement of direct expenses, such as travel, meals, messenger services, and overnight mail, and charges for court fees, stenographers, photocopying and faxes, printing, computerized legal research, expert witnesses, consultants, and private investigators
- Whether the client requires counsel to prepare an initial case assessment and evaluation early in the engagement, and what the content and format of the analysis should be; possible topics include overall litigation strategy, evaluation of the various theories of liability and defenses and their respective likelihoods of success, an estimate of the value of the case in terms of potential ranges of settlements and jury awards, what types of expert witnesses and consultants may be required, and the assistance and information needed from company employees
- The timing and content of status reports about the progress of the case
- Whether prior review by in-house counsel of draft pleadings, motions, and correspondence is required before filing or service on other parties

Fee Arrangements

Given the potential scope of Y2K litigation and the prospects for an economic recession, management and in-house counsel should consider whether they can obtain Year 2000 legal representation in more cost-effective ways than traditional hourly rates. Richard C. Reed's *Billing Innovations: New Win-Win Ways to End Hourly Billings* (American Bar Association, Law Practice Management Section, 1996), is an excellent reference about alternative fee structures for legal services. Further information is available on the Internet at the Litigation Cost Control Resource Center (Voltz, 1996a). Corporations may wish to consider the following major categories:

- Task-based billing (American Bar Association, 1995a)
- Flat fees
- Contingent fees
- Blended hourly rates
- Bonuses for increased recoveries or reduced costs
- Monthly retainers
- Volume billing
- Hybrid arrangements combining elements of any of the preceding methods

Litigation Budgets

Litigation budgets seem to go in and out of fashion, and law firms often view them with fear and loathing. It is certainly true that lawsuits are unpredictable to a very large degree, but it is equally true that trial lawyers just aren't very good at subjecting themselves to budgetary discipline. If your organization is one that would not authorize six- or seven-digit expenditures over several years for any other business activity without having some budgetary controls in place, it makes little sense to carve out an exception for lawsuits. The volatile nature of litigation does require that budgets be developed in less detail and that clients accept greater flexibility in modifying and even reassessing budgetary assumptions along the way. Many events that precipitate intense activity in the case and drive costs are beyond your counsel's control. The exercise of fashioning a budget, however, can impose a moderating influence on the cost of litigation and provide in-house counsel with greater leverage for controlling how the case is conducted.

Preparing the Initial Budget

There are two essential components to the litigation budget process: the initial budget projection and monthly reports that measure billings against budgetary targets. In addition, once the overall budget for the entire lawsuit is in place, bimonthly or quarterly budgets might help sharpen the accuracy of expenditure controls as the case progresses:

> More directly useful for containing costs [than overall case budgets] however are sixty day or ninety day budgets. It is in these budgets that you and your lawyers should be able to nail down anticipated costs with a reasonable degree of certainty. Although like any other major project, litigation is somewhat unpredictable, you

and your lawyers should be able to look at least sixty to ninety days ahead and come up with both a litigation strategy and a detailed litigation budget you can stick to for the short term. As in any major undertaking, unexpected events will occasionally require adjusting the budget, but if you want to get control of your litigation costs you need to have a detailed working budget for each case and strive to make any changes the exception rather than the rule (Voltz, 1996b).

The budget should be prepared as a spreadsheet with detailed worksheets supporting the overall budget for the case. The format shown in Figure 11.1 is one suggested approach.

Cost categories. In the left-most column, list the major phases of the litigation that correspond to cost categories. For example, the American Bar Association's "Uniform Task-Based Management System Litigation Code Set" breaks litigation costs into the following six groups (American Bar Association, 1995b):

- Case assessment, development, and administration
- Pre-trial pleadings and motions
- Discovery
- Trial preparation and trial
- Appeal
- Expenses

To avoid misunderstandings between the client and the firm, counsel should identify in a supporting worksheet the principal tasks that are to be performed in each phase. The ABA's *litigation code definitions* are very useful for this purpose (see Figure 11.2), even when task-based billing is not used (American Bar Association, 1995c).

Estimated duration. In the next column, provide an estimate in days or hours of the time anticipated for each phase. We recommend that the estimates be expressed in terms of a high and low range, in recognition of the inherent imprecision of litigation budgeting. The supporting worksheets should estimate the time during each phase for each class of personnel working on the case, such as senior partner, junior partner, senior associate, associate, law clerk, and paralegal. Time estimates are worthwhile even when compensation is not based on hourly rates, so that the client can gain an understanding of how long the case is expected to last and when it is likely to be in the various stages.

Building the summary time estimates based on the extent of the anticipated involvement of each lawyer and other staff forces the law firm to think in advance about cost-efficient staffing and enables the client to better understand what drives the cost in each phase. For example, discovery is expensive because it is so labor-intensive, but efficiencies are realized by having

LITIGATION BUDGET: ABC CORP. v. XYZ INC.

Court: Law Firm:

Docket No.:   Lead Counsel:

File No.:   Date:

Litigation Phase	Rate $ Per Hour	Time Requirements		Extended Cost	
		Low Estimate (Days)	High Estimate (Days)	Total Low Estimate	Total High Estimate
Case Assessment, Development, & Administration	250	10	20	20000	40000
Pre-Trial Pleadings & Motions	300	20	30	48000	72000
Discovery	200	100	150	160000	240000
Trial Preparation & Trial	300	20	30	48000	72000
Appeal	300	30	45	72000	108000
Expenses				50000	75000
Estimated Total		**180**	**275**	**$398000**	**$607000**

Figure 11.1   A sample Y2K litigation budget.

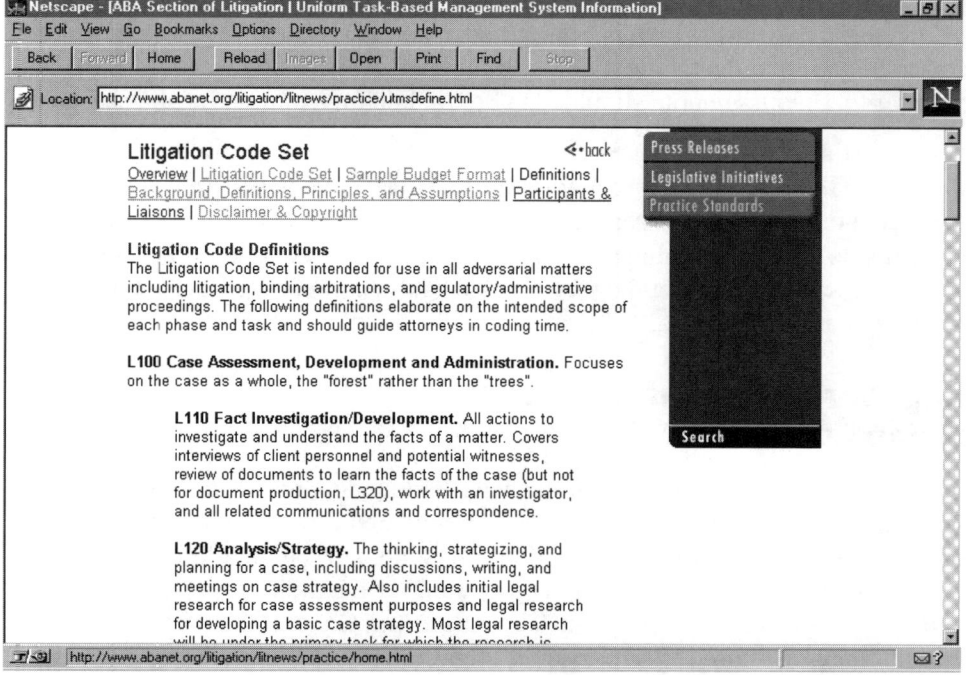

Figure 11.2   Litigation code definitions from the ABA.

junior associates and paralegals review voluminous documents for production to the other parties. Trial preparation requires less time, but much of the work must be performed by more experienced attorneys.

Estimated cost. Next, a range of estimated costs needs to be assigned to each phase of the lawsuit. When hourly rates are used, the time ranges allotted for each legal and non-legal professional on the worksheet of estimated durations can be multiplied by the corresponding rate, which can then be added together to derive the total estimated cost range for each phase. If something other than straight hourly rates is used, such as blended rates or hybrid fee arrangements, an appropriate adjustment can be made to calculate the extended cost. When flat fees are used for one or more phases, such as the initial assessment or the appeal, the agreed amount is used in place of the calculated cost.

Total duration and cost. The total time and cost are calculated as the sum of the ranges for each phase. Disbursements can be added as a lump sum to the total cost, with details provided in a supporting worksheet.

Submitting Budget-Based Bills

Once the case budget is prepared, the same format can be used to develop quarterly budgets. Monthly bills should include budget comparisons in the form of the cumulative amount billed to date and the cumulative amount billed for the quarter. Monthly budget comparisons are also possible, but the imprecision of litigation budgets might defeat their usefulness at too fine a level of granularity. Disbursements should also be tracked on a cumulative basis.

It is important to emphasize that a reasonable measure of flexibility must be tolerated when trying to predict and control litigation costs. Counsel should be prepared to explain the reasons for large or unexpected variances, and the client needs to view the objective as moderating the cost of litigation and not expect the same level of budgetary control as the company exercises over other corporate initiatives.

Allocating Work between In-House and Outside Counsel

The capabilities of in-house attorneys vary widely depending primarily on the size and expertise of the corporate legal department. In companies with just a few in-house lawyers, virtually all litigation is likely to be handled by outside law firms, and corporate counsel occupy their time handling transactional matters and advising management. The role of the General Counsel's office in lawsuits may be limited to supervising litigation counsel and setting up interviews with company employees.

In larger corporate law departments, the direct participation of in-house lawyers throughout the litigation can reduce costs and help achieve better results. Corporate attorneys already know the client's business, its people, and its external business dependencies, including its customers. Indeed, corporate counsel may well have long-standing working relationships with the in-house counsel for the other parties in cases such as supply-chain disputes. It makes no sense in such cases not to take full advantage of the lawyers who are already on the company's payroll for such tasks as formulating strategy and negotiating settlements.

In addition, there are important areas of responsibility where in-house attorneys can take the lead more effectively and at far less cost than outside counsel. Two obvious areas are factual investigations and document production. Company lawyers can most easily find out which employees have documents in their files that have been requested in discovery or that are otherwise relevant to the case. They can do many of the time-consuming tasks of compiling, indexing, and abstracting documents, as well as identifying records that may be protected by the attorney-client privilege or attorney work product doctrine. Corporate counsel can also identify which employees would make the best witnesses, participate in employee interviews, and help employees prepare for depositions. They can prepare detailed chronologies of relevant events, work with investigators, identify potential expert witnesses, ensure that all requested documents have been produced, and prepare draft interrogatory responses.

Of course, outside litigation counsel should not completely abdicate their responsibilities for these activities, but effective coordination can enable inside and outside lawyers to put their respective talents and resources to the highest and best use. In addition, an outside law firm has certain advantages for protecting privileged communications over in-house lawyers who also engage in nonprivileged discussions, so care should be taken not to compromise confidentiality in the interest of cutting costs.

Communications Planning

Year 2000 lawsuits will be played out not only in the courtroom, but also in the arena of public opinion and among networks of business partners. Rather than just reacting to adverse publicity when you've been sued—or even when you've suffered a financial loss that forces you to file suit—plan ahead for telling your side of the story to your company's stakeholders. Keep the following points in mind.

Audiences. When you become involved in a lawsuit, either as a plaintiff or a defendant, many different parties will want to know what's going on, including customers, stockholders, other suppliers, banks, insurers, parent companies and affiliates, and the media. Plan what kinds of information each audience will need and how best to deliver it to them. What Gillian Albers, CEO of Amroth Inc., has observed about Year 2000 communications in general also applies to Y2K lawsuits: "You will want your staff, your customers, your partners and your suppliers to feel confident that if a problem occurs, you can handle it" (Albers, 1998).

Coordination and control. Even if you need to speak to different audiences in different ways through different channels, establishing a consistent message is important. Your customer and media relations departments and your lawyers need to develop positive themes and useful information so that you're not speaking out of both sides of your mouth. Have your counsel educate your key employees and relationship managers about the issues in the case and alert them to sensitive subjects they should avoid discussing outside the company.

Dealing with the media. If the suit is likely to generate media interest, you should prepare in advance to get your story out and respond to press inquiries. Consider the following suggestions when dealing with reporters:

- Keep your message short and simple, and stick to it. Avoid legalese and long-winded explanations of complex legal arguments.
- Develop positive working relationships with reporters covering the case, but do not assume that informal comments or humorous remarks won't come back to bite you. Don't say anything that you wouldn't want to read about in the paper.
- Do not say anything "off the record" unless you have a long-standing relationship with a reporter whose integrity you trust.
- Provide information to the media that can help them understand your side of the case.
- Be sensitive to reporters' deadlines.
- Be patient with hostile or strident reporters—they always get the last word.
- For television or radio interviews, speak in short, coherent sound bites. You don't control how the story will be edited or how much of the interview will be aired, so use simple, complete sentences that stand on their own and persuasively state your position.
- Prepare a press release setting forth the basic facts of the case and your client's position in reasonable and temperate language.

Cost Recovery Suits

Private lawsuits to recover damages arising from Year 2000 will surely be the most common form of Y2K litigation. When the expense of remediation, business disruptions, and the attendant financial losses becomes too great to simply absorb as a cost of doing business, companies will have little choice but to seek compensation from those they believe caused their injuries. Indeed, directors and officers may well have fiduciary duties to file such actions to protect corporate assets. It makes sense for organizations on both sides to prepare for the wave of litigation that appears imminent. The risks from failing to anticipate and plan for cost recovery suits far outweigh the minimal cost.

Every lawsuit takes on a life of its own and progresses in unpredictable ways. There are, however, recognizable stages of litigation that correspond to the procedural framework under which courts operate. In the following sections we will look at the important—and costly—activities that take place in each phase of commercial lawsuits and the opportunities they present for planning and cost control.

Phase 1: A Loss Is Suffered

Lawsuits begin with some precipitating event that engenders a claim by one party against another. Litigation is an expensive and uncertain undertaking, so businesses do not lightly run into court unless they have suffered a loss that is great enough to justify the effort and expense. In the case of year 2000, that event is likely to be an IT failure or processing error inside your company or somewhere along the supply chain that is of sufficient magnitude to seriously disrupt a company's operations for at least a short period of time.

Assessing the Situation

The decision to file suit needs to be made with some care. It may be that a simple demand for compensation, made in an effective way, could achieve a result that would justify accepting "half a loaf" and forgoing litigation. It is often worthwhile to pay a law firm a flat fee of, say, $5,000 to $10,000, to make an initial assessment of the case in order to make an informed judgment about its strengths, weaknesses, and probable value. Some of the factors to consider in deciding whether to go to court include the following:

The contracts. Whether or not you conducted a legal audit before any Y2K failure occurred, it is essential to closely review the business agreements between the parties before filing suit. As we showed in Chapter 4, "Reducing Y2K Liability Exposure," there could be important provisions that limit or even foreclose rights of recovery, such as warranty disclaimers and remedy exclusions, that may permit only damage awards that fall substantially short of full compensation for the losses incurred. Indeed, depending on the wording of the contract, a shortened statute of limitations or a *force majeure* clause could make clear that your case would probably be dismissed. If so, a straightforward business-to-business approach might produce some tangible benefits, such as discounts, improved credit terms, or additional support services, even without any legal entitlement. If, on the other hand, you have contractual rights that support one or more claims for substantial monetary damages, an assessment of the contract language will guide your counsel to the most promising avenues of recovery and away from those that might yield little return despite considerable effort.

Cost of suit. The growth of litigation and frequent dissatisfaction with its outcomes have led most corporations to closely scrutinize the cost of litigation. One in-house lawyer recently observed that litigation "[c]ost control is the single most important priority in the corporate legal department" (Decker, 1998b). Before filing suit, ask the law firm to estimate the cost and value of the case under different scenarios, such as the case (1) settles within six months, (2) settles within two years. or (3) must be tried to a conclusion. These projections will be "ball park" guesses at best, but comparisons across different ranges of expense and recovery can and should be made as carefully as possible.

Availability of insurance. Certainly one of the most important considerations in deciding whether to sue someone and what kinds of claims to assert is the availability of insurance. A lawsuit against a small IT services company that has no assets other than some office equipment may be worth pursuing if it has $1 million of errors and omissions coverage. Of course, for the reasons explained in Chapter 9, "Insurance Issues," evaluating whether the policy is likely to apply to Year 2000 claims is crucial. It can be difficult, though, to find out whether coverage is available, in what amounts, and under what terms, even if the contract required the vendor to provide insurance. A putative defendant that does *not* have insurance or other assets sufficient to pay for the loss it may have caused might volunteer that information in the hope of discouraging you from embarking on a wasted effort. It is also important to find out whether the coverage has been depleted or even exhausted by other claims, whether coverage is provided on a *claims made* or *occurrence* basis, and whether dealing with an adjuster directly might promote a prompt settlement.

Value of business relationships. A Y2K calamity can easily end a long-standing business relationship, but that drastic result is by no means inevitable. The valued supplier that blew a giant hole in your just-in-time inventory and caused you to antagonize your customers and suffer a large revenue loss may have itself been a victim of someone else's Y2K failure. If so, you might decide to forgive and forget, depending on how the numbers work out. Your supplier might be encouraged to offer future price reductions or other concessions to keep your business and dissuade you from filing suit. A loss may simply be too large to bear, of course, but it may be worth taking the long view if your business has not been irretrievably damaged.

Cost-benefit analysis. Beyond the mere transaction costs of litigation, companies should consider the relative value of alternatives to litigation, including business negotiations without lawyers and ADR. Lawsuits are unpredictable, distracting, difficult to resolve, and prone to becoming acrimonious. They should be avoided whenever possible. If Year 2000 generates a great deal of litigation, Y2K suits could become even more difficult than ordinary commercial cases. Use decision-tree analysis to take a disciplined, objective look at the probabilities of various outcomes from alternative courses of action. Look before you leap.

First Steps

When a serious Y2K failure occurs, the first order of business is to get the situation under control and restore normal business operations as quickly as possible. In the excitement of an exigent situation, though, it can be hard to think clearly about what needs to be done in order to seek compensation from the responsible parties or to protect yourself from unreasonable or excessive claims. A systematic approach must be taken in the early days and weeks of a Year 2000 event to lay the proper foundation on either side of a cost recovery claim.

Demand. Once a substantial loss is incurred, a *demand* should be prepared immediately. Although the term carries a belligerent tone, it simply means that you must make a formal notification of the loss and request compensation from the responsible party. An effective demand (which can be presented in the form of a letter) should present a clear and compelling depiction of the nature and amount of the loss and summarize the reasons why the other party should make you whole without, of course, laying all of your cards on the table. Although a demand letter almost never generates payment in the full amount requested, success is achieved if the recipient comes to believe that your claim may have merit and deserves a serious response. If nothing else, a reasonable demand letter enables you to say you took the high road before rushing into court and, if properly drafted, sets a positive tone that is conducive to more productive discussions once litigation gets underway.

Notify insurers. Both the claimant and the recipient of a demand should immediately notify their respective insurance agents as soon as they become aware of any loss that might result in a liability claim. Ask your agent what you need to do to invoke your rights under the policy, but read the policy yourself and make absolutely sure you do not fail to take every step that is required to obtain coverage. Agents handle claims every day, and one probably looks the same as the next. A serious Year 2000 failure could embroil your company in a dispute that could jeopardize its survival and the well-being of its customers, stockholders, employees, and directors and officers. Do not assume that your insurer will overlook *any* minor deviation from the policy requirements when it comes to coverage for Y2K claims. This seemingly innocuous early step in the dispute resolution process—properly notifying your insurance company of a potentially insurable loss—may be the single most important thing you do to protect your enterprise. It is no time for casual inattention or informality.

Retain counsel. Whether or not you ultimately decide to sue, the earlier you retain litigation counsel, the better. The party who becomes better prepared sooner often has an advantage in the early stages of the case, and even experienced outside attorneys need time to get up to speed to provide the client with informed advice in the first frantic days leading up to possible litigation. It is not uncommon for lawyers to work virtually full time during the first couple of weeks on a new case seeking six- or seven-figure damages, so the legal bill for the first month can easily reach $10,000 to $20,000 or more. Any head start the client can give counsel by bringing them on board early to educate themselves about the history of the transaction and the facts of the dispute will facilitate a less hasty and more effective assessment, and more carefully considered judgments about recommended courses of action. Companies that have followed our advice about preparing business risk assessments and contingency plans and substantiating due diligence are likely to pleasantly surprise their lawyers with the usefulness of the materials they have already prepared.

Communication. Get the word out as quickly as possible to those who need to know that a loss has been suffered or that a claim has been filed, so that effective communications planning can begin immediately. Customers, stockholders, investment analysts, bankers, and reporters may be calling any number of officers and employees in your company with challenging questions, and it is important to have a consistent strategy for responding. IT companies, in particular, could face a barrage of inquiries about the potential impact of Year 2000 litigation on the firm's prospects, and finding oneself in a reactive mode without a forceful and coherent message could undermine confidence that could hurt business. Unless both sides agree to a moratorium on making public statements about their dispute, each should launch a communications campaign presenting their side of their story, including an immediate press release and answering questions from the media. This strategy should be coordinated with counsel, however, to ensure that no statements are made that might be inconsistent with later litigation strategies or that might lead to awkward questions during discovery.

Investigation. Once a serious Y2K failure occurs and a demand for compensation is made, the threat of litigation is no longer merely hypothetical and the need for intensive factual investigation becomes imperative. Again, any time lost in finding out what happened and why could create a competitive disadvantage that may be difficult to overcome, at least without considerable additional expense, under the sometimes unrelenting pressure of litigation. Once suit is filed, the plaintiffs—who can and will prepare their case before they go forward—have an opportunity to move aggressively to catch their opponents unprepared for early discovery requests. The defendants should not allow themselves to be caught flat-footed as volleys of document requests, interrogatories, and deposition notices come flying across the transom. As soon as counsel is retained, they need to be provided with organized sets of relevant documents, and interviews with employees and other friendly witnesses need to be scheduled. In addition, potential technical and financial experts need to be identified before they are snapped up by others, including expert witnesses and nontestimonial experts needed for case preparation. Litigation support consultants and private investigators also may need to be brought on board early in the process.

Litigation budget. Once counsel is retained and the initial investigation is complete, a preliminary litigation budget should be prepared so an informed decision can be made about the transaction costs that are likely to be incurred. Many clients rush headlong into lawsuits without any idea how long it will take or what it will cost. Much of the friction that sometimes develops between business clients and their counsel is attributable to the "sticker shock" that comes from unexpectedly large monthly legal bills.

Mitigate damages. An important requirement for almost any cause of action is that the injured party take reasonable measures to limit the losses for which it seeks recovery. The claimant must exercise the reasonable care of an ordinary person under the circumstances to prevent further damages it has the power to avoid. The reasonable costs to mitigate damages are usually recoverable, so document all such expenditures and their justification.

Responding to the demand. Just as the party suffering the loss needs to prepare a prompt and effective demand, so too does the party receiving the demand need to respond quickly and resolutely. This is not to say that a hard line is always the best response, but every rejoinder must be compelling and forceful in its own right. In most cases, the response should be shorter than the demand because the defense usually benefits from keeping its cards close to its vest. Enough information should be conveyed to convince the claimant that there are indeed two sides to every story and that the respondent is fully capable of defending itself, if necessary. For example, an IT vendor would not compromise any secrets by directing the customer's attention to the key clauses in the contract that limit the seller's liability or pointing out any actions by the customer that caused or contributed to the problem that is the subject of the dispute. At the same time, it is generally to both parties' benefit to avoid burning bridges with each other and to suggest instead that mature discussion of the issues would be worthwhile early on. Even if litigation proves unavoidable, lawsuits in which the parties continue to talk productively are almost always less destructive than cases in which open hostility rules.

ADR. Depending on the nature of the dispute, the time after an actual loss has been sustained and before a suit has been filed can be the most advantageous opportunity to pursue alternative dispute resolution. Informal techniques such as nonbinding mediation can be particularly useful because they are easy to put into motion and can generate results quickly. Potential defendants may be especially amenable to ADR as a way of keeping the lawyers at bay and promoting good will that can lead to more reasonable settlements. For example, an IT company could agree to work with its client to explain to the client's customers that the Y2K failure wasn't the client's fault and what is being done to correct the situation. The injured party, however, should hold off on final negotiations until the nature and extent of the damages can be fully ascertained. Moreover, both parties should consult with their respective insurers first.

Phase 2: Suit Is Filed

When a decision is made to proceed with litigation, the client should not simply delegate complete authority and responsibility to the outside lawyers. Litigation is an adversarial process, and even the plaintiff may be exposed to public accusations that it caused or contributed to the problem. Like Y2K itself, a business lawsuit is a business problem and should be treated as such.

Preparing the complaint. Most trial counsel find it difficult to resist the urge to throw in the kitchen sink when they develop the initial pleading in the case, called the *complaint*. In-house counsel can play a useful management role by helping to focus the factual allegations and legal claims that are the most straightforward to prove and have the greatest likelihood of generating a worthwhile recovery. Complaints can almost always be amended later on, and weeding out marginal claims can help prevent the case from becoming bogged down in ancillary issues and pointless motions. For their part, litigation counsel should anticipate and address the defenses that are likely to be raised, such as the statute of limitations and exclusions of remedies. The complaint should also identify all categories of damages to which the plaintiff believes it is entitled, which should be well documented before the complaint is filed as the defendant will ask for backup during discovery:

- Direct costs of remediation and software and hardware upgrades and replacements
- Reduced value of IT investments made before 2000 for which accelerated upgrades were required

- The time value of money for IT expenditures made earlier than planned (Ozenne, 1998)
- In-house and outsourced labor charges, especially those that had to be incurred at premium rates
- Lost sales, profits, and customer good will
- Expenses of mitigating damages, business continuity measures, contingency mode operations, and disaster recovery efforts

Choice of forum. Before filing the complaint, it is important to consider where to bring suit. Most cost recovery suits asserting common law or U.C.C. claims for breach of contract or breach of warranty, or statutory claims under consumer protection or unfair competition statutes, may be restricted to state court. If the plaintiffs are citizens of different states than all of the defendants, however, it may be possible to invoke federal court *diversity jurisdiction.* Federal courts sometimes provide procedural and other tactical advantages over state courts, including streamlined discovery, uniform rules of evidence, the assignment of a single judge or magistrate to the case from beginning to end, less crowded dockets, and, sometimes, more capable judges. Many contracts, though, specify not only what forum any suit must be filed in, but also which state's law will govern any disputes arising under the contract.

Responding to the complaint. Answering the allegations of the complaint is a reasonably straightforward exercise, especially if in-house and outside counsel conducted a thorough factual investigation as soon as they became aware of an incipient dispute. Beyond simply reacting to the plaintiff's charges, the defendants may have opportunities to seize the upper hand and turn the dynamics of the case in their favor. In lieu of answering the complaint, a motion to dismiss could be filed if dispositive legal defenses are available, such as filing suit after the statute of limitations has expired or ignoring mandatory dispute resolution procedures. Counterclaims for nonpayment or copyright infringement can be maintained that could substantially reduce or offset the plaintiff's damages. Most importantly, third parties that may be liable to either the plaintiff or the defendant can be brought into the suit as additional defendants to spread the costs of defense and contribute to any settlement.

ADR. Once the contours of the case have been established by the filing of the plaintiff's complaint and the defendant's response, including the joinder of any third-party defendants, the parties have an auspicious opportunity to consider alternative dispute resolution. Counsel should explain to their clients that the case is about to become expensive with the commencement of discovery, and spending a few weeks and a few thousand dollars on nonbinding mediation can be a worthwhile investment, provided that all of the parties have a genuine and good-faith interest in pursuing an early settlement. If that is not the case, ADR will just be a waste of time that is more likely to generate ill will toward the recalcitrant party than promote resolution.

Phase 3: Discovery

We have just three points to add to our discussion in Chapter 4, "Reducing Y2K Liability Exposure," of the discovery process. First, litigation costs cannot be controlled without managing discovery, inasmuch as discovery comprises about 65 to 75 percent of the cost of litigation (Katz, 1997a). Trial lawyers are both the perpetrators and victims of discovery abuse, including "(1) attorneys who seek discovery . . . of insignificant or unnecessary information; (2) attorneys who use discovery to increase the cost and/or burden of litigation for opponents; and (3) attorneys who unreasonably resist discovery" (Katz, 1997b).

Second, business clients, whether or not they employ in-house counsel, should require outside law firms to prepare discovery plans for the purpose of reining in the cost:

> Discovery should not be an open-ended exploration into uncharted territory. Rather, it should be a purposeful and focused process. No discovery should be taken before the lawyer has prepared a discovery plan, and the discovery plan should be grounded in a solid preliminary trial plan . . . Working backward, the lawyer should identify the evidence that needs to be presented at trial, taking into consideration the elements of each cause of action to be proved, the potential defenses, and the jury instructions or law the judge will apply. Then the lawyer should determine how the discovery process can best be used or not used to develop the necessary evidence (Becker, 1997).

The discovery plan should be covered in the litigation budget and monitored closely each month. As we noted earlier, a certain amount of flexibility is appropriate to accommodate the vagaries of individual lawsuits. But reasonable deviations from an agreed-upon plan are more likely to limit excessive discovery costs than bickering with outside counsel after the fact about why this month's bill is so high.

Third, Year 2000 litigation will probably generate much more discovery of electronic information than ordinary commercial cases. This is a complex and evolving area of procedure, and corporations and their counsel should prepare themselves accordingly. For example, companies may wish to take steps *before* suit is filed to ensure that computer files believed to be deleted are truly unrecoverable and are not maintained on a backup volume somewhere. Also, parties seeking electronic discovery must carefully consider what kinds and sources of information they should request.

Phase 4: Moving toward Resolution?

It is a well-known and much-ignored fact that well over 90 percent of all cases are resolved by settlement. Yet most cases are conducted as if they were headed for trial. A common litigation psychology requires all parties to act as if they are indifferent to settlement and assume that the party that seeks compromise lacks confidence in its case. But a business client that is actively managing an expensive Year 2000 lawsuit should always be on the lookout for an exit strategy. Litigation is a necessary evil of last resort, and it should be pursued as an instrument for resolving disputes, the sooner the better.

Once a Y2K suit has been underway for six months or so, we suggest that client and counsel revisit the assessments they made before filing suit and review whether their initial judgments about the need for litigation, the value of the case, the cost of suit, and the prospects for success still make sense. If so, carry on and repeat the exercise at the end of one year. If not, consider what midcourse corrections should be made. Have facts emerged that cast doubt on the viability of one or more claims or defenses? Is the case likely to drag on substantially longer and cost substantially more than planned? Is the other side's position more reasonable, or at least likely to appear more plausible to a judge or jury, than originally believed? Has the dynamic changed in ways that make settlement more or less likely? Are the parties more amenable to ADR than they were before they became embroiled in wearisome litigation?

Lawsuits tend to assume lives of their own, seemingly beyond anyone's control. Don't let that happen. Unless the case is making meaningful progress toward resolution, let your lawyers know you expect creative suggestions to improve the situation. Decision-tree analysis can be particularly helpful in comparing alternatives.

Phase 5: Preparing and Trying the Case

Case preparation takes place continuously after the suit is filed, of course, but it really begins in earnest as discovery nears completion. It is then that the lawyers for each side compile the body of information they have collected over the past year or two and start shaping the affirmative or defensive case they intend to present to the *trier of fact*: the judge or jury. This is usually a subtractive process in which counsel decide which witnesses, documents, and discovery responses they will use and which they will do without, in order to reduce their case to its most persuasive essentials.

Getting ready for trial is an extraordinarily time-consuming process, marked by 12- to 14-hour days and 7-day weeks. Unfortunately, there are usually few opportunities for reducing costs at this stage: A case that hasn't settled must be prepared for trial, and trial preparation must be exceedingly thorough. At the same time, however, this is when most cases settle. Both parties will have helped their cases and hurt their opponent's during discovery, and the parties come to recognize that the outcome is uncertain and risky. These conflicting impulses—the need to prepare for trial and the reluctance to leave one's fate in someone else's hands—often make the end game clumsy and difficult. If settlement talks are stalled, this is a good time to reconsider ADR. All parties have a much better idea of the facts, including the basis for the damages claims, making it possible to submit the case to mediation quickly and efficiently. A skilled neutral might help the parties get past the psychological barriers that frustrate compromise. Alternatively, a mini-trial is a useful evaluative tool that can provide a reality test of each side's case. If you are reluctant to raise the issue for fear of appearing to lack confidence in your case, the clerk will surely be willing to pass the suggestion along to the judge, who will be eager to find a way to remove a case from the trial list.

Phase 6: Post-Trial

Litigation is a disorderly business that often does not come to a decisive conclusion when the verdict is rendered. Post-trial motions for various kinds of procedural rulings and modifications of the judgment are common, and they may be necessary predicates to appeal. That process will take at least several weeks and possibly months to complete. The plaintiff may have to pursue further proceedings to obtain an *execution* to collect its monetary award, and, in extreme cases, the prospect of bankruptcy might loom. Either party might file an appeal, a process that can take an additional year or two or more. Appeals are less expensive than trials, but they are not inexpensive. Depending on the size of the case and the hourly rate charged, assembling and reviewing the record of the trial proceedings, researching and drafting a rigorous legal brief of 50 pages or more, and arguing the case before the appellate court can easily cost more than $50,000. For all of these reasons, post-trial settlements are not uncommon. Other opportunities for cost control include ADR and alternative fee arrangements for handling the appeal.

Managing Multiple Lawsuits

As if the prospect of hundreds of billions of dollars of Y2K litigation weren't troubling enough, many industries—including hardware and software, healthcare, financial services, insurance, utilities, and telecommunications—could face multiple lawsuits presenting common legal, technical, and factual issues. Coordinating litigation management in such cases can reduce overall liability exposure, generate substantial cost savings, and produce more efficient and effective use of counsel.

The Need for Coordination Counsel

The potential number and scope of Year 2000 lawsuits pose special risks over and above the risks of the litigation itself. Companies that face lawsuits across the country relating to similar products, services, and theories of liability may find themselves overwhelmed by the cost and logistical burdens of managing multiple lawsuits. For example, Dow Corning petitioned for bankruptcy protection in 1995 after it faced 30,000 breast implant claims and had 90 cases scheduled for trial in the following six months (Higgins, 1998). Different law firms may adopt inconsistent positions on the many factual and legal issues that must be addressed, or some may fail to take advantage of claims and defenses of which they are unaware.

The use of national or regional coordinating counsel has been successfully employed by defendants in asbestos and other toxic tort litigation to effectively respond to the unique demands of mass litigation:

> The sharing of information and resources on the national level will avoid defendants' needless duplication of each other's work. National coordinating counsel can jointly draft master discovery requests that can be filed in numerous jurisdictions. Similarly, national coordinating counsel can develop protocols for inspection and discovery activities and can prepare deposition outlines and source materials to assist local counsel in conducting technical discovery on complex issues . . .

> In addition to cost savings and the efficient utilization of resources, national coordination among defendants provides consistency in the defense of the cases in all jurisdictions and minimizes conflicts among co-defendants. Open communication among the defendants through national coordinating counsel allows each company to not only be apprised of important developments across the country, but it also allows the defendants to rely upon a favorable track record of rulings in other jurisdictions when presenting similar issues to a particular court (Cetrulo, 1989).

Factors to consider in deciding whether coordinating counsel may be needed include the following:

- The number and similarity of cases
- The number of class action suits and the number of plaintiffs participating in such actions
- The number of different jurisdictions in which the suits have been or are expected to be filed
- The existence of complex technical issues and novel legal theories
- The extent of the need for expert testimony
- The number of relevant documents
- The length and complexity of the factual history
- The need for coordinated media responses

Publicly traded IT companies, including large Y2K solutions providers, that might be named in multiple, large-scale litigation are likely to be most in need of coordinating counsel. Other industries that should consider engaging coordinating counsel in 1999 to prepare for the possible wave of post-2000 lawsuits include insurance companies, utilities, financial institutions, national healthcare corporations, national and international freight carriers and transportation companies, and publicly held corporations that are heavily dependent on foreign operations or suppliers.

Selecting Coordination Counsel

Inasmuch as coordinating counsel serve a management role that is distinct from that of trial counsel, corporations should consider retaining a law firm that has organized itself to perform those specialized administrative functions. The firm serving as coordinating counsel (also known as *liaison counsel*) is primarily responsible for organizing large amounts of information, developing systems for managing simultaneous cases, and coordinating communications among the various law firms that are directly handling lawsuits in disparate jurisdictions. Liaison counsel functions can be performed well by small specialty firms that understand complex technical and legal issues and have experience in managing complex litigation, leaving much of the brute-force trial work to larger firms that have the resources necessary to conduct extensive discovery and prepare for numerous court appearances and motions practice. In fact, many large law firms have neither the temperament nor the interest in serving in the supporting role of coordinating counsel. A law firm that will dedicate itself to collecting, organizing, and disseminating a large body of information and handling such matters as scheduling and coordinating communications among participating firms is the ideal candidate for liaison counsel.

One consideration for choosing coordination counsel may be the firm's ability to use technology platforms that can support the efficient sharing of information. Groupware and Internet applications such as Lotus *Notes* and *Domino Instant! Host* and Microsoft *Exchange* enable geographically dispersed law firms and clients to share information securely and reduce litigation costs. Examples of information that can be hosted on a secure server for the benefit of participating firms and corporations include model pleadings and discovery, research memoranda on common issues of law, bibliographies, checklists, deposition transcripts, resumes of expert witnesses, and briefing books.

Joint Defense Agreements

Sharing information among defendants can potentially undermine the confidentiality of communications that would otherwise be protected by the attorney-client privilege and expose counsel to difficult conflict-of-interest problems. To control these risks without sacrificing the benefits of sharing information and reducing defense costs, it is advisable to consider entering a written joint defense agreement among all parties who intend to share privileged information. Such agreements, when properly drafted, have been accepted by the courts (Scheininger, 1994). A joint defense agreement generally should include the following provisions:

Agreement to share information. Identify the legal proceedings in which the signatory parties and their counsel have agreed to share information and strategy in their common interest and for the purpose of preserving confidentiality.

Assertion of privilege. Stipulate that all shared information and strategy will (a) be governed by the attorney-client privilege, the work product doctrine, and all other applicable privileges, (b) be kept confidential from third parties, and (c) not be disclosed to any third party without the consent of the party who provided the information. State that the clients do not intend to waive their privileges by entering the agreement.

Responding to legal process. In the event that any of the clients or any of their attorneys are served with legal process, such as a subpoena, requiring testimony, production, or disclosure of any confidential information or strategy that has been acquired under the agreement, the client or attorney will (a) immediately inform the other parties and provide a copy of the process, (b) assert all available privileges, (c) not waive any privilege or objection without the consent of the party who provided the information, and (d) make every reasonable effort to prevent or limit disclosure.

Protection from inconsistent agreements. If any client engages in any discussions or enters any agreements with any third parties that are or may be inconsistent with the joint defense agreement, that client will (a) immediately inform the other parties, (b) promptly return all documents received from each other party, and (c) refrain from disclosing any confidential information or strategy to any third party. The parties should agree that entering any such agreement does not relieve them from the continuing obligation to maintain all privileges and protect the confidentiality of all information and strategy provided under the joint defense agreement.

Withdrawal. Each client is free to withdraw from the agreement upon giving prior written notice to counsel for the other parties. The agreement should state that it shall continue to operate with respect to all remaining clients and attorneys and shall continue to protect all communications, documents, and information disclosed prior to the withdrawal. The withdrawing client and counsel should be required to promptly return all documents received pursuant to the agreement.

Conflicts of interest. The parties and their counsel should agree that the joint defense agreement does not create an attorney-client relationship between any counsel and anyone other than the client of that counsel. Nor should the agreement preclude any attorney from representing any interest adverse to any party to the agreement or disqualify any counsel from representing any other party in the proceeding covered by the agreement or any other proceeding, now or in the future. The participating attorneys shall not be disqualified from examining or cross-examining any participating client. Each counsel should represent that he or she has discussed this provision with his or her respective client before signing the agreement.

Limitations of scope. Each attorney should be free to use shared information or strategy to obtain leads to other evidence that would not be subject to the agreement. The agreement does not affect employment or other relationships. An employer may not use information obtained under the agreement in a disciplinary proceeding against a participating employee, but the agreement does not prevent an employer from taking such action based on information obtained from other sources.

Extensions of scope. The agreement should expressly relate back to cover any information and strategy that was shared among any of the participants before the date of the agreement. Other attorneys and parties may be added to the agreement with the consent of all of the parties.

Conclusion

Year 2000 lawsuits may well represent the next major wave of litigation on a scale that exceeds environmental liability and toxic tort suits of years past. Thus, at the same time that companies exercise due diligence to try to avoid litigation, effective risk management requires corporations to develop and implement strategies to reduce the costs and optimize the outcomes of Y2K suits. 1999 presents a rare opportunity to gear up for the expected crush of Year 2000 cases by finding qualified counsel, exploring alternative fee arrangements, planning for cost recovery suits, and organizing to manage multiple lawsuits.

CHAPTER 12

Post-2000 Risk Management

"I think there is a world market for maybe five computers."

—THOMAS WATSON, CHAIRMAN OF IBM, 1943

As you can see from Mr. Watson's quote, predicting where technology will lead us can be quite difficult. Predicting the outcome of the Year 2000 crisis may be even more difficult because innumerable factors are still unknown. Even though no one has a crystal ball, we can assume that the period of time after the rollover will be filled with plenty of angst and even more work still to be done. First and foremost will be the need for *crisis management*, "what you do when there is indeed a smoky fire in the kitchen" (Ulrich, 1998). This time period can potentially be one where firms are operating in a contingency mode while waiting for stability in the business and consumer environments. Many will be nervously eyeing the government's response and waiting for other shoes to drop as disruptions ripple through the economy and corporate supply chains. We will be watching for disruptions on other key dates such as leap day (February 29, 2000) and cleaning up the mess that rushed remediation projects left behind. We will be working on permanent solutions and building new and more reliable environments. And, yes, we will be waiting for the expected flood of legal actions to be unleashed. This chapter discusses some of the issues that you can expect to arise in the post-2000 period.

We will begin by reviewing various assessments of the overall compliance situation that have been published as of late 1998. We will then offer some final observations and recommended strategies in three areas of post-2000 risk management: crisis management, financial, and legal.

Predictions for 2000

Many prognosticators have been trying to estimate the impact of Y2K on our future. At one end of the spectrum are those that downplay the seriousness of the issue, even to the point of calling it a hoax. At the other end of the spectrum is "the-end-of-life-as-we-know-it," doom and gloom crowd. In between those extremes, there continue to be serious warnings from knowledgeable experts that Y2K is likely to cause some serious disruptions.

Dr. Edward Yardeni, the respected chief economist at Deutsche Bank Securities, sees Year 2000 as a very serious threat to the global economy. According to Dr. Yardeni, "If the disruptions are significant and widespread, then a global recession is likely. Currently, I believe there is a 70% chance of such a worldwide recession, which could last at least 12 months starting in January 2000 and could be at least as severe as the 1973–74 global recession" (Yardeni, 1998). He goes on to say that ". . . it might be too optimistic to believe that the information gridlock won't be even more damaging, sending us further back in time, when the level of GDP that our information systems supported was even lower. Therefore, I predict that, in the United States, real GDP could fall 5% from peak to trough over a 12–24 month period starting late in 1999."

Capers Jones, in a paper titled "Probabilities of Year 2000 Damages" (Jones, 1998), takes an analytical approach looking at the fact that the overall U.S. average for software defect removal efficiency (finding and removing bugs) is only about 85 percent. Jones adds that the testing sequence is usually only about 70 percent efficient in finding latent errors. As a result, he sees the possibility of 5 percent to more than 20 percent of the Year 2000 problems still unrepaired and remaining in software after the century ends and the resulting high probability of significant damages. Jones uses this information to make a number of predictions, such as the following:

YEAR 2000 PROBLEM	PROBABILITY OF OCCURRENCE
Bad credit reports due to Year 2000 errors	70%
Cancellation of Year 2000 liability insurance	60%
Loss of local electric power (> 1 day)	55%
Litigation against corporate officers	55%
Loss of regional electric power (> 1 day)	40%

On the other hand, the Gartner Group is less concerned, at least domestically. In a report titled *Year 2000 Risk Assessment and Planning for Individuals* (1998), it states that, for strategic planning purposes, we should assume that only 10 percent of mission-critical failures will last three days or more and that 70 percent will likely last less than 48 hours (0.8 probability). But the Gartner Group ranks Argentina, Germany, Japan, and Venezuela as having 50 percent probabilities of experiencing a mission-critical Y2K failure, and it ranks Russia as having a 66 percent failure probability (Legard, 1998).

The North American Electric Reliability Council (NERC) has been asked by the U.S. Department of Energy to conduct an assessment of the continent's power systems. In a report titled *Preparing the Electric Power Systems of North America for Transition to the Year 2000*, NERC reported that its initial assessment found that ". . . the impacts of Y2K on electrical systems appear to be less than first anticipated (North American Electric Reliability Council, 1998)." The report acknowledges the many risks that may be present but concludes that it is too soon to tell what the risks are or if they will be significant.

We expect that various experts will continue to fine-tune these predictions as we approach the year 2000. What is missing to date is a comprehensive assessment of these threats by the government. Several grass-roots organizations are attempting to perform high-level risk assessments and system dynamics models of critical infrastructure and supply areas. We hope that an organized and credible effort will surface that will provide both the business and public sectors with these needed assessments. Information on the reliability of electricity and other critical dependencies such as processing financial transactions and telecommunications will be key, as will be the results of modeling the threat to interdependencies. Unfortunately, it appears at this late date that such assessments are unlikely to be completed in time.

Crisis Management

Even though we hope that the post-2000 period is one of only minor disruptions, much uncertainty remains. Most large organizations will have contingency plans in place that should help mitigate Year 2000 disruptions. Despite this, the post-2000 period is likely to be one of crisis management. Organizations large and small depend to varying degrees on suppliers, subcontractors, vendors, service providers, government agencies, and utilities that may have debilitating Y2K problems. These problems are likely to mount and may drag on for longer than anticipated, particularly if contaminated data spreads to once-compliant systems. It may take considerable time to resolve some of the larger problems while other new problems may be discovered at the same time.

This type of atmosphere will require strong crisis management skills. Management will have to provide the "cool heads" to lead your organizations through what may be a tumultuous period. It is possible that the crisis period may drag on for much longer than any type of crisis that you have dealt with in the past.

Disaster recovery may be made even more difficult by the fact that others on whom you depend can be expected to be similarly affected.

Under any scenario, a crisis period is a time that will need strong public communications skills. Your customers, employees, and stockholders are likely to be very anxious about what your planning efforts have encompassed, and, in the event of a crisis, they will want to know just what is going on in your organization. Your planning should take this into account by preemptively publicizing your planning and preparation and then making your best efforts to communicate to these groups through the difficult period.

Failure Scenarios

We have already discussed several ways in which Y2K failures are likely to occur. Two others deserve consideration: the possibility that predictions of a crisis will themselves engender a crisis and the prospect for breakdowns in government services.

Self-Fulfilling Prophecy

Many observers predict that actual Y2K failures will increase sharply in 1999 as organizations enter projected "00" date information into computer systems that have not been fully renovated. In effect, we will be "live" testing a large number of systems in a production environment that may not be ready to process twenty-first century data. The problem is made more immediate by the fact that many organizations, especially state governments, operate on a fiscal year basis that begins as early as July 1, 1999. This experience could prove informative if it reveals how Year 2000 failures will actually occur before the entire technology infrastructure crosses the date boundary.

It is also possible that serious failures in 1999 could fuel sensationalist media coverage, which in turn could lead individuals and businesses to take actions that would transform minor problems into self-fulfilling prophecies of severe economic dislocations. The most obvious example would be if large numbers of cash withdrawals were made in 1999 and 2000. Although the Federal Reserve Board has announced it will increase cash reserves by $50 billion, that amount would not be sufficient to control panic withdrawals. Similarly, hoarding of prescription medicines, electric generators, nonperishable foods, and personal computers could cascade into a serious situation if public anxiety gets out of hand.

Failure of Government Services

We will discuss the government's role in helping lead recovery from Y2K events in the following section. However, we could also find ourselves in a "reverse civil defense" situation, in which man-made disasters trigger the loss of essential federal, state, and local services on which businesses depend. The private and nonprofit sectors need to take such governmental Year 2000 failures into account as they plan their risk management strategies. Government services at risk fall into five general categories:

- Infrastructure—public utilities, airports, shipping links, traffic signals and controls, and public transportation
- Emergency services—police and fire, public hospitals, emergency management agencies, and snow removal
- Regulatory functions—permits, business filings, inspection services, and health and safety enforcement
- Funds transfers—medical insurance payments and tax refunds
- Proprietary functions—public contracts and capital project financing

Companies need to make sure that the public sector is on their risk management radar screens. Inventory your governmental dependencies, cross-reference them to the business functions they support, and prioritize them as you do other risks. For your mission-critical governmental dependencies, avoid damages by maintaining close communications with key government officials and exploring private sector alternatives before failures occur. Find out how to get in touch with the right person before an emergency arises.

Recovery Strategies

Crisis management is what you do when your contingency plan fails or overlooks something important. The planning process is similar to the ones we discussed earlier for contingency planning, but the focus is on immediate problem-solving rather than alternative business processes:

> Year 2000 crisis management requires that you form a team that includes tactical response units, business leaders, third-party managers, purchasing executives, legal counsel, hot-line support and communication coordinators. Tactical response units, composed of IS and business professionals paired by area of responsibility, will coordinate hundreds of decisions.
>
> Tactical response units must be able to make quick decisions without calling for group consensus, and they must have the grit to escalate strategic decisions to senior executives as needed.
>
> Crisis management teams must plan for high-volume end-user change requests, systems software and hardware failures, network outages and queries from business units experiencing desktop, embedded or non-IT systems failures. Those teams also must plan to respond to customer calls, regulatory inquiries, third-party delays, data contamination, power or telecommunications outages, supplier shortages and broader economic problems (Ulrich, 1998).

The Role of the Government

The role of government in post-2000 activities has yet to be clearly defined. Several progressive local government agencies are developing detailed emergency management plans that are looking at how to respond to emergencies during a Y2K-induced crisis and how to maintain and restore government services after a disruption. Depending on the level of disruptions, federal intervention is possible, but it was painfully clear in 1998 that the government had no publicized strategy for dealing with the potential crisis. Emergency preparedness agencies such as the Federal Emergency Management Agency have been largely silent as to plans or preparations.

Government officials have an obligation to make Y2K a top priority and to take appropriate actions to minimize the length and severity of these disruptions. It appears, however, that most local governments have been slow to realize the need to deal with Year 2000 within their organizations, let alone outside of the organization. Community impact planning is just evolving as a priority of government. We expect that 1999 will be a period of increased activity on these issues as government leaders realize that they have an important role to play. In the end, government officials will be judged by how well they understood the Y2K problem and, most importantly, by how well they responded to the challenge, informed and prepared their constituents, and planned for Year 2000 impacts.

Reestablishing Communications with Business Partners

After any period of disruption, reestablishing communications with your various business partners will be important. Your business continuity planning should incorporate a strategy for resuming normal business operations as soon as contingency modes conclude. Being in contact with customers and suppliers to gauge the flow of products and service into and out of your organization will be crucial. Work with your business partners early on to develop strategies for the resumption of normal business processes.

Financial Concerns

Even though the financial sector has made the most progress in Y2K preparedness, risks of significant failures will remain due to the complexities and interdependencies of the national and international financial networks.

Liquidity Shortages

As we noted earlier, cash shortages could arise because financial institutions might experience Year 2000 disruptions or simply because too many people withdraw funds out of concern that they might. Watch for banking regulators to provide information designed to reassure the public and forestall ruinous bank runs. CFOs should keep a close eye on cash flow, cash reserves, and accounts receivable during at least the first two quarters of 2000.

Possible Credit Crunch

For several reasons, there may be a credit crunch in early 2000. Banks will be maximizing liquidity in response to cash demands while at the same time reducing risk by refusing or reducing loans to firms that appear to be most vulnerable to Y2K problems. Both of these factors are likely to limit the availability of loans. As the Gartner Group has pointed out, other financial players will start paying closer attention to Y2K risks, including institutional fund managers, credit-rating agencies, auditors, and insurers. Companies that establish *reasonable* cash reserves or even lines of credit before 2000 can be expected to be in a much better position than those that are looking to borrow funds after the date rollover.

The Federal Financial Institutions Examination Council (FFIEC) has issued several statements that provide guidance to financial institutions on the Year 2000 problem. One such statement, issued March 17, 1998 and titled "Guidance Concerning the Year 2000 Impact on Customers," includes credit risk questionnaires for use by banks. It is clear from reading the credit risk questionnaires that it will be very easy for firms to be categorized as high risk credits, making it more difficult to obtain, renew, extend, or enlarge a business loan or line of credit. It is too early to say how strictly the FFIEC and the banks will rank and enforce Y2K credit risk ratings, but the framework is quite conservative. Businesses should make sure they are not failing to take steps now that they will need to complete or at least have underway in order to qualify for borrowing during 1999 and 2000.

Post-2000 Investment Opportunities

A number of possible but unpredictable factors will drive post-2000 investment opportunities. Without knowing just how disruptive Year 2000 failures might prove to be, it is impossible to predict exactly what opportunities will present themselves. Some plausible scenarios do suggest themselves.

The Stock Market

The stock market has been affected recently by global economic developments that, to date, have proven to be more significant than the Year 2000 problem. This situation may change, though, as we go through 1999 and as problems are likely to mount transitioning into the year 2000. Based on what we know today, several investment opportunity scenarios are possible. For instance, the markets may respond to reduced profits or simply because of fear of what may happen. It is conceivable that Y2K might dampen stock prices until investor confidence is regained, or, conversely, the market may rise if disruptions are less serious than some expect. In addition, promising investment opportunities could arise in those companies that do well in preparing for Y2K.

Profit Concerns

Heavy Year 2000 remediation costs as well as the distraction of Y2K-related risk management efforts are expected to lower corporate profits during 1999. Assuming that these anticipated profit reductions occur, and depending on other economic factors, stock prices may be driven down by the end of 1999. This would, in the eyes of most investors, present considerable investment opportunities in 2000. This opportunity must be reviewed in light of several factors:

- The key question will be when has the bottom been reached—when is the right time to invest?
- How will a loss of consumer and investor confidence affect the market?
- How will a credit crunch affect businesses and the market?
- Will federal regulators take action such as not allowing stock price movements except on a thin "flotation" band and on currency equivalencies? (Gartner Group, 1998)
- What are the profitability and survivability factors for certain industries such as IT consulting, electronic commerce, and Internet stocks?

Mergers and Acquisitions

Firms with solid Year 2000 programs may take the opportunity to acquire firms that have troubled projects. The firms that merge with or acquire these other firms stand to increase market share or, in some cases, dominate the market. Companies that are able to capitalize on the problems of others may represent good investment opportunities, provided they are able to overcome the difficulties of inheriting noncompliant IT systems from the acquired company.

Legal

It is certain that in the years 2000 and beyond Y2K failures will cause financial losses and that conflicts will arise over responsibility for those losses. We hope that many of the disputes that result can and will be resolved using alternative dispute resolution methods, instead of going to trial.

Post-2000 Litigation

Even though lawsuits certainly are not waiting for the year 2000, many experts are predicting a flood of Y2K-related actions:

> If the [Y2K] problem materializes with the magnitude that many predict, there is no question that there will be a lot more litigation. It will be on a much more diverse basis than the consumer or small business warranty or consumer protection based cases that have predominated so far. There will be cases that are more specifically contract based. There will be tort cases in product liability and other areas that will undoubtedly involve consequential damages in a way that class actions generally do not. I think that will expand the field of Y2K litigation in many different ways (Y2K Advisor, 1998).

As the courts become bogged down in legal actions, alternative dispute resolution and out-of-court settlements can be expected to be promoted as better ways to resolve these disputes. Directors and officers should be especially attentive to addressing Y2K problems as best they can in the hopes that they can bring themselves within the business judgment defense. The principal focus should be on how companies can maintain operations in the face of significant litigation. Consider hiring outside coordination counsel if your organization finds itself embroiled in multiple suits.

Insurance Claims and Coverage

Clearly, the post-2000 period can be expected to be a time of numerous insurance claims and legal actions regarding coverage. To the degree that significant property and business losses occur, and that other potentially insurable events arise, litigation and subrogation levels can be expected to be high. You can expect this greater volume of claims to take longer than usual to process, particularly if insurers are facing their own Y2K problems. Plan for maintaining operations without insurance funds. Insurance coverage lawsuits will take several years to resolve as the cases work their way through the appellate courts. Carriers should consider bringing some insurance disputes to ADR to avoid adverse court rulings in cases where ambiguous policy language might be read in favor of the insured.

Conclusion

We will all be waiting to see just what disruptions year 2000 brings, and we hope that the Gartner Group is correct that most disruptions will be short-lived. It is possible, though, that we will suffer from ongoing disruptions and economic downturns for years to come.

The best advice that we can give you at this point is to follow the best practices outlined in this book and strive for due diligence and reasonable business judgment in everything that you do. Remember to maintain thorough documentation of all important decisions and actions.

No matter what happens, the result should include a worldwide awareness of our dependence on technology and the fragile state of our complex and interdependent systems. We can expect a changed perception of the importance and risks present in information technology and the various companies that we depend on as partners in our businesses. We will have an improved understanding of our need for risk management in general but with our technology assets in particular. And we will likely have better inventories, better documentation, and a better understanding of the interrelationships and interdependencies among our many systems. But if there was ever a case where an ounce of prevention is worth a pound of cure, surely Y2K is it.

APPENDIX

Y2K Resources

Following are some useful Year 2000 Web sites and other Internet resources arranged by category.

General

www.year2000.com
: *Year 2000 Information Center.* Peter de Jager's ultimate Y2K site.

www.DavisLogic.com/impact.htm
: *Dealing with the Year 2000 Problem.* Author Steven Davis' site has information on risk management, contingency planning, and emergency management.

www.y2ktoday.com
: *Y2K Today.* New megasite that offers news, views, and things you can use. The site intends to be the number one Y2K site and includes forums and personalized news.

www.willitwork.com
: *Lab 2K, LLC.* Has a free search engine, which contains contact information for thousands of vendors with Year 2000 compliance issues.

www.y2k.gov
: *President's Year 2000 Conversion Council.* Includes information of the U.S. government progress and links by sector.

www.bog.frb.fed.us/y2k
   Federal Reserve Board. Video recordings of Presentations on the Year 2000 Problem: a collection of Y2K presentations for the Federal Reserve Board.

www.zdnet.com/zdy2k
   ZDY2K. Ziff-Davis contributes to the cause with numerous Y2K articles and papers.

www.itaa.org/year2000.htm
   Information Technology Association of America.

www.year2000.unt.edu
   The Society for Information Management Year 2000 Working Group.

www.y2kinvestor.com
   Y2k Investor. Investment advice and links.

www.spr.com/html/year_2000_problem.htm
   Global Economic Impact. Capers Jones' seminal piece on economic impacts of Y2K.

News

www.year2000.com/y2karticles.html
   Year 2000 Press Clippings. Year 2000 Information Center.

www.newsnow.co.uk
   NewsNow. Provides headlines from more than 20 top IT news sources, updated every 5 minutes.

Risk Management

www.consult2000.com
   Next Millennium Consulting (NMC), co-founded by author Andrew M. Pegalis, is the nation's first independent risk management consulting firm dedicated exclusively to providing complete Y2K risk management services.

www.y2k.gov.au/methodology/html/about.html
   Business Risk Analysis Methodology. Developed by the New South Wales Government (Australia).

www.year2000.com/archive/risky2k.html
   For Risk Managers, the Year 2000 Is Now. By Andrew M. Pegalis, reprinted from *Business Insurance,* December 23/30, 1996.

www.jks.co.uk/y2ki/recent/index.htm
   The Risks Matrix. A risks matrix compiled by Steve Wakeland, former head of Computer Audit at Abbey National plc.

www2.computerworld.com/home/online9697.nsf/All/971103worth3
Year 2000 Risk by Industry. Computerworld article on American Management Systems, Inc.'s rating of risks by industry.

Contingency Planning

www.business-continuity.com/business_continuity.html
Journal of Business Continuity. Provides information and news on business continuity.

www.zdnet.com/zdy2k/1998/09/4796.html
ZDY2K Web site. Includes several good articles on contingency planning and community preparedness including "Contingency Planning Step by Step."

www.gao.gov/special.pubs/cpguide.pdf
General Accounting Office. Year 2000 Computing Crisis: Business Continuity and Contingency Planning.

www.gsa.gov/gsacio/ssay2kb1.htm
Social Security Administration. Business Continuity and Contingency Plan.

www.gsa.gov/gsacio/ssamatr3.pdf
Social Security Administration. Business Continuity and Contingency Plan Matrices.

www.mitre.org/research/y2k/docs/CONTINGENCY_PLAN.html
Y2K Contingency Management Plans. Provided by Electronic Systems Center and The MITRE Corporation.

www.fws.gov/pullenl/security/contpln.html
Guidelines for Contingency Plan Development. The U.S. Fish and Wildlife Service.

www.fdic.gov/banknews/fils/1998/fil9851b.html
FDIC. Guidance Concerning Contingency Planning.

www.dir.state.tx.us/y2k/resources/guidebook2000
State of Texas. Guidelines for Contingency Planning.

www.y2kjournal.com/hot/contingency.htm
Year 2000 Journal Articles. Specializes in technical Year 2000 issues but has had several excellent articles on Y2K contingency planning.

www.energy.ca.gov/contingency/introduction.html
California Energy Shortage Contingency Plan. A good example of a complete contingency plan.

www.masp.com/Year2000.htm
Management Advisory Services & Publications. This site includes information on building an effective Year 2000 conversion plan, including strategies

and technical approaches. It also provides guidelines to plan and execute effective Y2K audits to ensure the adequacy of Y2K programs.

Disaster Recovery

www.dr.org/ppover.htm
Disaster Recovery Institute of Canada. "Professional Practices for Business Continuity Planners."

Legal

www.2000legal.com
Legal Resources for Avoiding Year 2000 Business Disruptions and Reducing Litigation Exposure. Author Steve Goldberg's site featuring extensive links to Y2K legal source materials.

www.dr2000.com
Dispute Resolution 2000. Author Steve Goldberg's site for Y2K alternative dispute resolution services.

www.y2k.com/legalpage.htm
The Y2K Law Site at Y2k.com. Great legal issues site, sponsored by William, Mullen, Christian & Dobbins.

www.year2000.com/y2klawcenter.html
Year 2000.Com Law Center. Focuses on the legal, accounting, and insurance aspects of the Year 2000 problem to avoid liability and maximize recovery.

www.itaa.org/script/2000vend.cfm
and
www.itaa.org/2000cert.htm
ITAA Y2K Information Center. Solution Providers Directory and Certification Program.

www.itaa.org/y2kadr.htm
ITAA's Y2K ADR Web Site. Articles and resources for Year 2000 alternative dispute resolution.

Future

www.angelfire.com/ca/rhomer/social.html
Social Issues. "The Year 2000: Social Chaos or Social Transformation?" by John L. Petersen, Margaret Wheatley, Myron Kellner-Rogers. This paper gives an excellent and detailed explanation of the current situation and advocates

collaboration—in communities, organizations, and governments—to engage in both preparedness planning and the creation of simplified systems.

www.arlinst.org/index.htm

Arlington Institute. A policy and research institute that has created a Year 2000 Fusion Center and is conducting systems modeling to assess the impact of Year 2000 problems. The Institute was founded by futurist John Petersen.

www.wfs.org

World Future Society. A nonprofit educational and scientific organization for people interested in how social and technological developments, including the Year 2000 Problem, are shaping the future.

Other Books to Read

De Jager, Peter and Bergeon, Richard. *Countdown Y2K: Business Survival Planning for the Year 2000.* New York: John Wiley & Sons, 1998.

Jones, Capers. *The Year 2000 Software Problem: Quantifying the Costs and Assessing the Consequences.* Reading, MA: Addison Wesley Longman, 1998.

Jones, Keith. *Year 2000 Software Crisis Solutions.* Boston: International Thomson Computer Press, 1997.

Kappelman, Leon (editor). *Solving the Year 2000 Problem.* Boston: International Thomson Computer Press, 1997.

Kappelman, Leon (editor). *Year 2000 Problem: Strategies and Solutions from the Fortune 100.* Boston: International Thomson Press, 1997.

Kappelman, Leon (editor). *Year 2000 Update: Key Issues and Research Reports.* Chicago: Society for Information Management (SIM) International, 1998.

Keyes, Tony. *The Year 2000 Computer Crisis: An Investor's Survival Guide.* Brookville, MD: The Y2K Investor, 1997.

Lefkon, Dick (editor). *Year 2000: Best Practices for Y2K Millennium Computing.* Upper Saddle River, NJ: Prentice Hall Computer Books, 1998.

Perry, William. *Year 2000 Software Testing.* New York: John Wiley & Sons, 1998.

Ragland, Bryce. *The Year 2000 Problem Solver.* New York: McGraw Hill, 1997.

Robbins, Brian and Rubin, Howard. *The Year 2000 Planning Guide.* Rubin Systems, Inc., Pound Ridge, NY, 1997.

Ulrich, William and Ian S. Hayes. *The Year 2000 Software Crisis: Challenge of the Century.* Upper Saddle River, NJ: Prentice Hall, Yourdon Press, 1997.

Ulrich, William and Ian S. Hayes. *The Year 2000 Software Crisis: The Continuing Challenge.* Upper Saddle River, NJ: Prentice Hall, Yourdon Press, 1998.

REFERENCES

Chapter 1

Ackerman, Joel M. 1997. "Prudent Paranoia." Rx2000 Solutions Institute. www.rx2000.org/Prudent.html.

Bailey, Janet L., Harry I. David, David C. Hall, and Leon A. Kappelman. 1997. "When the Chips Are Down" in *Year 2000 Problem: Strategies and Solutions from the Fortune 100*. Boston: Int'l. Thomson Computer Press, 135–6.

Caldwell, Bruce. 1998. "Gartner Survey Finds Year 2000 Efforts at Many Companies Lag." *InformationWeek Online, TechWeb News* (April 9).

Coffou, Ann K. 1997. "Year 2000 Risks: What Are the Consequences of Technology Failures?" Statement of Hearing Testimony, Subcommittee on Technology and Subcommittee on Government Management, Information and Technology, March 20). www.house.gov/science/couffou_3-20.html.

Coffou, Ann K. 1998. "Year 2000 Risks: Non-IT/Embedded Systems." Giga Information Group, presentation to Boston Millennium Association, April.

Cowles, Rick. 1998. *Electric Utilities and Y2K*, 12.

de Jager, Peter and Richard Bergeon. 1997. *Managing 00: Surviving the Year 2000 Computing Crisis*. New York: Wiley Computer Publishing, vii.

de Jager, Peter. 1998. "Moving to Zero—September 1998, How Time Flies When You're Having Fun …." www.year2000.com/archive/timeflies.html.

FFIEC. 1998. "Guidance Concerning the Year 2000 Impact on Customers," March 17.

Hagewood, Larry and Ken Owen. 1998. "PLANT Y2K: A White Paper That Discusses the Significance of the Effect of the Millennium Bug (Y2K) on Process Control, Factory Automation & Embedded Systems in Manufacturing Companies." TAVA Technologies, Inc., 2–5.

IEE. 1998. "What Is an Embedded Systems?" The Institution of Electrical Engineers. www.iee.org.uk/2000risk/guide/year2k10.htm.

Jinnett, Jeff. 1997a. "Year 2000 'Millennium Bug' Litigation." www.llgm.com/FIRM/article5.htm.

Jinnett, Jeff. 1997b. "Millennium Bug to Lead to Huge Claims-Lawyer." *The ZD Net News Channel*, June 19.

Jones, Capers. 1998a. "Probability of Year 2000 Damages." www.year2000.com/archive/proby2k.html.

Jones, Capers. 1998b. *The Year 2000 Software Problem: Quantifying the Costs and Assessing the Consequences*. Boston: Addison-Wesley, 153, 168, 207, 237.

Kizer, Kenneth W. 1998. Statement by the Honorable Kenneth W. Kizer, M.D., M.P.H., Under Secretary for Health, Department of Veterans Affairs, Before the U.S. Senate Special Committee on Year 2000, July 23, 1, 2.

Lynch, David J. 1998. "In Europe—Denial, Inaction Threaten USA." *USA Today*, April 13, 3B.

Mandel, Coy, Peter Coy, Paul C. Judge. 1998. "Zap! How the Year 2000 Bug Will Hurt the Economy." *Business Week*, March 2, 93.

Montagnolo, Anthony J. ECRI. 1998. "Medical Devices and the Year 2000 Problem." Presentation to American Society of Healthcare Materials Management, April.

Nolan, Richard L. 1998. "Connectivity and Control in the Year 2000 and Beyond." *Harvard Business Review*, July/August, 150

Reuters. 1998. "Cambridge Technology shares fall on slower growth report." *Boston Globe*, September 5, F1.

Sheinheit, Steve and Brian Robbins. 1998. "Connectivity and Control in the Year 2000 and Beyond." *Harvard Business Review*, July/August, 166.

Soat, John. 1998. "Companies Encounter Unexpected Y2K Problems." *Information Week Online, TechWeb News*, July 21.

Strassman, Paul A. 1998. "Year 2000 Opens Door to More Federal Rules for IT." *Computerworld*, August 31, 54.

Weil, Nancy. 1998. "Gartner's year-2000 survey finds widespread disruptions likely." *InfoWorld Electric*, August 5.

Yardeni, Ed. 1998. "Connectivity and Control in the Year 2000 and Beyond." *Harvard Business Review*, July/August, 162.

Yourdon, Ed. 1998. "Don't shoot the year 2000 lawyers." *Computerworld*, June 22. www.computerworld.com/home/features.nsf/all/980622y2k.

Chapter 4

American Institute of Certified Public Accountants, et al. 1997. "Eleven International Organizations Join Forces to Encourage Executive Attention to Year 2000 Computer Date Issue." *Press Release*, October 1. www.isaca.org/y2kpr.htm.

British Standards Institution. 1998. "A Definition of Year 2000 Conformity Requirements." *DISC PD2000-1*. ISBN 0-580-29746-2. www.bsi.org.uk/disc/year2000/2000.htm.

Cirillo, Gregory P. 1998. "Y2K Remediation Contracts: When Your Back is Against the Wall, You Do Not Need Leverage to Succeed." www.y2k.com/sequelgp.htm.

Commonwealth of Massachusetts. 1998a. "Agency Statement of Year 2000 Compliance." www.state.ma.us/y2k.

Commonwealth of Massachusetts, Information Technology Division. 1998b. "Year 2000 Independent Verification and Validation Services." *OSD RFR* No. ITS04, June 10, 14.

Feathers, Timothy J. 1998. "Year 2000 Warranty." www.year2000.com/archive/warranty.html.

Gergacz, John William. 1990. *Attorney-Corporate Client Privilege, 2nd ed.* New York: Garland Law Publishing, A-3 to A-5.

Harvey, William L. 1998. "Addressing Year 2000 Credit Risk through Loan Documentation Provisions" in *The Year 2000 Legal Guide*. New York: Bowne & Co., Inc., N207-8.

Microsoft Year 2000 Compliance Statement. 1998. www.microsoft.com/technet/topics/year2k/y2kcomply/y2kcomply.htm.

New York State Year 2000 Contract Language Guidelines. 1998. www.irm.state.ny.us/yr2000/contract.htm.

Nolan, Joseph R. and Michael J. Connolly, eds. 1979. *Black's Law Dictionary*, 5th ed. Eagan, Minnesota: West Publishing Company.

Office of the Inspector General, Department of Health and Human Services. 1998. *The Office of Inspector General, Compliance Program Guidance for Clinical Laboratories*, August 8, 6–7.

Paar, Randy and Joshua Gold. 1998. "Coverage Issues for Year 2000 Computer Losses and Liability" in *The Year 2000 Legal Guide*. Bowne & Co., Inc., E201-2.

Ricci, Chris. 1997. "High Technology Contractual Issues Related to the Year 2000" in *Year 2000 Computer Failures*. Boston: Mass. Continuing Legal Education, 246-8.

Rosenthal, Bob B. 1997. "Year 2000 Failures: General Contract Issues" in *Year 2000 Computer Failures*. Boston: Mass. Continuing Legal Education, 241-244.

U.S. General Services Administration. 1997. "Recommended Year 2000 Contract Language, Commercial Supply Products Warranty." www.itpolicy.gsa.gov/mks/yr2000/contlang.htm.

Chapter 5

Securities and Exchange Commission. 1997. *SEC Report to Congress on the Readiness of the United States Securities Industry and Public Companies to Meet the Information Processing Challenges of the Year 2000.* www.sec.gov/news/studies/yr2000.htm.

Securities and Exchange Commission. 1998. *Statement of the Commission Regarding Disclosure of Year 2000 Issues and Consequences by Public Companies, Investment Advisers, Investment Companies, and Municipal Securities Issuers.* www.sec.gov/rules/concept/33-7558.htm.

Chapter 6

Jones, Capers. 1998. *Probabilities of Year 2000 Damages*. SPR, Inc. February 27, 1998, www.year2000.com/y2karchive.html.

Lanza, Chuck. 1998. "Community Preparedness, Y2Kprep." Director, Miami-Dade County (Florida) Office of Emergency Management. www.chucklanza.com/emerprep.htm.

Marcoccio, Lou. 1998. Gartner Group, "Testimony before the United States Senate Special Committee on the Year 2000 Technology Problem," October 7, 1998. www.senate.gov/%7Ey2k/statements/100798marcoccio.html.

Myrick, David E. 1998. "Year 2000 Contingency Planning White Paper." Myrick Consulting Services. www.myrickconsulting.com/Y2KSELWP.HTM#Year 2000 Contingency Planning.

Chapter 8

AICPA. 1998. *The Year 2000 Issue—Current Accounting and Auditing Guidance*. www.aicpa.org/members/y2000/intro.htm (revised October 19).

Carvill, Wynne. 1998. "Management Use of Internal Audit to Assure Year 2000 Preparedness" in *The Year 2000 Legal Guide*. New York: Bowne & Co., Inc., B201.

Dec, Irene. 1997. *Proceedings*, Year 2000 Conference & Expo, Boston, November 18.

Gross, Ira. 1998. "Potential Claims and the Paper Trail in Compliance Efforts" in *The Year 2000 Legal Guide*. New York: Bowne & Co., Inc., H405.

Kyte, A. 1998. "Financial Markets Have Year 2000 Losses on Their Radar Screens." *Inside Gartner Group*, August 19. gartner4.gartnerweb.com/public/static/home/00071915.html.

Mandel, Michael J., Peter Coy, and Peter C. Judge. 1998. "Zap! How the Year 2000 Bug Will Hurt the Economy." *Business Week*, March 2, 93.

Mass. 1998. 426 Mass. 491, 1998 Mass. LEXIS 22.

Wakeland, Steve. 1998. "Year 2000 Programme: The Audit Contribution," www.jks.co.uk/y2ki/recent/index.htm.

Chapter 9

FFIEC. 1997. "Federal Financial Institutions Examination Council, Interagency Statement." www.FFIEC.gov/y2k/federal.htm.

FRB. 1997. SR 97-34; SR 97-29; SR 97-16; SR 96-16; "FFIEC Safety and Soundness Guidelines Concerning The Year 2000 Business Risk."

Gartner Group. 1996. "Time Marches On—Less than 900 Working Days to January 1, 2000," June 28, www.garter.com/cgi-bin/pforms.

ISO. 1984. ISO form CG 00 01 11 85. Copyright of the Insurance Services Office, Inc.

ISO. 1985. ISO form CG 00 01 11 85 Copyright of the Insurance Services Office, Inc.

ISO. 1997. ISO form CG 21 60 04 98. Copyright of the Insurance Services Office, Inc.

Jones, Capers. 1997. "Global Economic Impact of the Year 2000 Software Problem." Software Productivity Research, Inc. www.spr.com/html/year_2000_problem.htm.

Knepper, William E. and Dan A. Bailey. 1993. *Liability of Corporate Officers & Directors*. 2 vol., 5th ed. LEXIS Law Publishing.

SEC. 1997a. "Readiness of the United States Securities Industry and Public Companies to Meet the Information Processing Challenges of the Year 2000," SEC Report to Congress.

SEC. 1998. *Statement of the Commission Regarding Disclosure of Year 2000 Issues and Consequences by Public Companies, Investment Advisers, Investment Companies, and Municipal Securities Issuers*. www.sec.gov/rules/concept/33-7558.htm.

Souter, Gavin. 1998. "Lawyer Says Order May Aid Y2K Claims, Business Insurance." *Business Insurance*, January 19, www.businessinsurance.com.

Chapter 10

American Arbitration Association. 1994a. "Drafting Dispute Resolution Clauses—A Practical Guide," 7. www.adr.org/ftp.

American Arbitration Association. 1994b. "Drafting Dispute Resolution Clauses—A Practical Guide," 5. www.adr.org/ftp.

Baum, William J., Jr. 1998. "Speaking Their Language—Presenting an ADR Program to Corporate Management," May 6, 1. www.adr.org/ftp.

CPR Institute for Dispute Resolution. 1998. "Questions to Assess ADR Suitability Regarding Consensual ADR." www.cpradr.org/qaadr.htm.

Halket, Thomas D. and Pitegoff, Thomas M. 1998. "The Role of ADR in Resolving Y2K Disputes Outside of the Overcrowded Courts." *The American Lawyer's Corporate Counsel Magazine*, June, 76.

Hock, Steven L. 1997. "The Year 2000 Problem and the Legal Risks." Proceedings, Year 2000 Conference & Expo, Boston, MA, Nov. 17–19.

ITAA. 1998a. "Y2K + ADR = Smart Business." www.itaa.org/Y2KADR.HTM.

ITAA. 1998b. "Sample ADR Contract Clause." www.itaa.org/y2kadr1.htm#sample.

Katz, Robert R. and Philip Gold. 1997. *Justice Matters: Rescuing the Legal System for the Twenty-First Century.* Seattle, WA: Discovery Institute, p. 17.

Keen, Peter G.W. 1998. "A Backlash Is Coming—and IS will be Caught in It." *Computerworld*, July 13.

Minnesota Dept. of Administration, Technology Management Bureau. 1997. "Year 2000 Dispute Resolution Language." www.state.mn.us/ebranch/admin/ipo/dispute.html.

Supreme Judicial Court, Trial Court Standing Committee on Dispute Resolution for the Chief Justice for Administration and Management of the Trial Court. 1998. "Report to the Legislature on the Impact of Alternative Dispute Resolution on the Massachusetts Trial Court," 5–6.

Victor, Mark B. 1990. "Litigation Risk Analysis™ and ADR" in *Donovan Leisure Newton & Irvine ADR Practice Book.* New York: John Wiley & Sons, Inc.

Chapter 11

Albers, Gillian. 1998. "Communicating and Year 2000." www.year2000.com/y2kcurrent3.html.

American Bar Association. 1995a. "Uniform Task-Based Management System Litigation Code Set." www.abanet.org/litigation/litnews/practice/utmscodeset.html.

American Bar Association. 1995b. "Overview." *Uniform Task-Based Management System Litigation Code Set.* www.abanet.org/litigation/litnews/practice/utmsoverview.html.

American Bar Association. 1995c. "Litigation Code Definitions." *Uniform Task-Based Management System Litigation Code Set.* www.abanet.org/litigation/litnews/practice/utmsdefine.html.

American Corporate Counsel Association. 1997. "Report on Selection of Outside Counsel by Corporations." www.acca.com/chapters/reportext.html, 24–25.

Becker, Theodore M. 1997. "How to Limit Discovery Without Costing Your Client the Case." *Illinois Legal Times*, May, 13.

Cetrulo, Lawrence G. and Randolph L. Smith. 1989. "Defending Multiparty Lawsuits." *Asbestos Issues '89*, March, 81.

Decker, Randy L. 1998a. "Economics and Litigation: View from the Inside Looking Out." *Litigation*, 24:4, 40.

Decker, Randy L. 1998b. "Economics and Litigation: View from the Inside Looking Out." *Litigation*, 24:4, 37.

Higgins, Michael. 1998. "Mass Tort Makeover?" *ABA Journal*, November, 54.

Katz, Roberta R., and Philip Gold. 1997a. *Justice Matters—Rescuing the Legal System for the Twenty-First Century.* Seattle, WA: Discovery Institute, 68,

n. 31, citing Presentation of Cynthia Munger of Altman Weil Pensa, Inc., at Tulane Law Institute, March 31, 1995.

Katz, Roberta R., and Philip Gold. 1997b. *Justice Matters—Rescuing the Legal System for the Twenty-First Century*. Seattle, WA: Discovery Institute, 68, n. 30, citing Federal Bar Association of the Western District of Washington, "Professionalism Task Force Interim Report," December 1994, pp. 1–6.

Ozenne, James, Atanu Saha, and Roy Weinstein. 1998. "Measuring Year 2000 Damages: A General Approach to Estimating Losses Caused by Non-Compliant Software." Micronomics, February, 10.

Scheininger, Michael G. and Ray M. Aragon. 1994. "Joint Defense Agreements." *Litigation*, 20:3, 11.

Voltz, Stephen M. 1996a. *Litigation Cost Control Resource Center*. www.tiac.net/users/svoltz.

Voltz, Stephen M. 1996b. *Litigation Cost Control Resource Center*. www.tiac.net/users/svoltz/chap02.htm.

Chapter 12

Federal Financial Institutions Examination Council (FFIEC). 1998. "Guidance Concerning the Year 2000 Impact on Customers." www.ffiec.gov/y2k/impact.htm.

Gartner Group. 1998. *Strategic Analysis Report*, October 28. gartner5.gartnerweb.com/public/static/home/00073955.html.

Jones, Capers, 1998. "Probabilities of Year 2000 Damages." SPR, Inc, February 27, www.year2000.com/y2karchive.html.

Legard, David. 1998. "Gartner says Asia will face big Y2K hit." *Computerworld*, November 12. www.computerworld.com/home/news.nsf/all/9811124asia.

North American Electric Reliability Council. 1998. "Preparing the Electric Power Systems of North America for Transition to the Year 2000." www.nerc.com and ftp.nerc.com/pub/sys/all_updl/docs/y2k/y2kreport-doe.pdf.

Ulrich, William. 1998. "Coming Soon: Year 2000 SWAT Teams." *Computerworld*, March 9. www.computerworld.com/home/print.nsf/All/9803092FDE.

Y2K Advisor. 1998. "The Future of Y2K Litigation—An Interview with Michael C. Spencer of Milberg Weiss Bershad Hynes & Lerach, LLP." *Y2K Advisor*, Vol. 1, No. 5, p. 3 (Nov./Dec.).

Yardeni, Edward. 1998. *Year 2000 Recession?* "Prepare for the worst. Hope for the best." Version 9.1 (November 2). www.yardeni.com/y2kbook.html.

INDEX

A

Abacus Law, 174
accountants, Y2K legal risks faced by, 198, 199–202
ADP, 173
AIG D&O Gold, 230
Albers, Gillian, 266
alternative dispute resolution (ADR), 103, 231, 233–254, 259, 269, 275, 276, 289
  advantages over litigation, 242–243
  best times to pursue, 272, 273–274
  court-ordered, 254
  developing programs for, 245–252
  evaluative, 253
  gaining management support for, 246–247
  ITAA initiative on, 242
  reasons for pursuing, 242
  requirements for success, 253–254
  resources, 248
  roles of neutrals in, 244–245, 252, 276
  sample contract clauses, 249–252
  techniques for instituting, 252
  types of, 243–245
American Airlines, 131
American Arbitration Association, 248
  arbitration clause, 252
American Corporate Counsel Association, 259
American Institute of Certified Public Accountants (AICPA), 91, 123, 175, 203
  guidelines for auditors, 198–201
American International Group (AIG), 229–230
AM-Re Managers, 228
Amroth, 266
antitrust laws, 225
Aon Risk Services, 228, 229

arbitration, 243, 245
  uses of, 247
ARM2000 program, 228–229
assessment phase, 49, 58–59, 228
  checklist, 65
attorney-client privilege, 103, 104, 265, 279
attorneys. *See* lawyers
auditors
  external, 198–204
  guidelines for working with, 203–204
  internal, 194–198
  lawsuits against, 198
  liability risks of, 199–202
  roles of, 194
  Y2K responsibilities of, 194–198, 199–200
audits, 194–204
  consequences of, 200
  going concern issues of, 200–201
  internal, phases of, 195–198
  qualified, 200, 204
automation
  and level of Y2K risk, 28
  manual alternatives to, 158
  of testing, 39
awareness
  lack of, in executives, 91, 222
  successfully promoting, 57–58
awareness phase, 29, 43, 49, 57, 228
  checklist, 64–65

B

backup strategies, 39, 47, 59
backup systems, 151, 158
bad faith, 90
bankruptcies
  caused by capacity problems, 131
  resulting from insurance claims, 226
  resulting from Y2K failures, 8–9, 150, 231
  stemming from Y2K lawsuits, 16, 277
best practices, 25, 26, 28, 46, 57, 60, 61, 162, 177, 207, 228, 290

Billing Innovations: New Win-Win Ways to End Hourly Billings, 260
BNA, 256
boiler and machinery (B&M) insurance, 215
British Standards Institution, 105
budget breakdowns for Y2K projects, 53–55
business continuity, 61
  planning for, 25, 28, 29, 32, 37, 38
business improvement, 178–182
business income (BI) insurance, 214
business judgment defense, 90–92, 184, 217, 219, 289
business operations
  changes in, mandated by Y2K effects, 20
  effects of Y2K failures on, 8, 12–13, 24
  impact of Y2K lawsuits on, 16
  planning for Y2K effects on, 23, 25–26, 38
  risks caused by Y2K crisis, 24
business organizations
  assessing risk tolerance of, 28
  interdependency of, 129–130, 133
  responsibilities in Y2K compliance projects, 136–137
  size of, as determinant of Y2K strategies, 51
  size of, related to risk management planning, 27, 28
business partners
  assessing legal relations with, 101
  assessing Y2K risk of, 27
  effect of Y2K disclosure on relations with, 174
  ensuring Y2K compliance of, 25, 39
  importance of cooperation in avoiding Y2K problems, 33
  increasing risk awareness of, 29
  reestablishing relations with after Y2K failures, 286

business partners *(Continued)*
  seeking concessions from, to avoid litigation, 268
  See also external business dependencies
business recovery, 61
  issues of, 22, 26
  planning, 36, 38
Business Today, 207
Business Week, 222

C

California Energy Shortage Contingency Plan Web site, 171
Cap Gemini, 53, 175
Caremark decision, 87, 92
Carvill, Wynne, 195
case evaluation, 243, 244
  methods of, 244
cash flow problems from Y2K failures, 6, 220, 286–287
Cirillo, Gregory P., 113, 117
Citicorp, 174
class-action suits, 13, 14–15, 16, 78, 79, 88, 119, 277
  and consumer protection laws, 85
CNA, 230
collusion, 225
commercial general liability (CGL) insurance, 210–211, 215, 218
commercial off-the-shelf (COTS) applications, 47, 81, 158
common law, 80, 81, 273
  indemnification, 97–98
communications strategies
  in crisis situations, 284, 285
  in internal audits, 196
  in litigation, 265–266, 270, 278–280
complaints, 272–273
compliance certifications, 6, 25, 61
compression of data, 136
Computerworld, 241
conciliation, 244
confidentiality, 103, 104, 278–279
conflict of interest, 87, 279, 280
consultants, 260, 271
  checking Y2K status of, 180
  liability risks of, 115–117
  as project managers, 50
  role in business improvement process, 180–181
  strategies for avoiding liability exposure, 117–119
  using to resolve Y2K issues, 30, 32
consumer protection laws, 85
contamination of data, 5, 60, 61, 283

contingency plans, 140, 151–172, 180, 181, 283, 285
  for ADR, 243
  benefits of, 153, 176
  changes in, resulting from Y2K crisis, 37
  developing, 28, 29, 30, 32, 33, 154–168
  disclosure of, 191
  and EDBs, 148–149
  elements of, 162
  importance of, 23, 153–154
  importance of communicating to employees, 167
  legal ramifications of, 76, 89
  prioritizing, 37, 41, 153, 156–157
  versus remediation, 45–46, 47–48
  resources for, 171
  restarting after, 168
  revising, 37, 40, 61
  sample outline, 163–166
  scope of, 154, 157
  teams for, 155, 166
  traditional versus Y2K, 151–152, 153
  training for, 157, 158, 165, 166–167, 168
  trigger events for, 161–162, 164, 167
contract claims, 80–83
contracts
  ADR clauses in, 247–252
  breaches of, 81, 82, 83, 273
  changes in, as result of Y2K issues, 75–76
  damage provisions in, 88
  as factors in determining whether to pursue litigation, 267–268
  and indemnification, 98
  and insurance exceptions, 210
  lawsuits based on, 80–83
  legal provisions of, 273
  misrepresentation and fraud provisions, 84
  outcome-oriented clauses, 110
  problems with, as result of Y2K issues, 70
  process-oriented clauses, 111, 117
  unconscionability of, 116
  waiving rights through, 194
  warranty exclusion in, 88
  Y2K legal issues and, 105–118, 243
  for Y2K remediation, 112–115
copyright infringement, 86, 229, 273
core business processes (CBPs), 139, 180, 181

cost-benefit analysis, 23, 27, 269
  as basis for risk management strategies, 36–37
  of contingency plans, 161
cost estimates, 53–55, 57, 58
cost-recovery lawsuits, 14, 100, 104, 255, 266–276
countersuits, 85, 86, 88, 273
CPR Institute for Dispute Resolution, 248
crisis management, 281, 283–286
critical business operations/systems, 152, 154
  identifying, 156, 158
customers
  assessing legal relations with, 100, 119
  assessing Y2K risk of, 27, 75, 176
  effect of Y2K disclosure on relations with, 174
  increasing risk awareness of, 29
  legal strategies of, 115–117
  material, 189–190
  relations with, exacerbated by Y2K problems, 70

D

damages, 85, 225, 272, 285
  consequential, 88
  failure to mitigate, 89
  limitations of, 238
  mitigating, 271
  provisions in contracts, 88
date-event horizon (DEH), 156
date windows, 136
  fixed, 5, 59
  sliding, 59
Davenport, Thomas H., 181
Dealing with the Year 2000 Problem Web site, 171
Dec, Irene, 185
decision making, 183
  in fast-track projects, 56–57
decision tree analysis, 253, 269, 275
de Jager, Peter, 2–3
demands, 269
  responding to, 271–272
Department of Labor, 86, 125
Deutsche Bank Securities, 282
directors and officers (D&O) insurance, 212, 217–220, 221, 222
Disaster Recovery Institute of Canada Web site, 171
Dispute Resolution 2000, 248
diversity jurisdiction, 273
documentation
  of business continuity plans, 38
  of contingency plans, 162, 166

of decision making processes, 52, 139
of due diligence, 11, 20, 23, 77, 104
elements of, 185
importance of, 183, 290
in internal audits, 196
as means of avoiding liability, 116, 118, 222
needed for financial audits, 203
needed for Y2K legal audits, 101–102
objectives of, 185
storage policies, 137, 185–187
of testing and remediation, 23, 33
of Y2K compliance questionnaires, 143, 146
do-nothing approach, 47, 160
Dow Corning, 277
drills, 29, 39
for contingency plan implementation, 167
for Y2K disaster, 168–169
due diligence, 70–72, 99, 137, 185, 207, 228, 256, 259, 280, 290
elements of, 127–128, 183
establishing through Y2K remediation projects, 47–48
importance of, 42, 69, 71
and M&A, 175–176
necessity of documenting, 11, 20, 23, 77, 104, 183–185
purpose of, 176–177
and risk determination, 25, 27
strategies for achieving, 71–72, 243
substantiating, 183–204

E

electronic data exchange
as source of Y2K risk, 5, 61
types of, 5
ways in which Y2K problems can occur, 5
Electronic Data Interchange (EDI), 33, 73
Y2K problems caused by, 135–136
electronic data processing (EDP) insurance, 214
embedded systems, 229
categories of, 3
difficulty of solving Y2K problems in, 3–4
prevalence of, as contributor to Y2K problems, 3–4
range of vulnerability to Y2K risk, 3
remediation, 140
as sources of Y2K risk, 2–5, 60, 135, 215
triaging, 139
emergency preparedness, 29, 38, 168–170, 286
Employee Retirement Income Security Act (ERISA), 86, 221
encapsulation, 136
enterprise resource planning (ERP), 180, 181
equitable relief, 247
equitable remedies, 238
errors and omissions (E&O) insurance, 95, 99, 118, 212, 220, 221, 222
European Money Unit (EMU), 7, 27
Executive Risk Management Associates (ERMA), 174
executives
avoiding personal liability, 89, 90
career damage from Y2K failures, 10
defenses against liability, 90–93
effects of Y2K litigation on, 242
gaining support for ADR, 246–247
importance of understanding Y2K risks, 30
lack of Y2K awareness, 91, 222
liability risks of, 69–70, 85–86, 89–90, 91, 100
responsibilities in Y2K situations, 92, 283–284, 287
roles in business improvement process, 179–182
roles in fast-track projects, 46, 49, 51–52, 55
roles in liability protection, 73–74
roles in risk management, 26, 28, 31, 38, 40, 41
on steering committees, 31, 136
expert witnesses, 258, 260, 265
external business dependencies (EBDs), 129–130
assessing Y2K status of, 189
as factor in Y2K failures, 152
guidelines for dealing with, 148–149
inventorying, 137
levels of risk, 132–133
magnitude of Y2K threat posed by, 150
and outsourcing, 181
resolving disputes with, 233–254
risks of dealing with, 206
Y2K compliance strategies regarding, 129–150
See also business partners

F

failure scenarios, 155–156, 284–285
fast-tracking, 31, 45–68
accelerating processes to facilitate, 55–57, 62
budgeting for, 53–55
composition and roles of teams, 48–49
decision making in, 56–57
first steps in implementing, 48–49
importance of teamwork in, 49, 50
legal fallout from, 45
management's role in, 49
measuring success of, 49
organizing projects, 50–51
project management plans for, 49
risk analysis for, 46–47
roadblocks to, 55–56
shortcuts necessitated by, 46, 57
triaging and, 46–47
Federal Accounting Standards Board (FASB), 175
Federal Acquisitions Regulation
definition of Y2K compliance, 2, 105
Federal Deposit Insurance Company (FDIC), 123, 171
Federal Emergency Management Agency (FEMA), 286
Federal Financial Institutions Examination Council (FFIEC), 6, 123, 257, 287
insurance disclosure requirements of, 227–228
interagency statement of, 134–135
Y2K documents available from, 123–124
Federal Reserve Bank, 7, 123
fiduciary duties, 85–86, 89, 90, 92, 125, 221, 257, 259
breaches of, 217, 184
fiduciary liability insurance, 221
fiduciary suits, 80, 87–88
corporate, 87
derivative, 87–88, 175, 176, 223, 257
field expansion, 136
financial aspects of Y2K crisis, 6, 8–9, 12, 18, 19, 78, 134–135, 150, 176, 284, 286–288
effect on asset valuation, 18
effect on banking, 12, 18, 208–209, 219–220, 227–228, 287
effect on investments, 18, 25, 287–288

financial aspects of Y2K crisis *(Continued)*
    effect on tax planning, 18, 70, 86, 176
    level of Y2K threat to financial industry, 219
    possible global recession, 18–19, 282
    regulation system of, 126
    risks to assets, 24–25
fire alarm systems
    elements of, susceptible to Y2K risk, 3
    possible failure of in Y2K, 9
fix-on-failure approach, 47, 160
force majeure, 75, 88–89, 103, 112, 267
foreign countries
    level of Y2K preparation, 7–8
forward-looking statements, 192–193
fraud, 83–84, 116, 118, 145
    legal importance of, 84
fungible goods, 132

G

Gartner Group, 15, 40, 131, 134, 153, 175, 198, 282, 287, 289
General Electric, 174
generally accepted accounting principles (GAAP), 199
General Motors, 129–130, 132–133, 135, 206
General Services Administration
    procurement policies, 106–107
Giga Information Group, 3, 13
Globex Insurance, 230
government
    bodies issuing Y2K information, 124–125
    failure of services in Y2K crisis, 284–285
    possible Y2K lawsuits against, 14
    role after the turn of the new century, 281, 286
    role in IT industry after Y2K, 10–11
    role in preserving insurance industry, 231
    special supply-chain issues of, 41
    state, 126, 210, 284
    and Y2K information immunity, 122
Groupware, 278
"Guidance Concerning the Year 2000 Impact on Customers," 287

Guidelines for Contingency Plan Development, 171
Gulf, 201, 202

H

Harvard Business Review, 181
healthcare, 135
    level of Y2K threat to industry, 219
    possible effects of Y2K problems on, 4, 9–10
    regulation structure of, 126
    Y2K standards for industry, 207
    See also insurance industry; medical equipment
Health Care Financing Administration, 258
hexadecimal data, 136

I

IBM, 174
impaired property, 216, 217
implementation phase, 60–61, 228
    checklist, 67
indemnification, 103, 209
    benefits of, 97
    common law, 97–98
    contractual, 98
    of executives, 92–93
    of IT personnel, 97–98
    pros and cons, 98
    by vendors, 111
independent validation and verification (IV&V), 22, 32, 166
    contracts for, 114–115
industrial equipment
    effects of Y2K failures on, 8
    subject to Y2K problems, 4
Information Technology Association of America, 91
    Web site, 248
information technology (IT) industry
    and business improvements, 179
    government involvement with, in future, 10–11
    level of Y2K threat to, 219
    potential impact of Y2K on public attitudes toward, 18, 241
    risks of litigation, 241–242
infrastructures
    elements of, susceptible to Y2K risk, 3, 24
    interruption in, due to Y2K failures, 7, 8, 25, 282–283
    risks associated with Y2K failures, 28, 37
    See also electric power providers

Information Technology Association of America (ITAA), 177, 242
insurance industry, 5, 135
    debate about provision of coverage for Y2K claims, 14, 16–17, 213–221, 225–228
    financial capacity of, 226
    as force for Y2K resolution, 20
    lawsuits against, 80
    level of Y2K threat to, 219
    regulation system of, 126
    response to Y2K risks, 210–212, 231
    and Y2K compliance questionnaires, 143, 145, 212, 221–224
    Y2K risks to, 224–227
insurance policies, 39, 103, 205–232, 256, 289
    activating after Y2K failures, 269–270
    all risk, 209–210, 213, 214
    buyback of Y2K exclusions in, 212
    claims-made, 218, 220, 268
    coverage of misrepresentation and fraud, 84
    difficulties in getting Y2K coverage from, 27, 70, 77–78, 215–216, 230–231
    disclosure of coverage, 227–228
    due diligence issues of, 184
    errors and omissions (E&O), 95, 99, 118
    exclusions in, 214, 215–217, 219, 220, 221
    for executive liability, 92
    express coverage grants, 212
    extended reporting periods (ERPs), 218
    as factor in determining whether to pursue litigation, 268
    grounds for voiding, 222–224
    for IT personnel, 95
    as means of mitigating Y2K risk, 27
    named peril, 209–210
    occurrence-based, 218, 268
    recovery provisions allowed by, 89
    renewal requirements, 223
    retroactive dates, 218–219, 220
    as risk transfer vehicle, 209–212
    severability of covered persons, 224
    specifically for Y2K, 228–231
    underwriting criteria for, 219–220
    variation in terms of, 220

Index

Y2K coverage issues, 213–221, 225–228
Y2K exclusions in, 210–212
See also specific types of policies
Insurance Services Office (ISO), 211, 215, 216
internal systems
  disruption of, 180
  as sources of Y2K problems, 135
  triaging, 139
International Data Corporation, 134
Internet information sharing applications, 278
investors
  assessing legal relations with, 101
  opportunities after the turn of the new century, 287–288
  reactions to Y2K disclosure, 174
IT personnel
  changes in careers as result of Y2K, 10–11, 62
  cooperation with employers in Y2K litigation, 95–96, 97
  legal risks in Y2K crisis, 69–70, 95–96
  liability protection for, 95–98
  necessity of understanding Y2K and their companies, 30
IT system remediation, 22–23
  criteria for choosing solutions, 23
  responsibilities of teams, 30
  security concerns stemming from, 23
IT systems
  integration of, 177–178
  prioritizing, 22, 23, 28
  as sources of Y2K risk, 2

J

JAMS/Endispute, 248
J&H Marsh & McLennan (J&H), 229
Jinnett, Jeff, 13
joint defense agreements, 97, 278–280
Jones, Capers, 8, 13, 18, 152, 282
Journal of Business Continuity, 171
just-in-time inventory systems, 40, 130

K

Keen, Peter G.W., 241
KPMG Peat Marwick LLP, 201, 202

L

Lanza, Chuck, 169

lawsuits, 78–88
  class-action suits, 13, 14–15, 16, 78, 79, 88, 119
  against computer manufacturers, 13
  contract claims, 80–83
  disadvantages of, 269
  elements of, 78
  fiduciary claims, 80, 87–88
  filing, 272–274
  forums for, 273
  industries facing, 276–278
  multiple, 276–280, 289
  parties likely to bring, 79–80
  precipitating events for, 267
  preventing, 78–79
  regulating/limiting, 184–185
  statutory/legal claims, 80, 85–87
  tort claims, 80, 83–85, 89
  types of, involving Y2K issues, 79–88
  See also individual types of lawsuits
lawyers
  advantages of retaining early, 270
  choosing, 255–258, 278
  coordination counsel, 277–278, 289
  fee arrangments for, 260–261
  importance of business knowledge, 257–258
  in-house versus outside, 96–97, 104, 264–265
  involvement in document storage policies, 186
  necessity of ongoing involvement in Y2K issues, 73, 137
  roles in handling litigation documentation, 265, 271
  on Y2K committees, 136, 139, 145
leap day, 281
legal audits, 73, 98–104
  objectives of, 99–101
  steps in conducting, 101–104
legalities of Y2K crisis, 13–16, 42, 69–128, 288–289
  analysis of in Y2K legal audits, 102–103
  assessing legal relations with other parties, 100–101
  burden on court system, 16, 231, 240, 289
  changes in, after the new century, 137
  and contingency plans, 76
  of corporate communications, 77
  criminal prosecutions, possibility of, 86

  estimated cost of, 13, 20, 209, 226
  and fast-track projects, 46, 52
  information on developments in, 256–257
  involving Y2K project managers, 10, 11
  issues peculiar to Y2K problems, 70
  judges' view of, 240–241
  juries' view of, 241
  lawsuits occurring before the new century, 14–15
  levels of legal risk in different industries, 27
  minimizing risk of legal problems, 24
  special problems with Y2K lawsuits, 16
  types of lawsuits expected, 13–14, 24
  and vendor questionnaires, 6, 25
  See also due diligence; lawsuits; liability; litigation; reasonable business judgment
LEXIS, 256
Lexis-Nexis, 174
liability
  avoiding through ADR, 243
  checklist for executive risk management, 93–95
  control of, in non-Y2K-compliant businesses, 74
  defenses against, 88–89, 120–122, 256
  intercompany, 80
  professional (malpractice), 84, 184
  reducing exposure, 69–128
  risk management of, 72–78
  strict products, 83
liaison counsel, 278
litigation
  ADR as precursor to, 245
  alternatives to, 233–254, 269, 275
  appeals, 276
  budgets for, 261–264, 271, 274
  categories of, in Y2K cases, 80–88
  complex nature of, in Y2K cases, 79
  cost containment, 256, 259, 260–264, 265, 273, 274, 275, 276, 278, 280
  cost of, 268, 270
  deciding whether to pursue, 99–100, 267, 275
  disadvantages of, 237–241
  discovery process in, 238–240, 274

litigation *(Continued)*
  guidelines for attorneys, 259–260
  importance of investigation in, 270–271, 273
  and insurance coverage, 218
  planning and management of, 255–280
  preparing and trying cases, 275–276
  risks of, 255
  strategies for avoiding, 119
Litigation Cost Control Resource Center, 261
loss adjustment, 227

M

major corporate decision making, 173–182
malpractice, 84, 240
management. *See* executives
Management Advisory Services & Publications Web site, 171
Management's Discussion and Analysis of Financial Condition and Results of Operations (MD&A), 187, 188, 190
Marcoccio, Lou, 40, 134
masking techniques, 12
Massachusetts Standing Committee on Dispute Resolution, 253
Mealey's, 256
media, advice for dealing with, 266
mediation, 243, 244–245, 247
  nonbinding, 252, 272, 273
medical equipment
  effects of Y2K failure on, 9
  likelihood of Y2K failure, 9
  regulations applying to, 125
  types of, susceptible to Y2K risk, 3
mergers and acquisitions (M&A)
  due diligence for, 175–176
  opportunities after the turn of the new century, 288
  and Y2K compliance disclosure, 175–178
  and Y2K insurance disclosure, 228
Microsoft's "Statement of Year 2000 Compliance," 105–106
Millennium Insurance, 229–230
mini-trials, 244, 276
misrepresentation, 83–84, 116, 117, 118
  legal importance of, 84
  negligent, 84
mission-critical factors, 23, 31, 33, 174, 179
  defining, 34

levels of risk, 130, 132–133
prioritizing, 41, 51
Monitor Insurance, 230
monitoring
  as aid to liability protection, 92
  importance in contract management, 113–114
  as ingredient in Y2K success, 136, 137, 143
  systems, susceptible to Y2K risk, 3
Myrick, David, 157

N

negligence, 83, 89, 184
negotiation, 243, 244, 247
net present value (NPV), 36
Netscape Communications, 237–238
neutral evaluation, 244
New York Times, The, 222
Nolan, Richard L., 7
North American Electric Reliability Council (NERC), 283
Nycal, 201, 202

O

outsourcing, 178, 181

P

paper trail, 185
patent infringement, 86
plant automation. *See* automation; industrial equipment
portability provisions, 113
post-implementation phase, 61
  checklist, 67–68
prioritizing, 31
  contingency planning, 37, 52, 153, 154, 156–157
  EBDs, 139
  importance of, 28
  risk management, 52
  risks, 29, 157
  systems, 22, 23, 28, 51, 154
  using triage process, 37, 41, 46–47
  Y2K projects, 26, 34, 42
"Probabilities of Year 2000 Damages," 282
processing alternatives, 36
project checklist, 61, 62–68
project management plans, 49
  contents of, 49
  importance of, 49
project managers
  consulting firms as, 50
  necessary powers of, 50, 55
  qualifications for, 49–50
  roles of, 52
project scoping, 51–53

property damage, 215–216
property insurance, 213–217
  fortuity requirement, 184, 213–214, 216
Prudential Insurance, 185

Q

quick fix strategies, 39, 158
quid pro quo inquiries, benefits of, 146

R

rapid rewrite strategies, 39
reasonable business judgment, 47, 51, 52, 290
  and contingency planning, 153, 172
Reed, Richard C., 260
regulation of IT industry, 87
  avoiding penalties, 126
  changes in as result of Y2K crisis, 122–123
  effects of preexisting laws, 125
  ensuring compliance with, 75, 122–127
  increase due to Y2K crisis, 10
reinsurance, 225–226
remediation contingency planning, 47
renovation phase, 29, 59, 228
  checklist, 65–66
  infringement issues and, 86
  in internal audits, 197
residual risk, 205–207
resources
  allocation of, 23, 26, 52, 53, 90, 180
  alternatives, myths about, 130–132
  capacity issues, 130–131
  obstacles to securing alternatives, 132
  problems caused by switching providers, 131
restart costs, 36
retirement funds and Y2K compliance, 18, 19, 125
risk allocation, 70, 115, 203
risk assessment, 29, 30, 31, 32–33, 41, 154, 180
  of EBDs, 137
  for fast-track projects, 46–47, 51
  in internal audits, 195
  and legal issues, 73
risk finance techniques, 207–209
risk management, 21–43, 154, 259, 280, 290
  areas to be addressed, 22–26, 32–33, 183

composition and roles of teams, 22, 25, 26, 28, 30–33, 38, 40
data necessary for, 48
determining correct approach toward, 27–29
elements in success of, 38–39
first steps in, 39
importance of reviewing progress, 23, 31
importance of teamwork in, 22, 28
phases of planning for, 29
planning programs for, 21–22, 26–39
after the turn of the new century, 281–289
risk rating, 34–35, 156, 157
as protection against liability, 90
and triage, 41–42, 51
risk transfer, 201, 205, 209–212
Rx2000 Solutions Institute, 9

S

SABRE System, 131
safe harbors, 192–193
safety equipment, effects of Y2K failure on, 9
Securities Act of 1933, 190
Securities and Exchange Commission (SEC), 18, 19, 85, 88, 123, 134, 174, 177, 201, 203, 205, 221, 222
statement on Y2K readiness disclosure, 146, 148, 187–193, 256–257
Securities Exchange Act of 1934, 190
securities industry, 135
regulation structure of, 126
securities trading
changes in, as result of Y2K crisis, 241–242
vulnerability to Y2K problems, 5
security systems
susceptibility to Y2K risk, 3, 152
settlements of legal cases, 275–276, 289
sliding window, 5
Social Security Administration, 12, 171, 258
Special Wits and Technologies (SWAT) teams, 20, 159, 164
Staff Legal Bulletin No. 5, 187, 257
standards of care, 207
State of Minnesota, 248
State of Texas Web site, 171
statute of limitations, 89, 103, 185, 272
tolling, 252

statutory/regulatory claims, 80, 85–87
steering committees
composition and roles of, 31, 42, 52–53, 136–137
special authority in fast-track situations, 55
Strassman, Paul A., 10
subrogation, 215, 224, 226–227, 289
summary jury trials, 244
suppliers
affiliated, risks of relying on, 135
assessment of Y2K compliance, 6, 25, 39
determining Y2K risk of, 27
importance of cooperating in achieving Y2K compliance, 25
increasing risk awareness of, 29
material, 189–190
sole-source, deciding whether to assist in Y2K efforts, 149
sole-source, risks of relying on, 135
supply chain, 129, 202–203, 265

T

TAVA Technologies, 4
tax implications of Y2K crisis, 18, 70, 86
telecommunications equipment, 135
elements of, susceptible to Y2K risk, 3
as factor in Y2K failures, 152
10Q forms, 174, 222
termination, 113
rights, 112
testing, 38, 54, 180
automated, 39, 60
best ways of performing, 60, 61
and contingency planning, 157, 166, 168
contracts for, 114–115
costs of, 59
effectiveness of, 282
end-to-end, 5, 122
importance of, 1, 39, 61
in internal audits, 197–198
joint, with business partners, 25
keeping records of, 23, 29
live, 284
problems in embedded systems, 3
schedules for, 29
vendor responsibility for, 2
third-party business relations
in internal audits, 198
and legal audits, 99

risks for Y2K problems, 5, 189–190
and testing for business partner compliance, 25
tort claims, 80, 83–85
defenses against, 89
torts, 83, 202
examples of, 83–85
trade secrets, 84–85
triaging, 22, 31, 37, 39, 41–42, 54, 139, 157
and fast-track projects, 46–47, 51–53
and legal risks, 73
trier of fact, 275
Twenty-First Century Insurance Policy, 228–229
2000 Secure, 229

U

unfair business practices, 85
Uniform Commercial Code (UCC), 78, 83, 85, 89, 116, 273
contracts covered by, 82
purpose of, 81
United Parcel Service (UPS), 130–131
U.S. Senate Special Committee on the Year 2000 Technology Problem, 134, 153
utilities, 135
as factor in Y2K failures, 152
regulation system of, 126
vulnerability to Y2K problems, 4

V

validation phase, 29, 59–60, 228
checklist, 66–67
value-added network (VAN), 73
vendors, 39
assessing legal relations with, 101
avoiding liability exposure, 117–119
liability risks of, 115–117
material, 189–190
possible lawsuits against, 13, 15
possible lawsuits by, 14
relations with, exacerbated by Y2K crisis, 2, 30, 70
responsibilities for embedded systems, 3
surveying for Y2K compliance, 6, 18, 25
switching to avoid Y2K problems, 29
Y2K compliance responsibilities, 99
and Y2K warranties, 106–112

W

waivers, contractual, 194
Wakeland, Steve, 195
Wall Street Journal, The, 222
warranties
  analyzing, in Y2K legal audits, 102
  breaches of, 81, 82, 273
  commercial, 107–110
  disclaimers against, 82, 88, 102, 112, 121–122, 267
  failure of essential purpose of, 116–117
  and insurance policies, 223, 224
  types of, 82
  year 2000, 106–110
Web sites, 102
  legalities of posting Y2K information on, 121
work-product doctrine, 103, 104, 265, 279
World Wide Web
  as force for promoting Y2K awareness, 58

Y

Yardeni, Edward, 18, 282
Year 99 problems, 136, 211
Year 2000 (Y2K) compliance
  assessing, 6, 25, 139–145
  communication programs, 139–145
  contract provisions for, 110–111
  defining, 105–106, 110, 136
  determining own status, 118–119, 180
  developing programs for, 126–127
  establishing standards for, 61, 74
  guidelines issued by private organizations, 125–126
  importance of documenting, 11, 20, 23, 29
  and interdependencies of IT systems, 2
  international variation in, 7–8, 27, 283
  legal aspects of (*see* legalities of Y2K crisis)
  maintaining, 61
  methods for achieving, 136
  organizational, 140
  problems with incompatible solutions, 5, 136, 178, 179
  responsibilities of third parties in attaining, 99–100
  sharing information on, 242–243
  strategies for achieving, 59
  uncertainty of, 134, 153
  and valuation of corporate entities, 175–176
  variation by industry, 258
  See also external business dependencies
Year 2000 Information and Readiness Disclosure Act of 1998, 84, 101, 146, 184, 225, 242
  liability defenses provided under, 119–122, 194
  purpose and provisions of, 145
  and Y2K insurance coverage, 223
"The Year 2000 Issue—Current Accounting and Auditing Guidance," 199
Year 2000 Journal Articles, 171
"Year 2000 Programme: The Audit Contribution," 195
Year 2000 Residual Risk Insurance Policy, 230
Year 2000 Risk Assessment and Planning for Individuals, 282
Year 2000 Software Testing, 60
Yourdon, Ed, 20
Y2K compliance questionnaires, 6, 25, 139–142, 143
  responding to others', 143–145, 146, 194
  response rates to, 139–140, 143
  sample questionnaire, 140–142
  standardized responses to, 145–146
  tracking, 143
Y2K Contingency Management Plans Web site, 171
Y2K disclosure, 173–174, 256
  and due diligence, 183
  effect on business relationships, 174, 194
  effect on stock prices, 174
  SEC guidelines for, 188–192
Y2K failures
  before the new century, 11–12, 40, 219, 284
  consequences of, 8–11, 168, 176, 178, 219, 233, 284–285
  cost of, 225
  data transmission problems caused by, 135–136
  determining costs of, 34, 36
  differing perspectives on, 236–237
  disputes engendered by, 233–236
  and EBDs, 132–135
  effect on corporate decision making, 76
  effect on resource availability, 130–131
  extending into the new century, 12, 282, 283
  financial impact of (*see* financial aspects of Y2K crisis)
  identifying opportunities in, 149–150, 287–288
  importance of timely prevention efforts, 1
  and interdependency of systems, 283
  large-scale fallout from, 17–19, 21–22, 255–256, 282
  planning for, 21–26
  predictions about the seriousness of, 282–283
  probability of, 152, 153, 282
  recovery strategies, 285–286
  reducing damage from, 19–20, 23–25, 45
  regulatory consequences of, 126
  as self-fulfilling prophecies, 284
  service interruptions caused by, 152
  spreading nature of, 133–134, 137, 156, 281
  what to do when they occur, 269–272
Y2K-LAW, 248
Y2K remediation plans, 45
  versus contingency plans, 47
  effects on business partners, 136
  establishing, 57
  estimated costs of, 53, 175–176
  human resources elements of, 74, 132
  importance in proving due diligence, 47
  late versus early starting, 46, 57
  level of implementation in small businesses, 134
  parallelling risk management, 46
  in Y2K legal audits, 102–103
Y2K risks, 1–20
  additive nature of, 1–2, 21–22
  management of, 20, 21–43 (*see also* risk management)
  and personal safety, 23
  sources of, 2–8, 21–22
  types of, 23–25

Z

ZDY2K Web site, 171